Dr. Simon's Magic English Series© is the most systematic and scientific program designed to improve essential English comprehension skills for students.

United States Canada United Kingdom Australia Germany France Italy Japan India South Korea China

미국 영국 캐나다 호주 독일 프랑스 이탈리아 일본 인도 학생들이 공부하는 세계 최고의 주니어 영어교육 프로그램

AI 학습자료와 인강

DR. SIMON'S MAGIC ENGLISH

VOCABULARY BOOK
100-900
AGE 7-15

LanCom
Language & Communication

사이먼 미국교과서 100에서 900까지 어휘 총정리
세계 최고의 주니어 영어교육 프로그램 사이먼 미국교과서 전시리즈 한국 독점 출판

DR. SIMON'S MAGIC ENGLISH

KEY VOCABULARY | LEVEL 100 - UNIT 1

- ☐ **grumpy**: _____; in a bad mood or easily annoyed
- ☐ **visit**: _____; go to see someone
- ☐ **ghost**: _____; the spirit of a dead person, often believed to haunt or appear to the living
- ☐ **past**: _____; the time before the present; history
- ☐ **present**: _____; the time that is happening now
- ☐ **future**: _____; the time that has not yet happened
- ☐ **childhood**: _____; the period of a person's life when they are a child
- ☐ **affecting**: _____; having an impact on something or someone
- ☐ **poor**: _____; lacking money or resources
- ☐ **employee**: _____; a person who works for someone else in exchange for payment
- ☐ **family**: _____; a group consisting of one or two parents and their children
- ☐ **bleak**: _____; unpleasant, hopeless, and without any positive aspects
- ☐ **hurt**: _____; cause emotional or physical pain to someone
- ☐ **realize**: _____; become aware of something
- ☐ **change**: _____; make or become different
- ☐ **kinder**: _____; more friendly, generous, and considerate
- ☐ **make amends**: _____; do something to show that you are sorry for having done something wrong
- ☐ **begin**: _____; start to do something
- ☐ **give**: _____; provide something to someone without expecting anything in return
- ☐ **in need**: _____; lacking the necessities of life, such as food, shelter, or clothing

KEY VOCABULARY | LEVEL 100 - UNIT 2

- ☐ **named**: _____; given a particular name
- ☐ **fall**: _____; move downward from a higher position to a lower position
- ☐ **rabbit hole**: _____; a hole in the ground where rabbits live or hide
- ☐ **enter**: _____; go into a place
- ☐ **strange**: _____; unusual or unexpected in a way that is unsettling or hard to understand
- ☐ **magical**: _____; relating to magic or having special powers
- ☐ **world**: _____; the earth and all the people, places, and things on it
- ☐ **unusual**: _____; not commonly encountered or experienced
- ☐ **creature**: _____; a living being, especially an animal
- ☐ **including**: _____; containing as a part of a larger group
- ☐ **grinning**: _____; smiling widely
- ☐ **crazy**: _____; mentally deranged, especially as manifested in a wild or aggressive way
- ☐ **adventure**: _____; an exciting or unusual experience
- ☐ **like**: _____; similar to or in the same way as something else
- ☐ **growing**: _____; increasing in size, amount, or intensity
- ☐ **playing**: _____; engaging in an activity for enjoyment or competition
- ☐ **attending**: _____; being present at an event or function
- ☐ **tea party**: _____; a social gathering at which tea is served
- ☐ **learn**: _____; acquire knowledge or skill
- ☐ **important**: _____; of great significance or value
- ☐ **lesson**: _____; an amount of teaching given at one time; a period of learning or teaching
- ☐ **growing up**: _____; the process of maturing and becoming an adult
- ☐ **brave**: _____; ready to face and endure danger or pain; showing courage
- ☐ **eventually**: _____; in the end, especially after a long delay, dispute, or series of problems
- ☐ **wake up**: _____; become conscious after being asleep or unconscious
- ☐ **realize**: _____; become fully aware or cognizant of something
- ☐ **imagination**: _____; the faculty or action of forming new ideas, or images or concepts of external objects not present to the senses

DR. SIMON'S MAGIC ENGLISH

KEY VOCABULARY | LEVEL 100 - UNIT 3

- ☐ **group**: _____; a number of people or things that are located, gathered, or classed together
- ☐ **farm**: _____; a piece of land used for growing crops or raising animals
- ☐ **animal**: _____; a living organism that feeds on organic matter
- ☐ **rebel**: _____; rise in opposition or armed resistance against an established government or leader
- ☐ **take over**: _____; take control of something
- ☐ **create**: _____; bring something into existence
- ☐ **society**: _____; the aggregate of people living together in a more or less ordered community
- ☐ **equal**: _____; being the same in quantity, size, degree, or value
- ☐ **smartest**: _____; having or showing quick intelligence or ready mental capability
- ☐ **change**: _____; make or become different
- ☐ **rule**: _____; one of a set of explicit or understood regulations or principles governing conduct or procedure within a particular area of activity
- ☐ **benefit**: _____; an advantage or profit gained from something
- ☐ **greedy**: _____; having or showing an intense and selfish desire for something, especially wealth or power
- ☐ **cruel**: _____; willfully causing pain or suffering to others, or feeling no concern about it
- ☐ **afraid**: _____; feeling fear or anxiety
- ☐ **speak up**: _____; speak more loudly or clearly
- ☐ **eventually**: _____; in the end, especially after a long delay, dispute, or series of problems
- ☐ **human**: _____; people; a person
- ☐ **no longer**: _____; not now as formerly
- ☐ **teach**: _____; show or explain to someone how to do something
- ☐ **important**: _____; of great significance or value
- ☐ **lesson**: _____; an amount of teaching given at one time; a period of learning or teaching
- ☐ **danger**: _____; the possibility of suffering harm or injury
- ☐ **power**: _____; the ability to do something or act in a particular way, especially as a faculty or quality
- ☐ **corruption**: _____; dishonest or fraudulent conduct by those in power, typically involving bribery

4 | Literature Series

KEY VOCABULARY | LEVEL 100 - UNIT 4

- ☐ **bet**: _____; a wager or agreement between two parties that a certain outcome will occur
- ☐ **travel**: _____; go from one place to another, especially over a long distance
- ☐ **loyal**: _____; faithful, devoted, and dedicated to someone or something
- ☐ **servant**: _____; a person who performs duties for others, especially in a household
- ☐ **country**: _____; a nation or area of land that is politically controlled by a government
- ☐ **challenge**: _____; a difficult task or situation that requires effort and determination to overcome
- ☐ **ride**: _____; travel in or on a vehicle or animal
- ☐ **train**: _____; a series of connected railway cars or carriages pulled by a locomotive
- ☐ **boat**: _____; a small vessel for travel on water, propelled by oars, sails, or an engine
- ☐ **elephant**: _____; a large mammal with a long, curved trunk and tusks, native to Africa and Asia
- ☐ **interesting**: _____; arousing curiosity or interest; fascinating
- ☐ **adventure**: _____; an exciting or unusual experience; a bold, risky undertaking
- ☐ **pursue**: _____; follow or chase after someone or something
- ☐ **detective**: _____; a person whose job is to investigate and solve crimes
- ☐ **steal**: _____; take something without permission or legal right
- ☐ **innocence**: _____; the state of being not guilty of a crime or offense

DR. SIMON'S MAGIC ENGLISH

KEY VOCABULARY | **LEVEL 100 - UNIT 5**

- **knight**: _____; a man who served his sovereign or lord as a mounted soldier in armor
- **chivalry**: _____; the medieval knightly system with its religious, moral, and social code
- **obsessed**: _____; preoccupied or filled the mind of someone continually and to a troubling extent
- **decide**: _____; come to a resolution in the mind as a result of consideration or impulse
- **adventure**: _____; an unusual and exciting or daring experience
- **loyal**: _____; giving or showing firm and constant support or allegiance to a person or institution
- **squire**: _____; a young nobleman acting as an attendant to a knight before becoming a knight himself
- **comical**: _____; relating to or resembling comedy
- **disaster**: _____; a sudden event, such as an accident or a natural catastrophe, that causes great damage or loss of life
- **mistake**: _____; take someone or something for someone or something else wrongly
- **windmill**: _____; a building with sails or vanes that turn in the wind and generate power to grind corn, pump water, etc
- **attack**: _____; take aggressive action against someone or something
- **sword**: _____; a weapon with a long metal blade and a hilt with a handguard, used for thrusting or striking
- **believe**: _____; accept that something is true, especially without proof
- **imaginary**: _____; existing only in the imagination
- **enemy**: _____; a person who is actively opposed or hostile to someone or something
- **battle**: _____; a sustained fight between large, organized armed forces
- **reality**: _____; the world or the state of things as they actually exist, as opposed to an idealistic or notional idea of them
- **fantasy**: _____; the faculty or activity of imagining things that are impossible or improbable
- **inspire**: _____; fill someone with the urge or ability to do or feel something, especially to do something creative
- **classic**: _____; judged over a period of time to be of the highest quality and outstanding of its kind

Literature Series

KEY VOCABULARY | LEVEL 100 - UNIT 6

- ☐ **vampire**: _____; a mythical or supernatural creature typically depicted as a bloodsucking corpse that rises from the grave at night to prey on humans
- ☐ **count**: _____; a rank or title of nobility in various European countries, typically that of a British earl
- ☐ **castle**: _____; a large building, typically of the medieval period, fortified against attack with thick walls, battlements, towers, and in many cases a moat
- ☐ **attack**: _____; take aggressive action against someone or something
- ☐ **young**: _____; having lived or existed for only a short time; not old
- ☐ **woman**: _____; an adult female human
- ☐ **named**: _____; having a specified name
- ☐ **friend**: _____; a person whom one knows and with whom one has a bond of mutual affection
- ☐ **try**: _____; make an attempt or effort to do something
- ☐ **save**: _____; rescue or protect someone or something from harm or danger
- ☐ **become**: _____; begin to be
- ☐ **meanwhile**: _____; in the intervening period of time
- ☐ **too**: _____; also; in addition
- ☐ **help**: _____; give or provide assistance to someone
- ☐ **hunter**: _____; a person who hunts game or other wild animals
- ☐ **chase**: _____; pursue in order to catch or catch up with
- ☐ **back**: _____; in the direction opposite to the one that one is facing or traveling
- ☐ **finally**: _____; after a long time, typically involving difficulty or delay
- ☐ **kill**: _____; cause the death of

DR. SIMON'S MAGIC ENGLISH

KEY VOCABULARY | LEVEL 100 - UNIT 7

- ☐ **soldier**: _____; a person who serves in an army
- ☐ **fight**: _____; engage in a physical or verbal conflict
- ☐ **meet**: _____; come into the presence of someone
- ☐ **group**: _____; a number of people or things that are located, gathered, or classed together
- ☐ **fighter**: _____; a person or group of people who fights, especially as a soldier or a boxer
- ☐ **blow up**: _____; explode or destroy something with an explosive device
- ☐ **bridge**: _____; a structure carrying a pathway or roadway over a depression or obstacle
- ☐ **stop**: _____; prevent something from happening or progressing
- ☐ **enemy**: _____; a person or group that is opposed to or hostile towards someone or something
- ☐ **advance**: _____; move forward, typically in a purposeful way
- ☐ **help**: _____; give assistance to someone or something
- ☐ **plan**: _____; a detailed proposal for doing or achieving something
- ☐ **fall in love**: _____; develop a strong romantic or affectionate feeling towards someone
- ☐ **named**: _____; having a particular name
- ☐ **terrible**: _____; extremely bad or serious
- ☐ **successful**: _____; achieving or having achieved success
- ☐ **kill**: _____; cause the death of a person, animal, or other living thing
- ☐ **process**: _____; a series of actions or steps taken in order to achieve a particular end
- ☐ **hurt**: _____; cause physical pain or injury to someone or something
- ☐ **know**: _____; be aware of something through observation, inquiry, or information
- ☐ **survive**: _____; continue to live or exist, especially in spite of danger or hardship
- ☐ **stay behind**: _____; remain in a place after others have left
- ☐ **delay**: _____; cause to be late or slow
- ☐ **escape**: _____; break free from confinement or control
- ☐ **die**: _____; cease to exist or function
- ☐ **fight for**: _____; struggle or contend for a cause, ideal, or principle
- ☐ **believe in**: _____; have faith or confidence in the existence or abilities of something or someone

KEY VOCABULARY | LEVEL 100 - UNIT 8

- ☐ **fairy**: _____; a creature that looks like a very small human being, has magic powers, and sometimes has wings
- ☐ **tale**: _____; a story about imaginary events, an exciting or dramatic story
- ☐ **prince**: _____; male royalty, usually the son of a king or queen
- ☐ **princess**: _____; female royalty, usually the daughter of a king or queen
- ☐ **talking animals**: _____; animals that can speak like humans
- ☐ **magical creatures**: _____; mythical beings with magical powers
- ☐ **locked**: _____; unable to open or access something that is sealed or fastened
- ☐ **tower**: _____; a tall structure, often used for observation or defense
- ☐ **outsmart**: _____; beat someone in a clever or cunning way
- ☐ **scary**: _____; frightening, causing fear
- ☐ **giant**: _____; an imaginary creature, usually depicted as an enormous human-like figure
- ☐ **red hood**: _____; a garment worn on the head that covers the hair and has a red color
- ☐ **big, bad wolf**: _____; a fictional character in fairy tales who is often portrayed as the antagonist
- ☐ **triumph**: _____; win, achieve success
- ☐ **heroes**: _____; protagonists or main characters in stories who are admired for their bravery and noble qualities
- ☐ **heroines**: _____; female protagonists or main characters in stories who are admired for their bravery and noble qualities
- ☐ **rewarded**: _____; given something in return for doing something good or valuable
- ☐ **generation**: _____; a group of individuals born and living at the same time
- ☐ **teach**: _____; provide knowledge or instruction on a subject or skill
- ☐ **courage**: _____; the ability to face and overcome fear or danger
- ☐ **kindness**: _____; the quality of being friendly, generous, and considerate
- ☐ **never giving up**: _____; persisting in efforts or actions despite obstacles or setbacks

DR. SIMON'S MAGIC ENGLISH

KEY VOCABULARY | **LEVEL 100 - UNIT 9**

- ☐ **adventures**: _____; exciting experiences or journeys to different places
- ☐ **visit**: _____; go to see or spend time with someone or somewhere
- ☐ **strange**: _____; unusual, unfamiliar, or bizarre
- ☐ **unusual**: _____; not commonly seen or experienced, uncommon
- ☐ **lands**: _____; countries or territories, often used to describe a specific geographic area
- ☐ **meet**: _____; encounter or come into contact with someone or something
- ☐ **tiny**: _____; very small in size
- ☐ **people**: _____; human beings
- ☐ **giant**: _____; extremely large in size
- ☐ **talking**: _____; able to speak like humans
- ☐ **horse**: _____; a large four-legged mammal commonly used for riding or work
- ☐ **travel**: _____; journey or trip taken to different places
- ☐ **ruled**: _____; governed or controlled by someone or something
- ☐ **scientists**: _____; people who study or work in science
- ☐ **created**: _____; made or brought into existence
- ☐ **inventions**: _____; new or innovative devices, products, or processes
- ☐ **learn**: _____; gain knowledge or understanding through experience or study
- ☐ **cultures**: _____; the customs, beliefs, and social practices of a particular group or society
- ☐ **ways of life**: _____; the habits, customs, and practices that are typical of a particular person or group
- ☐ **important**: _____; significant, having great value or impact
- ☐ **lesson**: _____; a piece of knowledge or instruction that is learned through experience or study
- ☐ **kindness**: _____; the quality of being friendly, generous, and considerate
- ☐ **understanding**: _____; the ability to comprehend or empathize with someone else's feelings or situation

KEY VOCABULARY | LEVEL 100 - UNIT 10

- ☐ **hunchback**: _____; a person with a condition that causes their back to curve forward
- ☐ **named**: _____; called
- ☐ **live**: _____; reside or inhabit
- ☐ **big**: _____; large
- ☐ **cathedral**: _____; a large and important church
- ☐ **called**: _____; named
- ☐ **lonely**: _____; feeling sad because one has no friends or company
- ☐ **unhappy**: _____; feeling sad or not content
- ☐ **meet**: _____; encounter or come into contact with someone or something
- ☐ **beautiful**: _____; pleasing the senses or mind aesthetically
- ☐ **girl**: _____; a female child or young woman
- ☐ **kind**: _____; having or showing a friendly, generous, and considerate nature
- ☐ **being pursued**: _____; being chased or followed persistently
- ☐ **evil**: _____; morally wrong or wicked
- ☐ **want**: _____; have a desire to possess or do something; wish for
- ☐ **marry**: _____; take someone as a spouse in a formal ceremony
- ☐ **become**: _____; begin to be
- ☐ **friends**: _____; people with whom one has a bond of mutual affection
- ☐ **try**: _____; make an attempt or effort to do something
- ☐ **protect**: _____; keep safe from harm or injury
- ☐ **plan**: _____; a detailed proposal for doing or achieving something
- ☐ **in the end**: _____; eventually
- ☐ **fight**: _____; a violent confrontation or struggle
- ☐ **hurt**: _____; cause physical or emotional pain or harm
- ☐ **able**: _____; having the power, skill, means, or opportunity to do something
- ☐ **save**: _____; keep safe or rescue someone or something from harm or danger
- ☐ **hero**: _____; a person who is admired or idealized for courage, outstanding achievements, or noble qualities
- ☐ **remember**: _____; keep someone or something in one's mind as a memory
- ☐ **bravery**: _____; courageous behavior or character

DR. SIMON'S MAGIC ENGLISH

KEY VOCABULARY | **LEVEL 100 - UNIT 11**

- ☐ **sailor**: _____ ; a person who works on a ship
- ☐ **named**: _____ ; called
- ☐ **go on**: _____ ; embark on or board a ship
- ☐ **whaling ship**: _____ ; a ship used for hunting and catching whales
- ☐ **called**: _____ ; named
- ☐ **captained**: _____ ; led or commanded by a captain
- ☐ **obsession**: _____ ; an idea or thought that continually preoccupies or intrudes on a person's mind
- ☐ **catching**: _____ ; capturing or seizing
- ☐ **giant**: _____ ; of very great size or force; gigantic
- ☐ **previously**: _____ ; before or prior to a specified or implied time
- ☐ **leg**: _____ ; a limb on which a person or animal stands or walks
- ☐ **along the way**: _____ ; during the journey or process
- ☐ **meet**: _____ ; encounter or come into contact with someone or something
- ☐ **including**: _____ ; comprising or taking in
- ☐ **harpooner**: _____ ; a person who uses a harpoon to catch whales or large fish
- ☐ **encounter**: _____ ; a meeting, especially one that is unplanned, unexpected, or brief
- ☐ **different**: _____ ; not the same as another or each other; unlike in nature, form, or quality
- ☐ **finding**: _____ ; discovering or locating something that was previously unknown or hidden
- ☐ **crew**: _____ ; the people who work on a ship or aircraft
- ☐ **face**: _____ ; confront or deal with something difficult or unpleasant
- ☐ **challenge**: _____ ; a difficult task or problem
- ☐ **dangerous**: _____ ; able or likely to cause harm or injury
- ☐ **storm**: _____ ; a violent disturbance of the atmosphere with strong winds and usually rain, thunder, lightning, or snow
- ☐ **mutiny**: _____ ; an open rebellion against the proper authorities, especially by soldiers or sailors against their officers
- ☐ **finally**: _____ ; after a long time or some difficulty
- ☐ **engage**: _____ ; participate or become involved in
- ☐ **fierce**: _____ ; showing a heartfelt and powerful intensity
- ☐ **battle**: _____ ; a prolonged and intense fight or conflict
- ☐ **ultimately**: _____ ; finally or eventually
- ☐ **sink**: _____ ; descend or cause to descend below the surface of a liquid
- ☐ **die**: _____ ; go to the end of life; cease to exist
- ☐ **surviving**: _____ ; continuing to live or exist, especially in spite of danger or hardship

KEY VOCABULARY | LEVEL 100 - UNIT 12

- ☐ **orphan**: _____; a child whose parents are dead
- ☐ **grow up**: _____; become an adult
- ☐ **workhouse**: _____; a place where the poor were housed and put to work
- ☐ **escape**: _____; get away from a place where one is being held captive or detained
- ☐ **find**: _____; discover or perceive by chance or unexpectedly
- ☐ **fortune**: _____; chance or luck as an arbitrary force affecting human affairs
- ☐ **pickpocket**: _____; a person who steals from the pockets or purses of others in public places
- ☐ **lead**: _____; guide or conduct oneself or others along a particular course
- ☐ **criminal**: _____; a person who has committed a crime
- ☐ **join**: _____; become connected or united
- ☐ **gang**: _____; an organized group of criminals or troublemakers
- ☐ **innocent**: _____; not guilty of a crime or offense
- ☐ **know**: _____; have knowledge or information about something or someone
- ☐ **thieves**: _____; people who steal things
- ☐ **eventually**: _____; in the end, especially after a long time or a lot of effort or problems
- ☐ **send**: _____; cause or arrange for someone or something to go to a particular place
- ☐ **jail**: _____; a place for the confinement of people accused or convicted of a crime
- ☐ **trick**: _____; a cunning or skillful action or scheme intended to deceive someone
- ☐ **later**: _____; after a period of time or an event has happened
- ☐ **rescue**: _____; save someone from a dangerous or distressing situation
- ☐ **kind**: _____; having or showing a friendly, generous, and considerate nature
- ☐ **believe**: _____; accept that something is true, especially without proof
- ☐ **innocence**: _____; the state of being not guilty of a crime or offense
- ☐ **fight**: _____; use physical force to try to defeat another person or group
- ☐ **safety**: _____; the state of being protected from harm or danger
- ☐ **in the end**: _____; finally, after everything has been done or considered
- ☐ **truth**: _____; the quality or state of being in accordance with fact or reality
- ☐ **reveal**: _____; make known something that was previously secret or unknown
- ☐ **reunite**: _____; be brought together again after being apart

DR. SIMON'S MAGIC ENGLISH

KEY VOCABULARY | **LEVEL 100 - UNIT 13**

- ☐ **boy**: _____; a male child
- ☐ **grow up**: _____; become an adult
- ☐ **fly**: _____; move through the air using wings or other means
- ☐ **live**: _____; have one's home in a particular place
- ☐ **magical**: _____; having or using magic powers
- ☐ **island**: _____; a piece of land surrounded by water
- ☐ **adventure**: _____; an exciting or dangerous experience
- ☐ **fairy**: _____; a mythical being with magical powers
- ☐ **friend**: _____; a person whom one knows and with whom one has a bond of mutual affection
- ☐ **siblings**: _____; brothers and sisters
- ☐ **visit**: _____; go to see or stay at a place for a short time
- ☐ **family**: _____; a group of related people
- ☐ **mermaid**: _____; a mythical sea creature with the upper body of a woman and the tail of a fish
- ☐ **pirates**: _____; people who attack and rob ships at sea
- ☐ **exciting**: _____; causing great enthusiasm and eagerness
- ☐ **experience**: _____; practical contact with and observation of facts or events
- ☐ **miss**: _____; feel sad or unhappy because one is not with someone or in a particular place
- ☐ **home**: _____; the place where one lives
- ☐ **help**: _____; make it easier or possible for someone to do something by offering them one's services or resources
- ☐ **promise**: _____; assure someone that one will definitely do something

KEY VOCABULARY | LEVEL 100 - UNIT 14

- ☐ **wooden**: _____; made of wood
- ☐ **puppet**: _____; a movable model of a person or animal that is typically moved either by strings controlled from above or by a hand inside it
- ☐ **becoming**: _____; the process of coming to be something or of passing into a state
- ☐ **real**: _____; actually existing as a thing or occurring in fact
- ☐ **mischievous**: _____; causing or showing a fondness for causing trouble in a playful way
- ☐ **trouble**: _____; difficulty or problem
- ☐ **tell**: _____; communicate information or ideas by speaking or writing
- ☐ **lie**: _____; an intentionally false statement
- ☐ **grow**: _____; increase in size or number over a period of time
- ☐ **longer**: _____; measuring a greater distance from end to end
- ☐ **meet**: _____; come into the presence or company of someone
- ☐ **character**: _____; a person in a novel, play, or movie
- ☐ **including**: _____; with something or someone that is part of a larger group or class
- ☐ **talking**: _____; able to speak
- ☐ **cricket**: _____; a small jumping insect with long antennae
- ☐ **try**: _____; make an effort to do something
- ☐ **teach**: _____; show or explain to someone how to do something
- ☐ **adventure**: _____; an exciting or dangerous experience
- ☐ **kidnap**: _____; take someone away illegally by force
- ☐ **want**: _____; have a desire to possess or do something
- ☐ **rob**: _____; take property unlawfully from a person or place by force or threat of force
- ☐ **turn**: _____; cause to move around an axis or center; rotate
- ☐ **sell**: _____; exchange something for money
- ☐ **eventually**: _____; in the end, especially after a long delay, dispute, or series of problems
- ☐ **realize**: _____; become aware of something as a fact or understand something clearly
- ☐ **importance**: _____; the quality or state of being important
- ☐ **honest**: _____; free of deceit; truthful
- ☐ **brave**: _____; ready to face and endure danger or pain; showing courage

DR. SIMON'S MAGIC ENGLISH

KEY VOCABULARY | LEVEL 100 - UNIT 15

- ☐ **stranded**: _____; left without the means to move from a place
- ☐ **deserted**: _____; abandoned, empty, without people
- ☐ **survive**: _____; continue living or existing, especially in difficult circumstances
- ☐ **shelter**: _____; a place that provides protection from danger or bad weather
- ☐ **food**: _____; any nutritious substance that people or animals eat or drink or that plants absorb to maintain life and growth
- ☐ **clothes**: _____; items worn to cover the body
- ☐ **discover**: _____; find something that was previously unknown or hidden
- ☐ **people**: _____; human beings in general or considered collectively
- ☐ **friendly**: _____; kind and pleasant
- ☐ **save**: _____; rescue someone or something from danger or harm
- ☐ **man**: _____; an adult human male
- ☐ **cannibal**: _____; a person who eats the flesh of other human beings
- ☐ **friend**: _____; a person whom one knows and with whom one has a bond of mutual affection
- ☐ **boat**: _____; a small vessel for traveling on water
- ☐ **together**: _____; with or in proximity to another person or people
- ☐ **destroy**: _____; cause something to cease to exist or be completely ruined
- ☐ **storm**: _____; a violent disturbance of the atmosphere with strong winds, lightning, thunder, rain, or snow
- ☐ **rescue**: _____; save someone or something from a dangerous or difficult situation

KEY VOCABULARY | LEVEL 100 - UNIT 16

- ☐ **story**: _____; an account of imaginary or real people and events
- ☐ **named**: _____; give a name to
- ☐ **go**: _____; move from one place to another
- ☐ **adventure**: _____; an unusual or exciting experience
- ☐ **river**: _____; a large natural stream of water
- ☐ **friend**: _____; a person whom one knows and trusts
- ☐ **runaway**: _____; a person who has escaped from captivity or confinement
- ☐ **slave**: _____; a person who is the legal property of another and is forced to obey them
- ☐ **face**: _____; confront and deal with or accept
- ☐ **challenge**: _____; a call to take part in a contest or competition
- ☐ **meet**: _____; come into the presence or company of someone by chance or arrangement
- ☐ **interesting**: _____; arousing curiosity or interest
- ☐ **people**: _____; human beings in general or considered collectively
- ☐ **learn**: _____; gain or acquire knowledge of or skill in something by study, experience, or being taught
- ☐ **importance**: _____; the state or fact of being of great significance or value
- ☐ **friendship**: _____; the emotions or conduct of friends; the state of being friends
- ☐ **difficult**: _____; needing much effort or skill to accomplish, deal with, or understand
- ☐ **set**: _____; put, lay, or stand something in a specified place or position
- ☐ **slavery**: _____; the state of being a slave; the practice or system of owning slaves
- ☐ **legal**: _____; permitted by law
- ☐ **address**: _____; write the destination on an envelope
- ☐ **important**: _____; of great significance or value
- ☐ **issue**: _____; an important topic or problem for debate or discussion
- ☐ **race**: _____; a group of people identified as distinct from other groups because of supposed physical or genetic traits shared by the group
- ☐ **inequality**: _____; the state of being unequal; lack of equality

DR. SIMON'S MAGIC ENGLISH

KEY VOCABULARY | LEVEL 100 - UNIT 17

- ☐ **brave**: _____; showing courage
- ☐ **kind**: _____; having or showing a friendly, generous, and considerate nature
- ☐ **help**: _____; make it easier or possible for someone to do something by offering them one's services or resources
- ☐ **bow**: _____; a weapon for shooting arrows, typically made of curved wood
- ☐ **arrow**: _____; a thin, pointed stick with a sharp tip that is shot from a bow
- ☐ **fight**: _____; take part in a violent struggle involving the exchange of physical blows or the use of weapons
- ☐ **bad**: _____; of poor quality; inferior or defective
- ☐ **sheriff**: _____; a government official who enforces the law, especially in rural areas
- ☐ **steal**: _____; take another person's property without permission or legal right and without intending to return it
- ☐ **rich**: _____; having a great deal of money or assets; wealthy
- ☐ **mean**: _____; unkind, spiteful, or unfair
- ☐ **poor**: _____; lacking sufficient money to live at a standard considered comfortable or normal in a society
- ☐ **feast**: _____; a large meal, typically one in celebration of something
- ☐ **dance**: _____; move rhythmically to music, typically following a set sequence of steps
- ☐ **sing**: _____; make musical sounds with the voice, especially words with a set tune
- ☐ **clever**: _____; quick to understand, learn, and devise or apply ideas; intelligent
- ☐ **outsmart**: _____; defeat or get the better of someone by being clever or cunning
- ☐ **lady**: _____; a polite or formal way of referring to a woman
- ☐ **friend**: _____; a person whom one knows and with whom one has a bond of mutual affection
- ☐ **adventure**: _____; an unusual and exciting or daring experience
- ☐ **happily ever after**: _____; a phrase used to describe the ending of a story in which a happy future is predicted for the main characters

KEY VOCABULARY | LEVEL 100 - UNIT 18

- ☐ **adventures**: _____ ; exciting experiences
- ☐ **collection**: _____ ; a group of items gathered together
- ☐ **short stories**: _____ ; brief narratives that focus on a particular event or character
- ☐ **detective**: _____ ; a person who investigates crimes and mysteries
- ☐ **solve**: _____ ; find a solution to a problem or mystery
- ☐ **mysteries**: _____ ; events or situations that are difficult to explain or understand
- ☐ **crime**: _____ ; an action that break the law and are punishable by the legal system
- ☐ **Victorian England**: _____ ; a period in English history during the reign of Queen Victoria
- ☐ **incredible**: _____ ; hard to believe or extraordinary
- ☐ **powers**: _____ ; abilities or skills
- ☐ **observation**: _____ ; the act of noticing or watching carefully
- ☐ **deduction**: _____ ; the process of reasoning from general principles to specific conclusions
- ☐ **investigate**: _____ ; look into something in order to discover the truth
- ☐ **disappearance**: _____ ; the act of vanishing or going missing
- ☐ **racehorse**: _____ ; a horse bred and trained for racing
- ☐ **missing**: _____ ; not present or accounted for
- ☐ **fiance**: _____ ; a man who is engaged to be married
- ☐ **catch**: _____ ; capture or seize
- ☐ **thief**: _____ ; a person who steals
- ☐ **valuable**: _____ ; worth a lot of money or highly prized
- ☐ **jewel**: _____ ; a precious stone or a piece of jewelry
- ☐ **murder**: _____ ; the crime of killing someone unlawfully
- ☐ **intelligence**: _____ ; the ability to learn and understand
- ☐ **wit**: _____ ; mental sharpness and humor
- ☐ **admiration**: _____ ; a feeling of respect and approval

DR. SIMON'S MAGIC ENGLISH

KEY VOCABULARY | **LEVEL 100 - UNIT 19**

- ☐ **young**: _____; at an early stage of life or growth
- ☐ **boy**: _____; a male child or youth
- ☐ **live**: _____; remain alive
- ☐ **small**: _____; of limited size or scope
- ☐ **town**: _____; a densely populated area outside a city
- ☐ **mischievous**: _____; causing or showing a fondness for causing trouble in a playful way
- ☐ **love**: _____; feel a strong affection or enjoyment for
- ☐ **play**: _____; engage in activity for enjoyment and recreation
- ☐ **prank**: _____; a mischievous act or practical joke
- ☐ **brave**: _____; ready to face and endure danger or pain
- ☐ **kind-hearted**: _____; having or showing a friendly, generous, and considerate nature
- ☐ **adventure**: _____; an unusual and exciting or daring experience
- ☐ **best**: _____; of the most excellent, effective, or desirable type or quality
- ☐ **friend**: _____; a person whom one knows and with whom one has a bond of mutual affection
- ☐ **explore**: _____; travel through an unfamiliar area in order to learn about it
- ☐ **haunted**: _____; visited by ghosts
- ☐ **house**: _____; a building for human habitation
- ☐ **search**: _____; look for or seek
- ☐ **treasure**: _____; a quantity of precious metals, gems, or other valuable objects
- ☐ **way**: _____; a method, style, or manner of doing something
- ☐ **trouble**: _____; difficulty or problems
- ☐ **teacher**: _____; a person who teaches, especially in a school
- ☐ **escape**: _____; break free from confinement or control
- ☐ **dangerous**: _____; able or likely to cause harm or injury
- ☐ **criminal**: _____; a person who has committed a crime
- ☐ **story**: _____; an account of past events that are or purport to be true
- ☐ **funny**: _____; causing laughter or amusement; humorous
- ☐ **exciting**: _____; causing great enthusiasm and eagerness
- ☐ **moments**: _____; very brief periods of time
- ☐ **important**: _____; of great significance or value
- ☐ **lesson**: _____; an amount of teaching given at one time; a period of learning or teaching
- ☐ **friendship**: _____; a state of mutual trust and support between people
- ☐ **bravery**: _____; courageous behavior
- ☐ **right**: _____; morally good, justified, or acceptable

20 | Literature Series

KEY VOCABULARY | LEVEL 100 - UNIT 20

- ☐ **jungle**: _____; an area of land with dense forest and tangled vegetation
- ☐ **collection**: _____; a group of things or people gathered together
- ☐ **story**: _____; a narrative, either true or fictitious, in prose or verse, designed to interest, amuse, or instruct the hearer or reader
- ☐ **young**: _____; at an early stage of life or growth
- ☐ **boy**: _____; a male child or youth
- ☐ **name**: _____; give a name to someone or something
- ☐ **animal**: _____; a living organism that feeds on organic matter, typically having specialized sense organs and nervous system and able to respond rapidly to stimuli
- ☐ **kind**: _____; having or showing a friendly, generous, and considerate nature
- ☐ **wolf**: _____; a wild carnivorous mammal of the dog family
- ☐ **family**: _____; a group consisting of parents and their children living together
- ☐ **take someone in**: _____; accept someone into one's home and look after them
- ☐ **adventures**: _____; unusual and exciting or daring experiences
- ☐ **friend**: _____; a person whom one knows and with whom one has a bond of mutual affection
- ☐ **including**: _____; comprising as part of a larger whole
- ☐ **fight**: _____; engage in a physical conflict or struggle
- ☐ **against**: _____; in opposition to; contrary to
- ☐ **enemy**: _____; a person who is actively opposed or hostile to someone or something
- ☐ **want**: _____; have a desire to possess or do something; wish for
- ☐ **kill**: _____; cause the death of a person, animal, or other living thing
- ☐ **exciting**: _____; causing great enthusiasm and eagerness
- ☐ **adventurous**: _____; willing to take risks or try out new methods, ideas, or experiences
- ☐ **brave**: _____; ready to face and endure danger or pain
- ☐ **become**: _____; come to be something or someone

Dr. Simon's Magic English Level 100 | 21

DR. SIMON'S MAGIC ENGLISH

KEY VOCABULARY | LEVEL 100 - UNIT 21

- ☐ **brave**: _____; ready to face and endure danger or pain
- ☐ **long time ago**: _____; a period of time in the distant past
- ☐ **friend**: _____; a person whom one knows and with whom one has a bond of mutual affection
- ☐ **group**: _____; a number of people or things that are located, gathered, or classed together
- ☐ **Native Americans**: _____; the indigenous peoples of North America
- ☐ **last**: _____; coming after all the others
- ☐ **member**: _____; a person or thing belonging to a group or class
- ☐ **tribe**: _____; a social division in a traditional society consisting of families or communities linked by social, economic, religious, or blood ties
- ☐ **help**: _____; give assistance to; make it easier for someone to do something
- ☐ **people**: _____; human beings in general or considered collectively
- ☐ **lost**: _____; unable to find one's way or direction
- ☐ **wilderness**: _____; an uncultivated, uninhabited, and inhospitable region
- ☐ **chase**: _____; pursue or run after someone or something
- ☐ **ally**: _____; a person or group that gives help to another in achieving a goal
- ☐ **fight**: _____; engage in a physical conflict or struggle
- ☐ **battle**: _____; a sustained fight between large, organized armed forces
- ☐ **face**: _____; confront and deal with or accept
- ☐ **dangerous**: _____; able or likely to cause harm or injury
- ☐ **situation**: _____; a set of circumstances in which one finds oneself
- ☐ **story**: _____; an account of imaginary or real people and events told for entertainment
- ☐ **full of**: _____; containing a lot of
- ☐ **action**: _____; the fact or process of doing something, typically to achieve an aim
- ☐ **adventure**: _____; an unusual and exciting or daring experience
- ☐ **exciting**: _____; causing great enthusiasm and eagerness
- ☐ **moment**: _____; a very brief period of time
- ☐ **explore**: _____; inquire into or discuss a subject in detail
- ☐ **theme**: _____; a recurrent or unifying subject or idea
- ☐ **friendship**: _____; the emotions or conduct of friends; the state of being friends
- ☐ **loyalty**: _____; a strong feeling of support or allegiance
- ☐ **respect**: _____; a feeling of deep admiration for someone or something elicited by their abilities, qualities, or achievements
- ☐ **different**: _____; not the same as another or each other
- ☐ **cultures**: _____; the arts and other manifestations of human intellectual achievement regarded collectively

KEY VOCABULARY | LEVEL 100 - UNIT 22

- ☐ **universe**: _____; the whole of all things that exist, including planets, stars, galaxies, and all forms of matter and energy
- ☐ **creatures**: _____; living beings, animals, or monsters
- ☐ **learning**: _____; acquiring knowledge or skills through study, experience, or teaching
- ☐ **life lesson**: _____; an experience or observation that teaches someone how to do something better or more effectively
- ☐ **tiny**: _____; very small in size or amount
- ☐ **planet**: _____; a celestial body that orbits around a star
- ☐ **journey**: _____; the act of traveling from one place to another
- ☐ **fox**: _____; a carnivorous mammal with a pointed muzzle, bushy tail, and reddish-brown fur
- ☐ **importance**: _____; the quality of being significant or valuable
- ☐ **forming**: _____; creating or making something
- ☐ **bonds**: _____; connections or relationships between people or things
- ☐ **rose**: _____; a flower with a sweet fragrance and typically pink, red, or white petals
- ☐ **love**: _____; a strong feeling of affection or attachment towards someone
- ☐ **responsibility**: _____; the state or fact of being accountable for something
- ☐ **Earth**: _____; the third planet from the sun, the planet we live on
- ☐ **pilot**: _____; a person who operates an aircraft
- ☐ **crash**: _____; be involved in a serious accident, typically a collision, in which the vehicle is severely damaged
- ☐ **desert**: _____; a dry, barren area of land, especially one covered with sand, that is characteristically desolate, waterless, and without vegetation
- ☐ **friendship**: _____; a state of mutual trust and support between people
- ☐ **value**: _____; the worth or usefulness of something
- ☐ **relationship**: _____; the way in which two or more people or things are connected or behave towards each other

Dr. Simon's Magic English Level 100 | 23

DR. SIMON'S MAGIC ENGLISH

KEY VOCABULARY | **LEVEL 100 - UNIT 23**

- ☐ **old**: _____; having lived for a long time; no longer young
- ☐ **fisherman**: _____; a person who catches fish, either for a living or as a hobby
- ☐ **small**: _____; little in size
- ☐ **village**: _____; a group of houses and associated buildings, larger than a hamlet and smaller than a town
- ☐ **ocean**: _____; a large body of saltwater that covers most of the Earth's surface
- ☐ **catch**: _____; grab or take hold of something, often with effort or difficulty
- ☐ **big**: _____; large in size
- ☐ **difficult**: _____; not easy; requiring effort or skill
- ☐ **sea**: _____; the saltwater body of the Earth's surface
- ☐ **struggle**: _____; make great effort; have difficulty
- ☐ **three**: _____; the number 3
- ☐ **shark**: _____; a type of predatory fish that live in the ocean and have sharp teeth
- ☐ **attack**: _____; try to harm or injure someone or something
- ☐ **lose**: _____; no longer have something or fail to keep something
- ☐ **skeleton**: _____; the framework of bones that support the body of a human or animal
- ☐ **despite**: _____; even though; in spite of
- ☐ **loss**: _____; the fact or process of losing something or someone
- ☐ **realize**: _____; become fully aware of something as a fact
- ☐ **still**: _____; despite what has just been said; nevertheless
- ☐ **strong**: _____; physically powerful; able to withstand great force or pressure
- ☐ **continue**: _____; keep doing something; to persist in an activity or process

KEY VOCABULARY | LEVEL 100 - UNIT 24

- ☐ **prince**: _____; a male member of a royal family who is next in line to the throne
- ☐ **pauper**: _____; a very poor person who has no money or possessions
- ☐ **boys**: _____; young males, usually under the age of 18
- ☐ **look alike**: _____; have a similar physical appearance to someone else
- ☐ **background**: _____; a person's family, social, and economic status
- ☐ **poor**: _____; lacking sufficient money to live at a standard considered comfortable or normal in a society
- ☐ **wealthy**: _____; having a great deal of money, resources, or assets; rich
- ☐ **palace**: _____; a large, impressive building that is the official home of a king, queen, president, or other important person
- ☐ **switch places**: _____; exchange roles, positions, or locations with someone else
- ☐ **learn**: _____; gain knowledge or skill in a subject through experience or study
- ☐ **challenges**: _____; difficult tasks or situations that require effort, skill, or courage to overcome
- ☐ **adventures**: _____; exciting and unusual experiences or journeys, often involving danger or risk

DR. SIMON'S MAGIC ENGLISH

KEY VOCABULARY | **LEVEL 100 - UNIT 25**

- ☐ **king**: _____; a male ruler of a country
- ☐ **legendary**: _____; remarkable enough to be famous or very well known
- ☐ **day**: _____; a particular day of the year
- ☐ **young**: _____; in the early period of life, development, or growth
- ☐ **boy**: _____; a male child or youth
- ☐ **pull**: _____; use force to move something towards oneself
- ☐ **magical**: _____; possessing or using magic; enchanting
- ☐ **sword**: _____; a weapon with a long metal blade and a hilt with a handguard
- ☐ **stone**: _____; a hard solid non-metallic mineral matter
- ☐ **make**: _____; bring into existence or produce
- ☐ **rightful**: _____; having a just or legally recognized claim
- ☐ **help**: _____; give assistance to someone or something
- ☐ **brave**: _____; showing courage in the face of danger
- ☐ **knight**: _____; a man who served his sovereign or lord as a mounted soldier in armor
- ☐ **sir**: _____; a respectful or formal title used to address a man
- ☐ **exciting**: _____; creating a strong sense of anticipation or emotional reaction
- ☐ **adventure**: _____; an exciting or dangerous experience
- ☐ **fight**: _____; engage in a physical battle
- ☐ **against**: _____; in opposition to
- ☐ **evil**: _____; morally wrong or wicked
- ☐ **sorcerer**: _____; a person who practices magic, typically for evil purposes
- ☐ **dragon**: _____; a mythical creature typically depicted as a huge, serpentine or reptilian creature with wings, sharp claws, and fire breath
- ☐ **giant**: _____; an imaginary or mythical being of human form but of superhuman size
- ☐ **advisor**: _____; a person who gives advice, typically someone who is expert or influential
- ☐ **decision**: _____; a conclusion or resolution reached after consideration

KEY VOCABULARY | LEVEL 100 - UNIT 26

- ☐ **group**: _____ ; a number of people or things that are located, gathered, or classed together
- ☐ **friend**: _____ ; a person whom one knows and with whom one has a bond of mutual affection
- ☐ **travel**: _____ ; make a journey, typically of some length or abroad
- ☐ **watch**: _____ ; look at or observe attentively over a period of time
- ☐ **bullfighting**: _____ ; a traditional spectacle of Spain, Portugal, southern France, and some Latin American countries, in which a bull is fought in a ring by a matador for sport and entertainment
- ☐ **main**: _____ ; chief in size, importance, or rank
- ☐ **character**: _____ ; the mental and moral qualities distinctive to an individual
- ☐ **veteran**: _____ ; a person who has had long experience in a particular field
- ☐ **love**: _____ ; a strong feeling of affection
- ☐ **woman**: _____ ; an adult human female
- ☐ **name**: _____ ; give a particular name to
- ☐ **injured**: _____ ; harmed or damaged physically or mentally
- ☐ **unable**: _____ ; not able to do something
- ☐ **romantic**: _____ ; conducive to or characterized by the expression of love
- ☐ **relationship**: _____ ; the way in which two or more people or things are connected, or the state of being connected
- ☐ **drink**: _____ ; consume a liquid through the mouth
- ☐ **lot**: _____ ; a great deal; much
- ☐ **enjoy**: _____ ; take delight or pleasure in an activity or occasion
- ☐ **nightlife**: _____ ; social activities or entertainment available at night in a town or city
- ☐ **experience**: _____ ; encounter or undergo an event or occurrence
- ☐ **sadness**: _____ ; the condition or quality of being sad; sorrow; unhappiness
- ☐ **disappointment**: _____ ; the feeling of sadness or displeasure caused by the nonfulfillment of one's hopes or expectations

DR. SIMON'S MAGIC ENGLISH

KEY VOCABULARY | **LEVEL 100 - UNIT 27**

- ☐ **man**: _____; an adult human male
- ☐ **invent**: _____; create or design something that has not existed before
- ☐ **machine**: _____; an apparatus using or applying mechanical power and having several parts, each with a definite function and together performing a particular task
- ☐ **travel**: _____; go from one place to another, typically over a distance of some length
- ☐ **time**: _____; the indefinite continued progress of existence and events in the past, present, and future regarded as a whole
- ☐ **Time Traveler**: _____; the name of the man who invents the machine that can travel through time
- ☐ **far**: _____; at, to, or by a great distance
- ☐ **future**: _____; the time or a period of time following the moment of speaking or writing; time regarded as still to come
- ☐ **discover**: _____; find something out for the first time
- ☐ **world**: _____; the earth, together with all of its countries, peoples, and natural features
- ☐ **change**: _____; make or become different
- ☐ **evolve**: _____; develop gradually, especially from a simple to a more complex form
- ☐ **distinct**: _____; recognizably different in nature from something else of a similar type
- ☐ **species**: _____; a group of living organisms consisting of similar individuals capable of exchanging genes or interbreeding
- ☐ **small**: _____; of a size that is less than normal or usual
- ☐ **weak**: _____; lacking the power to perform physically demanding tasks; lacking strength
- ☐ **big**: _____; of considerable size or extent
- ☐ **strong**: _____; having the power to move heavy weights or perform other physically demanding tasks
- ☐ **try**: _____; make an attempt or effort to do something
- ☐ **understand**: _____; perceive the intended meaning of words, a language, or a speaker
- ☐ **figure out**: _____; succeed in understanding, solving, or finding something
- ☐ **own**: _____; belonging to oneself or itself; possessive pronoun used to indicate something belongs to the speaker or writer
- ☐ **get back**: _____; return to a place or situation that one has left

KEY VOCABULARY | LEVEL 100 - UNIT 28

- **young**: _____; having lived or existed for only a short time and not yet old
- **name**: _____; give a name to
- **want**: _____; have a desire to possess or do something; wish for
- **become**: _____; begin to be; grow into
- **musketeer**: _____; a soldier armed with a musket, especially one of the French royal foot soldiers of the 16th–18th centuries, typically having long hair and a flamboyant appearance
- **meet**: _____; come into the presence or company of someone by chance or arrangement
- **good**: _____; to be desired or approved of; satisfactory or pleasing in quality, quantity, or degree
- **friend**: _____; a person with whom one has a bond of mutual affection, typically one exclusive of sexual or family relations
- **together**: _____; with or in proximity to another person or people
- **many**: _____; a large number of
- **adventure**: _____; an unusual and exciting or daring experience
- **protect**: _____; keep safe from harm or injury
- **queen**: _____; the female ruler of an independent state, especially one who inherits the position by right of birth
- **fight**: _____; take part in a violent struggle involving the exchange of physical blows or the use of weapons
- **evil**: _____; profoundly immoral and wicked
- **fall in love**: _____; begin to feel a strong emotional attachment or deep romantic affection for someone
- **lady**: _____; a polite or formal way of referring to a woman
- **help**: _____; make it easier or possible for someone to do something by offering them one's services or resources
- **escape**: _____; break free from confinement or control
- **bad guys**: _____; the characters in the story who are portrayed as villains or the antagonists
- **end**: _____; the final part of something
- **work together**: _____; cooperate with each other
- **save the day**: _____; prevent a situation from turning into a disaster or resolve a difficult situation successfully

DR. SIMON'S MAGIC ENGLISH

KEY VOCABULARY | LEVEL 100 - UNIT 29

- ☐ **go**: _____; move or travel from one place to another
- ☐ **big**: _____; large in size or amount
- ☐ **adventure**: _____; an unusual, exciting, or dangerous experience
- ☐ **find**: _____; discover something or someone
- ☐ **treasure**: _____; valuable objects or money hidden or lost in a place
- ☐ **map**: _____; a diagrammatic representation of an area of land or sea
- ☐ **lead**: _____; be a route or means of access to a particular place or in a particular direction
- ☐ **set**: _____; put or place in a particular position
- ☐ **sail**: _____; travel on water in a ship or boat
- ☐ **crew**: _____; a group of people who work together on a ship or aircraft
- ☐ **sailor**: _____; a person whose job is sailing or working as a member of the crew on a ship
- ☐ **man**: _____; an adult human male
- ☐ **name**: _____; give a particular name to something or someone
- ☐ **long**: _____; extending a great distance from end to end
- ☐ **encounter**: _____; unexpectedly experience or be faced with something difficult or hostile
- ☐ **many**: _____; a large number of
- ☐ **obstacle**: _____; a thing that blocks one's way or prevents or hinders progress
- ☐ **way**: _____; a route or means to get somewhere or achieve something
- ☐ **including**: _____; comprising as part of a whole
- ☐ **storm**: _____; a violent disturbance of the atmosphere with strong winds and usually rain, thunder, lightning, or snow
- ☐ **battle**: _____; a sustained fight between large organized armed forces
- ☐ **pirate**: _____; a person who attacks and robs ships at sea
- ☐ **friend**: _____; a person whom one knows and with whom one has a bond of mutual affection
- ☐ **able**: _____; having the power, skill, means, or opportunity to do something
- ☐ **outsmart**: _____; win

KEY VOCABULARY | LEVEL 100 - UNIT 30

- ☐ **wolf-dog**: _____; a hybrid animal that is a cross between a wolf and a domesticated dog
- ☐ **live**: _____; remain alive or in existence
- ☐ **wild**: _____; living in a state of nature
- ☐ **learn**: _____; gain knowledge or skill through experience or study
- ☐ **survive**: _____; remain alive or continue to live
- ☐ **fighting**: _____; the action of engaging in a physical conflict with someone or something
- ☐ **hunting**: _____; the activity of pursuing and killing wild animals
- ☐ **eventually**: _____; in the end, especially after a long delay, dispute, or series of problems
- ☐ **capture**: _____; take someone as a prisoner or as if taken as a prisoner
- ☐ **human**: _____; a bipedal primate species that includes modern humans
- ☐ **hard**: _____;requiring a great deal of effort or endurance to endure
- ☐ **time**: _____; the indefinite continued progress of existence
- ☐ **adjust**: _____; become more suitable for new circumstances
- ☐ **life**: _____; the condition that distinguishes living organisms from non-living things
- ☐ **trust**: _____; believe in the reliability, truth, or ability of someone or something
- ☐ **become**: _____; begin to be something or to cause someone or something to become something
- ☐ **loyal**: _____; giving or showing firm and constant support or allegiance to a person or institution
- ☐ **companion**: _____; a person or animal with whom one spends a lot of time or with whom one travels
- ☐ **man**: _____; an adult human male
- ☐ **name**: _____; give a particular name to something or someone
- ☐ **treat**: _____; behave toward or deal with someone in a certain way
- ☐ **kindly**: _____; in a way that is kind or pleasant
- ☐ **love**: _____; feel a strong affection or deep attachment towards someone or something
- ☐ **family**: _____; a group of people related by blood or marriage
- ☐ **protect**: _____; keep someone or something safe from harm or injury
- ☐ **danger**: _____; the possibility of suffering harm or injury
- ☐ **end**: _____; the final part of something, especially a period of time or a story
- ☐ **loving**: _____; feeling or showing love or great care
- ☐ **faithful**: _____; remaining loyal and steadfast to someone or something
- ☐ **friend**: _____; a person whom one knows and likes and who is not related to one by blood or marriage

DR. SIMON'S MAGIC ENGLISH

KEY VOCABULARY | LEVEL 200 - UNIT 1

- ☐ **farewell**: _____; goodbye, the act of departing or leaving
- ☐ **arms**: _____; weapons or firearms
- ☐ **war**: _____; a state of armed conflict between nations, states, or societies
- ☐ **long time ago**: _____; a period in the distant past
- ☐ **help**: _____; assist, aid or support
- ☐ **fight**: _____; engage in a battle, struggle or conflict
- ☐ **against**: _____; in opposition or hostility to
- ☐ **injured**: _____; harmed, wounded or hurt
- ☐ **hospital**: _____; a medical facility where people receive treatment and care
- ☐ **meet**: _____; encounter or come across someone or something
- ☐ **nurse**: _____; a healthcare professional who provides medical care and support to patients
- ☐ **named**: _____; called or designated with a particular name
- ☐ **fall in love**: _____; develop strong romantic feelings for someone
- ☐ **spent**: _____; passed or used time
- ☐ **together**: _____; in each other's company or presence
- ☐ **still**: _____; continuing to exist or occur
- ☐ **going on**: _____; happening or continuing
- ☐ **try**: _____; attempt or make an effort
- ☐ **run away**: _____; escape or flee from a dangerous or unpleasant situation
- ☐ **safe place**: _____; a location where one can be protected from harm or danger
- ☐ **caught**: _____; apprehended or captured
- ☐ **have to**: _____; require or obligate to do something
- ☐ **back**: _____; to the place one was before or previously
- ☐ **later on**: _____; at a subsequent or later time
- ☐ **find out**: _____; discover or learn something
- ☐ **pregnant**: _____; carrying a developing fetus within the female body
- ☐ **get someone to safety**: _____; move someone to a secure or protected place
- ☐ **again**: _____; once more, another time
- ☐ **happen**: _____; occur
- ☐ **very**: _____; to a high degree or extent
- ☐ **say goodbye**: _____; bid farewell, to part from someone
- ☐ **forever**: _____; for all time or eternity

KEY VOCABULARY | LEVEL 200 - UNIT 2

- ☐ **night**: _____; a period of darkness that occurs between sunset and sunrise, typically from about 6 p.m. to 6 a.m.
- ☐ **famous**: _____; well-known, widely recognized or celebrated
- ☐ **book**: _____; a written or printed work consisting of pages bound together
- ☐ **story**: _____; a narrative or tale, either true or fictitious
- ☐ **Middle East**: _____; a region in western Asia and northeastern Africa
- ☐ **young**: _____; in the early years of life, growth or development
- ☐ **girl**: _____; a female child
- ☐ **named**: _____; designated or called by a particular name
- ☐ **tell**: _____; give an account of something, narrate or describe
- ☐ **king**: _____; a male monarch, the ruler of a kingdom or empire
- ☐ **save**: _____; rescue, protect or spare from harm or danger
- ☐ **own**: _____; belonging to oneself, not someone else
- ☐ **life**: _____; the state of being alive or living
- ☐ **habit**: _____; a regular practice or tendency, especially one that is hard to give up
- ☐ **marry**: _____; enter into the legal union of marriage with someone
- ☐ **new**: _____; recently made or produced, not existing before
- ☐ **wife**: _____; a married woman
- ☐ **every**: _____; each one of a group, occurring at regular intervals
- ☐ **only**: _____; and no more, just one thing
- ☐ **executed**: _____; put to death, killed as a punishment
- ☐ **next day**: _____; the day after today, following the present day
- ☐ **begin**: _____; start, commence
- ☐ **always**: _____; at all times, every time
- ☐ **leave**: _____; abandon, let remain, depart from
- ☐ **unfinished**: _____; not complete or finished
- ☐ **spare**: _____; refrain from killing or harming, to give mercy or leniency
- ☐ **many**: _____; a large number of, numerous
- ☐ **exciting**: _____; stimulating, thrilling, or stirring
- ☐ **like**: _____; such as, similar to
- ☐ **sailor**: _____; a person who works on a ship or boat, especially one who is skilled or experienced

Dr. Simon's Magic English Level 200 | 33

DR. SIMON'S MAGIC ENGLISH

KEY VOCABULARY | **LEVEL 200 - UNIT 3**

- ☐ **society**: _____; a community of people living together in a particular country or region
- ☐ **born**: _____; brought into existence through birth
- ☐ **raised**: _____; brought up or reared
- ☐ **factory**: _____; a building where goods are manufactured or assembled chiefly by machine
- ☐ **made**: _____; created or produced
- ☐ **happy**: _____; feeling or expressing joy or contentment
- ☐ **think**: _____; use one's mind to consider or reason about something
- ☐ **too much**: _____; to an excessive or unreasonable degree
- ☐ **group**: _____; a number of people or things that are located, classified, or considered together
- ☐ **called**: _____; named or referred to as
- ☐ **caste**: _____; a social class or system based on birth and rank
- ☐ **allowed**: _____; permitted or authorized to do something
- ☐ **move up or down**: _____; change one's social class or rank
- ☐ **follow**: _____; trace the course or direction of something
- ☐ **man**: _____; an adult human male
- ☐ **named**: _____; called or designated with a particular name
- ☐ **fit in**: _____; be accepted or belong to a group or society
- ☐ **rest of society**: _____; the other members of a community or social group
- ☐ **meet**: _____; encounter or come across someone or something
- ☐ **girl**: _____; a female child or young woman
- ☐ **start to fall in love**: _____; begin to have romantic feelings for someone
- ☐ **complicated**: _____; involved or intricate, difficult to understand or deal with
- ☐ **trip**: _____; a journey or excursion, typically for pleasure or vacation
- ☐ **place**: _____; a particular position, point, or area in space
- ☐ **reservation**: _____; a place in "Brave New World" where people still live in a traditional way
- ☐ **still**: _____; continuing to exist or occur
- ☐ **live**: _____; remain alive or have one's being
- ☐ **way**: _____; a method, style, or manner of doing something
- ☐ **bring back**: _____; return with something or someone
- ☐ **fascinated**: _____; strongly attracted and interested in something or someone
- ☐ **unhappy**: _____; not happy or content with a situation
- ☐ **born naturally**: _____; not created or manufactured artificially

34 | Literature Series

KEY VOCABULARY | LEVEL 200 - UNIT 4

- ☐ **generation**: _____; a group of individuals born and living at the same time
- ☐ **people**: _____; human beings
- ☐ **older**: _____; having lived for a long time
- ☐ **called**: _____; named or identified as
- ☐ **younger**: _____; being in an early stage of life or growth
- ☐ **story**: _____; a narrative, either true or fictitious, in prose or verse, designed to interest, amuse, or instruct the hearer or reader
- ☐ **follow**: _____; go or come after a person or thing proceeding ahead; move or travel behind
- ☐ **named**: _____; called; given a name
- ☐ **believe**: _____; accept something as true; feel sure of the truth of
- ☐ **science**: _____; the study of the natural world based on facts learned through experiments and observation
- ☐ **tradition**: _____; a long-established custom or belief that has been passed on from one generation to another
- ☐ **feeling**: _____; an emotional state or reaction
- ☐ **visit**: _____; go to see and spend time with someone socially
- ☐ **family**: _____; a group of people related to one another by blood or marriage
- ☐ **friend**: _____; a person whom one knows and with whom one has a bond of mutual affection
- ☐ **meet**: _____; come into the presence or company of someone by chance or arrangement
- ☐ **women**: _____; adult human females
- ☐ **start**: _____; begin or cause to begin to happen or exist
- ☐ **fall**: _____; move downward, typically rapidly and freely without control
- ☐ **love**: _____; an intense feeling of deep affection
- ☐ **same**: _____; exactly alike; not different
- ☐ **way**: _____; a method, style, or manner of doing something
- ☐ **meanwhile**: _____; in the intervening period of time; at the same time
- ☐ **get**: _____; come to have or hold something; receive
- ☐ **engaged**: _____; having formally agreed to marry
- ☐ **complicated**: _____; consisting of many interconnecting parts or elements; intricate
- ☐ **sick**: _____; affected by physical or mental illness
- ☐ **realize**: _____; become fully aware of something as a fact; understand clearly
- ☐ **life**: _____; the condition that distinguishes animals and plants from inorganic matter, including the capacity for growth, reproduction, functional activity, and continual change preceding death
- ☐ **than**: _____; introducing the second element in a comparison

DR. SIMON'S MAGIC ENGLISH

KEY VOCABULARY | LEVEL 200 - UNIT 5

- ☐ **scientist**: _____; a person who is studying or has expert knowledge of one or more of the natural or physical sciences
- ☐ **named**: _____; called; given a name
- ☐ **create**: _____; make something exist or happen; bring into being
- ☐ **monster**: _____; a large, ugly, and frightening imaginary creature
- ☐ **dead**: _____; no longer alive
- ☐ **body**: _____; the physical structure of a person or an animal, including the bones, flesh, and organs
- ☐ **part**: _____; a piece or segment of something
- ☐ **scary-looking**: _____; frightening in appearance
- ☐ **also**: _____; in addition; too
- ☐ **lonely**: _____; sad because one has no friends or company
- ☐ **want**: _____; have a desire to possess or do something
- ☐ **someone**: _____; an unknown or unspecified person; somebody
- ☐ **love**: _____; an intense feeling of deep affection
- ☐ **story**: _____; a narrative, either true or fictitious, in prose or verse, designed to interest, amuse, or instruct the hearer or reader
- ☐ **follow**: _____; go or come after a person or thing proceeding ahead; move or travel behind
- ☐ **try**: _____; make an attempt or effort to do something
- ☐ **find**: _____; discover or perceive by chance or unexpectedly
- ☐ **acceptance**: _____; the action of consenting to receive or undertake something offered
- ☐ **world**: _____; the earth, together with all of its countries, peoples, and natural features
- ☐ **people**: _____; human beings
- ☐ **scared**: _____; frightened; afraid
- ☐ **chase**: _____; pursue in order to catch or catch up with
- ☐ **away**: _____; to or at a distance from a particular place or person
- ☐ **realize**: _____; become fully aware of something as a fact; understand clearly
- ☐ **mistake**: _____; an action or judgment that is misguided or wrong
- ☐ **get rid of**: _____; dispose of; remove
- ☐ **very**: _____; used to emphasize the degree of something
- ☐ **sad**: _____; feeling or showing sorrow; unhappy
- ☐ **angry**: _____; feeling or showing strong annoyance, displeasure, or hostility
- ☐ **start**: _____; begin or cause to begin to happen or exist
- ☐ **bad**: _____; of poor quality or a low standard
- ☐ **thing**: _____; an object that one need not, cannot, or does not wish to give a specific name to

KEY VOCABULARY | LEVEL 200 - UNIT 6

- ☐ **live**: _____; have one's permanent home in a particular place or with a particular person
- ☐ **beautiful**: _____; pleasing the senses or mind aesthetically
- ☐ **love**: _____; feel a deep romantic or sexual attachment to someone
- ☐ **fun**: _____; enjoyment, amusement, or lighthearted pleasure
- ☐ **man**: _____; an adult human male
- ☐ **named**: _____; called; given a name
- ☐ **another**: _____; different from the one already mentioned or known about
- ☐ **woman**: _____; an adult human female
- ☐ **end up**: _____; finally arrive or do something after a lot of problems, effort, or delay
- ☐ **marry**: _____; take someone as one's wife or husband in marriage
- ☐ **first**: _____; before anything else in order or time
- ☐ **during**: _____; throughout the course or duration of a period of time
- ☐ **war**: _____; a state of armed conflict between nations, states, or societies
- ☐ **life**: _____; the condition that distinguishes animals and plants from inorganic matter
- ☐ **change**: _____; make or become different
- ☐ **lot**: _____; a great deal; much
- ☐ **work**: _____; activity involving mental or physical effort done in order to achieve a result
- ☐ **hard**: _____; with a great deal of effort
- ☐ **money**: _____; a current medium of exchange in the form of coins, banknotes, or digital currency
- ☐ **strong**: _____; having the power to move heavy weights or perform other physically demanding tasks
- ☐ **give up**: _____; stop trying; surrender
- ☐ **baby**: _____; a very young child, especially one newly or recently born
- ☐ **die**: _____; stop living of a person, animal, or plant
- ☐ **soon**: _____; in or after a short time
- ☐ **after**: _____; following in time or place; later than
- ☐ **born**: _____; brought into existence
- ☐ **end**: _____; the final part of something, especially a period of time, an activity, or a story
- ☐ **realize**: _____; become fully aware of something as a fact; understand clearly
- ☐ **too**: _____; to a higher degree than is desirable, permissible, or possible; excessively
- ☐ **late**: _____; after the expected, proper, or usual time
- ☐ **leave**: _____; go away from a place or situation

Dr. Simon's Magic English Level 200 | 37

DR. SIMON'S MAGIC ENGLISH

KEY VOCABULARY | **LEVEL 200 - UNIT 7**

- ☐ **prince**: _____; a male member of a royal family
- ☐ **sad**: _____; feeling unhappy or sorrowful
- ☐ **father**: _____; a male parent
- ☐ **king**: _____; a male ruler of a country or state
- ☐ **uncle**: _____; the brother of one's parent
- ☐ **new**: _____; recently made or produced
- ☐ **marry**: _____; become the husband or wife of someone
- ☐ **angry**: _____; feeling or showing strong annoyance or displeasure
- ☐ **revenge**: _____; the action of inflicting harm or punishment on someone for an injury or wrong suffered at their hands
- ☐ **know**: _____; have information or knowledge about something
- ☐ **pretend**: _____; behave as if something is true when it is not
- ☐ **crazy**: _____; mentally deranged or unstable
- ☐ **suspect**: _____; have an idea or impression of the existence, presence, or truth of something without certain proof
- ☐ **girlfriend**: _____; a regular female companion with whom a person is romantically or sexually involved
- ☐ **upset**: _____; make someone unhappy or disappointed
- ☐ **drown**: _____; die or kill by immersion in liquid
- ☐ **river**: _____; a large natural stream of water flowing in a channel to the sea, a lake, or another such stream
- ☐ **end**: _____; the final part of something
- ☐ **fight**: _____; a violent confrontation or struggle
- ☐ **die**: _____; cease to live
- ☐ **friend**: _____; a person whom one knows and with whom one has a bond of mutual affection
- ☐ **alive**: _____; living, not dead
- ☐ **tell**: _____; communicate information, facts or news to someone
- ☐ **happened**: _____; occurred, took place

KEY VOCABULARY | LEVEL 200 - UNIT 8

- ☐ **little**: _____; small in size or amount
- ☐ **girl**: _____; a female child
- ☐ **named**: _____; called
- ☐ **live**: _____; reside, exist
- ☐ **mountain**: _____; a large natural elevation of the earth's surface
- ☐ **grandfather**: _____; a parent's or a parent-in-law's father
- ☐ **very**: _____; extremely, to a high degree
- ☐ **happy**: _____; feeling or showing pleasure or contentment
- ☐ **love**: _____; like very much, have a great affection for
- ☐ **play**: _____; engage in activity for enjoyment and recreation
- ☐ **day**: _____; a period of 24 hours
- ☐ **aunt**: _____; the sister of one's parent
- ☐ **come**: _____; arrive or reach a place
- ☐ **take**: _____; carry or bring someone or something to a place
- ☐ **city**: _____; a large town or urban area
- ☐ **companion**: _____; a person or animal with whom one spends a lot of time or with whom one travels
- ☐ **sick**: _____; affected by illness
- ☐ **homesick**: _____; experiencing a longing for one's home during a period of absence from it
- ☐ **first**: _____; at the beginning
- ☐ **eventually**: _____; in the end, after a long time
- ☐ **become**: _____; start to be
- ☐ **friend**: _____; a person whom one knows and with whom one has a bond of mutual affection
- ☐ **teach**: _____; show or instruct someone how to do something
- ☐ **walk**: _____; move at a regular pace by lifting and setting down each foot in turn
- ☐ **much**: _____; to a great extent or degree
- ☐ **happier**: _____; feeling or showing pleasure or contentment to a greater extent than before
- ☐ **still**: _____; continuing to happen or take place
- ☐ **want**: _____; have a desire to possess or do something
- ☐ **go**: _____; move from one place to another
- ☐ **back**: _____; in the direction opposite to the one that is facing or is being faced
- ☐ **end**: _____; the final part of something

Dr. Simon's Magic English Level 200 | 39

DR. SIMON'S MAGIC ENGLISH

KEY VOCABULARY | LEVEL 200 - UNIT 9

- ☐ **invisible**: _____; unable to be seen or perceived
- ☐ **feel**: _____; experience a particular emotion or physical sensation
- ☐ **like**: _____; having the same characteristics or qualities as; similar to
- ☐ **because**: _____; for the reason that; since
- ☐ **people**: _____; human beings in general or considered collectively
- ☐ **see**: _____; perceive with the eyes; discern visually
- ☐ **grow**: _____; become larger or greater over a period of time; increases
- ☐ **experience**: _____; encounter, undergo or live through
- ☐ **racism**: _____; prejudice, discrimination, or antagonism directed against someone of a different race based on the belief that one's own race is superior
- ☐ **discrimination**: _____; the unjust or prejudicial treatment of different categories of people, especially on the grounds of race, age, or sex
- ☐ **move**: _____; change one's place of residence or work
- ☐ **try**: _____; make an attempt or effort to do something
- ☐ **find**: _____; discover or perceive by chance or unexpectedly
- ☐ **place**: _____; a particular position or point in space
- ☐ **world**: _____; the earth, together with all of its countries, peoples, and natural features
- ☐ **still**: _____; continuing to happen or take place
- ☐ **control**: _____; the power to influence or direct people's behavior or the course of events
- ☐ **tell**: _____; communicate information, facts, or news to someone
- ☐ **want**: _____; have a desire to possess or do something; wish for
- ☐ **own**: _____; belonging to oneself or itself
- ☐ **person**: _____; a human being regarded as an individual
- ☐ **join**: _____; become a member or part of a group, organization, or club
- ☐ **called**: _____; named or titled
- ☐ **gain**: _____; obtain or secure something wanted or desirable
- ☐ **equal**: _____; being the same in quantity, size, degree, or value
- ☐ **right**: _____; a moral or legal entitlement to have or do something
- ☐ **realize**: _____; become fully aware of something as a fact; understand clearly
- ☐ **care**: _____; feel concern or interest; attach importance to something
- ☐ **tool**: _____; a device or implement, especially one held in the hand, used to carry out a particular function
- ☐ **achieve**: _____; successfully bring about or reach a desired objective, level, or result by effort, skill, or courage
- ☐ **goal**: _____; the object of a person's ambition or effort; an aim or desired result

KEY VOCABULARY | LEVEL 200 - UNIT 10

- ☐ **early**: _____; happening or done near the beginning of a period of time
- ☐ **parents**: _____; mother and father
- ☐ **life**: _____; the condition that distinguishes organisms from inorganic substances and dead objects
- ☐ **aunt**: _____; the sister of someone's father or mother or the wife of someone's uncle
- ☐ **cousin**: _____; a child of one's uncle or aunt
- ☐ **treat**: _____; behave towards or deal with in a certain way
- ☐ **nicely**: _____; in a pleasant or correct way, well
- ☐ **love**: _____; an intense feeling of deep affection
- ☐ **read**: _____; look at and comprehend the meaning of written or printed matter by mentally interpreting the characters or symbols of which it is composed
- ☐ **boarding school**: _____; a school providing living accommodation for some or all of its pupils or students
- ☐ **governess**: _____; a woman employed to teach children in a private household
- ☐ **person**: _____; a human being regarded as an individual
- ☐ **take care of**: _____; be in charge of or responsible for someone or something
- ☐ **child**: _____; a young human being below the age of full physical development or below the legal age of majority
- ☐ **called**: _____; named or identified as
- ☐ **name**: _____; give a name to
- ☐ **start**: _____; begin or cause to begin
- ☐ **fall in love**: _____; begin to experience feelings of love towards someone
- ☐ **father**: _____; a male parent
- ☐ **find out**: _____; discover something
- ☐ **hide**: _____; put or keep out of sight; conceal from the view or notice of others
- ☐ **secret**: _____; something that is kept or meant to be kept unknown or unseen by others
- ☐ **end**: _____; the final part of something
- ☐ **leave**: _____; go away from
- ☐ **stop**: _____; come to an end; cease to happen
- ☐ **live**: _____; remain alive
- ☐ **eventually**: _____; in the end, especially after a long time or a series of problems or delays
- ☐ **back together**: _____; in reunited way after a separation

DR. SIMON'S MAGIC ENGLISH

KEY VOCABULARY | **LEVEL 200 - UNIT 11**

- ☐ **journey**: _____; a long and often difficult process of personal change and development
- ☐ **center**: _____; the middle point of something
- ☐ **Earth**: _____; the planet on which we live; the world
- ☐ **professor**: _____; a teacher of the highest rank in a college or university
- ☐ **nephew**: _____; a son of one's brother or sister or of one's brother-in-law or sister-in-law
- ☐ **mysterious**: _____; difficult or impossible to understand, explain, or identify
- ☐ **map**: _____; a diagrammatic representation of an area of land or sea showing physical features, cities, roads, etc
- ☐ **lead**: _____; cause someone to take a particular course of action
- ☐ **climb down**: _____; descend
- ☐ **discover**: _____; find unexpectedly or during a search
- ☐ **beneath**: _____; in a lower position; below
- ☐ **surface**: _____; the outside part or uppermost layer of something
- ☐ **underground**: _____; beneath the surface of the earth
- ☐ **ocean**: _____; a very large expanse of sea, in particular each of the main areas into which the sea is divided geographically
- ☐ **prehistoric**: _____; relating to or denoting the period before written records
- ☐ **mushroom**: _____; a fungal growth that typically takes the form of a domed cap on a stalk, with gills on the underside of the cap
- ☐ **forest**: _____; a large area covered chiefly with trees and undergrowth
- ☐ **solve**: _____; find an answer to, explanation for, or means of effectively dealing with a problem or mystery
- ☐ **puzzle**: _____; a game, toy, or problem designed to test ingenuity or knowledge
- ☐ **overcome**: _____; succeed in dealing with a problem or difficulty
- ☐ **obstacle**: _____; a thing that blocks one's way or prevents or hinders progress
- ☐ **continue**: _____; persist in an activity or process
- ☐ **guide**: _____; a person who shows the way to others, especially one employed to show tourists around places of interest
- ☐ **navigate**: _____; plan and direct the route or course of a ship, aircraft, or other form of transportation
- ☐ **dangerous**: _____; able or likely to cause harm or injury
- ☐ **terrain**: _____; a stretch of land, especially with regard to its physical features
- ☐ **witness**: _____; see an event, typically a crime or accident happen
- ☐ **volcanic**: _____; relating to or resulting from the action of volcanoes
- ☐ **eruption**: _____; an instance of a volcano erupting
- ☐ **incredible**: _____; unbelievable

42 | Literature Series

KEY VOCABULARY | LEVEL 200 - UNIT 12

- ☐ **jail**: _____; a place of confinement for those convicted of a crime
- ☐ **steal**: _____; take something that does not belong to you without permission
- ☐ **hire**: _____; employ someone for wages
- ☐ **ex-convict**: _____; a person who has been released from prison after serving a sentence
- ☐ **businessman**: _____; a man who works in business or commerce
- ☐ **catch**: _____; seize or capture
- ☐ **convict**: _____; a person who has been found guilty of a crime and sentenced to imprisonment
- ☐ **feed**: _____; provide food for someone or something
- ☐ **honest**: _____; truthful, sincere, and morally upright
- ☐ **imprison**: _____; put someone in jail or prison
- ☐ **inspector**: _____; a person who investigates or examines something
- ☐ **kindness**: _____; the quality of being friendly, generous, and considerate
- ☐ **lie**: _____; give false information with the intent to deceive
- ☐ **police**: _____; a civil force responsible for enforcing laws and maintaining order
- ☐ **repay**: _____; return something to someone or make amends for a debt or wrong
- ☐ **shelter**: _____; a place that provides protection or refuge
- ☐ **silverware**: _____; utensils made of silver, such as forks, knives, and spoons
- ☐ **successful**: _____; achieving or having achieved success
- ☐ **try**: _____; attempt or make an effort
- ☐ **woman**: _____; an adult female human
- ☐ **bishop**: _____; a high-ranking member of the Christian clergy who oversees a diocese
- ☐ **honest life**: _____; a way of living that is truthful, upright, and moral

DR. SIMON'S MAGIC ENGLISH

KEY VOCABULARY | **LEVEL 200 - UNIT 13**

- ☐ **live**: _____; have a place of residence
- ☐ **mother**: _____; a female parent
- ☐ **lawyer**: _____; a person who practices or studies law
- ☐ **come**: _____; move toward or to a place
- ☐ **house**: _____; a building for human habitation
- ☐ **tell**: _____; communicate information, facts or news to someone in spoken or written words
- ☐ **grandfather**: _____; the father of one's father or mother
- ☐ **earl**: _____; a British nobleman ranking above a viscount and below a marquess
- ☐ **heir**: _____; a person legally entitled to the property or rank of another on that person's death
- ☐ **title**: _____; a name that describes someone's position or job
- ☐ **fortune**: _____; a large amount of money or assets
- ☐ **travel**: _____; make a journey, typically of some length
- ☐ **meet**: _____; come into the presence or company of someone
- ☐ **learn**: _____; gain or acquire knowledge of or skill in something by study, experience, or being taught
- ☐ **friend**: _____; a person whom one knows and with whom one has a bond of mutual affection
- ☐ **people**: _____; human beings in general or considered collectively
- ☐ **work**: _____; activity involving mental or physical effort done in order to achieve a purpose or result
- ☐ **estate**: _____; an extensive area of land in the country, usually with a large house, owned by one person, family, or organization
- ☐ **including**: _____; comprising as part of a whole; being one of a number of things, parts, or aspects
- ☐ **name**: _____; give a particular title or epithet to
- ☐ **uncle**: _____; the brother of one's father or mother or the husband of one's aunt
- ☐ **supposed**: _____; considered to be true or real, based on what is known
- ☐ **inherit**: _____; receive money, property, or a title as an heir at the death of the previous holder
- ☐ **earldom**: _____; the rank, lands, or income

KEY VOCABULARY | LEVEL 200 - UNIT 14

- ☐ **little**: _____; small in size or quantity
- ☐ **women**: _____; adult female humans
- ☐ **sisters**: _____; female siblings
- ☐ **live**: _____; have one's permanent home in a particular place
- ☐ **away**: _____; not present at a particular place
- ☐ **during**: _____; throughout the course or duration of a particular time period
- ☐ **civil**: _____; relating to the ordinary citizens and their concerns, rather than military or ecclesiastical matters
- ☐ **war**: _____; a state of armed conflict between nations, states, or societies
- ☐ **eldest**: _____; oldest
- ☐ **like**: _____; have a preference for
- ☐ **proper**: _____; conforming to conventionally accepted standards of behavior or morals
- ☐ **tomboy**: _____; a girl who enjoys rough, noisy activities traditionally associated with boys
- ☐ **love**: _____; feel a deep affection or fondness for
- ☐ **writing**: _____; the activity or skill of writing
- ☐ **quiet**: _____; making little or no noise, done in a calm and gentle manner
- ☐ **playing**: _____; engaging in an activity for enjoyment or recreation
- ☐ **youngest**: _____; the least old in a group of siblings
- ☐ **paint**: _____; cover a surface with paint
- ☐ **follow**: _____; come after something in time or order
- ☐ **grow up**: _____; mature and become an adult
- ☐ **face**: _____; confront and deal with or accept
- ☐ **various**: _____; different from one another, having different characteristics
- ☐ **challenge**: _____; a call to take part in a contest or competition, especially a duel
- ☐ **illness**: _____; a disease or period of sickness affecting the body or mind
- ☐ **poverty**: _____; the state of being extremely poor
- ☐ **heartbreak**: _____; overwhelming distress, sorrow or pain caused by a relationship coming to an end
- ☐ **learn**: _____; acquire knowledge or skills through study, experience, or being taught
- ☐ **importance**: _____; the state or fact of being of great significance or value
- ☐ **family**: _____; a group consisting of parents and their children living together as a unit
- ☐ **friendship**: _____; the emotions or conduct of friends, the state of being friends
- ☐ **kindness**: _____; the quality of being friendly, generous, and considerate

KEY VOCABULARY | LEVEL 200 - UNIT 15

- ☐ **group**: _____; a number of people or things that are located, gathered, or classed together
- ☐ **stranded**: _____; left without the means to move from somewhere
- ☐ **island**: _____; a piece of land surrounded by water
- ☐ **adults**: _____; fully grown or developed people
- ☐ **range**: _____; the area or distance between limits
- ☐ **age**: _____; the length of time that a person has lived or a thing has existed
- ☐ **learn**: _____; acquire knowledge or skills through study, experience, or being taught
- ☐ **elect**: _____; choose someone to hold public office or some other position by voting
- ☐ **leader**: _____; a person who leads or commands a group or organization
- ☐ **shelter**: _____; a place giving temporary protection from bad weather or danger
- ☐ **hunt**: _____; search determinedly for someone or something
- ☐ **start**: _____; begin or be reckoned from a particular point in time or space
- ☐ **go wrong**: _____; not according to plan or expectation
- ☐ **argue**: _____; exchange or express diverging or opposite views, typically in a heated or angry way
- ☐ **fight**: _____; take part in a violent struggle involving the exchange of physical blows or the use of weapons
- ☐ **become**: _____; begin to be
- ☐ **violent**: _____; using or involving physical force intended to hurt, damage, or kill someone or something
- ☐ **worship**: _____; show reverence and adoration for a deity; honor with religious rites
- ☐ **beast**: _____; an animal, especially a large or dangerous four-footed one
- ☐ **act**: _____; take action; do something
- ☐ **savage**: _____; a person regarded as primitive or uncivilized
- ☐ **show**: _____; demonstrate or prove
- ☐ **lose**: _____; be deprived of or cease to have or retain something
- ☐ **sense**: _____; a feeling that something is the case
- ☐ **civilization**: _____; the stage of human social and cultural development and organization that is considered most advanced
- ☐ **isolated**: _____; far away from other places, buildings, or people; remote
- ☐ **society**: _____; the aggregate of people living together in a more or less ordered community

KEY VOCABULARY | LEVEL 200 - UNIT 16

- ☐ **iron**: _____; a strong, hard magnetic metal
- ☐ **mask**: _____; a covering for the face, typically used for protection, disguise, or performance
- ☐ **mysterious**: _____; difficult or impossible to understand, explain, or identify
- ☐ **prisoner**: _____; a person who is kept in prison as a punishment or while awaiting trial
- ☐ **prison**: _____; a building where people are held as punishment for a crime they have committed
- ☐ **take**: _____; lay hold of something with one's hands
- ☐ **place**: _____; a particular position, point, or area in space; a location
- ☐ **during**: _____; throughout the course or duration of a particular time period
- ☐ **century**: _____; a period of one hundred years
- ☐ **involve**: _____; include or contain something as a necessary part or result
- ☐ **political**: _____; relating to government or the public affairs of a country
- ☐ **intrigue**: _____; the secret planning of something illicit or detrimental
- ☐ **secret**: _____; not known or meant to be known by others
- ☐ **plot**: _____; a plan made in secret by a group of people to do something harmful or illegal
- ☐ **main**: _____; most important or significant
- ☐ **character**: _____; a person in a novel, play, or movie
- ☐ **musketeer**: _____; a soldier armed with a musket
- ☐ **use**: _____; employ or make use of something
- ☐ **together**: _____; in or into one gathering, company, mass, or place
- ☐ **uncover**: _____; reveal or bring to light something that was previously hidden or unknown
- ☐ **try**: _____; make an attempt or effort to do something
- ☐ **help**: _____; assist or support someone in need
- ☐ **escape**: _____; break free from confinement or control
- ☐ **adventure**: _____; an unusual and exciting or daring experience
- ☐ **face**: _____; confront or deal with a difficult or unpleasant situation
- ☐ **challenge**: _____; a call or summons to engage in any contest, as of skill, strength, etc
- ☐ **classic**: _____; judged over a period of time to be of the highest quality and outstanding of its kind
- ☐ **tale**: _____; a fictitious or true narrative or story, especially one that is imaginatively recounted
- ☐ **friendship**: _____; a state of mutual trust and support between individuals
- ☐ **loyalty**: _____; the quality of being faithful to a person, cause, or belief, showing constant support or allegiance

Dr. Simon's Magic English Level 200 | 47

DR. SIMON'S MAGIC ENGLISH

KEY VOCABULARY | **LEVEL 200 - UNIT 17**

- **hundred**: _____ ; the number 100
- **solitude**: _____ ; the state of being alone or secluded from others
- **story**: _____ ; a narrative or account of events
- **family**: _____ ; a group of people related by blood or marriage
- **life**: _____ ; the state of being alive or the way someone lives
- **magical**: _____ ; relating to or using magic or supernatural powers
- **town**: _____ ; a place where people live, smaller than a city
- **called**: _____ ; named or known as
- **interesting**: _____ ; arousing curiosity or attention; engaging
- **adventure**: _____ ; an exciting or unusual experience
- **experiences**: _____ ; things that happen to someone, often influencing their life
- **course**: _____ ; a series of events or a particular order in which something happens
- **fill**: _____ ; put or pour something into a container or space
- **realism**: _____ ; the attitude or practice of accepting a situation as it is and being prepared to deal with it accordingly
- **elements**: _____ ; parts or components of something
- **fantasy**: _____ ; the faculty or activity of imagining things, especially things that are impossible or improbable
- **mix**: _____ ; combine or put together to form one substance or mass
- **reality**: _____ ; the state of things as they actually exist
- **character**: _____ ; the individual who appears in a story, play, or movie
- **live**: _____ ; have life; exist
- **ghost**: _____ ; the spirit of a dead person, sometimes appearing to the living
- **haunt**: _____ ; visit frequently and persistently
- **explore**: _____ ; investigate or analyze thoroughly
- **theme**: _____ ; a unifying or dominant idea, motif, etc
- **love**: _____ ; an intense feeling of affection and connection to someone else
- **death**: _____ ; the end of life
- **passage**: _____ ; the process or an instance of passing from one place, condition, or stage to another
- **time**: _____ ; the indefinite continued progress of existence and events in the past, present, and future
- **show**: _____ ; make something visible or apparent
- **action**: _____ ; the fact or process of doing something, typically to achieve an aim
- **generation**: _____ ; all of the people born and living at about the same time
- **affect**: _____ ; produce a change or influence something

48 | Literature Series

KEY VOCABULARY | LEVEL 200 - UNIT 18

- ☐ **great**: _____; of an extent, amount, or intensity considerably above average
- ☐ **warrior**: _____; a person engaged in or experienced in warfare
- ☐ **fall**: _____; move downward, typically rapidly and freely without control
- ☐ **love**: _____; a strong feeling of affection
- ☐ **woman**: _____; an adult human female
- ☐ **named**: _____; having a name
- ☐ **however**: _____; nevertheless; on the other hand
- ☐ **happiness**: _____; the state of being happy
- ☐ **threaten**: _____; cause someone or something to be vulnerable or at risk
- ☐ **man**: _____; an adult human male
- ☐ **jealous**: _____; feeling or showing envy of someone or their achievements and advantages
- ☐ **success**: _____; the accomplishment of an aim or purpose
- ☐ **want**: _____; have a desire to possess or do something
- ☐ **ruin**: _____; cause the destruction of something
- ☐ **life**: _____; the condition that distinguishes living things from non-living things
- ☐ **trick**: _____; deceive or outwit someone
- ☐ **thinking**: _____; the process of considering or reasoning about something
- ☐ **unfaithful**: _____; not remaining loyal to someone or something
- ☐ **cause**: _____; make something happen
- ☐ **angry**: _____; having a strong feeling of or showing annoyance, displeasure, or hostility
- ☐ **upset**: _____; cause someone to feel unhappy, disappointed, or worried
- ☐ **treat**: _____; behave toward or deal with in a certain way
- ☐ **badly**: _____; in an unsatisfactory, inadequate, or unsuccessful way
- ☐ **eventually**: _____; in the end, especially after a long delay, dispute, or series of problems
- ☐ **kill**: _____; cause the death of a person, animal, or other living thing
- ☐ **story**: _____; an account of imaginary or real people and events told for entertainment
- ☐ **explore**: _____; inquire into or discuss in detail, analyze
- ☐ **theme**: _____; the subject of a talk, a piece of writing, a person's thoughts, or an exhibition
- ☐ **betrayal**: _____; the action of betraying one's country, a group, or a person; treachery
- ☐ **revenge**: _____; the action of inflicting hurt or harm on someone for an injury or wrong suffered at their hands
- ☐ **show**: _____; give evidence or show signs of
- ☐ **one**: _____; a single person or thing
- ☐ **person's**: _____; relating to a particular person
- ☐ **action**: _____; the fact or process of doing something, typically to achieve an aim
- ☐ **impact**: _____; the effect or influence of one person, thing, or action, on another

DR. SIMON'S MAGIC ENGLISH

KEY VOCABULARY | LEVEL 200 - UNIT 19

- ☐ **pride**: _____; a feeling of deep pleasure or satisfaction derived from one's achievements
- ☐ **prejudice**: _____; preconceived opinion that is not based on reason or actual experience
- ☐ **live**: _____; remain alive
- ☐ **late**: _____; the latter part of a period of time
- ☐ **eager**: _____; wanting to do or have something very much
- ☐ **married**: _____; the state of being united to a person of the opposite sex as husband or wife
- ☐ **follow**: _____; come after a particular person or thing in time, order, or space
- ☐ **navigate**: _____; plan and direct the route or course of a ship, aircraft, or other form of transportation
- ☐ **society**: _____; the aggregate of people living together in a more or less ordered community
- ☐ **main**: _____; the most important or principal in rank, importance, or degree
- ☐ **character**: _____; the mental and moral qualities distinctive to an individual
- ☐ **independent**: _____; free from outside control; not subject to another's authority
- ☐ **marry**: _____; become the legally recognized union of two people as partners in a personal relationship
- ☐ **initially**: _____; at first
- ☐ **dislike**: _____; regard with distaste or aversion; to feel uncomfortable or unhappy about something
- ☐ **arrogant**: _____; having or revealing an exaggerated sense of one's own importance or abilities
- ☐ **later**: _____; happening at a time subsequent to a reference time
- ☐ **realize**: _____; become aware of something as a fact or truth
- ☐ **wrong**: _____; not correct or true; unjust, dishonest, or immoral
- ☐ **explore**: _____; inquire into or discuss in detail, analyze
- ☐ **theme**: _____; the subject of a talk, a piece of writing, a person's thoughts, or an exhibition
- ☐ **marriage**: _____; the legally or formally recognized union of two people as partners in a personal relationship
- ☐ **social**: _____; relating to society or its organization
- ☐ **status**: _____; the relative social, professional, or other standing of someone or something
- ☐ **change**: _____; make or become different
- ☐ **opinion**: _____; a view or judgment formed about something, not necessarily based on fact or knowledge
- ☐ **action**: _____; the fact or process of doing something, typically to achieve an aim

KEY VOCABULARY | LEVEL 200 - UNIT 20

- **shipwrecked**: _____; having survived a shipwreck
- **deserted**: _____; abandoned or uninhabited
- **island**: _____; a piece of land surrounded by water
- **work**: _____, 일; do something to achieve a goal or result
- **together**: _____; with other people
- **survive**: _____; remain alive or continue to exist
- **build**: _____; construct something
- **shelter**: _____; a place that provides protection from weather or danger
- **find**: _____; discover something
- **clothes**: _____; items worn to cover the body
- **tools**: _____; instruments used to perform a task
- **animals**: _____; living organisms that feed on organic matter
- **pet**: _____; a domesticated animal kept for companionship
- **tame**: _____; not afraid of humans
- **parrot**: _____; a bird with bright colors and a curved beak
- **adventure**: _____; an exciting or unusual experience
- **explore**: _____; travel through an unfamiliar area
- **caves**: _____; natural underground chambers
- **building**: _____; the process of constructing something
- **discover**: _____; find something that was previously unknown
- **hidden**: _____; not visible or easily noticed
- **treasure**: _____; a collection of valuable or precious items
- **encounter**: _____; come across or meet with something
- **dangerous**: _____; able or likely to cause harm or injury
- **teach**: _____; impart knowledge or skill
- **important**: _____; of great significance or value
- **lesson**: _____; a piece of instruction or teaching
- **teamwork**: _____; working together as a team
- **problem-solving**: _____; finding a solution to a problem
- **power**: _____; the ability to do something
- **imagination**: _____; the ability to form mental images or concepts of things not present in reality
- **overcome**: _____; succeed in dealing with a problem or difficulty
- **difficult**: _____; needing skill or effort to accomplish or understand
- **challenge**: _____; a task or situation that tests someone's abilities
- **creativity**: _____; the ability to use imagination to produce something new or original

Dr. Simon's Magic English Level 200

DR. SIMON'S MAGIC ENGLISH

KEY VOCABULARY | LEVEL 200 - UNIT 21

- ☐ **born**: _____; come into existence or be brought into existence
- ☐ **child**: _____; a person's offspring
- ☐ **teenager**: _____; a person between the ages of 13 and 19
- ☐ **run away**: _____; leave a place suddenly or secretly
- ☐ **printing**: _____; the process of producing printed material
- ☐ **business**: _____; a commercial activity engaged in for profit
- ☐ **successful**: _____; achieving a desired aim or result
- ☐ **famous**: _____; known about by many people
- ☐ **inventor**: _____; a person who creates or designs new inventions
- ☐ **create**: _____; bring something into existence
- ☐ **bifocal glasses**: _____; eyeglasses with lenses that have two different sections for seeing near and far
- ☐ **lightning rod**: _____; a metal rod that protects buildings from lightning strikes
- ☐ **writer**: _____; a person who writes books, articles, or other texts
- ☐ **book**: _____; a written or printed work consisting of pages glued or sewn together along one side and bound in covers
- ☐ **article**: _____; a piece of writing included with others in a newspaper, magazine, or other publication
- ☐ **addition**: _____; the act of adding something
- ☐ **accomplishment**: _____; something that has been achieved successfully
- ☐ **important**: _____; of great significance or value
- ☐ **statesman**: _____; a person who is skilled in government or diplomacy
- ☐ **Declaration of Independence**: _____; a document stating that the 13 American colonies were no longer subject to British rule
- ☐ **signer**: _____; a person who signs a document
- ☐ **U.S. Constitution**: _____; the supreme law of the United States, outlining the government's framework and procedures

KEY VOCABULARY | LEVEL 200 - UNIT 22

- ☐ **housewife**: _____; a married woman who manages her household
- ☐ **mother**: _____; a female parent
- ☐ **photographer**: _____; a person who takes photographs
- ☐ **visit**: _____; go to a place temporarily
- ☐ **area**: _____; a particular place or region
- ☐ **picture**: _____; a representation of a person or thing in a photograph
- ☐ **covered bridge**: _____; a bridge with a roof and walls on each side
- ☐ **connection**: _____; a relationship between things or people
- ☐ **spend**: _____; use time doing something
- ☐ **several**: _____; more than two but not many
- ☐ **explore**: _____; travel around a place to learn about it
- ☐ **fall in love**: _____; start to feel romantic feelings for someone
- ☐ **leave**: _____; go away from a place
- ☐ **family**: _____; a group consisting of parents and children living together in a household
- ☐ **years later**: _____; after many years have passed
- ☐ **pass away**: _____; die
- ☐ **diary**: _____; a book in which one keeps a daily record of events and experiences
- ☐ **learn**: _____; gain knowledge or skill in a subject or activity
- ☐ **love affair**: _____; a romantic relationship between two people
- ☐ **letter**: _____; a written or printed message
- ☐ **explain**: _____; make something clear or easy to understand
- ☐ **feeling**: _____; an emotional state or reaction
- ☐ **ask**: _____; request something from someone
- ☐ **forgiveness**: _____; the action of forgiving or being forgiven for a mistake or wrongdoing
- ☐ **choice**: _____; an act of selecting or making a decision when faced with two or more possibilities
- ☐ **consequence**: _____; a result or effect of an action or decision
- ☐ **teach**: _____; give someone information or knowledge about something
- ☐ **loss**: _____; the fact or process of losing something or someone
- ☐ **importance**: _____; the state or fact of being important
- ☐ **true to ourselves**: _____; remaining faithful to one's own personality, spirit, or character

Dr. Simon's Magic English Level 200 | 53

DR. SIMON'S MAGIC ENGLISH

KEY VOCABULARY | **LEVEL 200 - UNIT 23**

- ☐ **brothers**: _____; male siblings
- ☐ **book**: _____; a written or printed work consisting of pages glued or sewn together along one side and bound in covers
- ☐ **family**: _____; a group of people related to each other by blood or marriage
- ☐ **father**: _____; a male parent
- ☐ **son**: _____; male offspring of parents
- ☐ **each**: _____; every one of two or more people or things
- ☐ **different**: _____; not the same as another or each other
- ☐ **personality**: _____; the combination of characteristics or qualities that form an individual's distinctive character
- ☐ **often**: _____; frequently, repeatedly
- ☐ **argue**: _____; express divergent or opposite views in a disagreement
- ☐ **other**: _____; the people or things not already mentioned or known
- ☐ **explore**: _____; investigate or analyze in detail
- ☐ **relationship**: _____; the way in which two or more people or things are connected
- ☐ **people**: _____; human beings in general or considered collectively
- ☐ **story**: _____; a narrative, either true or fictional
- ☐ **there**: _____; in that place, in a particular place
- ☐ **murder**: _____; the unlawful premeditated killing of one human being by another
- ☐ **suspect**: _____; a person thought to be guilty of a crime or offense
- ☐ **mystery**: _____; something that is difficult or impossible to understand or explain
- ☐ **committed**: _____; carried out or perpetrated
- ☐ **crime**: _____; an action or omission that constitutes an offense that may be punished by law
- ☐ **affect**: _____; have an effect on or influence something or someone

KEY VOCABULARY | LEVEL 200 - UNIT 24

- ☐ **group**: _____; a collection of people
- ☐ **traveling**: _____; moving from one place to another
- ☐ **religious**: _____; relating to religion
- ☐ **site**: _____; a location
- ☐ **called**: _____; named
- ☐ **walks**: _____; move with your legs at a speed that is slower than running
- ☐ **life**: _____; the condition that distinguishes animals and plants from inorganic matter
- ☐ **including**: _____; comprising or taking into account
- ☐ **knight**: _____; a person who serves a king or queen
- ☐ **nun**: _____; a member of a religious community of women
- ☐ **merchant**: _____; a person involved in trade or commerce
- ☐ **miller**: _____; a person who owns or operates a mill
- ☐ **tell**: _____; communicate something by speaking
- ☐ **stories**: _____; narratives or tales
- ☐ **each**: _____; every individual in a group
- ☐ **other**: _____; different or distinct from one previously mentioned
- ☐ **pass**: _____; spend or occupy time
- ☐ **time**: _____; the indefinite continued progress of existence
- ☐ **sorts**: _____; various types or kinds
- ☐ **like**: _____; similar to
- ☐ **adventure**: _____; an exciting or remarkable experience
- ☐ **humor**: _____; the quality of being amusing or comic
- ☐ **serious**: _____; significant or important
- ☐ **silly**: _____; lacking seriousness or good sense
- ☐ **give**: _____; provide or present
- ☐ **glimpse**: _____; a brief or partial view
- ☐ **during**: _____; throughout the course or duration of
- ☐ **century**: _____; a period of one hundred years
- ☐ **see**: _____; perceive with the eyes
- ☐ **different**: _____; not the same as another or each other
- ☐ **classes**: _____; groups or categories
- ☐ **backgrounds**: _____; personal or social circumstances that form the setting for an event or fact
- ☐ **interact**: _____; act in such a way as to have an effect on each other
- ☐ **thought**: _____; an idea, plan, opinion, picture, etc., that is formed in your mind; something that you think of
- ☐ **important**: _____; of great significance or value

Dr. Simon's Magic English Level 200 | 55

DR. SIMON'S MAGIC ENGLISH

KEY VOCABULARY | LEVEL 200 - UNIT 25

- ☐ **patient**: _____; a person receiving medical treatment or care
- ☐ **book**: _____; a written or printed work consisting of pages glued or sewn together along one side and bound in covers
- ☐ **man**: _____; an adult male human being
- ☐ **badly**: _____; in a severe or unfavorable manner
- ☐ **burned**: _____; affected or injured by fire or heat
- ☐ **plane**: _____; an aircraft with wings and one or more engines
- ☐ **crash**: _____; a violent collision, typically involving vehicles or objects
- ☐ **during**: _____; throughout the course or duration of
- ☐ **world**: _____; the earth, together with all of its countries, peoples, and natural features
- ☐ **war**: _____; a state of armed conflict between different nations or states
- ☐ **remember**: _____; have a recollection of something
- ☐ **come**: _____; arrive or move to a place
- ☐ **so**: _____; to such a great extent
- ☐ **other**: _____; different or distinct from one previously mentioned
- ☐ **characters**: _____; individuals in a story or narrative
- ☐ **call**: _____; give a name or title to someone or something
- ☐ **story**: _____; an account of imaginary or real people and events told for entertainment
- ☐ **take**: _____; carry or bring with one
- ☐ **place**: _____; a particular position, point, or area in space
- ☐ **villa**: _____; a large and luxurious country residence
- ☐ **care**: _____; feel concern or interest; attach importance to something
- ☐ **nurse**: _____; a person trained to care for the sick or infirm, especially in a hospital
- ☐ **named**: _____; having a particular name
- ☐ **also**: _____; in addition; too
- ☐ **living**: _____; having life; not dead or inanimate
- ☐ **including**: _____; comprising or taking into account
- ☐ **soldier**: _____; a person who serves in an army
- ☐ **work**: _____; perform or carry out tasks or duties
- ☐ **bombs**: _____; explosive devices used as weapons
- ☐ **unfold**: _____; reveal or disclose gradually
- ☐ **learn**: _____; acquire knowledge or skill
- ☐ **past**: _____; gone by in time and no longer existing
- ☐ **interact**: _____; act in such a way as to have an effect on each other
- ☐ **deal**: _____; cope or manage with something difficult or challenging
- ☐ **trauma**: _____; a deeply distressing or disturbing experience

KEY VOCABULARY | LEVEL 200 - UNIT 26

- ☐ **story**: _____; an account of imaginary or real people and events told for entertainment
- ☐ **war**: _____; a state of armed conflict between different nations or states
- ☐ **between**: _____; in or along the space separating two objects, regions, or points
- ☐ **groups**: _____; collections or sets of people or things
- ☐ **people**: _____; individuals
- ☐ **main**: _____; principal or most important
- ☐ **character**: _____; a person in a story, play, or movie
- ☐ **brave**: _____; showing courage or fearlessness
- ☐ **warrior**: _____; a person who fights in battles or wars
- ☐ **named**: _____; having a particular name
- ☐ **skilled**: _____; having or showing proficiency, expertise, or competence
- ☐ **fighting**: _____; engaging in combat or physical conflict
- ☐ **upset**: _____; unhappy, disappointed, or disturbed
- ☐ **leader**: _____; a person who leads or commands a group or organization
- ☐ **take**: _____; move or carry someone or something from one place to another
- ☐ **prize**: _____; something given as a reward for victory or success
- ☐ **won**: _____; had victory
- ☐ **battle**: _____; a sustained fight between large organized armed forces
- ☐ **decide**: _____; make a choice or reach a conclusion
- ☐ **stop**: _____; cease or halt an action or activity
- ☐ **tent**: _____; a portable shelter made of cloth, supported by one or more poles and stretched tight by cords or loops attached to pegs driven into the ground
- ☐ **start**: _____; begin or set in motion
- ☐ **win**: _____; be victorious or successful in a competition or conflict
- ☐ **get**: _____; come into possession or use of something
- ☐ **close**: _____; at or to a short distance away from someone or something
- ☐ **friends**: _____; people whom one knows and with whom one has a bond of mutual affection
- ☐ **set**: _____; a collection of objects or items that belong together
- ☐ **armor**: _____; protective clothing or equipment worn in warfare
- ☐ **fight**: _____; engage in combat or physical conflict
- ☐ **end**: _____; the final part of something
- ☐ **lose**: _____; be deprived of or cease to have or retain something
- ☐ **sad**: _____; feeling or showing sorrow; unhappy
- ☐ **die**: _____; cease to live; undergo death
- ☐ **killed**: _____; caused the death of someone or something

Dr. Simon's Magic English Level 200 | 57

DR. SIMON'S MAGIC ENGLISH

KEY VOCABULARY | **LEVEL 200 - UNIT 27**

- **pretend**: _____; behave so as to make it appear that something is the case when, in fact, it is not
- **someone**: _____: an unspecified or unknown person
- **else**: _____; in addition to; different from
- **more**: _____; a greater or additional amount or degree
- **fun**: _____; enjoyment, amusement, or lighthearted pleasure
- **named**: _____; having a particular name
- **city**: _____; a large town
- **without**: _____; not having or being affected by
- **anyone**: _____; any person at all
- **knowing**: _____; having knowledge or awareness of something
- **sick**: _____; affected by physical or mental illness
- **friend**: _____; a person whom one knows and with whom one has a bond of mutual affection
- **leave**: _____; go away from a place
- **town**: _____; a built-up area with a name, defined boundaries, and a local government, that is larger than a village and generally smaller than a city
- **whenever**: _____; at any time
- **want**: _____; desire or wish for something
- **both**: _____; the two of two considered together; the one and the other
- **fall**: _____; move downward, typically rapidly and freely without control
- **love**: _____; an intense feeling of deep affection
- **women**: _____; adult female human beings
- **marry**: _____; enter into a legally recognized marriage with someone
- **lead**: _____; cause someone to do something, typically something regarded as undesirable
- **lot**: _____; a large number or amount; a great deal
- **confusion**: _____; a lack of understanding; uncertainty
- **funny**: _____; causing laughter or amusement
- **situations**: _____; sets of circumstances; the conditions in which someone or something exists or operates
- **end**: _____; the final part of something
- **revealed**: _____; made known or disclosed
- **long-lost**: _____; not seen or heard of for a long time; lost or vanished for a long time
- **relative**: _____; a person connected by blood or marriage
- **real**: _____; actually existing as a thing or occurring in fact
- **still**: _____; up to and including the present or the time mentioned; even now
- **even**: _____; used to emphasize something surprising or extreme
- **though**: _____; despite the fact that; although

KEY VOCABULARY | LEVEL 200 - UNIT 28

- **sanatorium**: _____; a medical facility for long-term illness or recuperation
- **mountains**: _____; large natural elevations of the earth's surface
- **visit**: _____; go to see and spend time with someone
- **cousin**: _____; a child of one's uncle or aunt
- **sick**: _____; affected by physical or mental illness
- **end**: _____; come to a conclusion or finish
- **staying**: _____; remaining or continuing to be in a particular place
- **meet**: _____; encounter or become acquainted with someone for the first time
- **interesting**: _____; arousing curiosity or interest; fascinating
- **patients**: _____; people receiving medical treatment or care
- **talk**: _____; speak in order to give information or express ideas or feelings
- **lot**: _____; a large number or amount; a great deal
- **philosophy**: _____; the study of fundamental questions about existence, knowledge, values, reason, and more
- **politics**: _____; the activities, actions, and policies used to gain and hold power in a government or to influence the government
- **become**: _____; begin to be
- **named**: _____; having a particular name
- **writer**: _____; a person who has written a particular text or works in writing books, stories, or articles
- **philosopher**: _____; a person engaged or learned in philosophy
- **different**: _____; not the same as another or each other; unlike in nature, form, or quality
- **ideas**: _____; thoughts or concepts
- **fall**: _____, 가을; descend or move downwards
- **married**: _____; joined in marriage
- **someone**: _____; an unspecified or unknown person
- **spend**: _____; use time in a particular way
- **time**: _____; the indefinite continued progress of existence
- **thinking**: _____; using one's mind to consider or reason about something
- **relationship**: _____; the way in which two or more people or things are connected or the state of being connected
- **leave**: _____; depart or go away from a place
- **return**: _____; go or come back to a place
- **real**: _____; actually existing as a thing or occurring in fact
- **world**: _____; the earth, together with all of its countries, peoples, and natural features
- **really**: _____; in actual fact, as opposed to what is said or imagined to be true or possible
- **want**: _____; desire or wish for something
- **change**: _____; become different; undergo alteration or modification
- **life**: _____; the existence of an individual human being or animal

DR. SIMON'S MAGIC ENGLISH

KEY VOCABULARY | **LEVEL 200 - UNIT 29**

- ☐ **adventure**: _____; an exciting or unusual experience
- ☐ **try**: _____; attempt or make an effort to do something
- ☐ **return**: _____; go or come back to a place or person
- ☐ **fought**: _____; engaged in a physical or verbal conflict
- ☐ **war**: _____; a state of armed conflict between different nations or groups
- ☐ **away**: _____; at a distance from a particular place
- ☐ **journey**: _____; a long trip or process of traveling
- ☐ **face**: _____; confront or encounter
- ☐ **challenges**: _____; difficult tasks or situations
- ☐ **including**: _____; comprising or taking into account
- ☐ **sea**: _____; the expanse of saltwater that covers most of the Earth's surface
- ☐ **monster**: _____; a large, often imaginary creature that is frightening or dangerous
- ☐ **witch**: _____; a woman believed to have magical powers
- ☐ **cyclops**: _____; a member of a mythical race of giants with a single eye in the middle of their forehead
- ☐ **meet**: _____; encounter or come into contact with
- ☐ **helpful**: _____; providing assistance or aid
- ☐ **people**: _____; individuals
- ☐ **goddess**: _____; a female deity, often associated with supernatural powers and abilities
- ☐ **kind**: _____; having or showing a gentle and friendly nature
- ☐ **queen**: _____; the female ruler of an independent state
- ☐ **finally**: _____; at the end of a period of time or a series of events
- ☐ **find**: _____; discover or encounter
- ☐ **wife**: _____; a married woman in relation to her husband
- ☐ **waiting**: _____; staying in readiness or anticipation
- ☐ **fending off**: _____; defending or resisting something or someone
- ☐ **suitors**: _____; men who court or seek the affections of a woman with the intention of marrying her
- ☐ **want**: _____; desire or wish for something
- ☐ **marry**: _____; enter into a legally recognized marriage with someone
- ☐ **prove**: _____; demonstrate the truth or existence of something
- ☐ **real**: _____; actually existing as a thing or occurring in fact
- ☐ **imposter**: _____; a person who pretends to be someone else in order to deceive others
- ☐ **defeat**: _____; overcome or prevail over in a competition or conflict
- ☐ **reunite**: _____; come together again after being separated
- ☐ **rest**: _____; the remaining part or portion
- ☐ **life**: _____; the existence of an individual human being or animal
- ☐ **peace**: _____; freedom from disturbance; tranquility

KEY VOCABULARY | LEVEL 200 - UNIT 30

- ☐ **relatives**: _____; family members who are connected by blood or marriage
- ☐ **giant**: _____; an extremely large person, creature, or thing
- ☐ **wizard**: _____; a man who has magical powers
- ☐ **accepted**: _____; agreed to receive or take on something
- ☐ **witchcraft**: _____; the practice of magic, typically involving spells and potions
- ☐ **wizardry**: _____; the art, skill, or practice of a wizard
- ☐ **adventures**: _____; exciting or remarkable experiences
- ☐ **together**: _____; with or in proximity to one another
- ☐ **learned**: _____; gained knowledge or information
- ☐ **magic**: _____; the power of apparently influencing events by using supernatural forces
- ☐ **spells**: _____; words or incantations believed to have magical powers
- ☐ **flew**: _____; moved through the air using wings or aircraft
- ☐ **broomsticks**: _____; long sticks traditionally associated with witches, used for flying in the story
- ☐ **classes**: _____; lessons or periods of instruction
- ☐ **potions**: _____; substances with magical properties, often used in brewing medicines or spells
- ☐ **magical**: _____; relating to magic or having special powers
- ☐ **creatures**: _____; living beings, often of a fantastical or imaginary nature
- ☐ **faced**: _____; confronted or encountered a difficulty or challenge
- ☐ **challenges**: _____; difficult or demanding tasks or situations
- ☐ **fought**: _____; engaged in a physical or verbal struggle against someone or something
- ☐ **lord**: _____; a title given to someone of high rank or authority
- ☐ **followers**: _____; people who believe in and support someone or their cause
- ☐ **bravery**: _____; the quality or state of being brave or courageous
- ☐ **friendship**: _____; the state of being friends or having a friendly relationship
- ☐ **discovered**: _____; found or learned about something for the first time
- ☐ **secrets**: _____; things that are kept hidden or not known by others
- ☐ **own**: _____; belonging to oneself or itself
- ☐ **abilities**: _____; talents or skills that someone has
- ☐ **end**: _____; the final part or conclusion of something
- ☐ **battle**: _____; a fight between opposing forces
- ☐ **army**: _____; a large organized group of people trained for war
- ☐ **bravely**: _____; in a courageous and fearless manner
- ☐ **dark**: _____; without light, gloomy or sinister
- ☐ **forces**: _____; strength or energy exerted or brought to bear
- ☐ **bring**: _____; cause to come to a place or participate in an action
- ☐ **peace**: _____; a state of tranquility, calm, or harmony

Dr. Simon's Magic English Level 200

DR. SIMON'S MAGIC ENGLISH

KEY VOCABULARY | LEVEL 300 - UNIT 1

- ☐ **live**: _____; have one's permanent residence or home in a particular place
- ☐ **scary**: _____; causing fear or alarm
- ☐ **place**: _____; a particular position, point, or area in space; a location
- ☐ **called**: _____; named or identified as
- ☐ **government**: _____; the governing body of a nation, state, or community
- ☐ **control**: _____; exercise power or authority over
- ☐ **everything**: _____; all things or all aspects of something
- ☐ **people**: _____; individuals
- ☐ **allowed**: _____; permitted or given authorization to do something
- ☐ **think**: _____; have a particular opinion, belief, or idea
- ☐ **say**: _____; express in words or speech
- ☐ **really**: _____; actually or in truth
- ☐ **feel**: _____; experience an emotion or sensation
- ☐ **secretly**: _____; in a way that is not known or seen by others
- ☐ **hate**: _____; feel intense or passionate dislike for
- ☐ **want**: _____; desire or wish for something
- ☐ **rebel**: _____; resist or defy an established authority, control, or tradition
- ☐ **fall**: _____; move downward, typically rapidly and freely
- ☐ **named**: _____; having a particular name
- ☐ **together**: _____; with or in proximity to another person or people
- ☐ **start**: _____; begin or set out on a journey, activity, or process
- ☐ **life**: _____; the existence of an individual human being or animal
- ☐ **watching**: _____; keeping a close observation on someone or something
- ☐ **catch**: _____; capture or seize, especially after a chase or pursuit
- ☐ **change**: _____; make or become different
- ☐ **way**: _____; a method, style, or manner of doing something
- ☐ **torture**: _____; do the action or practice of inflicting severe pain or suffering on someone as a punishment or in order to force them to do or say something
- ☐ **until**: _____; up to the point in time or the event mentioned
- ☐ **believe**: _____; accept that something is true or existed
- ☐ **end**: _____; the final part of something
- ☐ **become**: _____; start to be or develop into something
- ☐ **loyal**: _____; faithful and devoted to someone or something
- ☐ **follower**: _____; a person who supports and admires someone or something
- ☐ **forget**: _____; fail to remember
- ☐ **rebellious**: _____; defying or resisting authority, control, or tradition
- ☐ **thoughts**: _____; the products of mental activity; ideas or opinions

KEY VOCABULARY | LEVEL 300 - UNIT 2

- ☐ **adventure**: _____; an exciting or unusual experience
- ☐ **submarine**: _____; a watercraft capable of operating underwater
- ☐ **captain**: _____; the person in command of a ship or boat
- ☐ **mysterious**: _____; difficult to understand or explain; enigmatic
- ☐ **under**: _____; located below or beneath
- ☐ **sea**: _____; the expanse of saltwater that covers most of the Earth's surface
- ☐ **creatures**: _____; living beings; animals
- ☐ **explore**: _____; travel through or investigate for discovery
- ☐ **ocean**: _____; a vast body of saltwater
- ☐ **fight**: _____; engage in a physical or verbal conflict
- ☐ **big**: _____; large in size or extent
- ☐ **octopus**: _____; a sea animal with eight tentacles
- ☐ **called**: _____; named or identified as
- ☐ **giant**: _____; exceptionally large in size
- ☐ **squid**: _____; a marine mollusk with a long body and ten arms
- ☐ **friends**: _____; people with whom one shares a bond of mutual affection
- ☐ **want**: _____; have a desire to possess or do something
- ☐ **leave**: _____; go away from a place
- ☐ **let**: _____; allow or permit
- ☐ **eventually**: _____; at some later time; in the end
- ☐ **escape**: _____; break free from confinement or control
- ☐ **back**: _____; returning to a previous position or condition
- ☐ **surface**: _____; the outside part or uppermost layer of something

DR. SIMON'S MAGIC ENGLISH

KEY VOCABULARY | **LEVEL 300 - UNIT 3**

- ☐ **grow**: _____; increase in size, develop
- ☐ **smart**: _____; intelligent, clever
- ☐ **like**: _____; enjoy, have a preference for
- ☐ **think**: _____; use the mind to consider or reason
- ☐ **lot**: _____; a large amount or number
- ☐ **school**: _____; an educational institution
- ☐ **learn**: _____; acquire knowledge or skills
- ☐ **religion**: _____; a belief system concerning the divine
- ☐ **good**: _____; morally right, virtuous
- ☐ **person**: _____; an individual
- ☐ **however**: _____; nevertheless, nonetheless
- ☐ **start**: _____; begin, initiate
- ☐ **own**: _____; belonging to oneself
- ☐ **ideas**: _____; thoughts or concepts
- ☐ **want**: _____; desire, wish for
- ☐ **artist**: _____; a person who creates art
- ☐ **instead**: _____; as an alternative or substitute
- ☐ **following**: _____; adhering to, obeying
- ☐ **rules**: _____; prescribed guidelines or regulations
- ☐ **experiences**: _____; events or incidents that one undergoes
- ☐ **shape**: _____; influence, mold
- ☐ **beliefs**: _____; convictions or principles
- ☐ **including**: _____; comprising, involving
- ☐ **church**: _____; a place of worship for Christians
- ☐ **hearing**: _____; the faculty or sense of perceiving sound
- ☐ **sin**: _____; an immoral act or wrongdoing
- ☐ **hell**: _____; a place of punishment or suffering after death
- ☐ **history**: _____; the study of past events
- ☐ **culture**: _____; the customs, arts, and social institutions of a particular group
- ☐ **struggle**: _____; face challenges or difficulties
- ☐ **identity**: _____; the qualities, beliefs, or characteristics that distinguish a person
- ☐ **expectations**: _____; anticipated outcomes or standards
- ☐ **decide**: _____; make a choice or resolution
- ☐ **leave**: _____; depart from a place
- ☐ **become**: _____; transform into, start being
- ☐ **ultimately**: _____; finally, eventually

KEY VOCABULARY | LEVEL 300 - UNIT 4

- **young**: _____; in the early stages of life; not old
- **fight**: _____; engage in a physical or verbal conflict
- **friends**: _____; people with whom one shares a bond of mutual affection
- **join**: _____; become a member or participant in
- **army**: _____; a large organized body of armed personnel
- **together**: _____; in association or companionship with others
- **excited**: _____; feeling enthusiastic or eager
- **realize**: _____; become aware or understand something
- **war**: _____; a state of armed conflict between nations or groups
- **fun**: _____; enjoyment, amusement
- **terrible**: _____; extremely bad or distressing
- **things**: _____; objects or matters
- **lose**: _____; be deprived of or cease to have
- **hungry**: _____; feeling or showing the need for food
- **tired**: _____; in need of rest or sleep
- **all the time**: _____; continuously; constantly
- **miss**: _____; feel sadness or longing for the absence of someone
- **family**: _____; a group of individuals related by blood or marriage
- **question**: _____; have doubts about or raise inquiries
- **enemy**: _____; a person or group that is hostile or opposed to another
- **soldiers**: _____; members of an army or military force
- **just like**: _____; similar to; in the same manner as
- **hurt**: _____; cause physical or emotional pain or harm
- **anymore**: _____; any longer; now
- **try**: _____; attempt to do something
- **sent**: _____; dispatched or caused to go
- **end**: _____; the final part or conclusion of something
- **kill**: _____; cause the death of someone or something
- **only**: _____; alone; solely
- **affect**: _____; influence or impact
- **change**: _____; make or become different
- **forever**: _____; for all future time; eternally
- **teach**: _____; impart knowledge or instruct
- **importance**: _____; significance or value
- **peace**: _____; a state of tranquility or harmony
- **consequences**: _____; the results or effects of an action or condition

Dr. Simon's Magic English Level 300

DR. SIMON'S MAGIC ENGLISH

KEY VOCABULARY | LEVEL 300 - UNIT 5

- ☐ **married**: _____; legally united in marriage
- ☐ **man**: _____; an adult human male
- ☐ **named**: _____; having a given name
- ☐ **fall in love**: _____; develop strong romantic feelings for someone
- ☐ **romantic affair**: _____; a secret or illicit relationship
- ☐ **husband**: _____; a married man
- ☐ **find out**: _____; discover information or a secret
- ☐ **upset**: _____; feeling distressed or unhappy
- ☐ **decide**: _____; make a choice or come to a resolution
- ☐ **leave**: _____; go away from a place
- ☐ **son**: _____; a male child
- ☐ **live**: _____; reside or dwell
- ☐ **together**: _____; in the company or presence of others
- ☐ **happy**: _____; feeling or showing pleasure or contentment
- ☐ **jealous**: _____; feeling or showing envy or resentment towards someone
- ☐ **other**: _____; different or distinct from the one or ones already mentioned or implied
- ☐ **women**: _____; adult human females
- ☐ **start**: _____; begin or commence
- ☐ **feel**: _____; experience an emotion or sensation
- ☐ **sad**: _____; feeling or showing sorrow or unhappiness
- ☐ **meanwhile**: _____; during the same time
- ☐ **another**: _____; one more person or thing
- ☐ **story**: _____; a narrative of real or imagined events
- ☐ **happening**: _____; an event or occurrence
- ☐ **realize**: _____; become fully aware of something
- ☐ **too**: _____; in addition; also
- ☐ **end**: _____; the final part or conclusion
- ☐ **unhappy**: _____; not happy or satisfied
- ☐ **kill**: _____; cause the death of
- ☐ **very**: _____; to a great extent or degree
- ☐ **continue**: _____; persist or carry on
- ☐ **life**: _____; the condition that distinguishes organisms from inorganic matter

KEY VOCABULARY | LEVEL 300 - UNIT 6

- ☐ **orphan**: _____; a child whose parents are both dead
- ☐ **real**: _____; genuine or authentic
- ☐ **home**: _____; a place where one lives or permanently resides
- ☐ **family**: _____; a group of people related to each other by blood or marriage
- ☐ **imaginative**: _____; having or showing creativity or inventiveness
- ☐ **love**: _____; have a strong affection or deep emotional attachment
- ☐ **read**: _____; look at and understand the meaning of written or printed matter by interpreting the characters or symbols
- ☐ **talk**: _____; speak or converse
- ☐ **originally**: _____; at first or at the beginning
- ☐ **wanted**: _____; expressed a desire or wish for something
- ☐ **adopt**: _____; take someone else's child legally and bring them up as one's own
- ☐ **boy**: _____; a male child or young man
- ☐ **help**: _____; assist or aid someone
- ☐ **farm**: _____; a piece of land used for growing crops or raising animals
- ☐ **work**: _____; activity involving mental or physical effort done to achieve a result
- ☐ **end**: _____; come to a final point or conclusion
- ☐ **instead**: _____; in place of something or someone else
- ☐ **excited**: _____; feeling or showing happiness or enthusiasm
- ☐ **hard**: _____; difficult or challenging
- ☐ **time**: _____; a period during which an action or process takes place
- ☐ **fitting**: _____; adapting or conforming to a particular situation or environment
- ☐ **children**: _____; young human beings regarded collectively
- ☐ **new**: _____; recently made, acquired, or experienced
- ☐ **town**: _____; a larger urban area
- ☐ **because**: _____; conjunction indicating the reason or cause of something
- ☐ **different**: _____; not the same as another or each other
- ☐ **lot**: _____; a great amount or quantity
- ☐ **best**: _____; of the most excellent or desirable type or quality
- ☐ **friends**: _____; people with whom one has a bond of mutual affection
- ☐ **girl**: _____; a female child or young woman

DR. SIMON'S MAGIC ENGLISH

KEY VOCABULARY | **LEVEL 300 - UNIT 7**

- ☐ **fall**: _____; move downward, typically rapidly and freely
- ☐ **family**: _____; a group consisting of parents and their children, considered as a unit
- ☐ **enemy**: _____; a person who is actively opposed or hostile to someone or something
- ☐ **different**: _____; not the same as another or each other
- ☐ **city**: _____; a large town
- ☐ **meet**: _____; come into the presence or company of someone
- ☐ **feud**: _____; a prolonged and bitter quarrel or dispute
- ☐ **relationship**: _____; the way in which two or more people or things are connected
- ☐ **difficult**: _____; not easy or straightforward
- ☐ **decide**: _____; come to a resolution or conclusion
- ☐ **secretly**: _____; in a way that is not known or seen by others
- ☐ **married**: _____; having a spouse or spouses
- ☐ **plan**: _____; a detailed proposal for doing or achieving something
- ☐ **foiled**: _____; prevented from succeeding or achieving something
- ☐ **banish**: _____; exile or send away
- ☐ **killing**: _____; the act of causing someone's death
- ☐ **cousin**: _____; a child of one's uncle or aunt
- ☐ **duel**: _____; a prearranged contest with deadly weapons between two people
- ☐ **desperate**: _____; feeling or showing a hopeless sense that a situation is so bad as to be impossible to deal with
- ☐ **fake**: _____; pretend or deceive
- ☐ **own**: _____; belonging exclusively to oneself
- ☐ **death**: _____; the permanent cessation of all vital functions
- ☐ **sleeping**: _____; the state or condition of being asleep
- ☐ **potion**: _____; a liquid with healing, magical, or poisonous properties
- ☐ **hoping**: _____; feeling a desire for a particular outcome or result
- ☐ **rescue**: _____; save someone from a dangerous or distressing situation
- ☐ **receive**: _____; be given or presented with something
- ☐ **message**: _____; a verbal, written, or recorded communication sent to or left for someone
- ☐ **dead**: _____; no longer alive
- ☐ **poison**: _____; a substance that can cause severe illness, injury, or death
- ☐ **die**: _____; cease to live
- ☐ **tomb**: _____; a large vault, typically an underground one, for burying the dead
- ☐ **wake**: _____; emerge or come to consciousness from sleep
- ☐ **stab**: _____; thrust a sharp or pointed object into someone or something
- ☐ **dagger**: _____; a short knife with a pointed and edged blade
- ☐ **lovers**: _____; people who are in a romantic relationship with each other

KEY VOCABULARY | LEVEL 300 - UNIT 8

- ☐ **young**: _____; in the early stages of life; not old
- ☐ **girl**: _____; a female child
- ☐ **named**: _____; given a particular name
- ☐ **travel**: _____; journey to another place
- ☐ **mother**: _____; a female parent
- ☐ **very**: _____; to a high degree; extremely
- ☐ **social**: _____; enjoying the company of others; outgoing
- ☐ **friends**: _____; people with whom one shares a bond of mutual affection
- ☐ **many**: _____; a large number or quantity
- ☐ **people**: _____; human beings in general
- ☐ **things**: _____; objects or matters
- ☐ **not acceptable**: _____; not meeting standards or approval
- ☐ **society**: _____; a community of individuals living together
- ☐ **like**: _____; similar to; such as
- ☐ **talking**: _____; engaging in conversation
- ☐ **men**: _____; adult human males
- ☐ **well**: _____; in a satisfactory manner
- ☐ **going out**: _____; leaving one's residence or usual location
- ☐ **alone**: _____; without others present
- ☐ **night**: _____; the period of darkness between sunset and sunrise
- ☐ **man**: _____; an adult human male
- ☐ **become interested**: _____; develop a curiosity or attraction towards
- ☐ **unsure**: _____; uncertain or doubtful
- ☐ **proper**: _____; appropriate or correct
- ☐ **lady**: _____; a polite or formal term for a woman
- ☐ **spend**: _____; use or pass time in a particular way
- ☐ **more time**: _____; additional duration
- ☐ **together**: _____; in association or companionship with others
- ☐ **sick**: _____; experiencing illness or poor health
- ☐ **realize**: _____; become aware of or understands something
- ☐ **care for**: _____; feel concern or affection towards
- ☐ **unfortunately**: _____; regrettably or sadly
- ☐ **too late**: _____; after the optimal or expected time
- ☐ **die**: _____; cease to live; pass away

Dr. Simon's Magic English Level 300 | 69

DR. SIMON'S MAGIC ENGLISH

KEY VOCABULARY | **LEVEL 300 - UNIT 9**

- **ups**: _____; positive or favorable experiences or situations
- **downs**: _____; negative or unfavorable experiences or situations
- **life**: _____; the existence or experience of being alive
- **born**: _____; brought into existence through birth
- **father**: _____; a male parent
- **die**: _____; cease to live; pass away
- **mother**: _____; a female parent
- **remarry**: _____; marry again after the end of a previous marriage
- **man**: _____; an adult human male
- **named**: _____; given a particular name
- **strict**: _____; enforcing rules or discipline firmly
- **punish**: _____; impose a penalty or consequence for wrongdoing
- **often**: _____; frequently or regularly
- **send**: _____; dispatch or direct someone to a place
- **work**: _____; engage in labor or employment
- **factory**: _____; a building or establishment where goods are produced
- **run away**: _____; flee or escape from a situation or place
- **meet**: _____; encounter or come across someone
- **aunt**: _____; the sister of one's parent
- **take care of**: _____; provide support, protection, or assistance to
- **school**: _____; an educational institution for instruction
- **friends**: _____; people with whom one shares a bond of mutual affection
- **including**: _____; comprising, involving
- **boy**: _____; a young male
- **finish**: _____; complete or conclude
- **writer**: _____; a person who produces literary or written work
- **also**: _____; in addition; as well
- **fall in love**: _____; develop strong affection or romantic feelings for someone
- **get married**: _____; enter into the state of marriage

KEY VOCABULARY | LEVEL 300 - UNIT 10

- ☐ **salesman**: _____; a person who sells goods or services
- ☐ **life**: _____; the existence or experience of being alive
- ☐ **trouble**: _____; difficulty or problems
- ☐ **selling**: _____; exchanging goods or services for money
- ☐ **used to**: _____; accustomed to; formerly did
- ☐ **want**: _____; desire or wish for
- ☐ **help**: _____; assist or support
- ☐ **own**: _____; belonging to oneself
- ☐ **problems**: _____; difficulties or challenges
- ☐ **seem**: _____; give the impression of
- ☐ **keep**: _____; maintain or retain
- ☐ **job**: _____; employment or occupation
- ☐ **always**: _____; at all times; consistently
- ☐ **trying**: _____; making an effort or attempting
- ☐ **impress**: _____; make a favorable impact or influence
- ☐ **hard time**: _____; difficulty or struggle
- ☐ **distinguishing**: _____; recognizing or differentiating
- ☐ **reality**: _____; the state of things as they actually exist
- ☐ **memories**: _____; recollections or remembrances
- ☐ **often**: _____; frequently or regularly
- ☐ **talk**: _____; engage in conversation or communication
- ☐ **passed away**: _____; died or deceased
- ☐ **flashbacks**: _____; vivid recollections of past experiences
- ☐ **younger**: _____; at a younger age or time
- ☐ **become**: _____; undergo a change or transformation
- ☐ **depressed**: _____; in a state of unhappiness or low spirits
- ☐ **feel**: _____; experience or have a sensation of
- ☐ **like**: _____; similar to; resembling
- ☐ **failure**: _____; lack of success or achievement
- ☐ **only way**: _____; the exclusive method or means
- ☐ **family**: _____; a group consisting of parents and children
- ☐ **play**: _____; a theatrical performance
- ☐ **end**: _____; conclude or finish
- ☐ **funeral**: _____; a ceremony for honoring and burying the dead
- ☐ **death**: _____; the cessation of life

DR. SIMON'S MAGIC ENGLISH

KEY VOCABULARY | **LEVEL 300 - UNIT 11**

- ☐ **democracy**: _____; a system of government in which power is vested in the people, who exercise it through elected representatives
- ☐ **written**: _____; expressed or communicated in writing
- ☐ **political thinker**: _____; a person who contemplates or studies political theories and ideas
- ☐ **early**: _____; happening or existing near the beginning
- ☐ **wanted**: _____; desired or wished for
- ☐ **learn**: _____; acquire knowledge or skill
- ☐ **system**: _____; a set of principles or procedures governing something
- ☐ **people**: _____; human beings in general
- ☐ **traveled**: _____; went on a journey or trip
- ☐ **country**: _____; a nation or state
- ☐ **talked**: _____; engaged in conversation or communication
- ☐ **including**: _____; comprising, involving
- ☐ **farmers**: _____; individuals who cultivate crops or raise livestock
- ☐ **politicians**: _____; individuals involved in politics or government
- ☐ **ordinary**: _____; with no special or distinctive features
- ☐ **citizens**: _____; members of a particular country or state
- ☐ **impressed**: _____; deeply or markedly affected or influenced
- ☐ **spirit**: _____; the prevailing or dominant attitude, character, or quality
- ☐ **equality**: _____; the state of being equal, especially in status, rights, and opportunities
- ☐ **believed**: _____; accepted as true or valid
- ☐ **key**: _____; crucial or essential
- ☐ **success**: _____; the accomplishment of an aim or purpose
- ☐ **wrote**: _____; produced or composed in writing
- ☐ **importance**: _____; significance or value
- ☐ **individual**: _____; a single human being, as opposed to a group
- ☐ **danger**: _____; potential harm or risk
- ☐ **government**: _____; the governing body of a nation, state, or community
- ☐ **control**: _____; the power to influence or direct people's behavior or the course of events
- ☐ **still**: _____; up to and including the present or the time mentioned
- ☐ **provide**: _____; supply or give
- ☐ **insight**: _____; deep understanding or perception
- ☐ **character**: _____; the mental and moral qualities distinctive to an individual or group
- ☐ **political system**: _____; the organization and structure of political institutions and processes

KEY VOCABULARY | LEVEL 300 - UNIT 12

- ☐ **East**: _____; a cardinal point of the compass, opposite west
- ☐ **eden**: _____; a place or state of great happiness; paradise
- ☐ **tell**: _____; narrate or relate information or a story
- ☐ **story**: _____; an account of imaginary or real people and events told for entertainment
- ☐ **family**: _____; a group consisting of parents and children living together in a household
- ☐ **live**: _____; have one's permanent residence or home in a particular place
- ☐ **early**: _____; happening or done before the usual or expected time
- ☐ **follow**: _____; come after or behind someone or something
- ☐ **lives**: _____; the ways in which a person lives or a particular type of life
- ☐ **brothers**: _____; male siblings
- ☐ **father**: _____; a male parent
- ☐ **own**: _____; belonging exclusively to oneself or itself
- ☐ **novel**: _____; a fictitious prose narrative of book length
- ☐ **explore**: _____; examine or investigate in detail
- ☐ **themes**: _____; subjects or topics of discussion or artistic representation
- ☐ **good**: _____; morally right or virtuous
- ☐ **evil**: _____; profoundly immoral and wicked
- ☐ **love**: _____; an intense feeling of deep affection
- ☐ **hate**: _____; feel intense or passionate dislike for someone
- ☐ **nature**: _____; the basic or inherent features of something
- ☐ **human**: _____; of, relating to, or characteristic of people or human beings
- ☐ **beings**: _____; living creatures
- ☐ **central**: _____; of, at, or forming the center
- ☐ **characters**: _____; the individuals in a story, play, or movie
- ☐ **woman**: _____; an adult female human
- ☐ **capable**: _____; having the ability or capacity to do something
- ☐ **great**: _____; of an extent, amount, or intensity considerably above average
- ☐ **cruelty**: _____; the desire to inflict pain, suffering, or hardship on others
- ☐ **deception**: _____; the action of deceiving someone; the state of being deceived
- ☐ **touch**: _____; briefly mention or deal with
- ☐ **biblical**: _____; related to or contained in the Bible

Dr. Simon's Magic English Level 300 | 73

DR. SIMON'S MAGIC ENGLISH

KEY VOCABULARY | LEVEL 300 - UNIT 13

- ☐ **named**: _____; given a particular name
- ☐ **becoming**: _____; the process of coming to be something or of passing into a state
- ☐ **gentleman**: _____; a chivalrous, courteous, or honorable man
- ☐ **escaped**: _____; having escaped from confinement or capture
- ☐ **convict**: _____; a person found guilty of a criminal offense and serving a sentence of imprisonment
- ☐ **threaten**: _____; express an intention to cause harm, pain, or trouble to someone
- ☐ **stealing**: _____; taking another person's property without permission or legal right and without intending to return it
- ☐ **file**: _____; a tool with a roughened surface or surfaces, typically of steel, used for smoothing or shaping a hard material
- ☐ **chains**: _____; a series of metal links or rings connected to or fitted into one another and used for various purposes
- ☐ **later**: _____; at some time in the future; subsequently
- ☐ **invite**: _____; formally request someone to be present or take part in an event
- ☐ **wealthy**: _____; having a great deal of money, resources, or assets; rich
- ☐ **strange**: _____; unusual or surprising; difficult to understand or explain
- ☐ **dressed**: _____; wearing clothes or garments
- ☐ **wedding**: _____; a marriage ceremony, especially considered as including the associated celebrations
- ☐ **gown**: _____; a long dress, typically worn by women
- ☐ **treat**: _____; behave toward or deal with someone or something in a certain way
- ☐ **poorly**: _____; in a way that is unsatisfactory or inadequate
- ☐ **soon**: _____; in or after a short time; before long
- ☐ **learn**: _____; acquire knowledge or skill
- ☐ **break**: _____; cause the failure or destruction of
- ☐ **heart**: _____; the central or innermost part of something
- ☐ **inform**: _____; give someone facts or information
- ☐ **fortune**: _____; a large amount of money or assets; wealth
- ☐ **unknown**: _____; not known or familiar
- ☐ **benefactor**: _____; a person who gives money or other help to a person or cause
- ☐ **pursue**: _____; follow or chase someone or something in order to catch or attack them
- ☐ **spend**: _____; use or expend money, time, or energy on something
- ☐ **lavishly**: _____; in a rich or luxurious manner
- ☐ **eventually**: _____; in the end, especially after a long delay, dispute, or series of problems
- ☐ **identity**: _____; the fact of being who or what a person or thing is
- ☐ **people**: _____; human beings in general, considered collectively
- ☐ **thought**: _____; an idea or opinion produced by thinking or occurring suddenly in the mind
- ☐ **knew**: _____; had information or knowledge about someone or something

KEY VOCABULARY | LEVEL 300 - UNIT 14

- ☐ **life**: _____; the capacity for growth, reproduction, functional activity, and continual change
- ☐ **experiences**: _____; events or occurrences that leave an impression on someone
- ☐ **steamboat**: _____; a boat propelled by steam power, especially a paddle-wheel craft of a type used widely on rivers in the 19th century
- ☐ **pilot**: _____; a person who operates the controls of an aircraft, spacecraft, or ship
- ☐ **river**: _____; a large natural stream of water flowing in a channel to the sea, a lake, or another such stream
- ☐ **talk**: _____; speak in conversation or discourse
- ☐ **growing**: _____; developing or maturing physically, mentally, or emotionally
- ☐ **small**: _____; of a size that is less than normal or usual
- ☐ **town**: _____; a place with a local government, typically larger than a village and smaller than a city
- ☐ **always**: _____; at all times; on all occasions
- ☐ **fascinated**: _____; extremely interested in or attracted by someone or something
- ☐ **wanted**: _____; desired or wished for
- ☐ **job**: _____; a paid position of regular employment
- ☐ **apprentice**: _____; a person who is learning a trade from a skilled employer, having agreed to work for a fixed period at low wages
- ☐ **full**: _____; containing or holding as much or as many as possible
- ☐ **stories**: _____; accounts of imaginary or real people and events told for entertainment
- ☐ **people**: _____; human beings in general or considered collectively
- ☐ **adventure**: _____; an unusual and exciting, typically hazardous, experience or activity
- ☐ **changed**: _____; made or became different
- ☐ **time**: _____; the indefinite continued progress of existence and events in the past, present, and future
- ☐ **important**: _____; of great significance or value; likely to have a profound effect

DR. SIMON'S MAGIC ENGLISH

KEY VOCABULARY | LEVEL 300 - UNIT 15

- ☐ **Scottish**: _____; relating to Scotland or its people
- ☐ **general**: _____; a high-ranking military officer
- ☐ **hear**: _____; perceive sound with the ear
- ☐ **prophecy**: _____; a prediction or foretelling of the future
- ☐ **witches**: _____; women who are believed to have magical powers
- ☐ **king**: _____; the male ruler of a country
- ☐ **encouragement**: _____; the act of giving support, confidence, or hope to someone
- ☐ **wife**: _____; a married woman
- ☐ **decide**: _____; make a choice or come to a conclusion about something
- ☐ **murder**: _____; kill someone unlawfully and intentionally
- ☐ **current**: _____; belonging to the present time
- ☐ **guilt**: _____; a feeling of remorse or responsibility for having committed a wrongdoing
- ☐ **paranoia**: _____; an irrational or excessive distrust or suspicion of others
- ☐ **series**: _____; a number of related events, actions, or things that come one after another
- ☐ **violent**: _____; involving or characterized by physical force intended to hurt, damage, or kill
- ☐ **acts**: _____; actions or deeds
- ☐ **maintain**: _____; keep in existence or continue
- ☐ **power**: _____; the ability or capacity to do something
- ☐ **defeat**: _____; win a victory over someone in a battle or contest
- ☐ **battle**: _____; a sustained fight between large, organized armed forces
- ☐ **order**: _____; the arrangement or disposition of people or things in relation to each other
- ☐ **restore**: _____; bring back or return something to its original state or condition
- ☐ **Scotland**: _____; a country in the northern part of the United Kingdom

KEY VOCABULARY | **LEVEL 300 - UNIT 16**

- ☐ **girl**: _____; a female child
- ☐ **named**: _____; having a name
- ☐ **move**: _____; change one's place of residence
- ☐ **live**: _____; have one's residence or dwelling in a particular place
- ☐ **uncle**: _____; the brother of one's father or mother, or the husband of one's aunt
- ☐ **old**: _____; having lived for a long time; no longer young
- ☐ **house**: _____; a building for human habitation
- ☐ **sad**: _____; feeling or showing sorrow or unhappiness
- ☐ **lonely**: _____; feeling alone or isolated
- ☐ **discover**: _____; find or become aware of something for the first time
- ☐ **hidden**: _____; concealed or out of sight
- ☐ **garden**: _____; a piece of ground, often near a house, used for growing flowers, fruit, or vegetables
- ☐ **no one**: _____; no person; nobody
- ☐ **friend**: _____; a person with whom one has a bond of mutual affection
- ☐ **work**: _____; activity involving mental or physical effort done to achieve a purpose or result
- ☐ **together**: _____; in company or association with others
- ☐ **make**: _____; bring into existence by shaping or changing material
- ☐ **beautiful**: _____; pleasing the senses or mind aesthetically
- ☐ **again**: _____; once more; another time
- ☐ **find**: _____; discover or perceive by chance or unexpectedly
- ☐ **sickly**: _____; in poor health; frequently ill
- ☐ **keep**: _____; have possession or control of something
- ☐ **away**: _____; at a distance from a particular place or person
- ☐ **bring**: _____; carry or accompany to a place
- ☐ **start**: _____; begin or set in motion
- ☐ **better**: _____; improved in health or other respects
- ☐ **spend**: _____; use up or consume
- ☐ **time**: _____; the indefinite continued progress of existence and events in the past, present, and future
- ☐ **outside**: _____; the external side or surface of something
- ☐ **grow**: _____; increase or develop in size, quantity, or degree
- ☐ **learn**: _____; acquire knowledge or skill through study, experience, or teaching
- ☐ **power**: _____; the ability or capacity to do something
- ☐ **nature**: _____; the phenomena of the physical world collectively
- ☐ **friendship**: _____; the emotions or conduct of friends; the state of being friends

DR. SIMON'S MAGIC ENGLISH

KEY VOCABULARY | **LEVEL 300 - UNIT 17**

- ☐ **follow**: _____; go or come after or behind someone or something
- ☐ **story**: _____; a narrative of real or imagined events
- ☐ **young**: _____; having lived or existed for only a short time
- ☐ **lovers**: _____; people who are in a romantic or sexual relationship
- ☐ **group**: _____; a number of people or things that are located, gathered, or classed together
- ☐ **amateur**: _____; a person who engages in a pursuit, especially a sport or a branch of the arts, as a pastime rather than as a profession
- ☐ **actors**: _____; people who perform in plays, movies, or television shows
- ☐ **mix up**: _____; be confused or mistaken
- ☐ **fairies**: _____; imaginary creatures with magical powers, often depicted as small and having wings
- ☐ **magical**: _____; relating to or using magic or sorcery
- ☐ **forest**: _____; a large area covered chiefly with trees and undergrowth
- ☐ **father**: _____; a male parent
- ☐ **want**: _____; have a desire to possess or do something
- ☐ **marry**: _____; become the legally recognized partner of someone in a formal ceremony
- ☐ **fight**: _____; a violent confrontation or struggle
- ☐ **wife**: _____; a married woman
- ☐ **each**: _____; every one of two or more people or things considered separately
- ☐ **revenge**: _____; the action of inflicting hurt or harm on someone for an injury or wrong suffered at their hands
- ☐ **see**: _____; perceive with the eyes; to observe or notice
- ☐ **argue**: _____; give reasons or cite evidence in support of an idea, action, or theory
- ☐ **help**: _____; give assistance or support to someone
- ☐ **spell**: _____; a form of words used as a magical charm or incantation
- ☐ **servant**: _____; a person who performs duties for others, especially a person employed in a house or as a personal attendant
- ☐ **fall in love**: _____; experience strong romantic or affectionate feelings toward someone
- ☐ **chaos**: _____; complete disorder and confusion
- ☐ **ensue**: _____; happen or occur afterward or as a result
- ☐ **eventually**: _____; in the end, especially after a long delay, dispute, or series of problems
- ☐ **couple**: _____; two people who are married, engaged, or otherwise romantically or sexually involved
- ☐ **end up**: _____; eventually reach or come to a specified place, condition, or situation
- ☐ **happily**: 행복하게; in a happy manner; with happiness or joy

KEY VOCABULARY | LEVEL 300 - UNIT 18

- ☐ **fables**: _____; short fictional stories that often feature animals and convey moral lessons
- ☐ **collection**: _____; a group of things gathered together
- ☐ **teach**: _____; impart knowledge or skill to someone through instruction or example
- ☐ **important**: _____; of great significance or value
- ☐ **lesson**: _____; an instructive or moral teaching
- ☐ **know**: _____; have information or awareness about something
- ☐ **write**: _____; form or inscribe letters, words, or symbols on a surface
- ☐ **around**: _____; in existence or available; near or accessible
- ☐ **long time**: _____; a lengthy period or duration
- ☐ **usually**: _____; most of the time; commonly
- ☐ **animals**: _____; living organisms that typically move, consume organic matter, and possess senses
- ☐ **honesty**: _____; the quality of being truthful, sincere, and upright in conduct
- ☐ **hard work**: _____; effortful labor or exertion
- ☐ **kindness**: _____; the quality of being friendly, generous, and considerate
- ☐ **most famous**: _____; widely recognized or well-known to a large extent
- ☐ **tortoise**: _____; a slow-moving land-dwelling reptile with a protective shell
- ☐ **hare**: _____; a fast-running mammal with long ears and powerful hind legs
- ☐ **beat**: _____; defeat or overcome in a contest or competition
- ☐ **race**: _____; a competition of speed
- ☐ **keep going**: _____; continue moving forward or progressing
- ☐ **give up**: _____; cease efforts or stop trying
- ☐ **ant**: _____; a small social insect that typically lives in organized colonies
- ☐ **grasshopper**: _____; an insect with long hind legs for jumping and producing chirping sounds
- ☐ **summer**: _____; the warmest season of the year
- ☐ **play**: _____; engage in recreational or enjoyable activities
- ☐ **sing**: _____; produce musical sounds with the voice
- ☐ **come**: _____; arrive or approach a certain time or situation
- ☐ **enough**: _____; sufficient or adequate in quantity or degree
- ☐ **food**: _____; substances consumed by living organisms to provide nourishment
- ☐ **survive**: _____; continue to live or exist
- ☐ **hungry**: _____; feeling or showing the need for food
- ☐ **be prepared**: _____; make ready or get ready beforehand
- ☐ **future**: _____; the time or period that will follow the present

Dr. Simon's Magic English Level 300

DR. SIMON'S MAGIC ENGLISH

KEY VOCABULARY | **LEVEL 300 - UNIT 19**

- ☐ **shipwrecked**: _____; having suffered a shipwreck; stranded or cast adrift as a result of a shipwreck
- ☐ **separate**: _____; move apart or be apart from someone or something
- ☐ **twin**: _____; one of two children or animals born at the same birth
- ☐ **brother**: _____; a male sibling
- ☐ **dress up**: _____; wear special clothes or costumes to appear different or in a particular way
- ☐ **boy**: _____; a male child
- ☐ **named**: _____; having a specified name
- ☐ **work**: _____; engage in physical or mental activity to accomplish a task or achieve a purpose
- ☐ **duke**: _____; a nobleman of the highest hereditary rank below a prince
- ☐ **lady**: _____; a title used before the name of a woman of noble rank or married to a lord
- ☐ **fall in love**: _____; develop strong romantic or affectionate feelings for someone
- ☐ **realize**: _____; become aware or conscious of something
- ☐ **actually**: _____; in reality; truly
- ☐ **girl**: _____; a female child
- ☐ **meanwhile**: _____; at the same time; in the meantime
- ☐ **also**: _____; in addition; too
- ☐ **some**: _____; an unspecified number or amount of people or things
- ☐ **other**: _____; different or distinct from the one or ones already mentioned or implied
- ☐ **funny**: _____; causing laughter or amusement; humorous
- ☐ **characters**: _____; the individuals who appear in a story, play, or movie
- ☐ **including**: _____; comprising as part of a larger whole
- ☐ **sir**: _____; a title of honor used before the name of a knight or baronet
- ☐ **eventually**: _____; at some later time; in the end
- ☐ **true**: _____; in accordance with fact or reality
- ☐ **identity**: _____; the distinguishing character or personality of an individual
- ☐ **reveal**: _____; make known or disclose something previously secret or unknown
- ☐ **end up**: _____; eventually reach or arrive at a specified place, situation, or result
- ☐ **right**: _____; morally or socially correct or acceptable
- ☐ **people**: _____; human beings in general

KEY VOCABULARY | LEVEL 300 - UNIT 20

- ☐ **betray**: _____; be disloyal or unfaithful to someone's trust or confidence
- ☐ **friends**: _____; people with whom one has a bond of mutual affection and trust
- ☐ **wrongfully**: _____; unjustly or unfairly
- ☐ **imprison**: _____; be confined or held captive in a prison or jail
- ☐ **many**: _____; a large number or amount
- ☐ **year**: _____; a unit of time equal to 365 days or 12 months
- ☐ **eventually**: _____; at some later time; finally
- ☐ **escape**: _____; break free or get away from confinement or danger
- ☐ **discover**: _____; find or become aware of something for the first time
- ☐ **treasure**: _____; valuable or precious objects or wealth
- ☐ **allow**: _____; give permission or opportunity for something to happen
- ☐ **become**: _____; undergo a change or transition into a different state or condition
- ☐ **rich**: _____; having a great amount of money, possessions, or resources
- ☐ **powerful**: _____; having great influence, control, or authority
- ☐ **man**: _____; an adult human male
- ☐ **new**: _____; recently made, acquired, or introduced
- ☐ **identity**: _____; the distinguishing character or personality of an individual
- ☐ **seek**: _____; try to find or discover something
- ☐ **revenge**: _____; the act of inflicting harm or punishment in return for an injury or wrongdoing
- ☐ **help**: _____; assist or support someone in need
- ☐ **kind**: _____; showing or characterized by benevolence, consideration, or generosity
- ☐ **way**: _____; a method, route, or course of action
- ☐ **fall in love**: _____; develop strong romantic or affectionate feelings for someone
- ☐ **learn**: _____; acquire knowledge or skill through study, experience, or being taught
- ☐ **important**: _____; significant or essential
- ☐ **lessons**: _____; instructive or moral teachings
- ☐ **forgiveness**: _____; the act of pardoning or letting go of resentment or blame
- ☐ **unintended**: _____; not planned or deliberate
- ☐ **consequences**: _____; the results or effects of an action or decision

DR. SIMON'S MAGIC ENGLISH

KEY VOCABULARY | **LEVEL 300 - UNIT 21**

- ☐ **travel**: _____; go on a journey or move from one place to another
- ☐ **through**: _____; moving in one side and out of the other side of something
- ☐ **parts**: _____; separate pieces or components of a whole
- ☐ **afterlife**: _____; the existence that is believed to follow death
- ☐ **hell**: _____; a place or state of punishment for the wicked or sinful after death
- ☐ **purgatory**: _____; a place or state of temporary suffering or purification
- ☐ **paradise**: _____; a place or state of bliss, happiness, or perfection
- ☐ **see**: _____; perceive with the eyes; observe
- ☐ **people**: _____; human beings in general
- ☐ **punish**: _____; be subjected to a penalty or suffering for wrongdoing
- ☐ **sins**: _____; immoral acts or transgressions against religious or moral principles
- ☐ **commit**: _____; carry out or perpetrate an act, typically a crime or wrongdoing
- ☐ **during**: _____; throughout the course or duration of a particular time or event
- ☐ **life**: _____; the condition that distinguishes organisms from inorganic objects
- ☐ **earth**: _____; the planet on which we live, the third from the sun in our solar system
- ☐ **purify**: _____; remove contaminants or impurities from something
- ☐ **before**: _____; in advance of or prior to a particular time or event
- ☐ **enter**: _____; come or go into a place
- ☐ **soul**: _____; the spiritual or immaterial part of a human being
- ☐ **blessed**: _____; endowed with divine favor or protection
- ☐ **enjoying**: _____; taking pleasure or satisfaction in something
- ☐ **eternal**: _____; without beginning or end; lasting forever
- ☐ **happiness**: _____; the state of being happy or content
- ☐ **throughout**: _____; from the beginning to the end of a particular period or situation
- ☐ **journey**: _____; a long and often difficult process of personal change or development
- ☐ **guide**: _____; lead, direct, or accompany someone
- ☐ **poet**: _____; a person who writes poems
- ☐ **named**: _____; having a specified name
- ☐ **later**: _____; after a particular point or time
- ☐ **woman**: _____; an adult human female

KEY VOCABULARY | LEVEL 300 - UNIT 22

- ☐ **novel**: _____; a fictional narrative in book form
- ☐ **tell**: _____; convey or relate information or a story
- ☐ **story**: _____; an account of imaginary or real people and events
- ☐ **poor**: _____; lacking sufficient money or resources
- ☐ **farmer**: _____; a person who cultivates land or raises crops and livestock
- ☐ **named**: _____; having a specified name
- ☐ **rural**: _____; relating to the countryside or agricultural areas
- ☐ **wife**: _____; a married woman
- ☐ **book**: _____; a written or printed work consisting of pages
- ☐ **follow**: _____; come after or go along behind someone or something
- ☐ **struggle**: _____; strive or fight against difficulties or obstacles
- ☐ **survive**: _____; continue to live or exist, especially in spite of danger or hardship
- ☐ **harsh**: _____; severe or strict
- ☐ **environment**: _____; the surroundings or conditions in which a person, animal, or plant lives or operates
- ☐ **relationship**: _____; the way in which two or more people or things are connected or involved with each other
- ☐ **work**: _____; exert effort or perform labor
- ☐ **hard**: _____; requiring a great deal of effort or endurance
- ☐ **provide**: _____; supply or make available something that is needed or wanted
- ☐ **family**: _____; a group consisting of parents and their children
- ☐ **eventually**: _____; at some later time; in the end
- ☐ **become**: _____; come to be or develop into something
- ☐ **wealthy**: _____; having a great deal of money, resources, or possessions
- ☐ **landowner**: _____; a person who owns land
- ☐ **however**: _____; nevertheless; on the other hand
- ☐ **come**: _____; arrive or approach a particular state or condition
- ☐ **temptation**: _____; a strong urge or desire to do something, especially something unwise or wrong
- ☐ **corruption**: _____; dishonest or fraudulent conduct by those in power, typically involving bribery
- ☐ **face**: _____; confront or deal with a difficult or challenging situation
- ☐ **consequences**: _____; the results or effects of an action or decision
- ☐ **actions**: _____; the things done or performed by someone
- ☐ **throughout**: _____; from the beginning to the end of a particular period or situation
- ☐ **themes**: _____; recurring subjects or ideas explored in a work of literature
- ☐ **importance**: _____; the quality or state of being significant or valuable
- ☐ **land**: _____; the solid part of the Earth's surface not covered by water
- ☐ **explore**: _____; investigate or analyze in detail

Dr. Simon's Magic English Level 300

DR. SIMON'S MAGIC ENGLISH

KEY VOCABULARY | **LEVEL 300 - UNIT 23**

- ☐ **story**: _____; an account of imaginary or real people and events
- ☐ **named**: _____; having a specified name
- ☐ **mansion**: _____; a large, impressive house
- ☐ **throw**: _____; project or propel something with force
- ☐ **amazing**: _____; causing great surprise, wonder, or admiration
- ☐ **parties**: _____; social gatherings or events
- ☐ **every**: _____; each; all possible instances of
- ☐ **already**: _____; before or by a specified time or period
- ☐ **married**: _____; having a spouse; united in wedlock
- ☐ **someone**: _____; an unknown or unspecified person
- ☐ **try**: _____; make an attempt or effort
- ☐ **win**: _____; achieve victory or success in a competition or endeavor
- ☐ **extravagant**: _____; exceeding what is reasonable or appropriate
- ☐ **buying**: _____; acquiring in exchange for money
- ☐ **expensive**: _____; costing a lot of money
- ☐ **gifts**: _____; items given to someone without payment
- ☐ **unfold**: _____; reveal or become revealed
- ☐ **learn**: _____; gain knowledge or information about something
- ☐ **past**: _____; the time before the present
- ☐ **money**: _____; a medium of exchange in the form of coins or banknotes
- ☐ **illegal**: _____; prohibited by law or rules
- ☐ **activities**: _____; actions or deeds performed by someone
- ☐ **husband**: _____; a married man
- ☐ **become**: _____; come to be or develop into something
- ☐ **jealous**: _____; feeling or showing envy or resentment
- ☐ **find**: _____; discover or perceive by chance or effort
- ☐ **eventually**: _____; at some later time; in the end
- ☐ **reconnect**: _____; establish a connection or relationship again
- ☐ **start**: _____; begin or set in motion
- ☐ **affair**: _____; a romantic or sexual relationship, typically secret or illicit
- ☐ **happiness**: _____; the state of being happy or content
- ☐ **short-lived**: _____; lasting for only a brief period
- ☐ **tragic**: _____; causing or characterized by extreme distress or sorrow
- ☐ **event**: _____; a thing that happens, especially one of importance
- ☐ **happen**: _____; take place or occur
- ☐ **kill**: _____; cause the death of someone

KEY VOCABULARY | LEVEL 300 - UNIT 24

- ☐ **book**: _____; a written or printed work consisting of pages glued or sewn together along one side and bound in covers
- ☐ **tell**: _____; give an account of something in spoken or written words
- ☐ **story**: _____; an account of imaginary or real people and events
- ☐ **hunting**: _____; the activity of pursuing and killing wild animals for food, sport, or profit
- ☐ **trip**: _____; a journey or excursion, especially for pleasure
- ☐ **famous**: _____; well-known; widely recognized
- ☐ **writer**: _____; a person who has written a particular text or works of literature
- ☐ **travel**: _____; go on a journey or trip
- ☐ **hunt**: _____; pursue and capture or kill wild animals
- ☐ **big game**: _____; large animals hunted for sport or food
- ☐ **animals**: _____; living organisms that typically move around, consume organic matter, and have specialized sense organs and nervous systems
- ☐ **such as**: _____; for example; as an illustration
- ☐ **lions**: _____; large, carnivorous felines found in Africa and Asia
- ☐ **zebras**: _____; African mammals with black-and-white striped coats
- ☐ **learn**: _____; gain knowledge or information about something
- ☐ **land**: _____; the solid part of the earth's surface
- ☐ **people**: _____; human beings considered collectively
- ☐ **divided**: _____; separated into parts or pieces
- ☐ **several**: _____; more than two but not many
- ☐ **chapters**: _____; main divisions of a book or literary work
- ☐ **each**: _____; every one of two or more people or things considered separately
- ☐ **describing**: _____; presenting or giving an account of something in words
- ☐ **different**: _____; not the same as another or each other
- ☐ **part**: _____; a piece or segment of a whole
- ☐ **journey**: _____; a traveling from one place to another, especially when involving a considerable distance
- ☐ **write**: _____; mark letters or words on a surface with a pen, pencil, or similar implement
- ☐ **challenges**: _____; difficulties or obstacles to overcome
- ☐ **faced**: _____; confronted with and dealt with
- ☐ **harsh**: _____; severe or demanding
- ☐ **terrain**: _____; a stretch of land, especially with regard to its physical features
- ☐ **dangers**: _____; conditions or situations that can cause harm or injury
- ☐ **met**: _____; encountered or come into contact with someone
- ☐ **local**: _____; relating to or occurring in a particular area or neighborhood
- ☐ **tribesmen**: _____; members of a tribe or indigenous community
- ☐ **helped**: _____; assisted or provided support to someone on their journey

DR. SIMON'S MAGIC ENGLISH

KEY VOCABULARY | **LEVEL 300 - UNIT 25**

- ☐ **young**: _____ ; in the early stage of life or development
- ☐ **named**: _____ ; given a particular name
- ☐ **live**: _____ ; exist or reside in a specific place
- ☐ **small**: _____ ; of a size that is less than average or usual
- ☐ **house**: _____ ; a building used as a dwelling or place to live
- ☐ **family**: _____ ; a group of people who are related by blood, marriage, or adoption
- ☐ **famous**: _____ ; well-known or widely recognized
- ☐ **reclusive**: _____ ; avoiding the company of others; solitary
- ☐ **candy**: _____ ; sweet food made with sugar or syrup
- ☐ **maker**: _____ ; a person or entity that creates or produces something
- ☐ **decide**: _____ ; make a choice or reach a conclusion
- ☐ **open**: _____ ; allow access or entry
- ☐ **chocolate**: _____ ; a food product made from roasted and ground cacao beans, often sweetened and flavored
- ☐ **factory**: _____ ; a building or facility where goods are manufactured or produced
- ☐ **lucky**: _____ ; fortunate or having good fortune
- ☐ **find**: _____ ; discover or locate something that was previously hidden or unknown
- ☐ **golden**: _____ ; having the color or shine of gold
- ☐ **ticket**: _____ ; a piece of paper or card that gives the holder the right to enter or access a particular event or place
- ☐ **bars**: _____ ; long, narrow, and solid objects, often made of metal or a similar material
- ☐ **able**: _____ ; having the capability, skill, or resources to do something
- ☐ **visit**: _____ ; go to or spend time in a place
- ☐ **amazing**: _____ ; causing wonder, astonishment, or great admiration
- ☐ **mysterious**: _____ ; difficult to understand or explain; enigmatic
- ☐ **witness**: _____ ; see or observe an event or situation
- ☐ **strange**: _____ ; unfamiliar, odd, or unusual
- ☐ **wonderful**: _____ ; inspiring delight, pleasure, or admiration
- ☐ **one by one**: _____ ; individually, in a sequence or order
- ☐ **misbehave**: _____ ; behave badly or inappropriately
- ☐ **disqualified**: _____ ; declared ineligible or not qualified to continue or participate
- ☐ **tour**: _____ ; a journey or series of visits to different places
- ☐ **leaving**: _____ ; departing or going away from a particular location or situation
- ☐ **end**: _____ ; the final part or conclusion of something
- ☐ **give**: _____ ; transfer the possession or ownership of something to someone else
- ☐ **kind**: _____ ; showing generosity, goodwill, or compassion
- ☐ **honest**: _____ ; truthful, sincere, or morally upright

KEY VOCABULARY | LEVEL 300 - UNIT 26

- ☐ **respected**: _____; admired, esteemed, or held in high regard
- ☐ **doctor**: _____; a person who is qualified to practice medicine and treat patients
- ☐ **secret**: _____; something that is kept hidden or not known by others
- ☐ **try**: _____; make an attempt or effort to do something
- ☐ **keep**: _____; maintain or retain possession or control of something
- ☐ **hidden**: _____; not visible or easily noticed
- ☐ **created**: _____; brought into existence or made something new
- ☐ **potion**: _____; a liquid or mixture, often with magical or medicinal properties
- ☐ **transform**: _____; change in form, appearance, or nature
- ☐ **violent**: _____; involving or characterized by physical force or aggression
- ☐ **terrible**: _____; extremely bad or severe
- ☐ **become**: _____; undergo a change or transition into something else
- ☐ **addicted**: _____; physically or psychologically dependent on a substance or behavior
- ☐ **control**: _____; have power or authority over something or someone
- ☐ **happening**: _____; occurring or taking place
- ☐ **own**: _____; belonging to oneself
- ☐ **kill**: _____; cause the death of someone or something
- ☐ **realize**: _____; become aware or conscious of something
- ☐ **taking**: _____; engaging in the act of consuming or using something
- ☐ **same**: _____; identical or not different
- ☐ **die**: _____; cease to live or exist
- ☐ **addiction**: _____; a strong dependence on a substance or behavior
- ☐ **temptation**: _____; a desire to do something, especially something that is considered wrong or unwise
- ☐ **resist**: _____; withstand or refuse to give in to something
- ☐ **effort**: _____; a vigorous or determined attempt to achieve something
- ☐ **transformation**: _____; a complete or significant change in form, appearance, or nature
- ☐ **undergo**: _____; experience or go through a process or change
- ☐ **transition**: _____; a process of changing from one state, condition, or form to another
- ☐ **dependent**: _____; relying on or influenced by something or someone else
- ☐ **authority**: _____; power or control over others
- ☐ **occurrence**: _____; an instance or happening of something
- ☐ **halt**: _____; stop or bring to a stop
- ☐ **cease**: _____; come to an end or stop happening
- ☐ **conclusion**: _____; the end or final part of something
- ☐ **existence**: _____; the fact or state of living or being present

Dr. Simon's Magic English Level 300 | 87

DR. SIMON'S MAGIC ENGLISH

KEY VOCABULARY | **LEVEL 300 - UNIT 27**

- ☐ **story**: _____; a narrative or tale
- ☐ **pig**: _____; a domesticated mammal with a stout body, short legs, and a snout used for rooting
- ☐ **friendship**: _____; a close relationship between two or more people characterized by trust, support, and mutual affection
- ☐ **spider**: _____; an eight-legged arachnid that spins webs to catch prey
- ☐ **destined**: _____; predetermined or fated to happen in a certain way
- ☐ **slaughtered**: _____; killed for food or other purposes
- ☐ **convinced**: _____; persuaded or made someone believe or agree to something
- ☐ **take care of**: _____; look after or provide for someone or something
- ☐ **fate**: _____; the development of events beyond a person's control, regarded as determined by a supernatural power
- ☐ **sad**: _____; feeling or showing sorrow or unhappiness
- ☐ **plan**: _____; a detailed proposal for doing or achieving something
- ☐ **save**: _____; rescue or protect from harm or danger
- ☐ **weave**: _____; create or form by interlacing threads or fibers
- ☐ **message**: _____; information or communication conveyed through words, signals, or symbols
- ☐ **web**: _____; a complex structure created by spiders for trapping prey or for other purposes
- ☐ **special**: _____; unique, different, or set apart from others
- ☐ **keep alive**: _____; ensure that someone or something continues to live or exist
- ☐ **love**: _____; a deep affection or fondness for someone or something
- ☐ **sacrifice**: _____; the act of giving up something valuable or important for the sake of someone or something else

KEY VOCABULARY | **LEVEL 300 - UNIT 28**

☐ **heartwarming**: _____; evoking feelings of warmth, affection, or sympathy
☐ **relationship**: _____; the way in which two or more people or things are connected or behave toward each other
☐ **tree**: _____; a tall plant with a trunk and branches made of wood
☐ **boy**: _____; a young male human
☐ **story**: _____; a narrative or tale
☐ **young**: _____; in an early stage of life or growth
☐ **play**: _____; engage in activity for enjoyment or recreation
☐ **eat**: _____; consume food by putting it in the mouth and chewing and swallowing it
☐ **apple**: _____; a round fruit with firm, crisp flesh and a green, yellow, or red skin
☐ **shade**: _____; a dark area or spot that is sheltered from the sun's direct rays
☐ **grow up**: _____; mature or develop into an adult
☐ **coming back**: _____; returning to a place or situation
☐ **various**: _____; different kinds or types
☐ **branches**: _____; the parts of a tree that grow out from the trunk and bear leaves, flowers, or fruit
☐ **give**: _____; provide or offer something to someone
☐ **everything**: _____; all things; all possible things
☐ **weaker**: _____; not as strong or powerful as before
☐ **less**: _____; a smaller amount or degree of something
☐ **beautiful**: _____; pleasing to the senses or mind, often associated with aesthetic qualities
☐ **eventually**: _____; at some later time; in the end
☐ **old**: _____; having lived for a long time; no longer young
☐ **asking**: _____; making a request or inquiring about something
☐ **place**: _____; a particular position, point, or area
☐ **rest**: _____; cease work or activity and relax or sleep
☐ **stump**: _____; the remaining part of a tree trunk after it has been cut down
☐ **left**: _____; remaining after others have gone or been used
☐ **teach**: _____; impart knowledge or lessons to someone
☐ **importance**: _____; the quality or state of being significant, valuable, or necessary
☐ **giving**: _____; the act of voluntarily providing or offering something to someone
☐ **grateful**: _____; feeling or showing appreciation or thanks
☐ **have**: _____; possess or own something

Dr. Simon's Magic English Level 300 | 89

DR. SIMON'S MAGIC ENGLISH

KEY VOCABULARY | LEVEL 300 - UNIT 29

- ☐ **girl**: _____; a young female human
- ☐ **named**: _____; given a particular name
- ☐ **family**: _____; a group consisting of parents and their children, living together in a household
- ☐ **live**: _____; have one's home in a particular place
- ☐ **town**: _____; a human settlement smaller than a city
- ☐ **called**: _____; named or known as
- ☐ **father**: _____; a male parent
- ☐ **lawyer**: _____; a person who practices or studies law; someone who provides legal advice or represents clients in legal matters
- ☐ **defend**: _____; protect or support someone or something against an accusation or attack
- ☐ **black**: _____; having the darkest color due to the absence or absorption of light; often used to refer to people of African descent
- ☐ **man**: _____; an adult human male
- ☐ **accused**: _____; charged with or declared to have committed a crime
- ☐ **crime**: _____; an act that is punishable by law as forbidden by statute or injurious to the public welfare
- ☐ **commit**: _____; be guilty of a particular offense or wrongdoing
- ☐ **make**: _____; cause something to happen or exist
- ☐ **some**: _____; an unspecified amount or number of people or things
- ☐ **people**: _____; human beings in general; individuals
- ☐ **angry**: _____; feeling or showing strong displeasure or hostility
- ☐ **treat**: _____; behave towards someone or something in a certain way
- ☐ **poorly**: _____; in a way that is not satisfactory or desirable; badly
- ☐ **brother**: _____; a male sibling
- ☐ **learn**: _____; acquire knowledge or skill through study, experience, or being taught
- ☐ **lessons**: _____; instructions, information, or experiences that provide knowledge or skill
- ☐ **life**: _____; the existence of an individual human being or animal
- ☐ **prejudice**: _____; preconceived opinion or feeling formed without knowledge, thought, or reason, often directed towards a particular group
- ☐ **watch**: _____; look at or observe attentively, typically over a period of time
- ☐ **trial**: _____; a formal examination of evidence in court to determine guilt or innocence
- ☐ **see**: _____; perceive with the eyes; become aware of something through observation
- ☐ **behave**: _____; act or conduct oneself in a particular way

KEY VOCABULARY | **LEVEL 300 - UNIT 30**

- ☐ **book**: _____; a written or printed work consisting of pages glued or sewn together along one side and bound in covers
- ☐ **family**: _____; a group consisting of parents and their children, living together in a household
- ☐ **live**: _____; have one's home in a particular place
- ☐ **called**: _____; named or known as
- ☐ **place**: _____; a particular position, point, or area in space
- ☐ **story**: _____; an account of imaginary or real people and events told for entertainment or to convey a message
- ☐ **mostly**: _____; mainly; for the most part
- ☐ **girl**: _____; a young female human
- ☐ **named**: _____; given a particular name
- ☐ **boy**: _____; a male child or young man
- ☐ **bring**: _____; cause someone or something to come to a place
- ☐ **become**: _____; begin to be or develop into something
- ☐ **close**: _____; near or intimate; having a strong emotional bond
- ☐ **friends**: _____; people whom one knows and with whom one has a bond of mutual affection
- ☐ **allowed**: _____; given permission to do something or have something
- ☐ **together**: _____; in each other's company; with or in proximity to one another
- ☐ **different**: _____; not the same as another or each other
- ☐ **social classes**: _____; divisions of society based on social and economic status
- ☐ **grow up**: _____; reach adulthood or full maturity
- ☐ **fall in love**: _____; develop strong romantic feelings towards someone
- ☐ **man**: _____; an adult human male
- ☐ **decide**: _____; make a choice or reach a conclusion
- ☐ **marry**: _____; legally join in marriage; become a husband or wife
- ☐ **instead of**: _____; in place of; as an alternative to
- ☐ **sad**: _____; feeling or showing sorrow or unhappiness
- ☐ **go away**: _____; leave or depart from a place
- ☐ **come back**: _____; return to a place
- ☐ **treat**: _____; behave towards someone or something in a certain way
- ☐ **people**: _____; human beings in general; individuals
- ☐ **well**: _____; in a good or satisfactory manner

Dr. Simon's Magic English Level 300

DR. SIMON'S MAGIC ENGLISH

KEY VOCABULARY | **LEVEL 400 - UNIT 1**

- ☐ **scientist**: _____; a person who studies and explores scientific knowledge
- ☐ **born**: _____; brought into existence through birth
- ☐ **loved**: _____; had a strong affection or fondness for
- ☐ **learn**: _____; acquire knowledge or skill
- ☐ **world**: _____; the planet Earth and everything on it
- ☐ **interested**: _____; having a curiosity or desire to know about something
- ☐ **astronomy**: _____; the scientific study of celestial objects and phenomena
- ☐ **study**: _____; acquire knowledge through learning or investigation
- ☐ **stars**: _____; massive celestial bodies that emit light and heat
- ☐ **planets**: _____; celestial bodies that orbit around a star
- ☐ **space**: _____; the vast expanse that exists beyond Earth's atmosphere
- ☐ **built**: _____; constructed or created something
- ☐ **telescope**: _____; an optical instrument used to observe distant objects
- ☐ **discovered**: _____; found or learned something new
- ☐ **amazing**: _____; causing wonder or astonishment
- ☐ **Earth**: _____; the planet we live on
- ☐ **move**: _____; change position or location
- ☐ **different**: _____; not the same or not alike
- ☐ **Jupiter**: _____; the largest planet in our solar system
- ☐ **named**: _____; gave a name to someone or something
- ☐ **discoveries**: _____; new findings or revelations
- ☐ **wrong**: _____; incorrect or not accurate
- ☐ **believe**: _____; accept as true or real
- ☐ **saying**: _____; expressing or stating something
- ☐ **trouble**: _____; difficulty or problem
- ☐ **church**: _____; a religious institution or building
- ☐ **jail**: _____; a place of confinement for prisoners
- ☐ **writing**: _____; the activity or process of composing written works
- ☐ **findings**: _____; results or conclusions obtained from research
- ☐ **inspired**: _____; filled someone with the urge or ability to do or feel something
- ☐ **other**: _____; additional or different from something mentioned
- ☐ **remembered**: _____; kept in one's memory or commemorated
- ☐ **greatest**: _____; of the highest rank, importance, or significance
- ☐ **helped**: _____; assisted or provided support to someone
- ☐ **change**: _____; make or become different
- ☐ **thought**: _____; the action or process of thinking

KEY VOCABULARY | LEVEL 400 - UNIT 2

- ☐ **scientist**: _____ ; a person who studies and explores scientific knowledge
- ☐ **discover**: _____ ; find or uncover something previously unknown
- ☐ **shape**: _____ ; the form or outline of an object
- ☐ **DNA**: _____ (Deoxyribo nucleic acid); a molecule that carries genetic information in living organisms
- ☐ **special**: _____ ; unique or distinct
- ☐ **molecule**: _____ ; a group of atoms bonded together
- ☐ **bodies**: _____ ; physical structures of living organisms
- ☐ **carry**: _____ ; transport or convey something
- ☐ **genetic**: _____ ; relating to genes or heredity
- ☐ **information**: _____ ; facts or knowledge about something
- ☐ **interested**: _____ ; having a curiosity or desire to know about something
- ☐ **science**: _____ ; the study of the natural world through observation and experimentation
- ☐ **curious**: _____ ; eager to know or learn something
- ☐ **questions**: _____ ; inquiries or queries
- ☐ **college**: _____ ; an institution of higher education
- ☐ **studied**: _____ ; pursued learning or knowledge in a specific field
- ☐ **biology**: _____ ; the study of living organisms and their interactions
- ☐ **living**: _____ ; having life or being alive
- ☐ **later**: _____ ; after a period of time
- ☐ **figure out**: _____ ; find a solution or understand something
- ☐ **experiments**: _____ ; tests or procedures conducted to gather data
- ☐ **won**: _____ ; achieved victory or success
- ☐ **Nobel Prize**: _____ ; a proper noun, a prestigious international award in various fields
- ☐ **teacher**: _____ ; a person who instructs or educates others
- ☐ **inspire**: _____ ; stimulate or motivate someone to do something
- ☐ **genetics**: _____ ; the study of genes and heredity
- ☐ **wrote**: _____ ; composed or penned written works
- ☐ **understand**: _____ ; comprehend or grasp the meaning of something
- ☐ **better**: _____ ; to a greater extent or degree
- ☐ **famous**: _____ ; widely known or recognized
- ☐ **funny**: _____ ; causing laughter or amusement
- ☐ **joke around**: _____ ; engage in playful or humorous behavior
- ☐ **sense of humor**: _____ ; the ability to appreciate or understand humor
- ☐ **laugh**: _____ ; produce sounds and expressions of amusement
- ☐ **retired**: _____ ; having ceased working or being employed
- ☐ **amazing**: _____ ; causing wonder or astonishment

DR. SIMON'S MAGIC ENGLISH

KEY VOCABULARY | LEVEL 400 - UNIT 3

- **important**: _____; of great significance or value
- **born**: _____; brought into existence through birth
- **became**: _____; came to be or assume a particular state or role
- **smart**: _____; having or showing quick intelligence or mental alertness
- **wanted**: _____; had a desire or wish for something
- **learn**: _____; acquire knowledge or skills
- **read**: _____; look at and comprehend written or printed matter
- **write**: _____; mark symbols on a surface to represent language
- **invented**: _____; created or designed something new
- **way**: _____; a method or manner of doing something
- **writing**: _____; the activity or process of composing written works
- **called**: _____; named or identified as
- **Hangul**: _____; the name of a writing system in Korea
- **easier**: _____; less difficult or complicated
- **understand**: _____; comprehend or grasp the meaning of something
- **built**: _____; constructed or created something
- **schools**: _____; institutions for educating students
- **libraries**: _____; buildings or collections of books for reading or research
- **well-educated**: _____; having a good education or high level of knowledge
- **country**: _____; a nation with its own government and institutions
- **grow**: _____; increase in size, number, or importance
- **stronger**: _____; having greater power, influence, or effectiveness
- **kind**: _____; having or showing a friendly, generous, or warm-hearted nature
- **poor**: _____; lacking sufficient money or resources
- **enough**: _____; as much or as many as required
- **thinking**: _____; the process of considering or reasoning about something
- **life**: _____; the existence of an individual human being or animal
- **remember**: _____; have in or be able to bring to one's mind an awareness of someone or something from the past
- **wise**: _____; having or showing experience, knowledge, and good judgment

KEY VOCABULARY | LEVEL 400 - UNIT 4

- ☐ **brilliant**: _____; exceptionally intelligent or talented
- ☐ **scientist**: _____; a person who studies and explores scientific knowledge
- ☐ **world**: _____; the planet Earth and everything on it
- ☐ **curious**: _____; eager to know or learn something
- ☐ **take apart**: _____; disassemble or separate into components
- ☐ **put back together**: _____; reassemble or restore to the original state
- ☐ **questions**: _____; inquiries or queries
- ☐ **seemed**: _____; appeared or gave the impression of being
- ☐ **silly**: _____; lacking in seriousness or intelligence
- ☐ **parents**: _____; a person's mother and father
- ☐ **encouraged**: _____; gave support, confidence, or hope to someone
- ☐ **curiosity**: _____; a strong desire to know or learn something
- ☐ **explore**: _____; travel through an unfamiliar area to learn about it
- ☐ **grew up**: _____; reached adulthood or maturity
- ☐ **physicist**: _____; a person who specializes in physics
- ☐ **tiny**: _____; very small in size or amount
- ☐ **particles**: _____; small portions of matter
- ☐ **called**: _____; named or identified as
- ☐ **atom**: _____; the basic unit of a chemical element
- ☐ **won**: _____; achieved victory or success
- ☐ **famous**: _____; widely known or recognized
- ☐ **funny**: _____; causing laughter or amusement
- ☐ **creative**: _____; having the ability to produce or use original and imaginative ideas
- ☐ **bongo**: _____; a pair of small drums of Afro-Cuban origin
- ☐ **draw**: _____; produce a picture or diagram by making lines or marks on paper
- ☐ **pictures**: _____; visual representations or images
- ☐ **design**: _____; plan or create something in a purposeful way
- ☐ **safe**: _____; free from harm or danger
- ☐ **transport**: _____; move or carry from one place to another
- ☐ **nuclear**: _____; relating to the nucleus of an atom or energy produced from it
- ☐ **material**: _____; the matter from which a thing is or can be made
- ☐ **passed away**: _____; died or ceased to exist
- ☐ **legacy**: _____; something handed down or left behind by a predecessor
- ☐ **live on**: _____; continue to exist or be remembered
- ☐ **inspired**: _____; filled someone with the urge or ability to do or feel something

DR. SIMON'S MAGIC ENGLISH

KEY VOCABULARY | LEVEL 400 - UNIT 5

- ☐ **famous**: _____; widely known or recognized
- ☐ **grew up**: _____; reached adulthood or maturity
- ☐ **lots of**: _____; a large number or amount of
- ☐ **smart**: _____; having or showing quick intelligence or mental alertness
- ☐ **curious**: _____; eager to know or learn something
- ☐ **printer**: _____; a person whose job is printing text and images
- ☐ **started**: _____; began or set in motion
- ☐ **own**: _____; belonging to oneself or itself
- ☐ **newspaper**: _____; a printed publication containing news, articles, and advertisements
- ☐ **life**: _____; the existence of an individual human being or animal
- ☐ **invented**: _____; created or designed something new
- ☐ **lightning rod**: _____; a metal rod or conductor mounted on a structure to protect it from lightning strikes
- ☐ **protect**: _____; keep safe from harm or injury
- ☐ **buildings**: _____; structures with a roof and walls, such as houses or offices
- ☐ **strike**: _____; an act or instance of hitting or attacking someone or something
- ☐ **created**: _____; brought into existence or produced
- ☐ **bifocal glasses**: _____; eyeglasses with lenses that have two distinct optical powers for near and far vision
- ☐ **near**: _____; at or to a short distance away
- ☐ **far**: _____; at or to a considerable distance away
- ☐ **important**: _____; of great significance or value
- ☐ **become**: _____; come to be or develop into something
- ☐ **country**: _____; a nation with its own government and institutions
- ☐ **write**: _____; mark on a surface using a pen or pencil to form letters or words
- ☐ **Declaration of Independence**: _____; a document that declared the United States' independence from Britain
- ☐ **ruled**: _____; governed or controlled by someone
- ☐ **busy**: _____; having a great deal to do; occupied with tasks or activities
- ☐ **fun**: _____; enjoyment, amusement, or lighthearted pleasure
- ☐ **swim**: _____; propel oneself through water using the limbs
- ☐ **chess**: _____; a strategic board game for two players
- ☐ **kite**: _____; an object flown in the air at the end of a string
- ☐ **remembered**: _____; kept or recalled in one's mind; not forgotten
- ☐ **history**: _____; the study of past events, particularly in human affairs
- ☐ **amazing**: _____; causing great surprise or wonder; astonishing

KEY VOCABULARY | LEVEL 400 - UNIT 6

- ☐ **famous**: _____; widely known or recognized
- ☐ **musician**: _____; a person who plays a musical instrument or sings
- ☐ **born**: _____; brought into existence through birth
- ☐ **talented**: _____; having a natural aptitude or skill in a particular area
- ☐ **playing**: _____; engaging in an activity for enjoyment or recreation
- ☐ **composing**: _____; creating or writing music
- ☐ **own**: _____; belonging to oneself or itself
- ☐ **teenager**: _____; a person aged between 13 and 19 years old
- ☐ **conductor**: _____; a person who directs the performance of an orchestra or choir
- ☐ **composer**: _____; a person who writes music
- ☐ **wrote**: _____; composed or expressed in writing
- ☐ **beautiful**: _____; pleasing the senses or mind aesthetically
- ☐ **symphonies**: _____; large-scale musical compositions for orchestra
- ☐ **pieces**: _____; separate parts of a whole
- ☐ **played**: _____; performed on a musical instrument
- ☐ **orchestra**: _____; a large group of musicians playing together
- ☐ **special**: _____; better, greater, or otherwise different from what is usual
- ☐ **different**: _____; not the same as another or each other
- ☐ **emotions**: _____; strong feelings deriving from one's circumstances, mood, or relationships with others
- ☐ **happiness**: _____; the state of being happy or feeling pleasure
- ☐ **sadness**: _____; the state of feeling sorrow or unhappiness
- ☐ **choirs**: _____; organized groups of singers
- ☐ **busy**: _____; having a great deal to do; occupied with tasks or activities
- ☐ **found**: _____; discovered or encountered by chance or intention
- ☐ **enjoyed**: _____; took delight or pleasure in something
- ☐ **hiking**: _____; the activity of walking in the countryside for pleasure or exercise
- ☐ **spend**: _____; use or give out time or money
- ☐ **nature**: _____; the physical world and everything in it
- ☐ **remembered**: _____; kept or recalled in one's mind; not forgotten
- ☐ **all time**: _____; the whole of recorded history or someone's life
- ☐ **still**: _____; up to and including the present or the time mentioned
- ☐ **world**: _____; the earth, together with all of its countries and peoples

DR. SIMON'S MAGIC ENGLISH

KEY VOCABULARY | **LEVEL 400 - UNIT 7**

- ☐ **queen**: _____; a female ruler of a country
- ☐ **lived**: _____; had one's home or permanent residence in a particular place
- ☐ **born**: _____; brought into existence through birth
- ☐ **young**: _____; having lived or existed for only a short time
- ☐ **fashionable**: _____; following or setting the latest trends in clothing, accessories, or style
- ☐ **loved**: _____; felt a deep affection or fondness for someone or something
- ☐ **wear**: _____; have on one's body as clothing or an accessory
- ☐ **beautiful**: _____; pleasing the senses or mind aesthetically
- ☐ **dresses**: _____; garments worn by women or girls
- ☐ **jewelry**: _____; personal ornaments, such as rings, necklaces, or bracelets, typically made of precious metals and gemstones
- ☐ **kind**: _____; having or showing a friendly, generous, or considerate nature
- ☐ **help**: _____; give assistance or support to someone
- ☐ **poor**: _____; lacking sufficient money or resources
- ☐ **palace**: _____; a large, impressive building used for the residence of a monarch or noble
- ☐ **called**: _____; named or referred to as
- ☐ **grand**: _____; magnificent or imposing in appearance, size, or style
- ☐ **parties**: _____; social gatherings or celebrations
- ☐ **invite**: _____; ask someone to go somewhere or do something
- ☐ **spent**: _____; used money, time, or energy
- ☐ **money**: _____; a medium of exchange in the form of coins and banknotes
- ☐ **clothes**: _____; items worn to cover the body
- ☐ **eventually**: _____; in the end, especially after a long delay, dispute, or series of problems
- ☐ **husband**: _____; a married man in relation to his spouse
- ☐ **prison**: _____; a building for the confinement of people accused or convicted of a crime
- ☐ **later**: _____; after the expected, usual, or proper time
- ☐ **executed**: _____; carried out a sentence of death on someone
- ☐ **means**: _____; a method or course of action used to achieve something
- ☐ **put**: _____; placed in a particular position or location
- ☐ **death**: _____; the end of life; the permanent cessation of vital functions
- ☐ **sad**: _____; feeling or showing sorrow; unhappy
- ☐ **ending**: _____; the final part of something
- ☐ **remembered**: _____; kept someone or something in one's mind as a memory or to bring to mind again
- ☐ **fashion sense**: _____; the ability to choose and wear stylish clothing and accessories
- ☐ **kindness**: _____; the quality of being friendly, generous, and considerate

Biography Series

KEY VOCABULARY | LEVEL 400 - UNIT 8

- **famous**: _____ ; known or recognized by many people
- **scientist**: _____ ; a person who conducts scientific research and studies various aspects of the natural world
- **known**: _____ ; recognized or familiar to someone
- **modern**: _____ ; relating to the present or recent times as opposed to the past
- **chemistry**: _____ ; the branch of science that deals with the properties, composition, and behavior of substances
- **different**: _____ ; not the same as another or each other
- **work**: _____ ; activity involving mental or physical effort done to achieve a purpose or result
- **oxygen**: _____ ; a chemical element with the symbol O and atomic number 8, constituting nearly 21 percent of the Earth's atmosphere
- **discovered**: _____ ; found or became aware of something for the first time
- **burned**: _____ ; underwent combustion or consumed by fire
- **combined**: _____ ; joined together to form a whole or greater unit
- **important**: _____ ; of great significance or value
- **discovery**: _____ ; the act or process of finding or learning something new
- **understand**: _____ ; comprehend or grasp the meaning or significance of something
- **invented**: _____ ; created or designed something that did not exist before
- **system**: _____ ; a set of connected things or parts forming a complex whole
- **chemical**: _____ ; relating to substances used in or produced by a chemical process
- **elements**: _____ ; substances that cannot be broken down into simpler substances by chemical means
- **rich**: _____ ; having a great deal of money or assets
- **French Revolution**: _____ ; a period of radical social and political upheaval in France from 1789 to 1799
- **accused**: _____ ; charged with a crime or wrongdoing
- **traitor**: _____ ; a person who betrays a country, group, or principle
- **sent**: _____ ; caused or enabled to go or be taken somewhere
- **prison**: _____ ; a building in which people are legally held as a punishment for a crime they have committed
- **later**: _____ ; after the expected or usual time
- **executed**: _____ ; carried out or performed a sentence, will, or other legal requirement
- **means**: _____ ; a method or course of action used to achieve something
- **death**: _____ ; the cessation of all biological functions that sustain a living organism
- **remembered**: _____ ; kept someone or something in one's mind as a memory or to bring to mind again
- **history**: _____ ; the study of past events, particularly in human affairs
- **invention**: _____ ; a unique or novel device, method, or process

Dr. Simon's Magic English Level 400 | 99

DR. SIMON'S MAGIC ENGLISH

KEY VOCABULARY | **LEVEL 400 - UNIT 9**

- ☐ **rich**: _____; having a great deal of money or assets
- ☐ **famous**: _____; known or recognized by many people
- ☐ **money**: _____; a medium of exchange in the form of coins and banknotes
- ☐ **starting**: _____; initiating or beginning something
- ☐ **company**: _____; an organization or business enterprise
- ☐ **sold**: _____; exchanged goods or services for money
- ☐ **oil**: _____; a viscous liquid derived from petroleum, used as a fuel or lubricant
- ☐ **called**: _____; named or designated as
- ☐ **became**: _____; came into existence or started to be
- ☐ **successful**: _____; accomplishing a desired aim or result
- ☐ **generous**: _____; showing a readiness to give more of something, especially money, than is strictly necessary or expected
- ☐ **gave**: _____; provided something to someone as a gift or contribution
- ☐ **charity**: _____; the voluntary giving of help, typically in the form of money, to those in need
- ☐ **build**: _____; construct or erect something
- ☐ **hospital**: _____; an institution providing medical and surgical treatment and nursing care for sick or injured people
- ☐ **believed**: _____; accepted that something is true or exists
- ☐ **important**: _____; of great significance or value
- ☐ **community**: _____; a group of people living in the same place or having a particular characteristic in common
- ☐ **simple**: _____; easily understood or done; presenting no difficulty
- ☐ **life**: _____; the condition that distinguishes animals and plants from inorganic matter
- ☐ **spend**: _____; pay out money in buying or hiring goods or services
- ☐ **fancy**: _____; elaborate in structure or decoration
- ☐ **preferred**: _____; liked one thing or person better than another or others
- ☐ **wear**: _____; have on one's body or a part of one's body as clothing, decoration, or protection
- ☐ **clothes**: _____; items worn to cover the body
- ☐ **remembered**: _____; kept someone or something in one's mind as a memory or to bring to mind again
- ☐ **businessman**: _____; a man who works in business, especially at a high level
- ☐ **history**: _____; a noun, the study of past events, particularly in human affairs
- ☐ **discovery**: _____; the action or process of making a new or important finding
- ☐ **invention**: _____; a unique or novel device, method, or process
- ☐ **powerful**: _____; having great power or strength
- ☐ **country**: _____; a nation with its own government, occupying a particular territory

KEY VOCABULARY | LEVEL 400 - UNIT 10

- ☐ **important**: _____; having great significance or value
- ☐ **grew up**: _____; developed or matured physically, mentally, or emotionally
- ☐ **treated**: _____; acted towards or dealt with in a certain way
- ☐ **unfairly**: _____; in a manner that is not just, equitable, or impartial
- ☐ **spent**: _____; used up or consumed
- ☐ **life**: _____; the condition that distinguishes animals and plants from inorganic matter
- ☐ **fighting**: _____; engaging in a battle or conflict
- ☐ **equality**: _____; the state of being equal, especially in status, rights, and opportunities
- ☐ **justice**: _____; the quality of being fair and reasonable
- ☐ **matter**: _____; physical substance in general, as distinct from mind and spirit
- ☐ **skin**: _____; the thin layer of tissue forming the natural outer covering of the body of a person or animal
- ☐ **prison**: _____; a building in which people are legally held as a punishment for a crime they have committed or while awaiting trial
- ☐ **belief**: _____; an acceptance that a statement is true or that something exists
- ☐ **gave up**: _____; stopped trying to do something
- ☐ **president**: _____; the elected head of a republic
- ☐ **worked**: _____; performed labor or exertion
- ☐ **hard**: _____; with a great deal of effort or endurance
- ☐ **unite**: _____; join together to form a single unit or group
- ☐ **equal**: _____; being the same in quantity, size, degree, or value
- ☐ **right**: _____; the legal or moral entitlement to have or do something
- ☐ **kind**: _____; having or showing a friendly, generous, or warm-hearted nature
- ☐ **compassionate**: _____; feeling or showing sympathy and concern for others
- ☐ **forgiveness**: _____; the action or process of forgiving or being forgiven
- ☐ **bring**: _____; cause someone or something to come to a place
- ☐ **together**: _____; with or in proximity to another person or people
- ☐ **enemy**: _____; a person who is actively opposed or hostile to someone or something
- ☐ **remembered**: _____; kept someone or something in one's mind as a memory or to bring to mind again
- ☐ **hero**: _____; a person who is admired or idealized for courage, outstanding achievements, or noble qualities
- ☐ **symbol**: _____; a thing that represents or stands for something else
- ☐ **hope**: _____; a feeling of expectation and desire for a particular thing to happen
- ☐ **legacy**: _____; something handed down by a predecessor or from the past
- ☐ **live on**: _____; continue to exist or be remembered
- ☐ **reminder**: _____; a thing that causes someone to remember something

DR. SIMON'S MAGIC ENGLISH

KEY VOCABULARY | LEVEL 400 - UNIT 11

- ☐ **talented**: _____; having a natural aptitude or skill in a particular area
- ☐ **musician**: _____; a person who plays a musical instrument or writes music
- ☐ **lived**: _____; had one's home or permanent residence in a particular place
- ☐ **born**: _____; brought into existence through birth
- ☐ **started**: _____; began or commenced an action or process
- ☐ **playing**: _____; engaging in activity for enjoyment and recreation
- ☐ **little**: _____; small in size, amount, or degree
- ☐ **musical**: _____; relating to music
- ☐ **genius**: _____; an exceptional intellectual or creative power or other natural ability
- ☐ **really**: _____; to a great extent; very
- ☐ **making**: _____; creating or producing
- ☐ **composed**: _____; created or written music
- ☐ **lots of**: _____; a large amount or number of
- ☐ **beautiful**: _____; pleasing the senses or mind aesthetically
- ☐ **piece**: _____; a part or portion of something
- ☐ **symphony**: _____; a long musical composition for full orchestra
- ☐ **opera**: _____; a dramatic work in one or more acts, set to music for singers and instrumentalists
- ☐ **sonata**: _____; a composition for an instrumental soloist, often with a piano accompaniment
- ☐ **amazing**: _____; causing great surprise or wonder; astonishing
- ☐ **people**: _____; human beings in general or considered collectively
- ☐ **still**: _____; up to and including the present or the time mentioned
- ☐ **listen**: _____; give attention to sound, pay attention to what someone is saying
- ☐ **easy**: _____; achieved without great effort; presenting few difficulties
- ☐ **struggled**: _____; made forceful or violent efforts to get free of restraint or constriction
- ☐ **money**: _____; a current medium of exchange in the form of coins and banknotes
- ☐ **sometimes**: _____; occasionally or at times
- ☐ **borrow**: _____; take and use something belonging to someone else with the intention of returning it
- ☐ **friend**: _____; a person whom one knows and with whom one has a bond of mutual affection
- ☐ **make ends meet**: _____; earn enough money to live without incurring debt
- ☐ **died**: _____; ceased to live; underwent the complete and permanent cessation of vital functions
- ☐ **loved**: _____; had a great affection or liking for someone or something

KEY VOCABULARY | LEVEL 400 - UNIT 12

- ☐ **important**: _____ ; of great significance or value
- ☐ **businessman**: _____ ; a person engaged in commercial or industrial activities with the aim of making a profit
- ☐ **lived**: _____ ; had one's home or permanent residence in a particular place
- ☐ **born**: _____ ; brought into existence through birth
- ☐ **working**: _____ ; engaging in labor or employment
- ☐ **smart**: _____ ; having or showing quick intelligence or mental alertness
- ☐ **hardworking**: _____ ; diligent in one's work or occupation
- ☐ **boat**: _____ ; a small vessel for traveling on water
- ☐ **owner**: _____ ; a person who possesses or has exclusive rights to something
- ☐ **shipping**: _____ ; the transport of goods by sea
- ☐ **company**: _____ ; a commercial business or enterprise
- ☐ **helped**: _____ ; assisted or provided aid to someone
- ☐ **build**: _____ ; construct or make by putting parts or materials together
- ☐ **railroad**: _____ ; a track or set of tracks made of steel rails along which trains run
- ☐ **rich**: _____ ; having wealth or abundant possessions
- ☐ **known**: _____ ; recognized or familiar to someone
- ☐ **tough**: _____ ; strong and resilient; not easily broken or defeated
- ☐ **sometimes**: _____ ; occasionally or at times
- ☐ **mean**: _____ ; unkind, spiteful, or unfair
- ☐ **like**: _____ ; find agreeable, enjoyable, or satisfactory
- ☐ **lose**: _____ ; be deprived of or cease to have or retain
- ☐ **looking**: _____ ; directing one's gaze or attention toward someone or something
- ☐ **ways**: _____ ; methods or means of doing something
- ☐ **money**: _____ ; a current medium of exchange in the form of coins and banknotes
- ☐ **forget**: _____ ; unintentionally cease to think or consider
- ☐ **importance**: _____ ; the quality or state of being of great significance or value
- ☐ **donated**: _____ ; gave or contributed money or goods to a charitable cause or organization
- ☐ **university**: _____ ; an institution of higher education and research that awards academic degrees
- ☐ **called**: _____ ; named or identified as
- ☐ **died**: _____ ; ceased to live; underwent the complete and permanent cessation of vital functions
- ☐ **legacy**: _____ ; something handed down by a predecessor or from the past
- ☐ **remembered**: _____ ; kept or recalled in one's mind, especially through honoring or commemorating
- ☐ **successful**: _____ ; accomplishing a desired aim or result; having achieved wealth, respect, or fame
- ☐ **history**: _____ ; the study of past events, particularly in human affairs

Dr. Simon's Magic English Level 400

DR. SIMON'S MAGIC ENGLISH

KEY VOCABULARY | **LEVEL 400 - UNIT 13**

- ☐ **author**: _____; a writer of a book, article, or document
- ☐ **professor**: _____; a teacher at a college or university
- ☐ **biochemistry**: _____; the branch of science that deals with the chemical processes and substances that occur within living organisms
- ☐ **born**: _____; brought into existence through birth
- ☐ **moved**: _____; changed one's place of residence or work to another
- ☐ **science**: _____; the intellectual and practical activity encompassing the systematic study of the structure and behavior of the physical and natural world through observation and experiment
- ☐ **began**: _____; started or commenced an action or process
- ☐ **writing**: _____; producing words, characters, or symbols on a surface
- ☐ **story**: _____; a narrative account of imaginary or real events
- ☐ **wrote**: _____; produced or composed written words, symbols, or sentences
- ☐ **science fiction**: _____; a genre of speculative fiction that typically deals with imaginative and futuristic concepts
- ☐ **non-fiction**: _____; prose writing that is based on facts, real events, and real people
- ☐ **taught**: _____; provided instruction or education to someone
- ☐ **passionate**: _____; having or expressing strong emotions or intense feelings
- ☐ **share**: _____; give a portion of something to another or others
- ☐ **knowledge**: _____; information, skills, and understanding acquired through experience, education, or training
- ☐ **addition**: _____; the action or process of adding something to something else
- ☐ **active**: _____; engaging or ready to engage in physically energetic pursuits
- ☐ **social**: _____; relating to society or its organization
- ☐ **political**: _____; relating to the government or public affairs of a country
- ☐ **cause**: _____; a principle, aim, or movement that, because of a deep commitment, one is prepared to defend or advocate
- ☐ **advocate**: _____; publicly recommend or support
- ☐ **civil rights**: _____; the rights of citizens to political and social freedom and equality
- ☐ **spoke out**: _____; expressed one's opinions or beliefs in a forceful and public manner
- ☐ **nuclear weapons**: _____; explosive devices that derive their destructive force from nuclear reactions
- ☐ **passed away**: _____; died
- ☐ **legacy**: _____; something handed down by a predecessor or from the past
- ☐ **live on**: _____; continue to exist or have significance
- ☐ **contribution**: _____; something given or supplied, such as money or effort, for a common purpose or to a common fund or project
- ☐ **society**: _____; the aggregate of people living together in a more or less ordered community

104 | Biography Series

KEY VOCABULARY | LEVEL 400 - UNIT 14

- ☐ **scientist**: _____; a person who conducts scientific research and studies the natural world
- ☐ **born**: _____; brought into existence through birth
- ☐ **interested**: _____; having or showing curiosity or concern about something or someone
- ☐ **nature**: _____; the physical world and everything in it, including plants, animals, and natural phenomena
- ☐ **trip**: _____; a journey or excursion, especially for pleasure
- ☐ **world**: _____; the earth, together with all of its countries, peoples, and natural features
- ☐ **called**: _____; named or designated as
- ☐ **visited**: _____; went to or spent time in a place
- ☐ **places**: _____; locations or destinations
- ☐ **observed**: _____; noticed or watched carefully
- ☐ **plants**: _____; living organisms such as trees, flowers, or grass
- ☐ **animals**: _____; living organisms that typically move, can feed on organic matter, and reproduce sexually
- ☐ **noticed**: _____; became aware of or paid attention to something
- ☐ **different**: _____; not the same as another or each other
- ☐ **similar**: _____; resembling or having a likeness to someone or something
- ☐ **began**: _____; started or commenced an action or process
- ☐ **think**: _____; have a particular opinion, belief, or idea
- ☐ **develop**: _____; grow or cause to grow and become more mature, advanced, or elaborate
- ☐ **theory**: _____; a system of ideas intended to explain something, especially one based on general principles independent of the thing to be explained
- ☐ **evolution**: _____; the process by which different kinds of living organisms have developed and diversified from earlier forms during the history of the Earth
- ☐ **believed**: _____; regarded as true or real
- ☐ **change**: _____; make or become different
- ☐ **adapt**: _____; make something suitable for a new use or purpose; modify
- ☐ **environment**: _____; the surroundings or conditions in which a person, animal, or plant lives or operates
- ☐ **wrote**: _____; produced or composed written words, symbols, or sentences
- ☐ **famous**: _____; widely known or recognized
- ☐ **explained**: _____; made an idea, situation, or problem clear to someone by describing it in more detail or revealing relevant facts or ideas
- ☐ **ideas**: _____; thoughts or concepts
- ☐ **fascinated**: _____; extremely interested in or attracted by someone or something
- ☐ **know**: _____; have developed a knowledge or understanding of
- ☐ **right**: _____; morally good, justified, or acceptable
- ☐ **important**: _____; of great significance or value

Dr. Simon's Magic English Level 400 | 105

DR. SIMON'S MAGIC ENGLISH

KEY VOCABULARY | **LEVEL 400 - UNIT 15**

- ☐ **scientist**: _____; a person who conducts scientific research and studies the natural world
- ☐ **grew up**: _____; became an adult or mature
- ☐ **wealthy**: _____; having a great deal of money, resources, or assets
- ☐ **interested**: _____; having or showing curiosity or concern about something or someone
- ☐ **conducted**: _____; organized and carried out
- ☐ **experiment**: _____; a scientific procedure undertaken to make a discovery, test a hypothesis, or demonstrate a known fact
- ☐ **famous**: _____; widely recognized or acclaimed to a great extent
- ☐ **gases**: _____; substances in a form that expands to fill the space available, such as the air we breathe
- ☐ **behave**: _____; act or conduct oneself in a particular way
- ☐ **different**: _____; not the same as another or each other
- ☐ **conditions**: _____; the circumstances or factors affecting the way people live or work
- ☐ **modern**: _____; relating to the present or recent times as opposed to the remote past
- ☐ **chemistry**: _____; the branch of science that deals with the composition, structure, properties, and reactions of substances
- ☐ **wrote**: _____; produced or composed written words, symbols, or sentences
- ☐ **argued**: _____; gave reasons or cited evidence in support of an idea, action, or theory
- ☐ **scientific**: _____; relating to or based on science
- ☐ **theory**: _____; a supposition or a system of ideas intended to explain something, especially one based on general principles independent of the thing to be explained
- ☐ **base**: _____; establish or found something on
- ☐ **evidence**: _____; the available body of facts or information indicating whether a belief or proposition is true or valid
- ☐ **curious**: _____; eager to know or learn something
- ☐ **subjects**: _____; areas of knowledge or study
- ☐ **including**: _____; comprising as part of a whole
- ☐ **medicine**: _____; the science or practice of the diagnosis, treatment, and prevention of disease
- ☐ **astronomy**: _____; the branch of science that deals with celestial objects, space, and the physical universe as a whole
- ☐ **philosophy**: _____; the study of fundamental questions about existence, knowledge, values, reason, and more
- ☐ **several**: _____; more than two but not many
- ☐ **language**: _____; a system of communication used by a particular country or community
- ☐ **interesting**: _____; arousing curiosity or interest; holding or catching the attention
- ☐ **lasting**: _____; enduring or able to endure over a long period of time
- ☐ **impact**: _____; the effect or influence of one person, thing, or action on another

KEY VOCABULARY | LEVEL 400 - UNIT 16

☐ **brave**: _____; showing courage and determination
☐ **determined**: _____; having made a firm decision and being resolved to achieve a goal
☐ **fought**: _____; engaged in a struggle or conflict
☐ **women's rights**: _____; the legal and social rights and entitlements claimed for women equal to those of men
☐ **believed**: _____; accepted or regarded as true
☐ **equal rights**: _____; the rights that are guaranteed to individuals without discrimination
☐ **vote**: _____; a formal expression of choice or opinion
☐ **own**: _____; possess
☐ **property**: _____; a thing or things belonging to someone; possessions collectively
☐ **paid**: _____; gave money in return for goods or services
☐ **change**: _____; make or become different
☐ **adult**: _____; a person who is fully grown or developed
☐ **involved**: _____; participated in an activity or event
☐ **speech**: _____; a formal address or discourse delivered to an audience
☐ **wrote**: _____; produced or composed written words, symbols, or sentences
☐ **article**: _____; a piece of writing included with others in a newspaper, magazine, or other publication
☐ **suffrage**: _____; the right to vote in political elections
☐ **organize**: _____; arrange or put into order
☐ **protest**: _____; a statement or action expressing disapproval or objection to something
☐ **rally**: _____; a mass meeting of people making a political protest or showing support for a cause
☐ **faced**: _____; confronted or dealt with a difficult or challenging situation
☐ **challenge**: _____; a call to take part in a contest or competition
☐ **arrested**: _____; seized by legal authority and taken into custody
☐ **voting**: _____; the action or process of expressing one's opinion or choice
☐ **illegally**: _____; in a way that is contrary to or forbidden by law
☐ **fine**: _____; a sum of money imposed as a penalty for an offense or breach of a law
☐ **gave up**: _____; ceased making an effort; surrendered
☐ **traveled**: _____; went on a journey or trip
☐ **country**: _____; a nation with its own government occupying a particular territory
☐ **speak out**: _____; express one's opinions or beliefs openly and publicly
☐ **death**: _____; the permanent ending of vital processes in a cell or tissue
☐ **passed**: _____; accepted or approved by a legislative body
☐ **hard work**: _____; strenuous physical or mental effort
☐ **determination**: _____; firmness of purpose; resoluteness
☐ **paid off**: _____; brought a beneficial result or reward

DR. SIMON'S MAGIC ENGLISH

KEY VOCABULARY | **LEVEL 400 - UNIT 17**

- ☐ **smart**: _____; intelligent or clever
- ☐ **interested**: _____; having or showing a curiosity or fascination about something
- ☐ **medicine**: _____; the science or practice of diagnosing, treating, and preventing disease
- ☐ **nursing**: _____; the profession or practice of providing care for the sick and infirm
- ☐ **common**: _____; occurring, found, or done often; prevalent
- ☐ **decided**: _____; made a firm decision about something
- ☐ **care**: _____; look after and provide for the needs of someone
- ☐ **injured**: _____; harmed or damaged
- ☐ **soldier**: _____; a person who serves in an army
- ☐ **improve**: _____; make or become better
- ☐ **condition**: _____; the state of something, especially with regard to its appearance, quality, or working order
- ☐ **hospital**: _____; an institution providing medical and surgical treatment and nursing care for sick or injured people
- ☐ **treated**: _____; gave medical care or attention to
- ☐ **healthy**: _____; in a good physical or mental condition
- ☐ **trained**: _____; taught a particular skill or type of behavior through practice and instruction
- ☐ **dedication**: _____; the quality of being dedicated or committed to a task or purpose
- ☐ **big difference**: _____; a significant change or impact
- ☐ **checking**: _____; examining or investigating something
- ☐ **patient**: _____; a person receiving or registered to receive medical treatment
- ☐ **returned**: _____; went or came back to a place or person
- ☐ **continued**: _____; persisted in an activity or process
- ☐ **article**: _____; a piece of writing included with others in a newspaper, magazine, or other publication
- ☐ **healthcare**: _____; the organized provision of medical care to individuals or a community
- ☐ **believed**: _____; accepted or regarded something as true or real
- ☐ **receive**: _____; be given, presented with, or paid something
- ☐ **medical care**: _____; the provision of medical services to patients
- ☐ **safe**: _____; protected from or not exposed to danger or risk
- ☐ **remembered**: _____; kept someone or something in one's mind as a memory or to show honor or respect
- ☐ **awarded**: _____; gave something to someone as a reward or recognition
- ☐ **honor**: _____; public recognition of achievement or distinction
- ☐ **inspired**: _____; stimulated to do or feel something, especially to do something creative
- ☐ **legacy**: _____; something handed down or received from an ancestor or predecessor

108 | Biography Series

KEY VOCABULARY | LEVEL 400 - UNIT 18

- ☐ **prophet**: _____; a person who delivers messages or teachings from a divine source
- ☐ **important**: _____; significant or of great importance
- ☐ **figure**: _____; a person who is well-known or influential in a particular field
- ☐ **religion**: _____; a set of beliefs and practices followed by a community or individuals
- ☐ **city**: _____; a large and permanent human settlement
- ☐ **known**: _____; familiar or recognized
- ☐ **honesty**: _____; the quality of being truthful, sincere, and free from deceit
- ☐ **kindness**: _____; the quality of being friendly, generous, and considerate
- ☐ **wisdom**: _____; the ability to discern and apply knowledge and experience
- ☐ **respect**: _____; a feeling of admiration or esteem for someone or something
- ☐ **merchant**: _____; a person involved in buying and selling goods
- ☐ **received**: _____; obtained or accepted
- ☐ **message**: _____; a verbal, written, or symbolic communication
- ☐ **God**: _____; a supreme being or divine entity worshipped in monotheistic religions
- ☐ **preaching**: _____; delivering religious or moral teachings in a public manner
- ☐ **follow**: _____; come after or adhere to someone or something
- ☐ **became**: _____; came into existence or started to be
- ☐ **foundation**: _____; the basis or underlying principle of something
- ☐ **simple**: _____; easy to understand or not complicated
- ☐ **worship**: _____; show reverence and devotion to a deity or religious entity
- ☐ **taught**: _____; instructed or educated someone in a particular subject or skill
- ☐ **poor**: _____; lacking sufficient money or resources
- ☐ **needy**: _____; in a condition of poverty or lacking basic necessities
- ☐ **treat**: _____; behave toward someone or something in a specific way
- ☐ **faced**: _____; confronted or encountered
- ☐ **challenges**: _____; difficulties or obstacles
- ☐ **lifetime**: _____; the period between a person's birth and death
- ☐ **remained**: _____; stayed or continued to be in a particular state
- ☐ **true**: _____; in accordance with fact or reality
- ☐ **led**: _____; guided or directed others
- ☐ **example**: _____; a person or thing that is considered worthy of imitation
- ☐ **showing**: _____; demonstrating or presenting something to others
- ☐ **righteous**: _____; morally upright or virtuous
- ☐ **celebrate**: _____; commemorate or honor an event or occasion
- ☐ **life**: _____; the state of being alive
- ☐ **teachings**: _____; lessons or principles taught by someone

DR. SIMON'S MAGIC ENGLISH

KEY VOCABULARY | **LEVEL 400 - UNIT 19**

- ☐ **famous**: _____; widely known or recognized
- ☐ **important**: _____; significant or of great importance
- ☐ **person**: _____; an individual human being
- ☐ **interested**: _____; having or showing curiosity or concern about something
- ☐ **technology**: _____; the application of scientific knowledge for practical purposes
- ☐ **own**: _____; belonging to oneself
- ☐ **grew up**: _____; became an adult or matured
- ☐ **moved**: _____; changed one's place of residence or location
- ☐ **college**: _____; an institution of higher education that grants degrees
- ☐ **started**: _____; established or initiated
- ☐ **different**: _____; not the same or distinct
- ☐ **companies**: _____; organizations or businesses engaged in commercial or industrial activities
- ☐ **created**: _____; brought something into existence
- ☐ **called**: _____; named or referred to as
- ☐ **send**: _____; cause to go or be taken to a particular destination
- ☐ **receive**: _____; be given or presented with something
- ☐ **wants**: _____; desires or wishes for something
- ☐ **space**: _____; the infinite expanse beyond the Earth's atmosphere, containing stars and galaxies
- ☐ **gasoline**: _____; a flammable liquid used as fuel in internal combustion engines
- ☐ **electric**: _____; powered by electricity
- ☐ **environment**: _____; the natural world and surroundings in which living beings exist
- ☐ **regular**: _____; conforming to a standard or usual pattern
- ☐ **smart**: _____; intelligent or clever
- ☐ **hardworking**: _____; diligent or industrious
- ☐ **give up**: _____; cease or stop trying to do something
- ☐ **world**: _____; the earth and all the people and things in it
- ☐ **better place**: _____; an improved or more desirable environment
- ☐ **using**: _____; employing or utilizing something
- ☐ **help**: _____; assist or aid someone or something

KEY VOCABULARY | LEVEL 400 - UNIT 20

- ☐ **emperor**: _____; a sovereign ruler of great power and rank
- ☐ **island**: _____; a piece of land surrounded by water
- ☐ **military**: _____; relating to the armed forces or warfare
- ☐ **officer**: _____; a person in a position of authority in the armed forces
- ☐ **army**: _____; a large organized body of armed personnel
- ☐ **leader**: _____; a person who leads or commands a group or organization
- ☐ **won**: _____; achieved victory in a competition or conflict
- ☐ **battles**: _____; engagements or encounters between armed forces
- ☐ **famous**: _____; widely known or recognized
- ☐ **world**: _____; the earth and all the people and things in it
- ☐ **skill**: _____; proficiency or ability in a particular field or activity
- ☐ **ruler**: _____; a person exercising government or dominion
- ☐ **powerful**: _____; having great strength, influence, or control
- ☐ **changes**: _____; alterations or modifications made to something
- ☐ **country**: _____; a nation with its own government and territory
- ☐ **stronger**: _____; having greater power, influence, or effectiveness
- ☐ **better place**: _____; an improved or more desirable environment
- ☐ **created**: _____; brought something into existence
- ☐ **laws**: _____; rules or regulations enacted by a governing authority
- ☐ **hospitals**: _____; medical institutions providing treatment and care for the sick or injured
- ☐ **peace**: _____; freedom from conflict or war
- ☐ **ambitious**: _____; having a strong desire for success, power, or achievement
- ☐ **rule**: _____; exercise ultimate power or authority over a territory or people
- ☐ **conquered**: _____; overcame or subjugated by force
- ☐ **eventually**: _____; in the end or after a long time
- ☐ **defeated**: _____; overcome or beaten in a contest or conflict
- ☐ **exiled**: _____; forced to leave one's home country or region
- ☐ **middle**: _____; the center or halfway point between two extremes
- ☐ **ocean**: _____; a vast body of saltwater
- ☐ **despite**: _____; in spite of or notwithstanding
- ☐ **flaws**: _____; imperfections or weaknesses
- ☐ **brilliant**: _____; exceptionally intelligent or talented
- ☐ **accomplished**: _____; successfully completed or achieved
- ☐ **remembered**: _____; kept in one's mind or memory

DR. SIMON'S MAGIC ENGLISH

KEY VOCABULARY | **LEVEL 400 - UNIT 21**

- ☐ **famous**: _____; known about by many people
- ☐ **known**: _____; recognized or familiar
- ☐ **inventing**: _____; creating or designing something for the first time
- ☐ **software**: _____; the programs and other operating information used by a computer
- ☐ **called**: _____; named or identified as
- ☐ **born**: _____; brought into existence by birth
- ☐ **loved**: _____; had a deep affection for
- ☐ **read**: _____; look at and comprehend the meaning of written or printed matter
- ☐ **play**: _____; engage in activity for enjoyment and recreation
- ☐ **started**: _____; began or set in motion
- ☐ **programming**: _____; the process of writing computer programs
- ☐ **dropped**: _____; stopped attending or participating
- ☐ **wanted**: _____; had a desire to do or have something
- ☐ **own**: _____; belonging to oneself or itself
- ☐ **company**: _____; a commercial business
- ☐ **friend**: _____; a person whom one knows and with whom one has a bond of mutual affection
- ☐ **successful**: _____; achieving or having achieved success
- ☐ **rich**: _____; having wealth or great possessions
- ☐ **used**: _____; employed for a purpose or to fulfill a need
- ☐ **money**: _____; a current medium of exchange in the form of coins and banknotes
- ☐ **world**: _____; the earth, together with all of its countries, peoples, and natural features
- ☐ **foundation**: _____; an organization established to promote or support a cause
- ☐ **need**: _____; require something because it is essential or very important
- ☐ **give**: _____; freely transfer the possession of something to someone
- ☐ **charities**: _____; organizations set up to provide help and raise money for those in need
- ☐ **organization**: _____; an organized group of people with a particular purpose
- ☐ **better**: _____; more desirable, satisfactory, or effective
- ☐ **place**: _____; a particular position or point in space
- ☐ **technology**: _____; the application of scientific knowledge for practical purposes
- ☐ **free**: _____; not under the control or in the power of another
- ☐ **time**: _____; the indefinite continued progress of existence and events in the past, present, and future

KEY VOCABULARY | LEVEL 400 - UNIT 22

- ☐ **smart**: _____; intelligent or clever
- ☐ **ancient**: _____; belonging to the very distant past
- ☐ **math**: _____; mathematics
- ☐ **famous**: _____; known about by many people
- ☐ **discovery**: _____; a person or thing discovered
- ☐ **figured out**: _____; worked out or understood by thinking or reasoning
- ☐ **measure**: _____; ascertain the size, amount, or degree of something by using an instrument or device marked in standard units
- ☐ **volume**: _____; the amount of space that a substance or object occupies, or that is enclosed within a container
- ☐ **object**: _____; a material thing that can be seen and touched
- ☐ **invented**: _____; created or designed something that has not existed before
- ☐ **machine**: _____; an apparatus using mechanical power and having several parts, each with a definite function and together performing a particular task
- ☐ **solve**: _____; find an answer to, explanation for, or means of effectively dealing with a problem or mystery
- ☐ **problem**: _____; a matter or situation regarded as unwelcome or harmful and needing to be dealt with and overcome
- ☐ **defend**: _____; resist an attack made on someone or something; protect from harm or danger
- ☐ **enemy**: _____; a person who is actively opposed or hostile to someone or something
- ☐ **attack**: _____; take aggressive action against a place or enemy forces with weapons or armed force
- ☐ **creating**: _____; bringing something into existence
- ☐ **clever**: _____; quick to understand, learn, and devise or apply ideas
- ☐ **protect**: _____; keep safe from harm or injury
- ☐ **curious**: _____; eager to know or learn something
- ☐ **experiment**: _____; a scientific procedure undertaken to make a discovery, test a hypothesis, or demonstrate a known fact
- ☐ **believe**: _____; accept that something is true or exists
- ☐ **possible**: _____; able to be done; within the power or capacity of someone or something
- ☐ **knowledge**: _____; facts, information, and skills acquired through experience, education, or training
- ☐ **determination**: _____; firmness of purpose; resoluteness
- ☐ **important**: _____; of great significance or value; likely to have a profound effect on success, survival, or well-being
- ☐ **engineer**: _____; a person who designs, builds, or maintains engines, machines, or public works
- ☐ **idea**: _____; a thought or suggestion as to a possible course of action

Dr. Simon's Magic English Level 400 | 113

DR. SIMON'S MAGIC ENGLISH

KEY VOCABULARY | **LEVEL 400 - UNIT 23**

- ☐ **important**: _____; of great significance or value; likely to have a profound effect on success, survival, or well-being
- ☐ **person**: _____; a human being regarded as an individual
- ☐ **history**: _____; the study of past events, particularly in human affairs
- ☐ **ride**: _____; sit on and control the movement of an animal, especially a horse
- ☐ **friend**: _____; a person whom one knows and with whom one has a bond of mutual affection
- ☐ **read**: _____; look at and understand written or printed matter by interpreting the characters or symbols of which it is composed
- ☐ **grew up**: _____; became larger or greater over a period of time; increased
- ☐ **brave**: _____; ready to face and endure danger or pain; showing courage
- ☐ **fought**: _____; took part in a violent struggle involving the exchange of physical blows or the use of weapons
- ☐ **war**: _____; a state of armed conflict between different nations or states or different groups within a nation or state
- ☐ **Revolutionary War**: _____; the war fought by American colonists to gain independence from Great Britain
- ☐ **become**: _____; begin to be
- ☐ **leader**: _____; a person who leads or commands a group, organization, or country
- ☐ **win**: _____; be successful or victorious in a contest or conflict
- ☐ **president**: _____; the elected head of a republican state
- ☐ **decision**: _____; a conclusion or resolution reached after consideration
- ☐ **famous**: _____; known about by many people
- ☐ **respected**: _____; admired or looked up to by someone; regarded with deep respect or admiration
- ☐ **country**: _____; a nation with its own government, occupying a particular territory
- ☐ **honest**: _____; free of deceit and untruthfulness; sincere
- ☐ **truth**: _____; the quality or state of being in accordance with fact or reality
- ☐ **hard**: _____; with a great deal of effort or force; strenuously
- ☐ **remember**: _____; have in or be able to bring to one's mind an awareness of someone or something from the past
- ☐ **hero**: _____; a person who is admired or idealized for courage, outstanding achievements, or noble qualities
- ☐ **celebrate**: _____; acknowledge a significant or happy day or event with a social gathering or enjoyable activity

Biography Series

KEY VOCABULARY | LEVEL 400 - UNIT 24

- ☐ **talented**: _____; having a natural aptitude or skill for something
- ☐ **musician**: _____; a person who plays a musical instrument, especially as a profession, or is musically talented
- ☐ **play**: _____; engage in activity for enjoyment and recreation rather than a serious or practical purpose
- ☐ **especially**: _____; used to single out one person, thing, or situation over all others
- ☐ **own**: _____; belonging to oneself or itself
- ☐ **become**: _____; begin to be
- ☐ **famous**: _____; known about by many people
- ☐ **piece**: _____; a portion of an object or of material, produced by cutting, tearing, or breaking the whole
- ☐ **lullaby**: _____; a soothing song, typically sung to young children before they sleep
- ☐ **sweet**: _____; having the pleasant taste characteristic of sugar or honey; not salt, sour, or bitter
- ☐ **hard**: _____; with a great deal of effort or force; strenuously
- ☐ **create**: _____; bring something into existence
- ☐ **beautiful**: _____; pleasing the senses or mind aesthetically
- ☐ **spent**: _____; passed time in a specified way or in a particular place
- ☐ **practice**: _____; perform an activity or exercise a skill repeatedly or regularly in order to improve or maintain one's proficiency
- ☐ **beard**: _____; a growth of hair on the chin and lower cheeks of a man's face
- ☐ **stroke**: _____; moved one's hand with gentle pressure over a surface, especially hair, fur, or skin, typically repeatedly; caressed
- ☐ **clap**: _____; strike the palms of one's hands together repeatedly, typically in order to applaud someone or something
- ☐ **cheer**: _____; shout for joy or in praise or encouragement
- ☐ **finish**: _____; bring a task or activity to an end; complete
- ☐ **passed away**: _____; died
- ☐ **enjoy**: _____; take delight or pleasure in an activity or occasion
- ☐ **reminder**: _____; a thing that causes someone to remember something
- ☐ **beauty**: _____; a combination of qualities, such as shape, color, or form, that pleases the aesthetic senses, especially the sight
- ☐ **joy**: _____; a feeling of great pleasure and happiness
- ☐ **found**: _____; discovered or perceived by chance or unexpectedly

DR. SIMON'S MAGIC ENGLISH

KEY VOCABULARY | **LEVEL 400 - UNIT 25**

- ☐ **important**: _____; of great significance or value
- ☐ **person**: _____; an individual human being
- ☐ **history**: _____; the study of past events, particularly in human affairs
- ☐ **machine**: _____; an apparatus using mechanical power and having several parts, each with a definite function and together performing a particular task
- ☐ **put**: _____; move to or place in a particular position
- ☐ **together**: _____; with or in proximity to another person or people
- ☐ **tool**: _____; a device or implement, especially one held in the hand, used to carry out a particular function
- ☐ **adult**: _____; a person who is fully grown or developed
- ☐ **own**: _____; belonging to oneself or itself
- ☐ **company**: _____; a commercial business
- ☐ **hard**: _____; with a great deal of effort or force; strenuously
- ☐ **affordable**: _____; inexpensive; reasonably priced
- ☐ **buy**: _____; obtain in exchange for payment
- ☐ **expensive**: _____; costing a lot of money
- ☐ **afford**: _____; have enough money to pay for
- ☐ **famous**: _____; known about by many people
- ☐ **simple**: _____; easily understood or done; presenting no difficulty
- ☐ **easy**: _____; achieved without great effort; presenting few difficulties
- ☐ **drive**: _____; operate and control the direction and speed of a motor vehicle
- ☐ **fix**: _____; fasten something securely in a particular place or position
- ☐ **cheap**: _____; low in price, especially in relation to similar items or services; inexpensive
- ☐ **clever**: _____; quick to understand, learn, and devise or apply ideas; intelligent
- ☐ **assembly**: _____; a group of people gathered together in one place for a common purpose
- ☐ **quickly**: _____; at a fast speed; rapidly
- ☐ **efficiently**: _____; in a way that achieves maximum productivity with minimum wasted effort or expense
- ☐ **produce**: _____; make or manufacture from components or raw materials
- ☐ **popular**: _____; liked, admired, or enjoyed by many people or by a particular person or group
- ☐ **legacy**: _____; an amount of money or property left to someone in a will
- ☐ **remember**: _____; have in or be able to bring to one's mind an awareness of someone or something from the past
- ☐ **pioneer**: _____; a person who is among the first to explore or settle a new country or area
- ☐ **industry**: _____; economic activity concerned with the processing of raw materials and manufacture of goods in factories
- ☐ **inventor**: _____; a person who invents or creates something, especially a process or device

KEY VOCABULARY | LEVEL 400 - UNIT 26

- ☐ **strong**: _____; having great physical or moral strength
- ☐ **intelligent**: _____; having or showing intelligence
- ☐ **knew**: _____; had knowledge or awareness of
- ☐ **languages**: _____; systems of communication used by a particular country or community
- ☐ **brave**: _____; ready to face and endure danger or pain; showing courage
- ☐ **always**: _____; at all times; on all occasions
- ☐ **stood up for**: _____; defended or supported
- ☐ **challenges**: _____; difficult tasks or situations
- ☐ **face**: _____; confront or deal with
- ☐ **lead**: _____; be in charge or command of
- ☐ **country**: _____; a nation with its own government, occupying a particular territory
- ☐ **war**: _____; a state of armed conflict between different nations or states or different groups within a nation or state
- ☐ **difficult**: _____; needing much effort or skill to accomplish, deal with, or understand
- ☐ **remain**: _____; stay in the same place or position; not move or change
- ☐ **calm**: _____; not showing or feeling nervousness, anger, or other strong emotions
- ☐ **achievement**: _____; a thing done successfully with effort, skill, or courage
- ☐ **defeating**: _____; winning a victory over someone in a battle or other contest; overcome or beat
- ☐ **fleet**: _____; a group of ships sailing together, engaged in the same activity, or under the same ownership
- ☐ **attack**: _____; take aggressive action against a place or enemy forces with weapons or armed force
- ☐ **navy**: _____; the branch of a nation's armed services that conducts military operations at sea
- ☐ **fashion**: _____; a popular trend, especially in styles of dress and ornament or manners of behavior
- ☐ **jewel**: _____; a precious stone, typically a single crystal or a piece of a hard lustrous or translucent mineral
- ☐ **own**: _____; belonging to oneself or itself
- ☐ **style**: _____; a manner of doing something
- ☐ **important**: _____; of great significance or value; likely to have a profound effect on success, survival, or well-being
- ☐ **rule**: _____; exercise ultimate power or authority over an area and its people
- ☐ **remember**: _____; have in or be able to bring to one's mind an awareness of someone or something from the past
- ☐ **greatest**: _____; of an extent, amount, or intensity considerably above average
- ☐ **monarch**: _____; a sovereign head of state, especially a king, queen, or emperor
- ☐ **history**: _____; the study of past events, particularly in human affairs

Dr. Simon's Magic English Level 400 | 117

DR. SIMON'S MAGIC ENGLISH

KEY VOCABULARY | **LEVEL 400 - UNIT 27**

- ☐ **famous**: _____; well-known, widely recognized
- ☐ **inventor**: _____; a person who creates or develops a new device, process, or invention
- ☐ **born**: _____; brought into life or existence
- ☐ **moved**: _____; changed one's place of residence or position
- ☐ **interested**: _____; having or showing curiosity, concern, or attention
- ☐ **sound**: _____; a vibration that travels through the air or another medium and can be heard when it reaches a person's or animal's ear
- ☐ **communication**: _____; the imparting or exchanging of information or news
- ☐ **find**: _____; discover or perceive by chance or unexpectedly
- ☐ **way**: _____; a method, style, or manner of doing something
- ☐ **talk**: _____; communicate or exchange ideas, information, or instructions by speaking
- ☐ **long distances**: _____; far distances
- ☐ **spent**: _____; used or consumed time or money
- ☐ **working**: _____; engaging in activity for the purpose of a particular aim or result
- ☐ **problem**: _____; a matter or situation regarded as unwelcome or harmful and needing to be dealt with and overcome
- ☐ **invented**: _____; created or designed something that did not exist before
- ☐ **telephone**: _____; a device used for communication, allowing people to talk to each other over a distance
- ☐ **device**: _____; an object or piece of equipment designed to fulfill a particular purpose
- ☐ **allowed**: _____; gave permission or opportunity
- ☐ **wire**: _____; a thin, flexible thread of metal
- ☐ **send**: _____; cause to go or be taken to a particular destination
- ☐ **message**: _____; a verbal, written, or recorded communication sent to or left for a recipient
- ☐ **telegraph**: _____; a system for transmitting messages over long distances, using coded signals
- ☐ **letter**: _____; a written or printed communication addressed to a person or organization
- ☐ **right away**: _____; immediately, without delay
- ☐ **changed**: _____; made or became different
- ☐ **communicated**: _____; conveyed or exchanged information or ideas
- ☐ **still**: _____; up to and including the present or the time mentioned
- ☐ **look**: _____; have the appearance or give the impression of being
- ☐ **different**: _____; not the same as another or each other
- ☐ **cell phones**: _____; portable telephones
- ☐ **curious**: _____; eager to know or learn something
- ☐ **creative**: _____; involving the use of imagination or original ideas to create something
- ☐ **solve**: _____; find an answer to, explanation for, or means of effectively dealing with a problem or mystery
- ☐ **kind**: _____; having or showing a friendly, generous, and considerate nature
- ☐ **loved**: _____; felt a deep affection or attachment for

Biography Series

KEY VOCABULARY | LEVEL 400 - UNIT 28

- ☐ **famous**: _____; well-known, widely recognized
- ☐ **writer**: _____; a person who uses written words in various styles and techniques to communicate ideas and stories
- ☐ **born**: _____; brought into life or existence
- ☐ **liked**: _____; found something enjoyable or satisfying
- ☐ **write**: _____; put thoughts, ideas, or information into written or printed form
- ☐ **stories**: _____; narratives or accounts of events, real or imaginary
- ☐ **young**: _____; having lived or existed for only a short time
- ☐ **fishing**: _____; the activity of catching fish
- ☐ **hunting**: _____; the activity of pursuing and killing wild animals for food, sport, or trade
- ☐ **play sports**: _____; participate in athletic activities or games
- ☐ **became**: _____; started to be or come to be
- ☐ **journalist**: _____; a person who writes for newspapers, magazines, or news websites or prepares news to be broadcast
- ☐ **wrote**: _____; composed or created written works
- ☐ **happened**: _____; occurred or took place
- ☐ **world**: _____; the earth, together with all of its countries, peoples, and natural features
- ☐ **later**: _____; at a time in the future or after the time previously mentioned
- ☐ **decided**: _____; made a resolution or determination
- ☐ **brave**: _____; ready to face and endure danger or pain; showing courage
- ☐ **strong**: _____; having great physical or moral strength
- ☐ **traveled**: _____; went on a journey or trip
- ☐ **countries**: _____; nations or sovereign states
- ☐ **experiences**: _____; events or occurrences that leave an impression on someone
- ☐ **safari**: _____; an expedition to observe or hunt animals in their natural habitat
- ☐ **won**: _____; achieved victory in a contest or competition
- ☐ **awards**: _____; honors or prizes given in recognition of achievement
- ☐ **Pulitzer Prize**: _____; a prestigious award for achievements in journalism, literature, and musical composition
- ☐ **Nobel Prize in Literature**: _____; a prestigious international literary award
- ☐ **sad**: _____; feeling or showing sorrow; unhappy
- ☐ **accidents**: _____; unfortunate incidents that happen unexpectedly and unintentionally
- ☐ **illnesses**: _____; conditions of being unwell or in poor health
- ☐ **died**: _____; ceased to live; passed away
- ☐ **read**: _____; look at and comprehend the meaning of written or printed matter by interpreting the characters or symbols of which it is composed

KEY VOCABULARY | LEVEL 400 - UNIT 29

- ☐ **important**: _____; of great significance or value; likely to have a profound effect on success, survival, or well-being
- ☐ **history**: _____; the study of past events, particularly in human affairs
- ☐ **powerful**: _____; having great strength or influence
- ☐ **samurai**: _____; a member of a powerful military caste in feudal Japan
- ☐ **warrior**: _____; a person who fights in battles or wars
- ☐ **smart**: _____; having or showing quick-witted intelligence
- ☐ **became**: _____; started to be or come to be
- ☐ **subordinate**: _____; a person under the authority or control of another
- ☐ **famous**: _____; well-known, widely recognized
- ☐ **died**: _____; ceased to live; passed away
- ☐ **ruler**: _____; a person exercising government or dominion
- ☐ **shogun**: _____; a hereditary military dictator of Japan
- ☐ **authority**: _____; the power or right to give orders, make decisions, and enforce obedience
- ☐ **organizing**: _____; arranging or putting in order
- ☐ **managing**: _____; being in charge of or controlling
- ☐ **castles**: _____; fortified buildings, typically with high walls and towers, used as residences and defensive structures
- ☐ **roads**: _____; routes or ways for traveling between places
- ☐ **treated**: _____; acted toward or dealt with in a certain way
- ☐ **fairly**: _____; in accordance with the rules or standards; justly
- ☐ **justly**: _____; in a fair and impartial manner
- ☐ **strict**: _____; demanding that rules, especially moral ones, be obeyed
- ☐ **fair**: _____; treating people equally without favoritism or discrimination
- ☐ **laws**: _____; rules established by a governing authority
- ☐ **chance**: _____; an opportunity or possibility
- ☐ **succeed**: _____; achieve the desired aim or result
- ☐ **matter**: _____; a physical substance that occupies space and possesses rest mass, especially as distinct from energy
- ☐ **leader**: _____; a person who leads or commands a group, organization, or country
- ☐ **invade**: _____; enter forcibly or hostilely into a place or domain
- ☐ **caused**: _____; made something happen
- ☐ **problems**: _____; difficulties or challenges
- ☐ **hurt**: _____; cause physical or emotional pain or injury to someone
- ☐ **persecute**: _____; subject someone to hostility and ill-treatment, especially because of their race, political, or religious beliefs
- ☐ **remember**: _____; have in or be able to bring to one's mind an awareness of someone or something from the past
- ☐ **shape**: _____; influence or determine the course or nature of

KEY VOCABULARY | LEVEL 400 - UNIT 30

- ☐ **writer**: _____; a person who uses written words in various styles and techniques to communicate ideas and stories
- ☐ **born**: _____; brought into life or existence
- ☐ **stories**: _____; narratives or accounts of events, real or imaginary
- ☐ **little**: _____; small in size, amount, or degree
- ☐ **grew up**: _____; became an adult or matured
- ☐ **famous**: _____; well-known, widely recognized
- ☐ **wrote**: _____; composed or created written works
- ☐ **named**: _____; given a particular name
- ☐ **happy**: _____; feeling or showing pleasure or contentment
- ☐ **tries**: _____; makes an attempt or effort to do something
- ☐ **find**: _____; discover or perceive by chance or unexpectedly
- ☐ **popularity**: _____; the state or condition of being liked, admired, or supported by many people
- ☐ **worked**: _____; engaged in physical or mental effort to achieve a purpose or result
- ☐ **hard**: _____; with a great deal of effort or endurance
- ☐ **thinking**: _____; using one's mind to consider or reason about something
- ☐ **making**: _____; the process of creating, forming, or producing something
- ☐ **right**: _____; morally good, justified, or acceptable
- ☐ **wanted**: _____; desired or wished for something to happen or be done
- ☐ **beautiful**: _____; pleasing the senses or mind aesthetically
- ☐ **meaningful**: _____; having significance or purpose
- ☐ **interested**: _____; showing curiosity or concern about something or someone
- ☐ **traveled**: _____; went on a journey or trip
- ☐ **different**: _____; not the same as another or each other
- ☐ **countries**: _____; nations or sovereign states
- ☐ **paintings**: _____; works of art created with paint on a surface
- ☐ **sculptures**: _____; three-dimensional works of art created by shaping or combining materials
- ☐ **believed**: _____; accepted or regarded something as true or real
- ☐ **connected**: _____; joined or linked together
- ☐ **inspire**: _____; fill someone with the urge or ability to do or feel something, especially to do something creative
- ☐ **each other**: _____; one another; used to refer to two or more people or things
- ☐ **died**: _____; ceased to live; passed away
- ☐ **still**: _____; up to and including the present or the time mentioned
- ☐ **admired**: _____; regarded with respect or warm approval
- ☐ **told**: _____; communicated information, a story, or an opinion to someone

Dr. Simon's Magic English Level 400 | 121

DR. SIMON'S MAGIC ENGLISH

KEY VOCABULARY | **LEVEL 500 - UNIT 1**

- ☐ **famous**: _____; well-known, widely recognized
- ☐ **scientist**: _____; a person who conducts scientific research to gain knowledge and understanding of the natural world
- ☐ **studied**: _____; examined closely and systematically
- ☐ **children**: _____; young human beings who are not yet adults
- ☐ **learn**: _____; acquire knowledge or skills through study, experience, or being taught
- ☐ **grow up**: _____; become an adult or mature
- ☐ **born**: _____; brought into life or existence
- ☐ **learning**: _____; the acquisition of knowledge or skills through study, experience, or being taught
- ☐ **nature**: _____; the physical world and its phenomena, including plants, animals, and landscapes
- ☐ **interested**: _____; showing curiosity or concern about something or someone
- ☐ **think**: _____; have a particular mental perception or opinion
- ☐ **spent**: _____; used or consumed time, effort, or resources
- ☐ **watching**: _____; observing closely and attentively
- ☐ **talking**: _____; engaging in conversation or discussion
- ☐ **discover**: _____; find something out or become aware of it for the first time
- ☐ **stages**: _____; distinct periods or phases of development
- ☐ **development**: _____; the process of growth, maturation, or progress
- ☐ **unique**: _____; being the only one of its kind; unlike anything else
- ☐ **understanding**: _____; the ability to comprehend or grasp the meaning or significance of something
- ☐ **world**: _____; the earth, together with all of its countries, peoples, and natural features
- ☐ **created**: _____; brought into existence or caused to happen
- ☐ **tests**: _____; assessments or evaluations to measure knowledge, skills, or abilities
- ☐ **own**: _____; belonging to oneself or itself
- ☐ **subjects**: _____; individuals or things being studied or investigated
- ☐ **experiments**: _____; tests or investigations conducted to gain scientific knowledge or evidence
- ☐ **educators**: _____; people who provide instruction or teaching
- ☐ **study**: _____; engage in the systematic and detailed examination of a subject
- ☐ **child development**: _____; the processes of physical, cognitive, emotional, and social growth and change in children
- ☐ **ideas**: _____; thoughts or concepts formed in the mind
- ☐ **teach**: _____; impart knowledge, skills, or information to someone
- ☐ **ways**: _____; methods, styles, or manners of doing something
- ☐ **best**: _____; of the most excellent or desirable type or quality
- ☐ **age**: _____; the length of time that a person has lived or a thing has existed

BIOGRAPHY Series

KEY VOCABULARY | LEVEL 500 - UNIT 2

- ☐ **scientist**: _____; a person who conducts scientific research to gain knowledge and understanding of the natural world
- ☐ **studied**: _____; examined closely and systematically
- ☐ **animals**: _____; living organisms that feed on organic matter, typically having specialized sense organs and nervous systems and able to respond rapidly to stimuli
- ☐ **learn**: _____; acquire knowledge or skills through study, experience, or being taught
- ☐ **born**: _____; brought into life or existence
- ☐ **playing**: _____; engaging in activity for enjoyment or recreation
- ☐ **grew up**: _____; became an adult or matured
- ☐ **interested**: _____; showing curiosity or concern about something or someone
- ☐ **behave**: _____; act or conduct oneself in a particular way
- ☐ **spending**: _____; using or consuming time, effort, or resources
- ☐ **watching**: _____; observing closely and attentively
- ☐ **discovered**: _____; found or ascertained information or knowledge for the first time
- ☐ **heard**: _____; perceived or received sound or information through the ears
- ☐ **saw**: _____; perceived or visually observed something
- ☐ **conditioning**: _____; the process of training or accustoming a person or animal to behave in a certain way in response to certain stimuli
- ☐ **experiment**: _____; a scientific procedure undertaken to make a discovery, test a hypothesis, or demonstrate a known fact
- ☐ **ringing**: _____; producing a clear resonant sound, typically by striking a bell or other metal object
- ☐ **fed**: _____; supplied with food or nourishment
- ☐ **salivate**: _____; secrete saliva, typically in response to the sight or smell of food
- ☐ **discovery**: _____; the act or process of finding or learning something for the first time
- ☐ **field**: _____; a particular branch of study or sphere of activity or interest
- ☐ **psychology**: _____; the scientific study of the human mind and behavior
- ☐ **wrote**: _____; composed or created written works
- ☐ **won**: _____; achieved victory or success in a competition, contest, or struggle
- ☐ **Nobel Prize**: _____; a prestigious international award given annually in several categories, including physics, chemistry, medicine, literature, and peace
- ☐ **still**: _____; up to and including the present or the time mentioned
- ☐ **use**: _____; employ or apply something for a purpose
- ☐ **ideas**: _____; thoughts or concepts formed in the mind
- ☐ **humans**: _____; individuals of the species Homo sapiens, distinguished from other animals by superior mental development, power of articulate speech, and upright stance

DR. SIMON'S MAGIC ENGLISH

KEY VOCABULARY | LEVEL 500 - UNIT 3

- ☐ **scientist**: _____; a person who conducts scientific research to gain knowledge and understanding of the natural world
- ☐ **lived**: _____; existed or had one's being in a specific time period
- ☐ **long time ago**: _____; in the distant past
- ☐ **born**: _____; brought into life or existence
- ☐ **studying**: _____; acquiring knowledge or information through systematic observation, inquiry, or instruction
- ☐ **stars**: _____; luminous celestial bodies consisting of a mass of gas held together by its own gravity and emitting light
- ☐ **planets**: _____; celestial bodies that orbit around a star
- ☐ **famous**: _____; well-known or widely recognized
- ☐ **discoveries**: _____; findings or revelations of something previously unknown or unseen
- ☐ **used**: _____; employed or applied something for a purpose
- ☐ **math**: _____; mathematics, the study of numbers, quantities, and shapes, and the relationships between them
- ☐ **figure out**: _____; solve or understand through reasoning or calculation
- ☐ **oval shape**: _____; a curved geometric shape that resembles an egg or ellipse
- ☐ **circle**: _____; a closed curve in which every point is equidistant from a fixed point called the center
- ☐ **discovered**: _____; found or ascertained information or knowledge for the first time
- ☐ **different**: _____; not the same as another or each other
- ☐ **speeds**: _____; rates of motion or movement
- ☐ **depending on**: _____; influenced or determined by
- ☐ **far**: _____; at or to a considerable distance away
- ☐ **wrote**: _____; composed or created written works
- ☐ **named**: _____; called or identified by a particular name
- ☐ **ideas**: _____; thoughts or concepts formed in the mind
- ☐ **help**: _____; assist or aid someone in doing something
- ☐ **learn**: _____; acquire knowledge or skills through study, experience, or being taught
- ☐ **space**: _____; the vast, seemingly infinite expanse that exists beyond the Earth
- ☐ **understand**: _____; comprehend or grasp the meaning or significance of something
- ☐ **universe**: _____; all existing matter, space, and energy as a whole

KEY VOCABULARY | LEVEL 500 - UNIT 4

- ☐ **famous**: _____; well-known or widely recognized
- ☐ **musician**: _____; a person who plays a musical instrument or sings
- ☐ **jazz music**: _____; a genre of music characterized by improvisation, syncopation, and a rhythmic and lively style
- ☐ **born**: _____; brought into life or existence
- ☐ **odd jobs**: _____; miscellaneous or casual work
- ☐ **play**: _____; perform on a musical instrument
- ☐ **cornet**: _____; a brass instrument similar to a trumpet but with a mellower tone
- ☐ **band**: _____; a group of musicians who play together
- ☐ **practiced**: _____; repeated an activity or skill to improve performance
- ☐ **became**: _____; started to be or develop into something
- ☐ **trumpet**: _____; a brass instrument with a flared bell and three valves
- ☐ **sang**: _____; produced musical sounds with the voice
- ☐ **deep**: _____; having a low pitch or tone
- ☐ **raspy**: _____; rough or hoarse in sound
- ☐ **voice**: _____; the sound produced in the larynx and uttered through the mouth
- ☐ **traveled**: _____; went on a journey or trip
- ☐ **perform**: _____; carry out an action or presentation before an audience
- ☐ **President**: _____; the elected head of a republic or nation
- ☐ **known**: _____; recognized or familiar
- ☐ **fun**: _____; enjoyment or amusement
- ☐ **personality**: _____; the combination of characteristics or qualities that form an individual's distinctive character
- ☐ **tell jokes**: _____; deliver humorous stories or anecdotes
- ☐ **world**: _____; the earth, together with all of its countries, peoples, and natural features
- ☐ **matter**: _____; physical substance or material in general
- ☐ **unfortunately**: _____; regrettably or sadly
- ☐ **passed away**: _____; died or ceased to exist
- ☐ **recordings**: _____; audio or video representations of sound or performance
- ☐ **inspired**: _____; motivated or influenced someone to do something
- ☐ **other**: _____; different or distinct from the one or ones already mentioned
- ☐ **too**: _____; also or in addition

DR. SIMON'S MAGIC ENGLISH

KEY VOCABULARY | **LEVEL 500 - UNIT 5**

- ☐ **architect**: _____; a person who designs buildings and oversees their construction
- ☐ **designed**: _____; created or planned the structure or form of something
- ☐ **buildings**: _____; structures with walls and a roof, such as houses, offices, or monuments
- ☐ **world**: _____; the earth, together with all of its countries, peoples, and natural features
- ☐ **born**: _____; brought into life or existence
- ☐ **draw**: _____; produce a picture or diagram by making lines and marks on paper or another surface
- ☐ **make models**: _____; create miniature representations of objects or structures
- ☐ **grew up**: _____; reached maturity or adulthood
- ☐ **studied**: _____; acquired knowledge or information through learning or research
- ☐ **architecture**: _____; the art and science of designing and constructing buildings
- ☐ **famous**: _____; well-known or widely recognized
- ☐ **interesting**: _____; arousing curiosity or interest
- ☐ **unusual**: _____; not habitually or commonly occurring
- ☐ **used for**: _____; employed or utilized for a specific purpose
- ☐ **swimming competitions**: _____; organized events where participants compete in swimming
- ☐ **Olympics**: _____; a major international multi-sport event
- ☐ **looks like**: _____; resembles or has a similar appearance to
- ☐ **giant**: _____; extremely large or of great size
- ☐ **wave**: _____; a long body of water curling into an arched form and breaking on the shore
- ☐ **curves**: _____; smoothly bending lines or shapes
- ☐ **shape**: _____; the external form or outline of something
- ☐ **win**: _____; achieve victory in a contest or competition
- ☐ **award**: _____; a prize or recognition given to honor achievement
- ☐ **proud**: _____; feeling deep pleasure or satisfaction as a result of one's achievements
- ☐ **showed**: _____; demonstrated or provided evidence of something
- ☐ **sadly**: _____; with regret or sorrow
- ☐ **passed away**: _____; died or ceased to exist
- ☐ **admire**: _____; regard with respect, pleasure, or approval
- ☐ **inspired**: _____; motivated or influenced someone to do something
- ☐ **other**: _____; different or distinct from the one or ones already mentioned
- ☐ **creative**: _____; having the ability to produce or use original and imaginative ideas
- ☐ **think outside the box**: _____; approach or solve problems in an unconventional or innovative way

126 | Biography Series

KEY VOCABULARY | LEVEL 500 - UNIT 6

- ☐ **explorer**: _____ ; a person who travels to unknown or remote areas to discover or investigate
- ☐ **traveled**: _____ ; went on a journey or trip
- ☐ **North and South Poles**: _____ ; the northernmost and southernmost points on Earth
- ☐ **born**: _____ ; brought into life or existence
- ☐ **adventure**: _____ ; an exciting or daring experience
- ☐ **teenager**: _____ ; a person between the ages of 13 and 19
- ☐ **sailed**: _____ ; traveled on water using sails or engines
- ☐ **world**: _____ ; the earth, together with all of its countries, peoples, and natural features
- ☐ **Atlantic Ocean**: _____ ; the body of water between North and South America to the east and Europe and Africa to the west
- ☐ **wanted**: _____ ; desired or wished for something
- ☐ **places**: _____ ; specific locations or areas
- ☐ **person**: _____ ; an individual human being
- ☐ **reach**: _____ ; arrive at or achieve something
- ☐ **team**: _____ ; a group of people who work together
- ☐ **skis**: _____ ; long, narrow pieces of wood or metal used for gliding over snow
- ☐ **sled dogs**: _____ ; dogs used for pulling sleds over snow or ice
- ☐ **brave**: _____ ; courageous or fearless
- ☐ **endure**: _____ ; withstand or tolerate difficult conditions
- ☐ **cold temperatures**: _____ ; low levels of atmospheric heat
- ☐ **made it**: _____ ; successfully accomplished or arrived at a destination
- ☐ **sail through**: _____ ; navigate or pass through a body of water
- ☐ **Arctic Ocean**: _____ ; the smallest and shallowest of the world's five major oceans, located around the North Pole
- ☐ **skills**: _____ ; abilities or expertise
- ☐ **accomplish**: _____ ; achieve or complete successfully
- ☐ **difficult**: _____ ; challenging or not easy
- ☐ **tasks**: _____ ; activities or assignments to be completed
- ☐ **unfortunately**: _____ ; regrettably or sadly
- ☐ **cut short**: _____ ; ended abruptly or prematurely
- ☐ **disappeared**: _____ ; vanished or went missing
- ☐ **flight**: _____ ; a journey made by air
- ☐ **bravery**: _____ ; courageous behavior or character
- ☐ **achievements**: _____ ; notable accomplishments or successes
- ☐ **remembered**: _____ ; recalled or kept in memory

Dr. Simon's Magic English Level 500

DR. SIMON'S MAGIC ENGLISH

KEY VOCABULARY | **LEVEL 500 - UNIT 7**

- ☐ **nun**: _____; a woman who has taken religious vows and lives in a convent
- ☐ **kind**: _____; showing benevolence or goodwill
- ☐ **caring**: _____; showing concern and consideration for others
- ☐ **world**: _____; the Earth or human society
- ☐ **better**: _____; improved or superior
- ☐ **place**: _____; a location or area
- ☐ **founded**: _____; established or created
- ☐ **type**: _____; category or kind
- ☐ **convent**: _____; a community of nuns or monks
- ☐ **simple**: _____; not elaborate or complicated
- ☐ **life**: _____; the existence of a living being
- ☐ **spent**: _____; used or utilized
- ☐ **praying**: _____; communicating with a deity through words or thoughts
- ☐ **writer**: _____; a person who produces literary work or written content
- ☐ **wrote**: _____; composed or penned
- ☐ **experiences**: _____; events or occurrences in one's life
- ☐ **famous**: _____; well-known or renowned
- ☐ **talks**: _____; discusses or explores
- ☐ **grow**: _____; develop or progress
- ☐ **closer**: _____; nearer or in proximity
- ☐ **God**: _____; a supreme being or deity
- ☐ **visions**: _____; supernatural or mystical experiences
- ☐ **believed**: _____; held as true or had faith in
- ☐ **spoke**: _____; communicated or conveyed a message
- ☐ **known**: _____; recognized or familiar
- ☐ **sense of humor**: _____; the ability to perceive and appreciate humor
- ☐ **chocolate**: _____; a sweet food made from roasted and ground cacao beans
- ☐ **died**: _____; passed away or ceased to live
- ☐ **saint**: _____; a person recognized by the Catholic Church for exceptional holiness
- ☐ **kindness**: _____; the quality of being friendly, generous, and considerate towards others
- ☐ **devotion**: _____; a strong dedication or loyalty, especially towards a religious belief or practice

KEY VOCABULARY | LEVEL 500 - UNIT 8

- ☐ **writer**: _____; a person who creates written works, such as books or stories
- ☐ **Ireland**: _____; a country located in western Europe
- ☐ **born**: _____; brought into existence through birth
- ☐ **loved**: _____; had a strong affection or fondness for
- ☐ **books**: _____; written or printed works consisting of pages bound together
- ☐ **older**: _____; of greater age or more advanced in years
- ☐ **famous**: _____; well-known or recognized by many people
- ☐ **difficult**: _____; not easy; requiring effort or skill
- ☐ **interesting**: _____; engaging or intriguing
- ☐ **smart**: _____; intelligent or clever
- ☐ **big**: _____; large in size or quantity
- ☐ **play**: _____; engage in an activity for enjoyment or recreation
- ☐ **language**: _____; a system of communication consisting of sounds, words, and grammar
- ☐ **make up**: _____; create or invent
- ☐ **long time ago**: _____; in the distant past
- ☐ **important**: _____; significant or of great value
- ☐ **study**: _____; examine closely or analyze
- ☐ **understand**: _____; comprehend or grasp the meaning of

DR. SIMON'S MAGIC ENGLISH

KEY VOCABULARY | **LEVEL 500 - UNIT 9**

- ☐ **queen**: _____; a female ruler of a kingdom or country
- ☐ **Russia**: _____; a country located in Eastern Europe and Northern Asia
- ☐ **born**: _____; brought into existence through birth
- ☐ **married**: _____; entered into a legal union with another person, typically in a formal ceremony
- ☐ **king**: _____; a male ruler of a kingdom or country
- ☐ **smart**: _____; intelligent or clever
- ☐ **loved**: _____; had a strong affection or fondness for
- ☐ **read**: _____; look at and understand the meaning of written or printed matter by interpreting the characters or symbols
- ☐ **learn**: _____; acquire knowledge or skills through study, experience, or teaching
- ☐ **changes**: _____; alterations or modifications made to something
- ☐ **reign**: _____; the period of time during which a monarch rules
- ☐ **famous**: _____; well-known or recognized by many people
- ☐ **art**: _____; creative works, such as paintings, sculptures, or music, that express emotions or ideas
- ☐ **paintings**: _____; pictures or artwork created using paint on a surface
- ☐ **sculptures**: _____; three-dimensional works of art created by carving, modeling, or molding materials
- ☐ **museum**: _____; a building or institution where objects of artistic, cultural, or historical significance are displayed
- ☐ **improvements**: _____; changes made to something in order to enhance or make it better
- ☐ **schools**: _____; institutions where education is provided to students
- ☐ **hospitals**: _____; institutions where medical treatment and care are provided to the sick or injured
- ☐ **life**: _____; the condition or state of living organisms
- ☐ **animals**: _____; living organisms that are not human and are often capable of movement
- ☐ **pets**: _____; domesticated animals kept for companionship or pleasure
- ☐ **dogs**: _____; domesticated canines kept as pets or working animals
- ☐ **cats**: _____; domesticated felines kept as pets or working animals
- ☐ **elephant**: _____; a large, intelligent mammal with a long trunk and tusks, native to Africa and Asia
- ☐ **died**: _____; ceased to live or exist
- ☐ **remembered**: _____; kept in the memory as an act of honoring or commemorating
- ☐ **greatest**: _____; of the highest degree or extent; utmost

KEY VOCABULARY | LEVEL 500 - UNIT 10

- ☐ **composer**: _____; a person who writes music
- ☐ **Germany**: _____; a country located in central Europe
- ☐ **born**: _____; brought into existence through birth
- ☐ **playing**: _____; producing music or sound on a musical instrument
- ☐ **music**: _____; organized sound or a sequence of notes and tones
- ☐ **young**: _____; at an early stage of life or development
- ☐ **talented**: _____; having a natural aptitude or skill
- ☐ **wrote**: _____; composed or created through written or musical expression
- ☐ **beautiful**: _____; pleasing to the senses or mind, often used to describe something aesthetically pleasing
- ☐ **songs**: _____; musical compositions with lyrics that are sung
- ☐ **pieces**: _____; individual compositions or sections of music
- ☐ **famous**: _____; well-known or recognized by many people
- ☐ **works**: _____; compositions or pieces of music created by a composer
- ☐ **include**: _____; contain or have as a part
- ☐ **brave**: _____; showing courage or bravery
- ☐ **lose**: _____; no longer have possession or control of something
- ☐ **hearing**: _____; the faculty or sense by which sound is perceived
- ☐ **deaf**: _____; lacking the ability to hear
- ☐ **serious**: _____; thoughtful, solemn, or earnest in manner or nature
- ☐ **person**: _____; an individual human being
- ☐ **worked**: _____; engaged in physical or mental activity to achieve a result
- ☐ **break**: _____; a pause or interruption in an activity
- ☐ **sense of humor**: _____; the ability to appreciate and understand humor
- ☐ **liked**: _____; had a favorable opinion or attitude towards
- ☐ **play**: _____; engage in activity for enjoyment or recreation
- ☐ **pranks**: _____; playful tricks or practical jokes
- ☐ **friends**: _____; people with whom one has a bond of mutual affection or trust
- ☐ **died**: _____; ceased to live or exist
- ☐ **popular**: _____; liked, admired, or enjoyed by many people
- ☐ **listen**: _____; give attention or focus to sound or music
- ☐ **love**: _____; have a deep affection or strong liking for

Dr. Simon's Magic English Level 500

DR. SIMON'S MAGIC ENGLISH

KEY VOCABULARY | **LEVEL 500 - UNIT 11**

- ☐ **invented**: _____ ; created or designed something for the first time
- ☐ **special**: _____ ; unique or different from what is usual or ordinary
- ☐ **blind**: _____ ; lacking the sense of sight
- ☐ **write**: _____ ; form letters or words on a surface using a pen, pencil, or keyboard
- ☐ **born**: _____ ; brought into existence through birth
- ☐ **village**: _____ ; a small community or settlement, typically located in a rural area
- ☐ **playing**: _____ ; engaging in an activity for enjoyment or recreation
- ☐ **tools**: _____ ; instruments or devices used to carry out a particular task or function
- ☐ **accidentally**: _____ ; happening unintentionally or by chance
- ☐ **poked**: _____ ; prodded or jabbed with force
- ☐ **awl**: _____ ; a small pointed tool used for making holes, typically in wood or leather
- ☐ **caused**: _____ ; brought about or resulted in a particular effect or outcome
- ☐ **infection**: _____ ; the invasion and multiplication of microorganisms, leading to harmful effects on the body
- ☐ **spread**: _____ ; extended or distributed over an area or range
- ☐ **completely**: _____ ; entirely or wholly
- ☐ **wanted**: _____ ; desired or wished for something
- ☐ **system**: _____ ; a set of principles or procedures for accomplishing a specific purpose or function
- ☐ **teenager**: _____ ; a person aged between thirteen and nineteen years old
- ☐ **uses**: _____ ; employs or utilizes for a specific purpose
- ☐ **raised**: _____ ; lifted or elevated
- ☐ **dots**: _____ ; small round marks or spots
- ☐ **feel**: _____ ; perceive through touch or physical sensation
- ☐ **fingertips**: _____ ; the ends of the fingers
- ☐ **quickly**: _____ ; at a fast pace or without delay
- ☐ **became**: _____ ; came to be or started to be
- ☐ **popular**: _____ ; liked, admired, or enjoyed by many people
- ☐ **world**: _____ ; the earth or all of human civilization
- ☐ **last**: _____ ; coming after all others in time or order
- ☐ **talented**: _____ ; having a natural aptitude or skill
- ☐ **musician**: _____ ; a person who plays a musical instrument or composes music
- ☐ **played**: _____ ; performed music on an instrument or produced sound from a musical device
- ☐ **organ**: _____ ; a keyboard instrument with pipe-like structures that produce sound
- ☐ **taught**: _____ ; provided instruction or education to others
- ☐ **died**: _____ ; ceased to live or exist
- ☐ **millions**: _____ ; a very large number, consisting of one thousand thousands

KEY VOCABULARY | LEVEL 500 - UNIT 12

- ☐ **famous**: _____; well-known or widely recognized
- ☐ **doctor**: _____; a person who is trained and licensed to practice medicine and treat illnesses
- ☐ **lived**: _____; existed or resided in a specific place or period of time
- ☐ **ideas**: _____; concepts or thoughts
- ☐ **mind**: _____; the faculty of consciousness and thought
- ☐ **works**: _____; operates or functions
- ☐ **lot**: _____; a large amount or quantity
- ☐ **thoughts**: _____; mental processes or ideas
- ☐ **feelings**: _____; emotions or sensations
- ☐ **come from**: _____; originate or arise from
- ☐ **unconscious**: _____; the part of the mind that is not directly accessible to conscious awareness
- ☐ **hidden**: _____; concealed or not easily noticed or understood
- ☐ **brain**: _____; the organ inside the head that controls the body's functions and processes information
- ☐ **believed**: _____; held a particular conviction or opinion
- ☐ **early**: _____; occurring or existing before the usual or expected time
- ☐ **experiences**: _____; events or occurrences that leave an impression or have an impact on someone
- ☐ **affect**: _____; influence or have an impact on
- ☐ **feel**: _____; experience or have an emotional response to something
- ☐ **behave**: _____; act or conduct oneself in a particular way
- ☐ **adults**: _____; fully grown or developed individuals
- ☐ **talked**: _____; engaged in conversation or discussion
- ☐ **patients**: _____; individuals receiving medical or psychological treatment
- ☐ **understand**: _____; comprehend or grasp the meaning of something
- ☐ **behaviors**: _____; actions or conduct
- ☐ **talking therapy**: _____; a form of therapy in which a person talks about their thoughts, feelings, and experiences
- ☐ **psychoanalysis**: _____; a psychological therapy that aims to uncover unconscious conflicts and motives
- ☐ **wrote**: _____; composed or authored written works
- ☐ **today**: _____; the present time or era
- ☐ **studied**: _____; examined or analyzed in detail
- ☐ **psychologists**: _____; professionals who study the human mind and behavior
- ☐ **all over**: _____; in various locations or places
- ☐ **world**: _____; the earth or all of human civilization

DR. SIMON'S MAGIC ENGLISH

KEY VOCABULARY | **LEVEL 500 - UNIT 13**

- ☐ **famous**: _____; well-known or widely recognized
- ☐ **inventor**: _____; a person who creates or develops something new
- ☐ **lived**: _____; existed or resided in a specific place or period of time
- ☐ **known**: _____; recognized or familiar
- ☐ **inventing**: _____; creating or devising something new
- ☐ **steam engine**: _____; a machine that uses steam to generate power or mechanical motion
- ☐ **machine**: _____; a device with moving parts that performs tasks or converts energy
- ☐ **turn**: _____; convert or transform
- ☐ **heat**: _____; thermal energy or warmth
- ☐ **energy**: _____; the capacity to do work or produce power
- ☐ **power**: _____; the ability to do or act
- ☐ **trains**: _____; vehicles that run on tracks and transport people or goods
- ☐ **powered**: _____; supplied with power or energy
- ☐ **animals**: _____; living organisms that are not humans
- ☐ **more**: _____; a greater amount or degree
- ☐ **less**: _____; a smaller amount or degree
- ☐ **time**: _____; a period or interval
- ☐ **helped**: _____; assisted or aided
- ☐ **factories**: _____; buildings or facilities where goods are produced
- ☐ **produce**: _____; manufacture or create
- ☐ **transportation**: _____; the act of moving people or goods from one place to another
- ☐ **faster**: _____; at a higher speed or rate
- ☐ **way**: _____; a method, manner, or means
- ☐ **measure**: _____; determine the size, amount, or degree of something
- ☐ **called**: _____; named or referred to as
- ☐ **horsepower**: _____; a unit of power equal to 550 foot-pounds per second
- ☐ **today**: _____; the present time or era
- ☐ **still**: _____; up to and including the present or a specified time
- ☐ **unit**: _____; a standard quantity used as a measurement
- ☐ **engines**: _____; machines or devices that convert energy into mechanical motion
- ☐ **changed**: _____; altered or modified
- ☐ **world**: _____; the earth or all of human civilization
- ☐ **remembered**: _____; recalled or held in memory
- ☐ **important**: _____; significant or of great significance
- ☐ **history**: _____; the study of past events or the whole series of past events

Biography Series

KEY VOCABULARY | LEVEL 500 - UNIT 14

- ☐ **scientist**: _____; a person who studies or practices science, especially in a specific field
- ☐ **lived**: _____; existed or resided in a specific place or period of time
- ☐ **known**: _____; recognized or familiar
- ☐ **discovering**: _____; finding or uncovering something for the first time
- ☐ **traits**: _____; distinguishing characteristics or qualities of an organism
- ☐ **passed down**: _____; transmitted or inherited from one generation to the next
- ☐ **parents**: _____; biological mother and father of an individual
- ☐ **worked**: _____; performed labor or research
- ☐ **pea plants**: _____; plants of the pea family used for scientific study
- ☐ **garden**: _____; an outdoor area for cultivating plants
- ☐ **study**: _____; the act of acquiring knowledge or information through examination or investigation
- ☐ **color**: _____; visual property of objects perceived by the sense of sight
- ☐ **height**: _____; measurement of vertical distance
- ☐ **inherited**: _____; received genetically from one's parents
- ☐ **dominant**: _____; having more influence or control over others
- ☐ **showed up**: _____; appeared or became visible
- ☐ **offspring**: _____; the product of reproduction, such as a child or young animal
- ☐ **recessive**: _____; not expressed or manifested unless inherited from both parents
- ☐ **helped**: _____; assisted or aided
- ☐ **understand**: _____; comprehend or grasp the meaning of something
- ☐ **genetics**: _____; the branch of biology that deals with heredity and variation of organisms
- ☐ **learn**: _____; acquire knowledge or skills through study, experience, or teaching
- ☐ **inherited diseases**: _____; genetic disorders or medical conditions transmitted through genes
- ☐ **important**: _____; significant or of great significance
- ☐ **lifetime**: _____; the period of time during which a person is alive
- ☐ **after**: _____; following in time or place
- ☐ **died**: _____; ceased to live or exist
- ☐ **realized**: _____; became aware of or understood something

DR. SIMON'S MAGIC ENGLISH

KEY VOCABULARY | LEVEL 500 - UNIT 15

- ☐ **artist**: _____; a person who creates visual art
- ☐ **lived**: _____; existed or resided in a specific place or period of time
- ☐ **born**: _____; brought into existence through birth
- ☐ **drawing**: _____; creating images or designs using lines on a surface
- ☐ **painting**: _____; the act or technique of applying paint to a surface to create a picture or artwork
- ☐ **created**: _____; brought into existence through artistic or creative efforts
- ☐ **famous**: _____; widely known or recognized
- ☐ **including**: _____; encompassing or involving as part of a whole
- ☐ **shows**: _____; displays or represents visually
- ☐ **horrors**: _____; extreme or distressing events or experiences
- ☐ **war**: _____; a state of armed conflict between different nations or groups
- ☐ **sculptures**: _____; three-dimensional artworks created by shaping or combining materials
- ☐ **ceramics**: _____; objects made from clay or other nonmetallic minerals through the process of firing
- ☐ **curious**: _____; eager to learn or know more about something
- ☐ **experiment**: _____; try out new ideas or methods to discover or learn something
- ☐ **different**: _____; not the same as another or each other
- ☐ **styles**: _____; distinctive approaches or characteristics in art
- ☐ **cubism**: _____; a style of art developed by Picasso and others that uses geometric shapes and abstract forms
- ☐ **geometric**: _____; relating to or characterized by shapes with straight lines and angles
- ☐ **abstract**: _____; not representing a realistic depiction of visual reality
- ☐ **amazed**: _____; filled with wonder or astonishment
- ☐ **unique**: _____; one of a kind or distinct
- ☐ **worth**: _____; having monetary or personal value
- ☐ **millions**: _____; a large number or quantity
- ☐ **dollar**: _____; the currency of the United States
- ☐ **travel**: _____; go on a journey or visit different places
- ☐ **inspired**: _____; influenced or stimulated creatively
- ☐ **places**: _____; locations or destinations
- ☐ **visited**: _____; went to or stayed in a particular place for a period of time
- ☐ **influenced**: _____; affected or impacted by someone or something
- ☐ **admired**: _____; regarded with respect, pleasure, or approval
- ☐ **legacy**: _____; something handed down or left behind by a previous generation
- ☐ **died**: _____; ceased to live or exist
- ☐ **age**: _____; the length of time a person or organism has lived, typically measured in years

KEY VOCABULARY | LEVEL 500 - UNIT 16

- ☐ **important**: _____; having great significance or influence
- ☐ **figures**: _____; significant or notable persons
- ☐ **history**: _____; the study of past events and their significance
- ☐ **pharaoh**: _____; a ruler or king in ancient Egypt
- ☐ **mean**: _____; cruel or unkind
- ☐ **ordered**: _____; commanded or directed
- ☐ **floated**: _____; moved gently on the surface of a liquid
- ☐ **found**: _____; discovered or came across
- ☐ **raised**: _____; brought up or nurtured
- ☐ **own**: _____; belonging to oneself or itself
- ☐ **grew up**: _____; matured or became an adult
- ☐ **discovered**: _____; found or learned something previously unknown
- ☐ **treated**: _____; how someone is dealt with or regarded
- ☐ **knew**: _____; had knowledge or awareness of something
- ☐ **God**: _____; a supreme being or deity
- ☐ **spoke**: _____; communicated verbally
- ☐ **burning**: _____; on fire or aflame
- ☐ **bush**: _____; a shrub or small tree
- ☐ **lead**: _____; guide or direct
- ☐ **journey**: _____; a long trip or travel
- ☐ **desert**: _____; a dry, barren, and often sandy region
- ☐ **faced**: _____; confronted or encountered
- ☐ **challenges**: _____; difficult tasks or situations
- ☐ **perform**: _____; carry out or execute
- ☐ **miracles**: _____; extraordinary events attributed to divine intervention
- ☐ **parting**: _____; dividing or separating
- ☐ **cross**: _____; go across or pass over
- ☐ **safely**: _____; without danger or harm
- ☐ **finally**: _____; at last or in conclusion
- ☐ **arrived**: _____; reached or reached a destination
- ☐ **Ten Commandments**: _____; a set of biblical principles or moral guidelines
- ☐ **rules**: _____; regulations or guidelines for conduct
- ☐ **lives**: _____; the existence or way of living
- ☐ **strength**: _____; the quality or state of being physically or mentally strong
- ☐ **courage**: _____; the ability to face and overcome fear or difficulties

DR. SIMON'S MAGIC ENGLISH

KEY VOCABULARY | **LEVEL 500 - UNIT 17**

- ☐ **entrepreneur**: _____; a person who starts and operates a business, taking on financial risks in the hope of making a profit
- ☐ **animator**: _____; a person who creates animated cartoons or animations
- ☐ **created**: _____; brought into existence or invented
- ☐ **beloved**: _____; greatly loved or cherished
- ☐ **cartoon characters**: _____; fictional characters portrayed in animated cartoons
- ☐ **grew up**: _____; matured or developed from childhood to adulthood
- ☐ **siblings**: _____; brothers or sisters
- ☐ **showed**: _____; demonstrated or displayed
- ☐ **talent**: _____; natural aptitude or skill
- ☐ **drawing**: _____; the act or skill of creating pictures or images with lines and marks
- ☐ **sell**: _____; exchange goods or services for money
- ☐ **neighbors**: _____; people who live near or next to each other
- ☐ **moved**: _____; changed one's place of residence or location
- ☐ **began**: _____; started or initiated
- ☐ **making**: _____; creating or producing
- ☐ **animated**: _____; characterized by movement or action
- ☐ **own**: _____; belonging to oneself or itself
- ☐ **animation**: _____; the technique of creating moving images or cartoons
- ☐ **studio**: _____; a workplace or facility for artistic production or recording
- ☐ **eventually**: _____; finally or in the end
- ☐ **world-renowned**: _____; famous or recognized throughout the world
- ☐ **company**: _____; an organization or business enterprise
- ☐ **famous**: _____; well-known or widely recognized
- ☐ **creation**: _____; something that is brought into existence or made
- ☐ **appeared**: _____; came into view or became visible
- ☐ **characters**: _____; fictional individuals or personalities in a narrative or work of art
- ☐ **classic**: _____; widely recognized and enduringly popular
- ☐ **films**: _____; motion pictures or movies
- ☐ **passed away**: _____; a euphemism for "died"
- ☐ **legacy**: _____; a person's impact or influence that continues after their death

BIOGRAPHY Series

KEY VOCABULARY | LEVEL 500 - UNIT 18

☐ **architect**: _____; a person who designs and oversees the construction of buildings
☐ **grew up**: _____; matured or developed from childhood to adulthood
☐ **rector**: _____; a clergyman in charge of a parish or church
☐ **smart**: _____; intelligent or clever
☐ **learned**: _____; acquired knowledge or skills through study or experience
☐ **professor**: _____; a senior academic position at a university or college
☐ **astronomy**: _____; the scientific study of celestial objects, space, and the universe
☐ **famous**: _____; well-known or widely recognized
☐ **building**: _____; a structure or edifice constructed with walls and a roof
☐ **St. Paul's Cathedral**: _____; a famous cathedral in London, designed by Christopher Wren and known for its architectural grandeur
☐ **math**: _____; short for mathematics, the study of numbers, quantities, and shapes
☐ **science**: _____; the systematic study of the physical and natural world through observation and experimentation
☐ **skills**: _____; abilities or proficiencies acquired through practice or experience
☐ **design**: _____; plan or create the appearance and structure of something
☐ **practical**: _____; useful or functional in a realistic sense
☐ **churches**: _____; buildings used for religious worship and gatherings
☐ **houses**: _____; buildings used as dwellings or residences
☐ **public buildings**: _____; structures used for public purposes, such as government offices or cultural institutions
☐ **project**: _____; a planned undertaking or task
☐ **proud**: _____; feeling a sense of satisfaction or accomplishment
☐ **scientist**: _____; a person who conducts scientific research or studies in a specific field
☐ **writer**: _____; a person who uses written words to express ideas or tell stories
☐ **remembered**: _____; recalled or kept in one's memory
☐ **greatest**: _____; highest in quality, extent, or importance
☐ **history**: _____; the study of past events and human affairs

DR. SIMON'S MAGIC ENGLISH

KEY VOCABULARY | **LEVEL 500 - UNIT 19**

- ☐ **scientist**: _____; a person who conducts scientific research or studies in a specific field
- ☐ **discovering**: _____; finding or uncovering something for the first time
- ☐ **penicillin**: _____; a group of antibiotics that can destroy or inhibit the growth of bacteria
- ☐ **interested**: _____; having a desire to learn or know more about something
- ☐ **science**: _____; the systematic study of the physical and natural world through observation and experimentation
- ☐ **plants**: _____; living organisms that typically have roots, stems, leaves, and produce their own food through photosynthesis
- ☐ **insects**: _____; small invertebrate animals with a segmented body and often with wings
- ☐ **doctor**: _____; a person who is qualified to practice medicine and treat illnesses
- ☐ **professor**: _____; a senior academic position at a university or college
- ☐ **bacteriology**: _____; the branch of biology that studies bacteria
- ☐ **experimenting**: _____; conducting tests or investigations to gather data and learn more about something
- ☐ **bacteria**: _____; microscopic single-celled organisms that can be beneficial or harmful to humans
- ☐ **mold**: _____; a type of fungus that grows in multicellular filaments and reproduces by forming spores
- ☐ **antibiotic**: _____; a substance that can kill or inhibit the growth of bacteria
- ☐ **cure**: _____; relieve or eliminate a disease or ailment
- ☐ **infection**: _____; the invasion and multiplication of harmful microorganisms in the body
- ☐ **revolutionized**: _____; radically changed or transformed something
- ☐ **medicine**: _____; the science and practice of diagnosing, treating, and preventing diseases and injuries
- ☐ **millions**: _____; a very large number
- ☐ **saved**: _____; preserved or rescued from harm or danger
- ☐ **awarded**: _____; given or presented as a reward or recognition
- ☐ **physiology**: _____; the branch of biology that deals with the functions and activities of living organisms and their parts
- ☐ **funding**: _____; providing financial support or resources for a project or endeavor
- ☐ **research**: _____; the systematic investigation of materials, sources, or information to discover or establish facts
- ☐ **uses**: _____; the practical applications or purposes of something
- ☐ **died**: _____; ceased to live or exist
- ☐ **age**: _____; the length of time that a person has lived, typically measured in years

Biography Series

KEY VOCABULARY | LEVEL 500 - UNIT 20

- ☐ **smart**: _____; having or showing intelligence or quick thinking
- ☐ **started**: _____; began or initiated something
- ☐ **company**: _____; a business or organization that sells goods or services
- ☐ **called**: _____; named or referred to as
- ☐ **kid**: _____; a child or young person
- ☐ **loved**: _____; had a strong affection or deep interest in something
- ☐ **play**: _____; engage in activities for enjoyment or recreation
- ☐ **interested**: _____; having a desire to learn or know more about something
- ☐ **older**: _____; of a greater age or more advanced in years
- ☐ **college**: _____; an institution of higher education that offers degrees and specialized courses
- ☐ **studied**: _____; acquired knowledge or information through learning and education
- ☐ **computer science**: _____; the study of computers and computing technology
- ☐ **graduated**: _____; completed a course of study and received a degree or diploma
- ☐ **working**: _____; engaging in activities to perform a job or tasks
- ☐ **different**: _____; not the same as another or each other
- ☐ **idea**: _____; a thought or concept that represents something
- ☐ **create**: _____; bring something into existence by combining or organizing various elements
- ☐ **online**: _____; connected to or accessed through a computer or the internet
- ☐ **store**: _____; a place where goods are kept for sale
- ☐ **buy**: _____; acquire or obtain in exchange for payment
- ☐ **leaving**: _____; going away or departing from a place
- ☐ **sold**: _____; exchanged goods or services for money
- ☐ **soon**: _____; in a short time or without much delay
- ☐ **added**: _____; included or introduced something additional
- ☐ **clothes**: _____; garments or apparel worn on the body
- ☐ **electronics**: _____; devices or equipment that operate using electric current or electromagnetic fields
- ☐ **delivered**: _____; brought or carried something to a destination
- ☐ **right**: _____; in a correct or appropriate manner
- ☐ **biggest**: _____; largest in size, extent, or importance
- ☐ **richest**: _____; having the greatest wealth or financial resources
- ☐ **likes**: _____; has a preference or enjoyment for something
- ☐ **fly**: _____; move through the air using wings or other mechanisms
- ☐ **spaceship**: _____; a vehicle designed for travel or operation in outer space
- ☐ **charities**: _____; organizations that provide assistance or support to those in need

Dr. Simon's Magic English Level 500

DR. SIMON'S MAGIC ENGLISH

KEY VOCABULARY | LEVEL 500 - UNIT 21

- ☐ **astronomer**: _____; a scientist who studies celestial objects, such as stars, planets, and galaxies
- ☐ **important**: _____; significant or of great significance
- ☐ **discoveries**: _____; findings or revelations about something previously unknown
- ☐ **universe**: _____; all of space and everything in it, including stars, planets, galaxies, and other celestial objects
- ☐ **college**: _____; an institution of higher education that offers degrees and specialized courses
- ☐ **mathematics**: _____; the study of numbers, quantities, and shapes, and the relationships between them
- ☐ **astronomy**: _____; the scientific study of celestial objects and phenomena
- ☐ **lawyer**: _____; a professional who provides legal advice and services
- ☐ **gave up**: _____; relinquished or abandoned something
- ☐ **expanding**: _____; growing larger in size, extent, or scope
- ☐ **found**: _____; discovered or came upon something
- ☐ **moving**: _____; changing position or location
- ☐ **each other**: _____; one another or reciprocally
- ☐ **farther**: _____; at or to a greater distance or more advanced point
- ☐ **apart**: _____; separated or at a distance from each other
- ☐ **changing**: _____; undergoing alteration, transformation, or modification
- ☐ **scientists**: _____; experts in a particular branch of science
- ☐ **formed**: _____; brought into existence or created
- ☐ **discovered**: _____; found or encountered something previously unknown
- ☐ **besides**: _____; in addition to or apart from
- ☐ **Milky Way**: _____; the galaxy that contains our solar system, consisting of billions of stars and various celestial objects
- ☐ **previously**: _____; before a particular time or event
- ☐ **believed**: _____; accepted or regarded as true or real
- ☐ **located**: _____; situated or positioned in a particular place or area
- ☐ **planets**: _____; celestial bodies that orbit around stars and do not produce their own light
- ☐ **received**: _____; obtained or was given something
- ☐ **awards**: _____; honors or recognition given to someone for their achievements or contributions
- ☐ **honors**: _____; distinctions or privileges conferred as a result of achievements or actions
- ☐ **highest**: _____; of the greatest height, level, or rank
- ☐ **civilian**: _____; a person not in the armed services or the police force
- ☐ **passed away**: _____; died or departed from life
- ☐ **continue**: _____; persist or endure without interruption
- ☐ **shape**: _____; influence the development or form of something
- ☐ **understanding**: _____; comprehension or knowledge about something

Biography Series

KEY VOCABULARY | LEVEL 500 - UNIT 22

- ☐ **African-American**: _____; relating to people of African descent living in the United States
- ☐ **leader**: _____; a person who guides or directs others
- ☐ **activist**: _____; a person who campaigns for social or political change
- ☐ **civil rights**: _____; the rights of citizens to political and social freedom and equality
- ☐ **harassed**: _____; subjected to aggressive pressure or intimidation
- ☐ **white supremacists**: _____; individuals who believe in the superiority of the white race and promote discriminatory practices
- ☐ **murdered**: _____; killed unlawfully and intentionally
- ☐ **racism**: _____; the belief that some races are superior or inferior to others, leading to discrimination and prejudice
- ☐ **inequality**: _____; a lack of fairness or equal opportunities, often based on factors such as race, gender, or socioeconomic status
- ☐ **criminal activity**: _____; involvement in illegal actions or behavior
- ☐ **arrested**: _____; taken into custody by law enforcement
- ☐ **sentenced**: _____; officially declared punishment by a court of law
- ☐ **prison**: _____; a place of confinement for individuals convicted of crimes
- ☐ **teachings**: _____; principles or lessons taught by someone
- ☐ **heritage**: _____; cultural, historical, or ancestral background or inheritance
- ☐ **prominent**: _____; well-known or widely recognized
- ☐ **speaker**: _____; a person who gives speeches or addresses an audience
- ☐ **racial inequality**: _____; disparities and unfair treatment based on race
- ☐ **identity**: _____; the characteristics, beliefs, and values that define an individual or group
- ☐ **disagreements**: _____; differences of opinion or conflict
- ☐ **evolved**: _____; developed or changed over time
- ☐ **working with**: _____; collaborating or cooperating with
- ☐ **nonviolence**: _____; the use of peaceful means rather than force or violence
- ☐ **assassinated**: _____; murdered for political or ideological reasons
- ☐ **speech**: _____; a formal address or oral presentation

Dr. Simon's Magic English Level 500 | 143

DR. SIMON'S MAGIC ENGLISH

KEY VOCABULARY | **LEVEL 500 - UNIT 23**

- ☐ **born**: _____; brought into existence by birth
- ☐ **smart**: _____; intelligent or clever
- ☐ **school**: _____; an institution for educating students
- ☐ **law**: _____; a system of rules and regulations enforced by a governing authority
- ☐ **politician**: _____; a person involved in politics or government
- ☐ **president**: _____; the head of a country or organization
- ☐ **elected**: _____; chosen by voting or a formal process of selection
- ☐ **life**: _____; the existence of a living being
- ☐ **better**: _____; improved or of higher quality
- ☐ **build**: _____; construct or create something
- ☐ **houses**: _____; dwellings or structures where people live
- ☐ **children**: _____; young human beings
- ☐ **make sure**: _____; ensure or guarantee something
- ☐ **enough**: _____; sufficient or adequate in quantity or degree
- ☐ **food**: _____; nourishment consumed by living organisms for sustenance
- ☐ **eat**: _____; consume food for nourishment
- ☐ **love**: _____; a deep affection or strong liking for someone or something
- ☐ **art**: _____; creative expression or visual creations
- ☐ **music**: _____; organized sound or melodies produced by instruments or voices
- ☐ **concerts**: _____; live performances of music in front of an audience
- ☐ **galleries**: _____; exhibition spaces for displaying art
- ☐ **read**: _____; comprehend written or printed words
- ☐ **books**: _____; written or printed literary works
- ☐ **kind**: _____; showing compassion, generosity, or benevolence
- ☐ **always**: _____; at all times or continuously
- ☐ **tried**: _____; made an effort or attempt
- ☐ **help**: _____; assist or support others in need
- ☐ **died**: _____; ceased to live or exist
- ☐ **remembered**: _____; kept in the memory or honored
- ☐ **great**: _____; remarkable or outstanding
- ☐ **cared**: _____; showed concern or interest about something or someone

Biography Series

KEY VOCABULARY | LEVEL 500 - UNIT 24

- ☐ **born**: _____; brought into existence by birth
- ☐ **study**: _____; acquire knowledge or skills through learning
- ☐ **people's**: _____; belonging to or associated with individuals
- ☐ **minds**: _____; the intellectual or cognitive faculties of a person
- ☐ **think**: _____; have thoughts or engage in mental processes
- ☐ **grew up**: _____; reached adulthood or matured
- ☐ **doctor**: _____; a medical professional who treats and heals patients
- ☐ **helped**: _____; provided assistance or support to someone in need
- ☐ **sick**: _____; unwell or suffering from an illness or disease
- ☐ **interested**: _____; having a desire or curiosity about something
- ☐ **studying**: _____; engaging in systematic learning or investigation
- ☐ **dreams**: _____; mental experiences or thoughts during sleep
- ☐ **felt**: _____; experienced or perceived emotions or sensations
- ☐ **believed**: _____; held as true or accepted as a concept or idea
- ☐ **different**: _____; not the same or distinct from others
- ☐ **parts**: _____; components or elements of a whole
- ☐ **conscious**: _____; awake and able to understand what is happening around you
- ☐ **unconscious**: _____; the part of the mind that is not directly accessible to conscious awareness
- ☐ **mind**: _____; the faculty of consciousness, thought, and perception
- ☐ **learn**: _____; acquire knowledge or information through study or experience
- ☐ **lot**: _____; a large amount or quantity
- ☐ **ideas**: _____; concepts, thoughts, or theories
- ☐ **wrote**: _____; created written works or authored books
- ☐ **books**: _____; written or printed literary works
- ☐ **famous**: _____; well-known or recognized by many people
- ☐ **all around**: _____; in various or diverse locations or regions
- ☐ **world**: _____; the planet Earth or human society in general
- ☐ **still**: _____; continuing to exist or be relevant
- ☐ **read**: _____; comprehend written or printed words
- ☐ **today**: _____; the present time or current era
- ☐ **understand**: _____; comprehend or grasp the meaning of something
- ☐ **better**: _____; improved or of higher quality

Dr. Simon's Magic English Level 500 | 145

DR. SIMON'S MAGIC ENGLISH

KEY VOCABULARY | **LEVEL 500 - UNIT 25**

☐ **born**: _____; brought into existence by birth
☐ **now**: _____; at the present time or currently
☐ **modern-day**: _____; belonging to the current era or time period
☐ **smart**: _____; intelligent or clever
☐ **man**: _____; an adult human male
☐ **loved**: _____; felt deep affection or strong liking for
☐ **invent**: _____; create or design something new
☐ **grew up**: _____; reach adulthood or mature
☐ **moved**: _____; changed one's place of residence
☐ **work**: _____; engage in labor or occupation
☐ **together**: _____; in collaboration or jointly
☐ **helped**: _____; provided assistance or support to someone
☐ **later on**: _____; at a subsequent time or stage
☐ **disagreement**: _____; a difference of opinion or conflict
☐ **stopped**: _____; ceased or discontinued an action
☐ **discoveries**: _____; findings or revelations
☐ **alternating current**: _____; a type of electric current that periodically reverses direction
☐ **electricity**: _____; a form of energy resulting from the existence of charged particles
☐ **still**: _____; continuing to exist or be in use
☐ **used**: _____; utilized or employed for a specific purpose
☐ **make**: _____; cause something to happen or exist
☐ **through**: _____; from one side or end to another
☐ **air**: _____; the invisible gaseous substance surrounding the earth
☐ **kind**: _____; having or showing a benevolent or gentle nature
☐ **vegetarian**: _____; a person who does not consume meat or animal products
☐ **means**: _____; a method or mechanism for achieving something
☐ **eat**: _____; consume food
☐ **meat**: _____; the flesh of animals used as food
☐ **died**: _____; ceased to live or exist
☐ **remembered**: _____; being kept or held in memory
☐ **amazing**: _____; inspiring awe, admiration, or astonishment
☐ **inventions**: _____; created or designed objects or processes
☐ **heart**: _____; the organ that pumps blood through the circulatory system

Biography Series

KEY VOCABULARY | LEVEL 500 - UNIT 26

- ☐ **born**: _____; brought into existence by birth
- ☐ **farm**: _____; an area of land used for cultivating crops or raising animals
- ☐ **machines**: _____; mechanical devices used to perform tasks or operations
- ☐ **invent**: _____; create or design something new
- ☐ **grew up**: _____; reached adulthood or matured
- ☐ **wanted**: _____; desired or wished for something
- ☐ **help**: _____; assist or aid someone or something
- ☐ **family**: _____; a group of individuals related by blood or marriage
- ☐ **farming**: _____; the activity or practice of cultivating crops or raising animals
- ☐ **noticed**: _____; became aware of something
- ☐ **took**: _____; required or consumed a certain amount of time or effort
- ☐ **harvest**: _____; gather or collect a crop or yield
- ☐ **wheat**: _____; a cereal grain used as a staple food
- ☐ **crops**: _____; plants cultivated for food, fiber, or other purposes
- ☐ **started**: _____; initiated or began an action or process
- ☐ **easier**: _____; less difficult or demanding
- ☐ **faster**: _____; at a higher rate of speed or efficiency
- ☐ **save**: _____; keep or preserve for future use
- ☐ **money**: _____; a medium of exchange for goods or services
- ☐ **invention**: _____; a new, useful, and non-obvious process, machine, or composition of matter
- ☐ **popular**: _____; widely liked, admired, or accepted
- ☐ **sell**: _____; exchange goods or services for money
- ☐ **successful**: _____; achieving the desired results or outcomes
- ☐ **rich**: _____; having wealth or abundant resources
- ☐ **died**: _____; ceased to live or exist
- ☐ **change**: _____; make or become different
- ☐ **forever**: _____; for all future time; eternally
- ☐ **reaper**: _____; a machine used for cutting or harvesting crops
- ☐ **food**: _____; any nutritious substance that is eaten or drunk to sustain life
- ☐ **production**: _____; the process of manufacturing or growing something
- ☐ **cheaper**: _____; costing less money or resources
- ☐ **world**: _____; the earth and all its inhabitants

DR. SIMON'S MAGIC ENGLISH

KEY VOCABULARY | **LEVEL 500 - UNIT 27**

- ☐ **born**: _____ ; brought into existence by birth
- ☐ **smart**: _____ ; having or showing intelligence or quick-wittedness
- ☐ **invent**: _____ ; create or design something new
- ☐ **curious**: _____ ; eager to know or learn something
- ☐ **apart**: _____ ; separated or disconnected
- ☐ **put**: _____ ; place or position something somewhere
- ☐ **learn**: _____ ; acquire knowledge or skill through study, experience, or teaching
- ☐ **older**: _____ ; having lived for a longer time or existed for a greater period
- ☐ **inventor**: _____ ; a person who creates or designs something new
- ☐ **important**: _____ ; of great significance or value
- ☐ **discoveries**: _____ ; findings or revelations
- ☐ **light bulb**: _____ ; an electric device that produces light
- ☐ **see**: _____ ; perceive with the eyes; discern visually
- ☐ **dark**: _____ ; the absence of light
- ☐ **phonograph**: _____ ; a device that records and plays back sound
- ☐ **machine**: _____ ; a mechanical device with moving parts designed to perform a specific task
- ☐ **record**: _____ ; make a permanent reproduction or documentation of sound or visual images
- ☐ **play back**: _____ ; reproduce or replay previously recorded sound or visual material
- ☐ **sound**: _____ ; a vibration that travels through the air and can be heard when it reaches a person's or animal's ear
- ☐ **hard-working**: _____ ; industrious or diligent in effort or labor
- ☐ **gave up**: _____ ; ceased making an effort; surrendered
- ☐ **genius**: _____ ; an exceptionally intelligent or creative person
- ☐ **inspiration**: _____ ; a sudden brilliant or timely idea
- ☐ **perspiration**: _____ ; the process of sweating; the excretion of moisture from the skin
- ☐ **means**: _____ ; a method or course of action used to achieve a particular result
- ☐ **lot**: _____ ; a large amount or quantity
- ☐ **hard work**: _____ ; diligent and sustained effort or labor
- ☐ **successful**: _____ ; achieving the desired results or outcomes
- ☐ **died**: _____ ; ceased to live or exist
- ☐ **amazing**: _____ ; causing great surprise or wonder; astonishing
- ☐ **invention**: _____ ; the action of inventing something new
- ☐ **remembered**: _____ ; recalled or kept in the memory

KEY VOCABULARY | LEVEL 500 - UNIT 28

- ☐ **born**: _____ ; brought into existence by birth
- ☐ **special**: _____ ; distinguished or unique
- ☐ **artist**: _____ ; a person who creates works of art
- ☐ **painted**: _____ ; created or produced a picture using paint
- ☐ **beautiful**: _____ ; pleasing to the senses or aesthetic
- ☐ **pictures**: _____ ; visual representations or images
- ☐ **famous**: _____ ; widely known or recognized
- ☐ **paintings**: _____ ; artworks created using paint on a surface
- ☐ **liked**: _____ ; had a preference or enjoyment for something
- ☐ **draw**: _____ ; create a picture or diagram by making lines or marks on paper
- ☐ **machines**: _____ ; mechanical devices or contraptions
- ☐ **inventions**: _____ ; novel or original creations
- ☐ **scientist**: _____ ; a person who conducts scientific research or studies natural phenomena
- ☐ **inventor**: _____ ; a person who creates or designs something new
- ☐ **study**: _____ ; engage in learning or acquiring knowledge
- ☐ **worked**: _____ ; engaged in effort or labor
- ☐ **ideas**: _____ ; concepts or notions formed in the mind
- ☐ **designed**: _____ ; created or planned out the structure or form of something
- ☐ **flying machine**: _____ ; a device or apparatus designed for flight
- ☐ **curious**: _____ ; eager to know or learn something
- ☐ **subjects**: _____ ; areas of study or disciplines
- ☐ **math**: _____ ; the study of numbers, quantities, and shapes
- ☐ **science**: _____ ; the systematic study of the natural world
- ☐ **music**: _____ ; an art form consisting of sound and rhythm
- ☐ **write**: _____ ; mark or record information using symbols or characters
- ☐ **special way**: _____ ; a unique or distinctive manner
- ☐ **left behind**: _____ ; left something for others to find or observe
- ☐ **amazing**: _____ ; causing great surprise or wonder; astonishing
- ☐ **see**: _____ ; perceive with the eyes; discern visually
- ☐ **learn**: _____ ; acquire knowledge or skill through study, experience, or teaching
- ☐ **remembered**: _____ ; recalled or kept in the memory
- ☐ **genius**: _____ ; an exceptionally intelligent or creative person
- ☐ **greatest thinkers**: _____ ; individuals who have made significant contributions to intellectual or philosophical thought
- ☐ **all time**: _____ ; throughout history or for all generations

DR. SIMON'S MAGIC ENGLISH

KEY VOCABULARY | LEVEL 500 - UNIT 29

- ☐ **famous**: _____; widely known or recognized
- ☐ **studying**: _____; engaging in learning or acquiring knowledge in a specific subject
- ☐ **language**: _____; the system of communication using words, sounds, and gestures
- ☐ **born**: _____; brought into existence by birth
- ☐ **young**: _____; in an early stage of life or development
- ☐ **loved**: _____; felt deep affection or strong liking for
- ☐ **read**: _____; look at and understand the meaning of written or printed matter
- ☐ **learn**: _____; acquire knowledge or skill through study, experience, or teaching
- ☐ **linguist**: _____; a person who studies language and its structure
- ☐ **written**: _____; produced or composed in written form
- ☐ **ideas**: _____; concepts or notions formed in the mind
- ☐ **world**: _____; the earth and all its inhabitants
- ☐ **talk**: _____; communicate or express ideas or information through speech
- ☐ **politics**: _____; the activities, actions, and policies used to gain and hold power in a government or to influence the government
- ☐ **government**: _____; the governing body of a nation, state, or community
- ☐ **power**: _____; the ability or capacity to do something or act in a particular way
- ☐ **important**: _____; of great significance or value
- ☐ **people**: _____; human beings in general
- ☐ **think**: _____; use thought or logical reasoning to form opinions or judgments
- ☐ **ask**: _____; pose a question or make a request
- ☐ **questions**: _____; inquiries or queries seeking information or clarification
- ☐ **smart**: _____; intelligent or clever
- ☐ **won**: _____; achieved victory or success in a competition or endeavor
- ☐ **award**: _____; recognition or honor bestowed on someone for their achievements
- ☐ **work**: _____; activity involving mental or physical effort done to achieve a purpose or result
- ☐ **professor**: _____; a senior teacher or academic at a university or college
- ☐ **university**: _____; an institution of higher education offering degrees in various subjects
- ☐ **getting older**: _____; aging or advancing in age
- ☐ **likes**: _____; has a preference or enjoyment for something
- ☐ **inspire**: _____; fill someone with the urge or ability to do or feel something
- ☐ **critically**: _____; in a manner that involves careful evaluation or analysis
- ☐ **live**: _____; have life or be alive

KEY VOCABULARY | LEVEL 500 - UNIT 30

- ☐ **man**: _____; an adult human male
- ☐ **lived**: _____; had one's residence or dwelling place in a specific location
- ☐ **place**: _____; a particular position or area occupied by someone or something
- ☐ **born**: _____; brought into existence by birth
- ☐ **died**: _____; ceased to live or exist
- ☐ **young**: _____; in an early stage of life or development
- ☐ **loved**: _____; felt deep affection or strong liking for
- ☐ **learn**: _____; acquire knowledge or skill through study, experience, or teaching
- ☐ **school**: _____; an institution for educating children or young adults
- ☐ **studied**: _____; engaged in learning or acquiring knowledge in a specific subject
- ☐ **different**: _____; not the same as another or each other
- ☐ **subjects**: _____; areas of knowledge or study
- ☐ **smart**: _____; intelligent or clever
- ☐ **became**: _____; started to be or develop into something
- ☐ **teacher**: _____; a person who educates or instructs others
- ☐ **interested**: _____; having or showing a curiosity or fascination in something
- ☐ **religion**: _____; the belief in and worship of a superhuman controlling power, especially a personal God or gods
- ☐ **wanted**: _____; had a desire or wish for something
- ☐ **more**: _____; a greater or additional amount or degree
- ☐ **God**: _____; the creator and ruler of the universe, as believed in many religions
- ☐ **priest**: _____; a person ordained for religious duties, especially in Christianity
- ☐ **wrote**: _____; produced or composed in written form
- ☐ **known**: _____; recognized or familiar to someone
- ☐ **important**: _____; of great significance or value
- ☐ **thinkers**: _____; individuals who engage in serious thought or intellectual activity
- ☐ **thought**: _____; the process of considering or reasoning about something
- ☐ **meant**: _____; intended to express or convey
- ☐ **person**: _____; an individual human being
- ☐ **think**: _____; use thought or logical reasoning to form opinions or judgments
- ☐ **ideas**: _____; concepts or notions formed in the mind
- ☐ **still**: _____; up to and including the present or the time mentioned
- ☐ **remembered**: _____; kept or recalled in one's mind as knowledge or information

DR. SIMON'S MAGIC ENGLISH

KEY VOCABULARY | **LEVEL 600 - UNIT 1**

- **powerful**: _____; having great strength or influence
- **leader**: _____; a person who guides or directs a group of people
- **enemies**: _____; individuals or groups who are opposed to or hostile toward someone or something
- **forced**: _____; compelled or obliged to do something against one's will
- **poverty**: _____; the state of being extremely poor
- **warrior**: _____; a brave or experienced soldier or fighter
- **united**: _____; brought together or combined into one
- **tribes**: _____; social groups typically consisting of families or communities sharing common customs, language, and culture
- **brilliant**: _____; exceptionally clever or talented
- **military**: _____; relating to or characteristic of soldiers, arms, or war
- **strategist**: _____; a person skilled in planning actions or processes to achieve a specific goal
- **led**: _____; guided or directed a group of people
- **armies**: _____; large organized groups of soldiers
- **victories**: _____; achievements or successes in a battle or competition
- **conquered**: _____; successfully invaded and took control of a place or people by force
- **created**: _____; brought into existence or caused to exist
- **empire**: _____; an extensive group of states or countries under a single supreme authority
- **reputation**: _____; the beliefs or opinions that are generally held about someone or something
- **fierce**: _____; having or displaying an intense or ferocious aggressiveness
- **wisdom**: _____; the quality of having experience, knowledge, and good judgment
- **kindness**: _____; the quality of being friendly, generous, and considerate
- **laws**: _____; rules or regulations enforced by authority
- **protect**: _____; keep safe from harm or danger
- **treated**: _____; behaved toward or dealt with in a certain way
- **fairly**: _____; in accordance with the rules or standards; without bias or favoritism
- **allowed**: _____; gave permission or consent to do something
- **religious**: _____; relating to or believing in a particular religion or religious system
- **freedom**: _____; the power or right to act, speak, or think as one wants without hindrance or restraint
- **unusual**: _____; not habitually or commonly occurring or done
- **legacy**: _____; something handed down or received from a predecessor
- **lasted**: _____; continued to exist or be in force for a certain period
- **centuries**: _____; periods of one hundred years
- **impact**: _____; the effect or influence of one person, thing, or action on another
- **admire**: _____; regard with respect or warm approval
- **respect**: _____; a feeling of deep admiration for someone or something

KEY VOCABULARY | LEVEL 600 - UNIT 2

- ☐ **famous**: _____; well-known or widely recognized
- ☐ **leader**: _____; a person who guides or directs a group of people
- ☐ **place**: _____; a particular position or area occupied by someone or something
- ☐ **wealthy**: _____; having a great deal of money, resources, or assets
- ☐ **general**: _____; a high-ranking military officer
- ☐ **politician**: _____; a person engaged in politics or holding a political office
- ☐ **bravery**: _____; courageous behavior or character
- ☐ **leadership**: _____; the action of leading a group of people or an organization
- ☐ **battlefield**: _____; a place where a military confrontation or engagement takes place
- ☐ **army**: _____; a large organized group of soldiers
- ☐ **victories**: _____; achievements or successes in a battle or competition
- ☐ **conquered**: _____; successfully invaded and took control of a place or people by force
- ☐ **speaker**: _____; a person who delivers a speech or addresses an audience
- ☐ **powerful**: _____; having great strength or influence
- ☐ **eventually**: _____; in the end, especially after a long delay, dispute, or series of problems
- ☐ **named**: _____; officially or publicly known as
- ☐ **emperor**: _____; a sovereign ruler of great power and rank, especially one ruling an empire
- ☐ **buildings**: _____; structures with roofs and walls
- ☐ **improving**: _____; making or becoming better or more satisfactory
- ☐ **city**: _____; a large town or urban area
- ☐ **infrastructure**: _____; the basic physical and organizational structures and facilities needed for the operation of a society or enterprise
- ☐ **unfortunately**: _____; used to introduce or signify a statement expressing regret or disappointment
- ☐ **thought**: _____; considered or regarded in a particular way
- ☐ **plotted**: _____; planned secretly or in a scheming way
- ☐ **assassinated**: _____; murdered, typically for political reasons
- ☐ **senators**: _____; members of a senate or other legislative bodies
- ☐ **opposed**: _____; in conflict or disagreement with someone or something
- ☐ **rule**: _____; exercise ultimate power or authority over a country, people, or organization
- ☐ **untimely**: _____; happening or done at an inappropriate or inconvenient time
- ☐ **death**: _____; the end of life
- ☐ **legacy**: _____; something handed down or received from a predecessor
- ☐ **remembered**: _____; kept in one's mind as a memorial or tribute to someone or something
- ☐ **symbol**: _____; a thing that represents or stands for something else
- ☐ **power**: _____; the ability or capacity to do something or act in a particular

DR. SIMON'S MAGIC ENGLISH

KEY VOCABULARY | **LEVEL 600 - UNIT 3**

- ☐ **important**: _____; significant or of great significance
- ☐ **leader**: _____; a person who guides or directs a group of people
- ☐ **different**: _____; not the same as another or each other
- ☐ **skin**: _____; the thin layer of tissue that covers the body
- ☐ **color**: _____; the visible hue of objects when light is reflected or emitted
- ☐ **treated**: _____; behaved toward or dealt with in a certain way
- ☐ **unfairly**: _____; in a manner that is not just or impartial
- ☐ **believed**: _____; regarded something as true or real
- ☐ **equally**: _____; to the same degree or extent
- ☐ **matter**: _____; be of importance; have significance
- ☐ **understand**: _____; comprehend or grasp the meaning or knowledge of something
- ☐ **deserves**: _____; has a claim to or is worthy of reward or punishment
- ☐ **respect**: _____; a feeling of deep admiration for someone or something
- ☐ **kindness**: _____; the quality of being friendly, generous, and considerate
- ☐ **speaker**: _____; a person who delivers a speech or addresses an audience
- ☐ **gave**: _____; provided or offered something to someone
- ☐ **speeches**: _____; formal addresses delivered to an audience
- ☐ **message**: _____; a verbal, written, or recorded communication sent to someone
- ☐ **equality**: _____; the state of being equal, especially in status, rights, or opportunities
- ☐ **famous**: _____; well-known or widely recognized
- ☐ **vision**: _____; an idea or mental image of what the future could be
- ☐ **races**: _____; distinct groups within the human species distinguished by physical traits
- ☐ **peace**: _____; freedom from disturbance; tranquility
- ☐ **led**: _____; guided or showed the way to others
- ☐ **peaceful**: _____; characterized by peace or the absence of violence
- ☐ **protests**: _____; public expressions of objection, disapproval, or dissent
- ☐ **marches**: _____; organized walks or demonstrations by a large group of people
- ☐ **raise**: _____; cause to increase or become higher
- ☐ **awareness**: _____; knowledge or perception of a situation or fact
- ☐ **unfair**: _____; not based on or behaving according to the principles of justice and equality
- ☐ **treatment**: _____; the manner in which someone is handled, managed, or treated
- ☐ **violence**: _____; behavior involving physical force intended to hurt, damage, or kill
- ☐ **assassinated**: _____; murdered, typically for political reasons
- ☐ **commitment**: _____; a pledge or undertaking to do something
- ☐ **nonviolence**: _____; the use of peaceful means, not force, to bring about political or social change
- ☐ **inspire**: _____; fill someone with the urge or ability to do or feel something

KEY VOCABULARY | LEVEL 600 - UNIT 4

- ☐ **famous**: _____; widely known or recognized
- ☐ **person**: _____; an individual human being
- ☐ **lifetime**: _____; the duration of a person's life
- ☐ **doctor**: _____; a qualified medical practitioner
- ☐ **musician**: _____; a person who plays or composes music
- ☐ **philosopher**: _____; a person who seeks wisdom and knowledge through rational inquiry
- ☐ **age**: _____; the length of time that a person has lived or a thing has existed
- ☐ **concerts**: _____; public performances of music
- ☐ **decided**: _____; made a resolution or determined a course of action
- ☐ **medicine**: _____; the science and practice of diagnosing, treating, and preventing diseases
- ☐ **sick**: _____; affected by illness or disease
- ☐ **became**: _____; came to be or started to be
- ☐ **access**: _____; the opportunity or right to use or benefit from something
- ☐ **healthcare**: _____; the organized provision of medical care
- ☐ **built**: _____; constructed or assembled something
- ☐ **hospital**: _____; a place where medical treatment and care are provided to the sick or injured
- ☐ **village**: _____; a small community in a rural area
- ☐ **spent**: _____; used or passed time in a particular way
- ☐ **treating**: _____; providing medical care or attention to someone
- ☐ **patients**: _____; people who receive medical treatment or care
- ☐ **community**: _____; a group of people living in the same area or sharing common interests
- ☐ **means**: _____; a method or way of doing something
- ☐ **thought**: _____; engaged in the process of thinking or considering
- ☐ **life**: _____; the condition that distinguishes living organisms from inanimate objects
- ☐ **believed**: _____; regarded something as true or real
- ☐ **reverence**: _____; deep respect or admiration
- ☐ **valuable**: _____; having great worth or importance
- ☐ **treated**: _____; behaved toward or dealt with in a certain way
- ☐ **respect**: _____; a feeling of deep admiration for someone or something
- ☐ **kindness**: _____; the quality of being friendly, generous, and considerate
- ☐ **inspired**: _____; filled with the urge or ability to do or feel something
- ☐ **ideas**: _____; concepts or thoughts that come to mind
- ☐ **won**: _____; achieved victory or success in a competition or endeavor
- ☐ **Nobel Peace Prize**: _____; an international award given annually to individuals or organizations who have made notable contributions to peace

DR. SIMON'S MAGIC ENGLISH

KEY VOCABULARY | **LEVEL 600 - UNIT 5**

- ☐ **born**: _____; brought into existence by birth
- ☐ **lived**: _____; had one's home or permanent residence in a particular place
- ☐ **politician**: _____; a person who is professionally involved in politics and holds a government position
- ☐ **leader**: _____; a person who leads or commands a group, organization, or country
- ☐ **decisions**: _____; conclusions or resolutions reached after consideration
- ☐ **country**: _____; a nation with its own government and territory
- ☐ **Prime Minister**: _____; the head of government in some countries
- ☐ **scary**: _____; causing fear or anxiety
- ☐ **war**: _____; a state of armed conflict between different nations or states or different groups within a nation or state
- ☐ **lasted**: _____; continued in existence or operation for a specified period
- ☐ **gave**: _____; provided or offered something to someone
- ☐ **speeches**: _____; formal talks given to an audience
- ☐ **radio**: _____; a device used for transmitting and receiving radio broadcasts
- ☐ **encourage**: _____; give support, confidence, or hope to someone
- ☐ **keep**: _____; continue or cause to continue in a specified condition, position, or course
- ☐ **fighting**: _____; engaging in a physical conflict or struggle
- ☐ **famous**: _____; widely known or recognized
- ☐ **called**: _____; named or referred to as
- ☐ **bombed**: _____; attacked with bombs
- ☐ **enemy**: _____; a person or group that is hostile to another or holds an opposing view
- ☐ **surrender**: _____; cease resistance to an enemy or opponent and submit to their authority
- ☐ **means**: _____; a method or way of doing something
- ☐ **talented**: _____; having a natural aptitude or skill in a particular area
- ☐ **writer**: _____; a person who has written a particular text or piece of literature
- ☐ **won**: _____; achieved victory or success in a competition or endeavor
- ☐ **actually**: _____; in fact; really
- ☐ **important**: _____; of great significance or value
- ☐ **person**: _____; an individual human being
- ☐ **world**: _____; the earth, together with all of its countries, peoples, and natural features
- ☐ **remembered**: _____; kept in one's memory or thought about again
- ☐ **read**: _____; look at and comprehend the meaning of written or printed matter by interpreting the characters or symbols
- ☐ **studied**: _____; examined closely or analyzed

KEY VOCABULARY | LEVEL 600 - UNIT 6

☐ **hero**: _____; a person who is admired or idealized for courage, outstanding achievements, or noble qualities
☐ **soldier**: _____; a person who serves in an army
☐ **sailing**: _____; the action of traveling in a boat or ship
☐ **fighting**: _____; engaging in a physical conflict or struggle
☐ **battles**: _____; sustained fights between large, organized armed forces
☐ **navy**: _____; the branch of a nation's armed services that conducts military operations at sea
☐ **victories**: _____; the acts of defeating an enemy in a battle or contest
☐ **brave**: _____; ready to face and endure danger or pain
☐ **smart**: _____; having or showing a quick-witted intelligence
☐ **plan**: _____; a detailed proposal for doing or achieving something
☐ **win**: _____; be successful or victorious in a contest or conflict
☐ **special**: _____; better, greater, or otherwise different from what is usual
☐ **sink**: _____; cause to go down below the surface of the water or another liquid
☐ **thick**: _____; having a large distance between opposite surfaces or sides
☐ **iron plates**: _____; metal sheets made of iron
☐ **outside**: _____; the external side or surface of something
☐ **protect**: _____; keep safe from harm or injury
☐ **sailors**: _____; people who work on ships or boats
☐ **inside**: _____; the inner side or part of something
☐ **attacked**: _____; take aggressive action against someone or something with the intention of causing harm or damage
☐ **huge**: _____; extremely large or extensive
☐ **fleet**: _____; a group of ships sailing together
☐ **tricked**: _____; deceived or outwitted someone using cunning or skill
☐ **different**: _____; not the same as another or each other
☐ **position**: _____; the location or arrangement of people or things
☐ **lost**: _____; be deprived of or cease to have or retain something
☐ **fair**: _____; treating people equally and without favoritism
☐ **treated**: _____; behaved towards or dealt with in a certain way
☐ **enough**: _____; as much or as many as required
☐ **end**: _____; the final part of something
☐ **legacy**: _____; something handed down from an ancestor or predecessor
☐ **symbol**: _____; a thing that represents or stands for something else, especially a material object representing something abstract
☐ **bravery**: _____; courageous behavior or character

DR. SIMON'S MAGIC ENGLISH

KEY VOCABULARY | **LEVEL 600 - UNIT 7**

- ☐ **famous**: _____; known or recognized by many people
- ☐ **musician**: _____; a person who plays a musical instrument or sings
- ☐ **village**: _____; a group of houses and associated buildings, larger than a hamlet and smaller than a town
- ☐ **play**: _____; perform on a musical instrument
- ☐ **writing**: _____; the activity or skill of marking coherent words on paper and composing text
- ☐ **peace**: _____; freedom from disturbance; tranquility
- ☐ **equality**: _____; the state of being equal, especially in status, rights, and opportunities
- ☐ **spread**: _____; cause to cover a larger area; extend over a wider area
- ☐ **message**: _____; a verbal, written, or recorded communication sent to or left for a recipient
- ☐ **hope**: _____; a feeling of expectation and desire for a certain thing to happen
- ☐ **unity**: _____; the state of being united or joined as a whole
- ☐ **band**: _____; a group of musicians playing popular music
- ☐ **popular**: _____; liked or admired by many people
- ☐ **reggae**: _____; a style of popular music with a strong offbeat rhythm, originating in Jamaica
- ☐ **different**: _____; not the same as another or each other
- ☐ **belief**: _____; acceptance that something exists or is true, especially without proof
- ☐ **value**: _____; the regard that something is held to deserve; the importance, worth, or usefulness of something
- ☐ **kind**: _____; having or showing a friendly, generous, and considerate nature
- ☐ **generous**: _____; showing a readiness to give more of something, especially money, than is strictly necessary or expected
- ☐ **community**: _____; a group of people living in the same place or having a particular characteristic in common
- ☐ **world**: _____; the earth, together with all of its countries, peoples, and natural features
- ☐ **gave**: _____; freely transferred the possession of something to someone
- ☐ **need**: _____; require something because it is essential or very important
- ☐ **spoke out**: _____; expressed one's opinions or feelings openly and confidently, especially in public
- ☐ **against**: _____; in opposition to
- ☐ **injustice**: _____; lack of fairness or justice
- ☐ **sadly**: _____; in a way that expresses sadness or regret
- ☐ **passed away**: _____; died
- ☐ **loved**: _____; felt deep affection or a strong liking for someone or something
- ☐ **listened to**: _____; gave attention to sound with the ear; hear with intent or purpose

KEY VOCABULARY | LEVEL 600 - UNIT 8

- ☐ **taught**: _____; gave instruction or lessons to someone
- ☐ **honest**: _____; free of deceit; truthful and sincere
- ☐ **leader**: _____; a person who leads or commands a group, organization, or country
- ☐ **spoke out**: _____; expressed one's opinions or feelings openly and confidently, especially in public
- ☐ **unfair**: _____; not based on or behaving according to the principles of equality and justice
- ☐ **laws**: _____; rules or regulations recognized by a community as binding
- ☐ **treated**: _____; acted or behaved toward someone in a certain way
- ☐ **skin color**: _____; the natural color of a person's skin, especially when it is other than white
- ☐ **fight**: _____; take part in a violent struggle involving physical force or weapons
- ☐ **believed**: _____; accepted that something is true, especially without proof
- ☐ **peacefully**: _____; without violence or disturbance
- ☐ **non-violent**: _____; using peaceful means rather than force or violence
- ☐ **methods**: _____; particular procedures for accomplishing or approaching something
- ☐ **make change**: _____; bring about a difference or alteration
- ☐ **organize**: _____; arrange or set up an event or activity
- ☐ **march**: _____; a procession of people walking together, often for a specific purpose
- ☐ **protest**: _____; a statement or action expressing disapproval or objection to something
- ☐ **hold hands**: _____; grasp or grip each other's hands
- ☐ **show support**: _____; demonstrate or express approval, agreement, or encouragement
- ☐ **hunger strike**: _____; a prolonged refusal to eat, undertaken as a means of protest
- ☐ **gain**: _____; obtain or secure something desired, favorable, or profitable
- ☐ **independence**: _____; the state or condition of being free from outside control or support
- ☐ **sadly**: _____; in a way that expresses sadness or regret
- ☐ **assassinated**: _____; murdered an important person for political or ideological reasons
- ☐ **remembered**: _____; kept in one's mind as a memory or thought
- ☐ **hero**: _____; a person admired or idealized for courage, outstanding achievements, or noble qualities
- ☐ **symbol**: _____; a thing that represents or stands for something else, especially a material object representing something abstract
- ☐ **peace**: _____; freedom from disturbance; tranquility
- ☐ **teachings**: _____; ideas or principles taught by someone
- ☐ **inspired**: _____; filled someone with the urge or ability to do or feel something
- ☐ **stand up**: _____; assert one's rights or defend one's beliefs in a firm or obstinate way
- ☐ **love**: _____; an intense feeling of deep affection

Dr. Simon's Magic English Level 600 | 159

DR. SIMON'S MAGIC ENGLISH

KEY VOCABULARY | **LEVEL 600 - UNIT 9**

- **brave**: _____; showing courage and determination
- **teenager**: _____; a person between the ages of 13 and 19
- **voice**: _____; the sound produced in a person's larynx and uttered through the mouth
- **God**: _____; the creator and ruler of the universe, believed in monotheistic religions to be the supreme being
- **war**: _____; a state of armed conflict between different nations or states or different groups within a nation or state
- **against**: _____; in opposition to
- **dangerous**: _____; able or likely to cause harm or injury
- **believed**: _____; accepted that something is true, especially without proof
- **put on**: _____; dress oneself in clothes
- **armor**: _____; protective covering worn by soldiers in battle
- **led**: _____; caused a person or animal to go with one by holding them by the hand, a halter, a rope, etc., while moving forward
- **army**: _____; a large organized body of armed personnel trained for war
- **victory**: _____; an act of defeating an enemy or opponent in a battle, game, or other competition
- **get crowned**: _____; have a crown placed on one's head as a symbol of authority or sovereignty
- **soldier**: _____; a person who serves in an army
- **fought**: _____; engaged in a war or battle
- **gave up**: _____; ceased making an effort; surrendered
- **battle**: _____; a sustained fight between large organized armed forces
- **captured**: _____; taken as a prisoner of war or an enemy, especially by force
- **accused**: _____; charged someone with an offense or crime
- **witch**: _____; a person who is believed to have magical powers and who uses them to harm or help others
- **put on trial**: _____; subject to a formal examination of evidence before a court
- **found guilty**: _____; determined by a court of law to have committed a crime
- **innocent**: _____; not guilty of a crime or offense
- **sentenced to death**: _____; officially ordered to be executed as a punishment for a crime
- **burned at the stake**: _____; killed by tying someone to a stake and setting them on fire
- **remembered**: _____; kept in one's mind as a memory or thought
- **belief**: _____; acceptance that something exists or is true, especially one without proof
- **symbol**: _____; a thing that represents or stands for something else, especially a material object representing something abstract
- **bravery**: _____; courageous behavior or character
- **courage**: _____; the ability to do something that frightens one; bravery
- **stood up**: _____; asserted one's rights or defended one's beliefs in a firm or obstinate way

Biography Series

KEY VOCABULARY | LEVEL 600 - UNIT 10

- ☐ **born**: _____; brought into existence by birth
- ☐ **grew up**: _____; matured or developed physically, mentally, or emotionally
- ☐ **interested**: _____; showing curiosity or concern about something or someone
- ☐ **medicine**: _____; the science or practice of the diagnosis, treatment, and prevention of disease
- ☐ **back then**: _____; at that time in the past
- ☐ **believed**: _____; accepted that something is true, especially without proof
- ☐ **worked**: _____; engaged in physical or mental activity in order to achieve a purpose or result
- ☐ **hard**: _____; with a great deal of effort or endurance
- ☐ **studied**: _____; acquired knowledge of or skill in by study, instruction, or experience
- ☐ **eventually**: _____; in the end, especially after a long delay, dispute, or series of problems
- ☐ **graduate**: _____; successfully complete an academic degree, course of training, or high school
- ☐ **medical school**: _____; an institution that provides education and training in medicine
- ☐ **opened**: _____; started the operation of; established or began
- ☐ **hospital**: _____; an institution providing medical and surgical treatment and nursing care for sick or injured people
- ☐ **teach**: _____; impart knowledge to or instruct someone in how to do something
- ☐ **access**: _____; the means or opportunity to approach or enter a place
- ☐ **healthcare**: _____; the organized provision of medical care to individuals or a community
- ☐ **matter**: _____; physical substance in general, as distinct from mind and spirit
- ☐ **make sure**: _____; take action so as to be certain that something is done or happens as intended or expected
- ☐ **care**: _____; the provision of what is necessary for the health, welfare, maintenance, and protection of someone or something
- ☐ **needed**: _____; requiring something because it is essential or very important
- ☐ **today**: _____; on or in the course of this present day
- ☐ **remembered**: _____; kept in one's mind as a memory or thought
- ☐ **hero**: _____; a person admired or idealized for courage, outstanding achievements, or noble qualities
- ☐ **trailblazer**: _____; a person who makes a new track through wild country or wilderness
- ☐ **showed**: _____; caused or allowed something to be seen
- ☐ **world**: _____; the earth, together with all of its countries, peoples, and natural features
- ☐ **anyone**: _____; any person or people
- ☐ **difference**: _____; a point or way in which people or things are dissimilar
- ☐ **believe**: _____; accept that something is true, especially without proof

DR. SIMON'S MAGIC ENGLISH

KEY VOCABULARY | **LEVEL 600 - UNIT 11**

- ☐ **famous**: _____; well-known, widely recognized
- ☐ **born**: _____; brought into existence by birth
- ☐ **country**: _____; a nation with its own government, occupying a particular territory
- ☐ **war**: _____; a state of armed conflict between different nations or groups
- ☐ **strategy**: _____; a plan of action designed to achieve a particular goal
- ☐ **smart**: _____; having or showing quick intelligence or sharp-wittedness
- ☐ **taught**: _____; provided knowledge, instruction, or guidance to someone
- ☐ **greatest**: _____; of the highest quality, importance, or degree
- ☐ **teacher**: _____; a person who instructs or educates others, especially as a profession
- ☐ **conquer**: _____; overcome and take control of a place or people by military force
- ☐ **ruler**: _____; a person exercising government or dominion
- ☐ **world**: _____; the earth, together with all of its countries, peoples, and natural features
- ☐ **led**: _____; guided or directed a group of people
- ☐ **army**: _____; a large organized body of armed personnel
- ☐ **battle**: _____; a sustained fight between large organized armed forces
- ☐ **victory**: _____; an act of defeating an enemy or opponent in a battle or competition
- ☐ **traveled**: _____; went on a journey or trips to different places
- ☐ **ideas**: _____; thoughts, concepts, or mental images
- ☐ **cultures**: _____; the ideas, customs, and social behavior of a particular people or society
- ☐ **brave**: _____; ready to face and endure danger or pain; showing courage
- ☐ **soldier**: _____; a person who serves in an army
- ☐ **forgot**: _____; failed to remember something
- ☐ **remembered**: _____; kept in one's mind as a memory or thought
- ☐ **made sure**: _____; took action to ensure or confirm that something happened or was the case
- ☐ **take care of**: _____; look after or provide for the needs or well-being of someone
- ☐ **sadly**: _____; in a sad, regrettable, or unfortunate manner
- ☐ **died**: _____; ceased to live; underwent biological death
- ☐ **left**: _____; departed from a place or position
- ☐ **legacy**: _____; something handed down by a predecessor or from the past
- ☐ **behind**: _____; remaining in a place or situation that has been left
- ☐ **thousands of years**: _____; a long span of time
- ☐ **leader**: _____; a person who leads or commands a group, organization, or country
- ☐ **inspired**: _____; filled someone with the urge or ability to do or feel something
- ☐ **learning**: _____; the acquisition of knowledge or skills through study, experience, or teaching
- ☐ **exploring**: _____; traveling through an unfamiliar area to learn about it

KEY VOCABULARY | LEVEL 600 - UNIT 12

- ☐ **famous**: _____; well-known, widely recognized
- ☐ **writer**: _____; a person who uses written words in various styles and techniques to communicate ideas
- ☐ **college**: _____; an institution of higher education that awards degrees and certificates
- ☐ **philosophy**: _____; the study of fundamental questions about existence, knowledge, values, reason, and more
- ☐ **subject**: _____; a branch of knowledge studied or taught in a school, college, or university
- ☐ **asks**: _____; puts a question to someone
- ☐ **question**: _____; a sentence worded or expressed to elicit information or to prompt thought or discussion
- ☐ **world**: _____; the earth, together with all of its countries, peoples, and natural features
- ☐ **became**: _____; started to be or come to be something specified
- ☐ **essay**: _____; a short piece of writing on a particular subject
- ☐ **different**: _____; not the same as another or each other; unlike in nature, form, or quality
- ☐ **art**: _____; the expression or application of human creative skill and imagination
- ☐ **politics**: _____; the activities, actions, and policies used to gain and hold power in a government or to influence the government
- ☐ **way**: _____; a method, style, or manner of doing something
- ☐ **think**: _____; have a particular opinion, belief, or idea about someone or something
- ☐ **feel**: _____; experience an emotion or sensation
- ☐ **smart**: _____; having or showing quick intelligence or sharp-wittedness
- ☐ **challenge**: _____; invite someone to engage in a contest or difficult undertaking
- ☐ **change**: _____; make or become different
- ☐ **travel**: _____; go on a journey or trip, typically to a distant or unfamiliar place
- ☐ **visited**: _____; went to see or spend time at a place
- ☐ **country**: _____; a nation with its own government, occupying a particular territory
- ☐ **cultures**: _____; the ideas, customs, and social behavior of a particular people or society
- ☐ **sadly**: _____; in a sad, regrettable, or unfortunate manner
- ☐ **died**: _____; ceased to live; underwent biological death
- ☐ **left behind**: _____; remained in a place after someone has left
- ☐ **ideas**: _____; thoughts or concepts that are produced by thinking or occurring suddenly in the mind
- ☐ **powerful**: _____; having great power or influence
- ☐ **encouraged**: _____; gave support, confidence, or hope to someone to do or continue something
- ☐ **deeply**: _____; to a great or profound extent
- ☐ **always**: _____; at all times; on all occasions

DR. SIMON'S MAGIC ENGLISH

KEY VOCABULARY | LEVEL 600 - UNIT 13

- ☐ **famous**: _____; well-known, widely recognized
- ☐ **artist**: _____; a person who creates art, especially paintings or drawings
- ☐ **village**: _____; a small community or group of houses in a rural area
- ☐ **draw**: _____; produce a picture or diagram by making lines and marks, especially with a pen or pencil, on paper
- ☐ **paint**: _____; apply color, pigment, or paint to a surface
- ☐ **outside**: _____; the external side or surface of something
- ☐ **beautiful**: _____; pleasing the senses or mind aesthetically
- ☐ **countryside**: _____; the land and scenery of a rural area
- ☐ **grew up**: _____; became an adult or matured
- ☐ **moved**: _____; changed one's place of residence or work
- ☐ **study**: _____; apply one's mind to the acquisition of knowledge
- ☐ **art**: _____; the expression or application of human creative skill and imagination
- ☐ **become**: _____; start to be or come to be something specified
- ☐ **make**: _____; create or construct
- ☐ **painting**: _____; a picture or design made with paint
- ☐ **love**: _____; have a great affection or liking for someone or something
- ☐ **different**: _____; not the same as another or each other; unlike in nature, form, or quality
- ☐ **real**: _____; actually existing as a thing or occurring in fact; not imagined or supposed
- ☐ **pretty**: _____; attractive in a delicate way without being truly beautiful or handsome
- ☐ **picture**: _____; a painting or drawing
- ☐ **ordinary**: _____; with no special or distinctive features; normal
- ☐ **working**: _____; engaging in activity to achieve a result
- ☐ **field**: _____; an area of open land, especially one planted with crops or pasture
- ☐ **fishing**: _____; the activity of catching fish, either for food or as a sport
- ☐ **river**: _____; a large natural stream of water flowing in a channel to the sea, a lake, or another river
- ☐ **ugly**: _____; unpleasant or repulsive, especially in appearance
- ☐ **showed**: _____; demonstrated or revealed
- ☐ **truth**: _____; the quality or state of being in accordance with fact or reality
- ☐ **life**: _____; the existence of an individual human being or animal
- ☐ **burial**: _____; the act or ceremony of burying a dead person
- ☐ **funeral**: _____; a ceremony or service held shortly after a person's death
- ☐ **hometown**: _____; the town or city where a person was born or grew up
- ☐ **unusual**: _____; not habitually or commonly occurring or done
- ☐ **remembered**: _____; kept something in one's mind as a reminder of someone or something
- ☐ **great**: _____; of an extent, amount, or intensity considerably above average
- ☐ **world**: _____; the earth, together with all of its countries, peoples, and natural features

KEY VOCABULARY | LEVEL 600 - UNIT 14

- ☐ **wise**: _____; having or showing experience, knowledge, and good judgment
- ☐ **teacher**: _____; a person who instructs or educates others, often in a school or academic setting
- ☐ **town**: _____; a human settlement smaller than a city
- ☐ **called**: _____; named or identified as
- ☐ **grew up**: _____; became an adult or matured
- ☐ **became**: _____; started to be or came to be something specified
- ☐ **traveled**: _____; went on a journey or trip
- ☐ **teaching**: _____; the profession or activity of imparting knowledge or skills
- ☐ **importance**: _____; the quality or state of being important or significant
- ☐ **kind**: _____; having or showing a friendly, generous, or considerate nature
- ☐ **respectful**: _____; showing admiration or deference toward someone or something
- ☐ **believed**: _____; held a strong conviction or acceptance of something as true
- ☐ **always**: _____; at all times; on all occasions
- ☐ **right**: _____; morally or socially correct or acceptable
- ☐ **thought**: _____; had a particular opinion, belief, or idea about someone or something
- ☐ **treat**: _____; behave toward or deal with in a certain way
- ☐ **admired**: _____; regarded with respect and warm approval
- ☐ **learn**: _____; gain or acquire knowledge or skill in a subject through study, experience, or teaching
- ☐ **including**: _____; comprising as part of a whole
- ☐ **leader**: _____; a person who leads or commands a group, organization, or country
- ☐ **live**: _____; have one's permanent home in a particular place
- ☐ **wrote**: _____; marked letters, words, or other symbols on a surface
- ☐ **teachings**: _____; the ideas or principles taught or advocated as part of a belief system or philosophy
- ☐ **popular**: _____; liked, admired, or enjoyed by many people or a particular group
- ☐ **today**: _____; the present day or time
- ☐ **follow**: _____; come after in time or order; engage in or be interested in
- ☐ **idea**: _____; a thought or suggestion as to a possible course of action
- ☐ **greatest**: _____; of an extent, amount, or intensity considerably above average
- ☐ **history**: _____; the study of past events, particularly in human affairs
- ☐ **influenced**: _____; had an effect on the character, development, or behavior of someone or something

Dr. Simon's Magic English Level 600

DR. SIMON'S MAGIC ENGLISH

KEY VOCABULARY | LEVEL 600 - UNIT 15

- ☐ **spiritual**: _____; relating to the soul, spirit, or religious matters
- ☐ **leader**: _____; a person who leads or commands a group, organization, or country
- ☐ **born**: _____; brought into existence by birth
- ☐ **country**: _____; a nation with its own government, occupying a particular territory
- ☐ **real**: _____; genuine or authentic
- ☐ **name**: _____; a word or set of words used to identify a person, animal, place, or thing
- ☐ **young**: _____; in the early stage of life, growth, or development
- ☐ **chosen**: _____; selected or picked out as the best or most appropriate
- ☐ **important**: _____; of great significance or value; noteworthy
- ☐ **religious**: _____; relating to or believing in a particular religion or faith
- ☐ **believes**: _____; accepts that something is true or exists
- ☐ **kindness**: _____; the quality of being friendly, generous, and considerate
- ☐ **compassion**: _____; sympathetic pity and concern for the sufferings or misfortunes of others
- ☐ **non-violence**: _____; the practice or principle of avoiding violence or harm to others
- ☐ **teaches**: _____; instructs or imparts knowledge or skills to others
- ☐ **need**: _____; require something because it is essential or very important
- ☐ **flee**: _____; run away from a place or danger in order to escape or find safety
- ☐ **government**: _____; the group of people with the authority to govern a country or state
- ☐ **take control**: _____; assume or assert authority or control over something
- ☐ **live**: _____; have one's permanent home in a particular place
- ☐ **continues**: _____; persists or carries on without interruption
- ☐ **known**: _____; recognized or familiar to many people
- ☐ **world**: _____; the earth, together with all of its countries and peoples
- ☐ **teachings**: _____; the ideas or principles taught or advocated as part of a belief system or philosophy
- ☐ **peace**: _____; freedom from disturbance or war; tranquility
- ☐ **travels**: _____; journeys or goes on trips to different places
- ☐ **talking**: _____; speaking or having a conversation with someone
- ☐ **spreading**: _____; distributing or disseminating widely
- ☐ **message**: _____; a verbal, written, or recorded communication sent to someone
- ☐ **love**: _____; a strong affection or deep attachment toward someone or something
- ☐ **look up to**: _____; regard with respect, admiration, or aspiration
- ☐ **role model**: _____; a person whose behavior, example, or success is or can be emulated by others
- ☐ **admire**: _____; regard with respect, warm approval, or pleasure
- ☐ **life**: _____; the existence of an individual human being or animal

166 | Biography Series

KEY VOCABULARY | LEVEL 600 - UNIT 16

- ☐ **scientist**: _____; a person who studies or specializes in science, especially a branch of natural or physical science
- ☐ **died**: _____; ceased to live; passed away
- ☐ **stars**: _____; luminous celestial objects consisting of a mass of gas held together by its own gravity
- ☐ **planets**: _____; celestial bodies that orbit around a star and do not produce light of their own
- ☐ **understand**: _____; comprehend the meaning or significance of something
- ☐ **universe**: _____; all existing matter, space, and energy, including the planets, stars, galaxies, and the entirety of space and time
- ☐ **famous**: _____; well-known or widely recognized
- ☐ **ideas**: _____; concepts or thoughts about something
- ☐ **black holes**: _____; regions of space with gravitational forces so strong that nothing, not even light, can escape from them
- ☐ **gravity**: _____; the force that attracts objects toward each other
- ☐ **escape**: _____; break free from or get away from something
- ☐ **light**: _____; the natural agent that stimulates sight and makes things visible
- ☐ **wheelchair**: _____; a chair fitted with wheels, used by people with mobility impairments
- ☐ **computerized**: _____; operated or controlled by a computer
- ☐ **voice**: _____; the sound produced in a person's larynx and uttered through the mouth, as speech or song
- ☐ **disease**: _____; a disorder of structure or function in a human, animal, or plant, especially one that produces specific symptoms
- ☐ **hard**: _____; difficult; not easy
- ☐ **science**: _____; the systematic study of the structure and behavior of the physical and natural world through observation and experiment
- ☐ **world**: _____; the earth, together with all of its countries and peoples
- ☐ **taught**: _____; provided instruction or lessons to others
- ☐ **anyone**: _____; any person or people
- ☐ **look like**: _____; have a similar appearance or resemblance
- ☐ **move**: _____; change position or place; go in a specified direction or manner
- ☐ **give up**: _____; cease making an effort; surrender or quit
- ☐ **dreams**: _____; a series of thoughts, images, and sensations occurring in a person's mind during sleep; also, aspirations or goals one desires to achieve

DR. SIMON'S MAGIC ENGLISH

KEY VOCABULARY | LEVEL 600 - UNIT 17

- ☐ **president**: _____; the head of state and government
- ☐ **served**: _____; fulfilled a duty or role
- ☐ **term**: _____; a fixed or limited period for which someone holds a particular office or position
- ☐ **passed away**: _____; died
- ☐ **actor**: _____; a person who performs in plays, movies, or television shows
- ☐ **starred**: _____; had the main role in a movie or play
- ☐ **popular**: _____; liked or admired by many people
- ☐ **prosperous**: _____; successful, flourishing, or thriving
- ☐ **believed**: _____; accepted as true or real
- ☐ **freedom**: _____; the power or right to act, speak, or think as one wants without hindrance or restraint
- ☐ **democracy**: _____; a system of government by the people, typically through elected representatives
- ☐ **opportunity**: _____; a favorable or advantageous circumstance or chance
- ☐ **succeed**: _____; achieve a desired aim or result
- ☐ **safer**: _____; free from harm, risk, or danger
- ☐ **period**: _____; a length or portion of time
- ☐ **tension**: _____; a state of mental or emotional strain
- ☐ **met**: _____; came into the presence or company of someone
- ☐ **leader**: _____; a person who leads or commands a group, organization, or country
- ☐ **reduce**: _____; make smaller or less in amount, degree, or size
- ☐ **threat**: _____; a statement or indication of an intention to inflict harm, injury, or damage
- ☐ **nuclear**: _____; relating to the energy released by reactions within atomic nuclei
- ☐ **war**: _____; a state of armed conflict between different nations or states or different groups within a nation or state
- ☐ **optimistic**: _____; hopeful and confident about the future
- ☐ **attitude**: _____; a settled way of thinking or feeling about something
- ☐ **speech**: _____; a formal address or discourse delivered to an audience
- ☐ **communicator**: _____; a person who conveys information or ideas to others effectively
- ☐ **inspire**: _____; fill someone with the urge or ability to do or feel something
- ☐ **left**: _____; departed or ceased to be in a place
- ☐ **office**: _____; a room, set of rooms, or building used as a place for commercial, professional, or bureaucratic work
- ☐ **continue**: _____; persist in an activity or process
- ☐ **important**: _____; of great significance or value
- ☐ **figure**: _____; a person who is important or influential in a particular sphere or area
- ☐ **ideas**: _____; concepts, thoughts, or plans
- ☐ **spirit**: _____; the nonphysical part of a person that is the seat of emotions and character

KEY VOCABULARY | LEVEL 600 - UNIT 18

- ☐ **famous scientist**: _____; a well-known researcher or expert in the field of science
- ☐ **studied**: _____; examined closely in order to gain knowledge or understanding
- ☐ **dreamed**: _____; indulged in a series of thoughts, images, or sensations during sleep or while awake
- ☐ **one day**: _____; at some point in the future
- ☐ **chance**: _____; an opportunity or possibility
- ☐ **afraid**: _____; feeling fear or apprehension
- ☐ **slowly**: _____; at a slow pace or speed
- ☐ **gained**: _____; obtained or acquired
- ☐ **trust**: _____; a firm belief in the reliability, truth, or ability of someone or something
- ☐ **spent**: _____; used or consumed time or energy
- ☐ **observing**: _____; watching carefully and attentively
- ☐ **behavior**: _____; the way in which someone or something acts or conducts oneself
- ☐ **discovered**: _____; found or became aware of something for the first time
- ☐ **knew**: _____; had information or awareness about something
- ☐ **tools**: _____; devices or implements used to carry out a particular function or task
- ☐ **sticks**: _____; long, thin pieces of wood or other materials
- ☐ **surprising**: _____; causing a feeling of astonishment or disbelief
- ☐ **used to**: _____; habitually did or had in the past but no longer do or have
- ☐ **noticed**: _____; observed or perceived with attention
- ☐ **emotions**: _____; strong feelings deriving from one's circumstances, mood, or relationships
- ☐ **humans**: _____; members of the species Homo sapiens
- ☐ **sad**: _____; feeling or showing sorrow or unhappiness
- ☐ **saw**: _____; perceived with the eyes
- ☐ **hug**: _____; hold someone closely in one's arms, especially as a sign of affection
- ☐ **kiss**: _____; touch or caress with the lips as a sign of love, sexual desire, or greeting
- ☐ **hold hands**: _____; grip or clasp one another's hands, typically as a sign of affection
- ☐ **work**: _____; activity involving mental or physical effort done to achieve a purpose or result
- ☐ **understand**: _____; comprehend the meaning or significance of something
- ☐ **written**: _____; expressed in writing or print
- ☐ **given**: _____; provided or offered
- ☐ **talks**: _____; speeches or presentations given to an audience
- ☐ **share**: _____; give a portion of something to others
- ☐ **knowledge**: _____; facts, information, and skills acquired through experience or education
- ☐ **important**: _____; of great significance or value
- ☐ **protect**: _____, 막다; keep safe from harm, injury, or loss
- ☐ **habitat**: _____; the natural environment in which an organism or species lives, providing the necessary conditions for its existence and growth

DR. SIMON'S MAGIC ENGLISH

KEY VOCABULARY | LEVEL 600 - UNIT 19

- ☐ **astronaut**: _____; a person trained for traveling in space
- ☐ **pilot's license**: _____; an official document or certification permitting someone to operate an aircraft
- ☐ **joined**: _____; became a member of or participated in
- ☐ **U.S. Navy**: _____; the naval warfare service branch of the United States Armed Forces
- ☐ **fighter planes**: _____; fast military aircraft designed for air-to-air combat
- ☐ **NASA**: _____; National Aeronautics and Space Administration
- ☐ **space**: _____; the boundless, three-dimensional extent in which objects and events occur and have relative position and direction
- ☐ **deal with**: _____; take action to solve or handle a problem or situation
- ☐ **emergency**: _____; a serious, unexpected, and often dangerous situation requiring immediate action
- ☐ **spacecraft**: _____; a vehicle designed for travel or operation in outer space
- ☐ **spin**: _____; rotate quickly and smoothly around a central point or axis
- ☐ **control**: _____; the power to influence or direct people's behavior or the course of events
- ☐ **fix**: _____; repair or mend something
- ☐ **safely**: _____; in a way that is not likely to cause harm or danger
- ☐ **surface**: _____; the outside part or uppermost layer of something
- ☐ **famously**: _____; in a way that is well known or recognized
- ☐ **small step**: _____; a minor or incremental action or progress
- ☐ **giant leap**: _____; a significant or substantial advancement or achievement
- ☐ **mankind**: _____; the human race; human beings collectively
- ☐ **huge**: _____; extremely large or great
- ☐ **accomplishment**: _____; something that has been achieved successfully
- ☐ **inspired**: _____; filled with the urge or ability to do or feel something creative or worthwhile
- ☐ **explore**: _____; travel in or through an unfamiliar area in order to learn about it
- ☐ **retiring**: _____; leaving one's job or ceasing to work, typically upon reaching a certain age
- ☐ **aerospace engineering**: _____; the branch of engineering concerned with the design, development, testing, and production of aircraft and spacecraft
- ☐ **served on**: _____; participated or worked as a member of
- ☐ **several**: _____; more than two but not many
- ☐ **committee**: _____; a group of people appointed for a specific function, typically consisting of members of a larger organization
- ☐ **related to**: _____; connected or associated with
- ☐ **space exploration**: _____; the discovery and exploration of outer space beyond Earth's atmosphere
- ☐ **legacy**: _____; something handed down or received from a predecessor or past generations
- ☐ **pioneering**: _____; involving new ideas, methods, or techniques that have not been used before
- ☐ **forgotten**: _____; no longer remembered or thought about

Biography Series

KEY VOCABULARY | LEVEL 600 - UNIT 20

- ☐ **scientist**: _____; a person who conducts scientific research and studies the natural world
- ☐ **learning**: _____; the process of acquiring knowledge or skills through study, experience, or teaching
- ☐ **questions**: _____; inquiries made to obtain information or clarify understanding
- ☐ **world**: _____; the planet Earth and all life and objects on it
- ☐ **child**: _____; a young human being
- ☐ **figure out**: _____; understand or solve something by thinking or reasoning
- ☐ **experiment**: _____; a scientific procedure carried out to make a discovery or test a hypothesis
- ☐ **objects**: _____; things that can be seen or touched
- ☐ **materials**: _____; substances or things from which something can be made
- ☐ **curious**: _____; eager to know or learn something
- ☐ **stars**: _____; massive, luminous balls of plasma held together by gravity and emitting light and heat
- ☐ **planets**: _____; large celestial bodies that orbit around a star
- ☐ **college**: _____; an institution of higher education that offers undergraduate and sometimes postgraduate courses
- ☐ **math**: _____; short for mathematics, the study of numbers, quantities, and shapes and their relationships
- ☐ **discoveries**: _____; new findings or breakthroughs in knowledge or understanding
- ☐ **laws**: _____; principles or rules that describe or govern a particular phenomenon or behavior
- ☐ **motion**: _____; the action or process of moving or being moved
- ☐ **gravity**: _____; the force that attracts objects toward the center of the Earth or other celestial bodies
- ☐ **equation**: _____; a mathematical statement that shows the equality of two expressions
- ☐ **universal**: _____; applicable or common to all cases or situations
- ☐ **gravitation**: _____; the force of attraction between two objects with mass
- ☐ **reflecting telescope**: _____; a telescope that uses a combination of mirrors to gather and focus light to create an image
- ☐ **inventions**: _____; new creations or devices that are made for the first time
- ☐ **type**: _____; a particular category or kind of something
- ☐ **calculus**: _____; a branch of mathematics that deals with rates of change and the accumulation of quantities
- ☐ **complex**: _____; complicated or intricate
- ☐ **problems**: _____; situations or tasks that require a solution or resolution
- ☐ **ideas**: _____; concepts, thoughts, or notions
- ☐ **understand**: _____; comprehend or grasp the meaning or significance of something

DR. SIMON'S MAGIC ENGLISH

KEY VOCABULARY | **LEVEL 600 - UNIT 21**

- ☐ **explorer**: _____; a person who travels to unknown places to discover new lands, resources, or information
- ☐ **discovery**: _____; the act of finding or uncovering something for the first time
- ☐ **America**: _____; the continents of North and South America
- ☐ **Italy**: _____; a country in southern Europe
- ☐ **sailor**: _____; a person who works on a ship, especially as a member of the crew
- ☐ **navigate**: _____; plan and direct the course of a ship or other vehicle
- ☐ **sea**: _____; a large body of saltwater that is partly or entirely enclosed by land
- ☐ **route**: _____; a way or course taken in getting from one place to another
- ☐ **Asia**: _____; the largest continent, located primarily in the eastern and northern hemispheres
- ☐ **Atlantic Ocean**: _____; the second-largest ocean in the world, separating the Americas from Europe and Africa
- ☐ **voyage**: _____; a long journey, especially by sea or in space
- ☐ **ships**: _____; large vessels used for transportation on water
- ☐ **land**: _____; the solid ground or surface of the Earth
- ☐ **Caribbean Sea**: _____; a sea in the western Atlantic Ocean, bounded by the islands of the Caribbean
- ☐ **island**: _____; a piece of land surrounded by water
- ☐ **Central America**: _____; the region between North America and South America, consisting of several countries
- ☐ **South America**: _____; the continent located in the western hemisphere, south of North America
- ☐ **continent**: _____; a large, continuous landmass, typically separated by oceans
- ☐ **treatment**: _____; the way in which someone is treated, especially in terms of their well-being or rights
- ☐ **native**: _____; belonging to or originating from a particular place or region
- ☐ **encountered**: _____; came across or met with someone or something unexpectedly
- ☐ **advantage**: _____; a favorable or superior circumstance or condition
- ☐ **forced**: _____; compelled or coerced someone to do something against their will
- ☐ **harsh**: _____; severe or cruel
- ☐ **celebrated**: _____; publicly recognized or acknowledged with festivities or ceremonies
- ☐ **negative**: _____; unfavorable or detrimental
- ☐ **impact**: _____; the effect or influence of one thing on another

BIOGRAPHY SERIES

KEY VOCABULARY | LEVEL 600 - UNIT 22

- ☐ **special**: _____; exceptional, unique, or distinct
- ☐ **Italy**: _____; a country in southern Europe
- ☐ **love**: _____; a strong affection or deep feeling of care towards someone or something
- ☐ **nature**: _____; the physical world and its phenomena, including plants, animals, landscapes, and natural processes
- ☐ **outdoors**: _____; the natural environment outside buildings or enclosed spaces
- ☐ **connection**: _____; a relationship or association between two or more things
- ☐ **devote**: _____; dedicate or commit oneself to a particular purpose or cause
- ☐ **God**: _____; a supreme being or deity in various religions, often believed to be the creator and ruler of the universe
- ☐ **monk**: _____; a member of a religious community, typically living in a monastery or convent, who has taken vows of poverty, chastity, and obedience
- ☐ **simple**: _____; uncomplicated, plain, or without unnecessary complexities
- ☐ **prayer**: _____; a solemn request or expression of thanks addressed to a deity or spiritual entity
- ☐ **vision**: _____; an experience of seeing something that is not physically present or perceptible
- ☐ **rebuild**: _____; construct or restore something that has been damaged or destroyed
- ☐ **church**: _____; a building used for public Christian worship
- ☐ **religious order**: _____; a community of individuals who live according to specific religious rules or principles
- ☐ **teachings**: _____; ideas, beliefs, or principles that are taught or shared as part of a religious or philosophical system
- ☐ **peace**: _____; a state of harmony, tranquility, and freedom from conflict or violence
- ☐ **humility**: _____; a modest or low view of one's own importance; humbleness
- ☐ **creatures**: _____; living beings or organisms
- ☐ **depicted**: _____; represented or portrayed in a picture, painting, or other visual form
- ☐ **paintings**: _____; visual artworks created with pigments on a surface, such as canvas or paper
- ☐ **surrounding**: _____; being present or located all around someone or something
- ☐ **celebrate**: _____; honor or mark a special occasion or event with festivities or ceremonies
- ☐ **blessings**: _____; prayers or invocations asking for divine favor, protection, or guidance
- ☐ **pets**: _____; domesticated animals kept for companionship or pleasure
- ☐ **feast day**: _____; a day dedicated to the commemoration or celebration of a saint or religious event
- ☐ **died**: _____; ceased living or existing
- ☐ **legacy**: _____; something that is handed down or transmitted from a predecessor or past generation
- ☐ **kind**: _____; showing benevolence, consideration, or gentleness
- ☐ **gentle**: _____; having a mild, tender, or compassionate nature

Dr. Simon's Magic English Level 600 | 173

DR. SIMON'S MAGIC ENGLISH

KEY VOCABULARY | LEVEL 600 - UNIT 23

- ☐ **wealthy**: _____; having a great amount of money, possessions, or resources
- ☐ **working**: _____; engaging in labor or employment
- ☐ **hard**: _____; requiring a lot of effort, energy, or endurance
- ☐ **intelligence**: _____; the ability to acquire, understand, and apply knowledge and skills
- ☐ **jobs**: _____; tasks or activities done to earn money or a livelihood
- ☐ **cotton mill**: _____; a factory where cotton is processed or spun into thread or fabric
- ☐ **telegraph**: _____; a communication system that transmits messages over long distances using coded electrical signals
- ☐ **messenger**: _____; a person who carries and delivers messages or documents
- ☐ **president**: _____; the highest-ranking executive officer in an organization or country
- ☐ **invested**: _____; allocated money or resources into something with the expectation of future gain or profit
- ☐ **richest**: _____; having the greatest amount of wealth or resources
- ☐ **important**: _____; significant, notable, or having great value or impact
- ☐ **donated**: _____; gave or contributed something, usually money or goods, to a charitable cause or organization
- ☐ **charities**: _____; organizations that provide assistance, support, or resources to those in need
- ☐ **build**: _____; construct or create something, typically a physical structure
- ☐ **libraries**: _____; buildings or institutions that house collections of books and other materials for reading, research, and learning
- ☐ **universities**: _____; institutions of higher education that offer academic programs and degrees in various fields of study
- ☐ **wrote**: _____; composed or produced written content
- ☐ **articles**: _____; written pieces of non-fiction or informative content published in newspapers, magazines, or other publications
- ☐ **teach**: _____; impart knowledge, skills, or information to others through instruction or guidance
- ☐ **successful**: _____; achieving a desired outcome, goal, or level of accomplishment
- ☐ **businessman**: _____; a person engaged in commercial or industrial activities, usually to earn a profit
- ☐ **philanthropist**: _____; a person who seeks to promote the welfare of others, often through charitable donations or actions
- ☐ **opportunity**: _____; a favorable or advantageous circumstance or chance
- ☐ **succeed**: _____; achieve a desired outcome or accomplish a goal
- ☐ **dies**: _____; ceases living or existing
- ☐ **disgraced**: _____; having lost honor, respect, or reputation

KEY VOCABULARY | LEVEL 600 - UNIT 24

- ☐ **remarkable**: _____; deserving of attention or admiration due to exceptional qualities or achievements
- ☐ **overcame**: _____; successfully dealt with or conquered a difficulty or obstacle
- ☐ **obstacles**: _____; things that stand in the way of progress or achievement
- ☐ **achieve**: _____; successfully reach or accomplish a desired goal or outcome
- ☐ **lost**: _____; no longer possessing or having something
- ☐ **sight**: _____; the ability to see or perceive visual stimuli
- ☐ **severe**: _____; extremely intense or serious
- ☐ **illness**: _____; a state of poor health or disease
- ☐ **communicate**: _____; share or exchange information, ideas, or feelings
- ☐ **frustrated**: _____; feeling or expressing annoyance or dissatisfaction
- ☐ **hired**: _____; engaged the services of someone in return for payment
- ☐ **method**: _____; a particular way of doing something
- ☐ **involved**: _____; included as part of something
- ☐ **sign language**: _____; a system of communication using visual gestures and signs
- ☐ **quick**: _____; done or happening in a short amount of time
- ☐ **learner**: _____; a person who is acquiring knowledge or skills
- ☐ **understand**: _____; comprehend the meaning or significance of something
- ☐ **raised**: _____; lifted to a higher position or level
- ☐ **dots**: _____; small round marks or points
- ☐ **special**: _____; better, greater, or otherwise different from what is usual or expected
- ☐ **technique**: _____; a method or way of doing something
- ☐ **vibrations**: _____; rapid back-and-forth movements or oscillations
- ☐ **determined**: _____; having a strong and unwavering commitment to achieving a goal or outcome
- ☐ **hard-working**: _____; characterized by diligence and persistence in one's efforts
- ☐ **graduate**: _____; successfully complete a course of study and receive a degree or diploma
- ☐ **college**: _____; an institution of higher education that typically offers undergraduate degrees
- ☐ **well-known**: _____; widely recognized or familiar to many people
- ☐ **public speaker**: _____; a person who delivers speeches or presentations to an audience
- ☐ **tirelessly**: _____; with great effort, determination, and energy
- ☐ **promote**: _____; support or actively encourage the growth or development of something
- ☐ **rights**: _____; entitlements or legal protections granted to individuals or groups
- ☐ **disabilities**: _____; physical, mental, or sensory impairments that may limit a person's abilities or functioning
- ☐ **inspiration**: _____; a person or thing that motivates or stimulates creative or productive activity
- ☐ **enormous**: _____; extremely large in size, quantity, or degree
- ☐ **challenges**: _____; difficult tasks or situations that require effort or skill to overcome

DR. SIMON'S MAGIC ENGLISH

KEY VOCABULARY | **LEVEL 600 - UNIT 25**

- ☐ **famous**: _____; widely recognized or known
- ☐ **painter**: _____; an artist who creates paintings
- ☐ **draw**: _____; create a picture or design using lines and marks on paper or another surface
- ☐ **struggled**: _____; made great efforts or experienced difficulty
- ☐ **mental illness**: _____; a condition that affects a person's thinking, feeling, behavior, or mood
- ☐ **different**: _____; not the same; distinct or separate
- ☐ **jobs**: _____; paid positions of regular employment
- ☐ **preacher**: _____; a person who delivers religious sermons or speeches
- ☐ **enjoy**: _____; take pleasure in or find satisfaction in
- ☐ **decided**: _____; made a choice or reached a resolution
- ☐ **become**: _____; begin to be or develop into something
- ☐ **taught**: _____; imparted knowledge or skills to someone
- ☐ **bright**: _____; having a strong, vivid, or intense color
- ☐ **bold**: _____; showing a willingness to take risks or be daring
- ☐ **colors**: _____; hues or shades perceived through the sense of vision
- ☐ **paintings**: _____; pictures or works of art created using paint
- ☐ **nature**: _____; the physical world and its phenomena
- ☐ **life**: _____; the existence of an individual human being or animal
- ☐ **pictures**: _____; visual representations or images
- ☐ **sunflowers**: _____; large, yellow flowers with a dark center
- ☐ **landscape**: _____; natural scenery or the view of rural or natural surroundings
- ☐ **portraits**: _____; artistic representations or images of a person
- ☐ **sadly**: _____; in a way that evokes sadness or regret
- ☐ **lifetime**: _____; the period of time during which a person is alive
- ☐ **appreciated**: _____; recognized the value, quality, or significance of
- ☐ **considered**: _____; thought of or regarded in a particular way
- ☐ **important**: _____; of great significance, value, or influence
- ☐ **artists**: _____; individuals who create art, especially visual art
- ☐ **history**: _____; the study of past events and the course of human development
- ☐ **worth**: _____; having a value, importance, or significance
- ☐ **money**: _____; a medium of exchange used for buying and selling goods and services
- ☐ **visit**: _____; go to see or spend time at a place
- ☐ **museums**: _____; institutions that preserve, exhibit, and study objects of artistic, cultural, or historical significance
- ☐ **artwork**: _____; creative or artistic works, such as paintings, sculptures, or photographs

176 | Biography Series

KEY VOCABULARY | LEVEL 600 - UNIT 26

- ☐ **scientist**: _____; a person who conducts scientific research and studies the natural world
- ☐ **famous**: _____; widely recognized or known
- ☐ **late**: _____; occurring near or towards the end of a particular period
- ☐ **learning**: _____; the acquisition of knowledge or skills through study, experience, or teaching
- ☐ **smart**: _____; having or showing quick intelligence or mental sharpness
- ☐ **hard**: _____; with a great deal of effort or energy
- ☐ **college**: _____; an educational institution offering higher education and granting degrees
- ☐ **studied**: _____; engaged in the investigation or analysis of a subject
- ☐ **physics**: _____; the branch of science that deals with matter, energy, and the interactions between them
- ☐ **chemistry**: _____; the branch of science that deals with the composition, properties, and reactions of substances
- ☐ **amazing**: _____; causing great surprise, wonder, or astonishment
- ☐ **discovered**: _____; found or learned something for the first time
- ☐ **elements**: _____; basic substances that cannot be broken down into simpler substances by chemical means
- ☐ **polonium**: _____; a chemical element with the symbol Po and atomic number 84
- ☐ **radium**: _____; a chemical element with the symbol Ra and atomic number 88
- ☐ **figured out**: _____; understood or solved a problem or mystery
- ☐ **radioactivity**: _____; the emission of radiation or particles from the nucleus of an unstable atom
- ☐ **treat**: _____; provide medical care or attention to
- ☐ **cancer**: _____; a disease characterized by the uncontrolled growth of abnormal cells
- ☐ **disease**: _____; a disorder of structure or function in a living organism
- ☐ **sick**: _____; affected by illness or disease
- ☐ **important**: _____; of great significance, value, or influence
- ☐ **awarded**: _____; presented with an honor, prize, or recognition
- ☐ **special**: _____; better, greater, or otherwise different from what is usual
- ☐ **challenges**: _____; difficulties or obstacles that require effort to overcome
- ☐ **scientists**: _____; individuals who study and investigate the natural world through scientific methods
- ☐ **education**: _____; the process of receiving or giving systematic instruction
- ☐ **research**: _____; the systematic investigation into and study of materials and sources to establish facts and reach new conclusions
- ☐ **money**: _____; a medium of exchange used for buying goods and services
- ☐ **passed away**: _____; died or ceased to exist
- ☐ **remembered**: _____; kept in one's mind as a memory or tribute
- ☐ **inspiration**: _____; a person or thing that stimulates or encourages creative thought or action
- ☐ **become**: _____; begin to be or develop into something

Dr. Simon's Magic English Level 600

DR. SIMON'S MAGIC ENGLISH

KEY VOCABULARY | LEVEL 600 - UNIT 27

- ☐ **duke**: _____; a nobleman of the highest hereditary rank below a prince or king
- ☐ **died**: _____; ceased to live; passed away
- ☐ **longest-reigning**: _____; having the longest period of rule or tenure
- ☐ **monarch**: _____; a sovereign head of state, especially a king, queen, or emperor
- ☐ **history**: _____; the study of past events, particularly in human affairs
- ☐ **death**: _____; the end of life; the cessation of existence or the process of dying
- ☐ **independent**: _____; free from outside control; not subject to another's authority
- ☐ **sense**: _____; a faculty by which the body perceives an external stimulus
- ☐ **duty**: _____; a moral or legal obligation; a responsibility
- ☐ **upset**: _____; feeling unhappy, disappointed, or worried
- ☐ **interested**: _____; having or showing a curiosity or desire to know or learn about something
- ☐ **literature**: _____; written works, especially those considered of superior or lasting artistic merit
- ☐ **accomplished**: _____; highly skilled or proficient in a particular activity or field
- ☐ **library**: _____; a building or room containing collections of books, periodicals, and sometimes films and recorded music for people to read, borrow, or refer to
- ☐ **patron**: _____; a person who gives financial or other support to a person, organization, or cause
- ☐ **support**: _____; provide assistance, encouragement, or comfort to someone or something
- ☐ **strict**: _____; demanding that rules concerning behavior are obeyed and observed
- ☐ **morality**: _____; principles concerning the distinction between right and wrong or good and bad behavior
- ☐ **importance**: _____; the quality or state of being important; significance
- ☐ **religion**: _____; the belief in and worship of a superhuman controlling power, especially a personal God or gods
- ☐ **promote**: _____; support or actively encourage the furtherance of something
- ☐ **values**: _____; principles or standards of behavior; one's judgment of what is important in life
- ☐ **national**: _____; relating to or characteristic of a nation; common to a whole nation
- ☐ **pride**: _____; a feeling of deep pleasure or satisfaction derived from one's achievements
- ☐ **strengthen**: _____; make or become stronger or more resilient
- ☐ **empire**: _____; an extensive group of states or countries under a single supreme authority, formerly especially an emperor or empress
- ☐ **overall**: _____; taking everything into account; as a whole
- ☐ **influential**: _____; having great influence on someone or something
- ☐ **leader**: _____; a person who leads or commands a group, organization, or country
- ☐ **progress**: _____; forward or onward movement toward a destination or goal
- ☐ **change**: _____; make or become different
- ☐ **remembered**: _____; kept in one's mind as a memory or tribute

KEY VOCABULARY | LEVEL 600 - UNIT 28

- ☐ **president**: _____; the elected head of a country or state
- ☐ **born**: _____; brought into existence or life
- ☐ **grew up**: _____; raised or brought up in a particular environment or upbringing
- ☐ **wealthy**: _____; having a great deal of money, resources, or assets
- ☐ **playing sports**: _____; engaging in physical activities or games that involve skill and competition
- ☐ **graduated**: _____; successfully completed a course of study and received a degree or diploma
- ☐ **degree**: _____; an academic qualification awarded by a college or university
- ☐ **government**: _____; the governing body of a nation, state, or community
- ☐ **navy**: _____; the branch of a country's armed services that conducts military operations at sea
- ☐ **hero**: _____; a person admired or idealized for courage, outstanding achievements, or noble qualities
- ☐ **congressman**: _____; a member of the United States House of Representatives
- ☐ **senator**: _____; a member of the United States Senate
- ☐ **ran for president**: _____; competed as a candidate in the presidential election
- ☐ **elected**: _____; chosen by voting or a formal process to hold a position or office
- ☐ **important**: _____; of great significance or value; crucial
- ☐ **Peace Corps**: _____; a volunteer program run by the United States government that provides assistance to developing countries
- ☐ **volunteers**: _____; individuals who offer themselves for a service or activity without being compelled or paid
- ☐ **countries**: _____; nations or sovereign states
- ☐ **improve**: _____; make or become better or of higher quality
- ☐ **relationship**: _____; the way in which two or more people, groups, or countries are connected or interact with each other
- ☐ **crisis**: _____; a time of intense difficulty, trouble, or danger
- ☐ **led**: _____; guided or directed a group or organization
- ☐ **difficult time**: _____; a period characterized by challenges or hardships
- ☐ **removed**: _____; taken away or eliminated
- ☐ **assassinated**: _____; murdered by a surprise attack for political or ideological reasons
- ☐ **shock**: _____; a sudden upsetting or surprising event or experience
- ☐ **mourning**: _____; the expression of sorrow or grief following a loss or death
- ☐ **great leader**: _____; an individual who inspires and guides others towards a common goal or vision
- ☐ **inspired**: _____; motivated or encouraged someone to do something positive or creative
- ☐ **peace**: _____; the absence of war or violence
- ☐ **progress**: _____; forward or onward movement toward a destination or goal

Dr. Simon's Magic English Level 600

DR. SIMON'S MAGIC ENGLISH

KEY VOCABULARY | **LEVEL 600 - UNIT 29**

- ☐ **kind**: _____; having or showing a gentle and generous nature
- ☐ **caring**: _____; displaying concern and empathy for others
- ☐ **dedicated**: _____; committed or devoted to a task or purpose
- ☐ **life**: _____; the existence of a living being
- ☐ **helping**: _____; providing assistance or support to someone
- ☐ **born**: _____; brought into existence or life
- ☐ **religious**: _____; relating to or believing in a system of faith or worship
- ☐ **attending**: _____; being present at or participating in an event or activity
- ☐ **church**: _____; a building used for Christian religious worship
- ☐ **poor**: _____; lacking sufficient money or resources
- ☐ **nun**: _____; a woman who has taken religious vows and lives in a convent
- ☐ **teach**: _____; impart knowledge or instruct someone
- ☐ **shocked**: _____; greatly surprised or disturbed
- ☐ **poverty**: _____; the state of being extremely poor
- ☐ **suffering**: _____; the state of undergoing pain, distress, or hardship
- ☐ **decide**: _____; make a resolution or determination about something
- ☐ **devote**: _____; give all or a large part of one's time or resources to a cause, activity, or person
- ☐ **sick**: _____; affected by physical or mental illness
- ☐ **homeless**: _____; without a home or a permanent place of residence
- ☐ **dying**: _____; approaching death; terminal
- ☐ **provide**: _____; supply or make available for use
- ☐ **shelter**: _____; a place giving protection from weather, such as a house or a tent
- ☐ **medical care**: _____; the provision of medical services or treatment
- ☐ **famous**: _____; widely known or recognized
- ☐ **world**: _____; the earth and all its people and nations
- ☐ **award**: _____; a prize or other mark of recognition given in honor of an achievement
- ☐ **honor**: _____; public recognition or respect for someone's achievements or qualities
- ☐ **compassion**: _____; sympathetic concern and care for the suffering or misfortune of others
- ☐ **faith**: _____; complete trust or confidence in someone or something
- ☐ **simple**: _____; not complicated or elaborate; easy to understand or do
- ☐ **legacy**: _____; something handed down or left behind by a predecessor
- ☐ **care**: _____; provision of what is necessary for the health, welfare, maintenance, and protection of someone or something
- ☐ **inspiration**: _____; the process of being mentally stimulated to do or feel something, especially to do something creative
- ☐ **better**: _____; of superior quality or more desirable or suitable

Biography Series

KEY VOCABULARY | LEVEL 600 - UNIT 30

- ☐ **engineer**: _____; a person who designs, builds, or maintains engines, machines, or public works
- ☐ **built**: _____; constructed or erected
- ☐ **famous**: _____; widely known or recognized
- ☐ **landmarks**: _____; prominent or well-known features of a landscape or area
- ☐ **world**: _____; the earth and all its people and nations
- ☐ **born**: _____; brought into existence or life
- ☐ **interested**: _____; showing curiosity or concern about something or someone
- ☐ **engineering**: _____; the branch of science and technology concerned with the design, building, and use of engines, machines, and structures
- ☐ **completing**: _____; finishing or bringing to an end
- ☐ **railway company**: _____; an organization that operates a system of trains for transportation of goods or passengers
- ☐ **projects**: _____; planned or proposed undertakings, often with specific goals and tasks
- ☐ **designing**: _____; creating a plan or specification for the construction or implementation of something
- ☐ **bridges**: _____; structures built to span physical obstacles such as rivers or valleys
- ☐ **viaduct**: _____; a long elevated bridge-like structure that carries a road or railway over a valley or other obstacles
- ☐ **World's Fair**: _____; an international exhibition showcasing achievements of nations, held periodically in different countries
- ☐ **iron**: _____; a strong, hard, magnetic metallic element used to make various products and structures
- ☐ **tallest**: _____; of great or more than average height
- ☐ **structure**: _____; something that has been built or constructed
- ☐ **excited**: _____; feeling or showing enthusiasm, eagerness, or anticipation
- ☐ **energy**: _____; the capacity or power to do work
- ☐ **completed**: _____; finished or brought to an end
- ☐ **immediate**: _____; happening or done without delay
- ☐ **success**: _____; the accomplishment of an aim or purpose
- ☐ **throughout**: _____; in every part or aspect of
- ☐ **life**: _____; the existence of a living being
- ☐ **framework**: _____; a basic structure or support
- ☐ **ideas**: _____; thoughts or concepts that come to mind
- ☐ **attention**: _____; the action of carefully observing or listening
- ☐ **detail**: _____; an individual feature, fact, or item
- ☐ **passed away**: _____; a euphemism for "died"

DR. SIMON'S MAGIC ENGLISH

KEY VOCABULARY | **LEVEL 700 - UNIT 1**

- ☐ **Cro-magnon**: _____; a prehistoric human population that lived in Europe about 40,000 years ago
- ☐ **cave paintings**: _____; artworks created on the walls of caves
- ☐ **created**: _____; made or brought into existence
- ☐ **express**: _____; convey or communicate a thought, feeling, or idea
- ☐ **interesting**: _____; arousing curiosity or attention
- ☐ **forms**: _____; different types or varieties
- ☐ **knew**: _____; possessed knowledge or awareness of something
- ☐ **read**: _____; interpret and understand written or printed matter
- ☐ **write**: _____; mark symbols or letters on a surface to represent words or ideas
- ☐ **found**: _____; discovered or came across something
- ☐ **ways**: _____; methods or means of doing something
- ☐ **incredible**: _____; extraordinary or astonishing
- ☐ **walls**: _____; vertical surfaces that enclose or divide spaces
- ☐ **natural**: _____; existing in or caused by nature
- ☐ **pigments**: _____; colored substances used for coloring or painting
- ☐ **clay**: _____; a type of soil or earth that is malleable when wet
- ☐ **charcoal**: _____; a black, porous form of carbon used as a drawing material
- ☐ **iron oxide**: _____; a compound of iron and oxygen used as a pigment
- ☐ **used**: _____; employed or utilized
- ☐ **apply**: _____; put to use or bring into operation
- ☐ **images**: _____; visual representations or pictures
- ☐ **bison**: _____; large, wild oxen native to North America and Europe
- ☐ **deer**: _____; hoofed grazing animals, often with antlers
- ☐ **horses**: _____; large, domesticated mammals used for riding, racing, or work
- ☐ **handprints**: _____; impressions made by the hand on a surface
- ☐ **communicate**: _____; convey information or exchange ideas or feelings
- ☐ **tell**: _____; convey information or give an account of something
- ☐ **belief**: _____; acceptance or conviction that something is true or exists
- ☐ **world**: _____; the earth and all its inhabitants and phenomena
- ☐ **exist**: _____; have objective reality or being
- ☐ **oldest**: _____; having lived or existed for the longest time
- ☐ **important**: _____; having significant meaning, value, or influence
- ☐ **works**: _____; artistic creations or compositions
- ☐ **scientists**: _____; experts in a particular branch of science
- ☐ **historians**: _____; scholars who study and interpret the past
- ☐ **learn**: _____; acquire knowledge or information about something

KEY VOCABULARY | LEVEL 700 - UNIT 2

- ☐ **neolithic revolution**: _____ ; a significant change in human society characterized by the transition from hunting and gathering to settled farming communities
- ☐ **change**: _____ ; alteration or transformation
- ☐ **nomads**: _____ ; people who move from place to place without a permanent home
- ☐ **traveled**: _____ ; went on a journey or moved from one place to another
- ☐ **place**: _____ ; a specific location or area
- ☐ **looking**: _____ ; searching or seeking
- ☐ **amazing**: _____ ; causing great surprise or wonder
- ☐ **learned**: _____ ; acquired knowledge or skills through study, experience, or teaching
- ☐ **farm**: _____ ; cultivate land and raise crops or animals for food or other resources
- ☐ **stay**: _____ ; remain or continue in a particular place or state
- ☐ **grow**: _____ ; cultivate or produce by natural processes
- ☐ **own**: _____ ; belonging to oneself or itself
- ☐ **plant**: _____ ; put or place seeds in the ground to grow
- ☐ **seeds**: _____ ; small, dormant plants enclosed in a protective outer covering
- ☐ **raise**: _____ ; breed or care for animals for a specific purpose
- ☐ **build**: _____ ; construct or create
- ☐ **houses**: _____ ; structures used as dwellings for human beings
- ☐ **happened**: _____ ; occurred or took place
- ☐ **different**: _____ ; not the same or not alike
- ☐ **parts**: _____ ; separate regions or sections
- ☐ **world**: _____ ; the earth and all its inhabitants and phenomena
- ☐ **later**: _____ ; after a period of time or after the usual or expected time
- ☐ **important**: _____ ; having significant meaning, value, or influence
- ☐ **human**: _____ ; relating to or characteristic of human beings
- ☐ **history**: _____ ; the study of past events, particularly in human affairs
- ☐ **led**: _____ ; served as a cause or catalyst for something
- ☐ **form**: _____ ; establish or create
- ☐ **communities**: _____ ; groups of people living in the same area or having a particular characteristic in common
- ☐ **cities**: _____ ; large and densely populated urban areas
- ☐ **tools**: _____ ; implements or devices used to carry out a particular function or task
- ☐ **weapons**: _____ ; instruments or objects used for attack or defense in combat
- ☐ **metal**: _____ ; a solid material that is typically hard, shiny, malleable, fusible, and ductile
- ☐ **easier**: _____ ; less difficult or demanding
- ☐ **communicate**: _____ ; convey information or exchange ideas or feelings

DR. SIMON'S MAGIC ENGLISH

KEY VOCABULARY | LEVEL 700 - UNIT 3

- ☐ **rise**: _____; the act of going up or becoming higher or greater
- ☐ **class**: _____; a social group or category of people sharing similar characteristics, such as wealth, occupation, or status
- ☐ **ancient**: _____; belonging to the very distant past, typically before the fall of the Roman Empire
- ☐ **civilizations**: _____; advanced societies characterized by complex social and cultural development
- ☐ **divided**: _____; separated or split into different parts or groups
- ☐ **based**: _____; established or founded on
- ☐ **create**: _____; bring into existence or give rise to
- ☐ **emerged**: _____; came into existence or prominence
- ☐ **ruling**: _____; exercising authority or control
- ☐ **charge**: _____; having responsibility or control over something or someone
- ☐ **government**: _____; the governing body of a nation, state, or community
- ☐ **decisions**: _____; choices or judgments made after consideration or discussion
- ☐ **rest**: _____; the remaining part or majority
- ☐ **wealthy**: _____; having a great deal of money, resources, or possessions
- ☐ **fancy**: _____; elaborate or decorative in design, structure, or appearance
- ☐ **owned**: _____; possessed or had legal title to something
- ☐ **businesses**: _____; commercial or industrial enterprises
- ☐ **clothes**: _____; garments worn on the body
- ☐ **merchants**: _____; people involved in buying and selling goods, typically on a large scale
- ☐ **artisans**: _____; skilled workers who produce goods by hand
- ☐ **farmers**: _____; people who cultivate land and raise crops or livestock for food production
- ☐ **support**: _____; provide assistance, comfort, or sustenance to someone or something
- ☐ **slaves**: _____; people who are owned by others and forced to work without pay or freedom
- ☐ **peasants**: _____; agricultural workers or farmers of low social status
- ☐ **freedom**: _____; the power or right to act, speak, or think as one wants
- ☐ **important**: _____; of great significance or value
- ☐ **allowed**: _____; permitted or given authorization to do something
- ☐ **specialize**: _____; focus on a particular area or activity and become highly skilled or knowledgeable in it
- ☐ **different**: _____; not the same as another or each other
- ☐ **experts**: _____; individuals with a high level of knowledge, skill, or proficiency in a particular field
- ☐ **fields**: _____; areas or subjects of study or activity
- ☐ **system**: _____; a set of connected parts forming a complex whole
- ☐ **order**: _____; a state in which everything is arranged or organized according to a particular system or sequence
- ☐ **organization**: _____; a structured arrangement or system of tasks, roles, and relationships within a group or society

KEY VOCABULARY | LEVEL 700 - UNIT 4

- ☐ **invention**: _____; the act or process of creating or discovering something new
- ☐ **communicate**: _____; exchange information or ideas with others
- ☐ **symbols**: _____; visual representations that represent ideas, objects, or concepts
- ☐ **system**: _____; a set of connected parts or elements working together to achieve a common purpose
- ☐ **spoke**: _____; communicated orally or verbally
- ☐ **gestures**: _____; physical movements or signals used to express ideas or emotions
- ☐ **ancient**: _____; belonging to a time long past, typically before the Middle Ages
- ☐ **modern-day**: _____; contemporary; existing or occurring at the present time
- ☐ **created**: _____; brought into existence; made
- ☐ **cuneiform**: _____; a writing system used in ancient Mesopotamia, characterized by wedge-shaped marks
- ☐ **wedge-shaped**: _____; having the shape of a wedge, with a wide end and a pointed end
- ☐ **marks**: _____; distinctive symbols or signs
- ☐ **pressed**: _____; applied pressure to something
- ☐ **clay tablets**: _____; flat pieces of clay used as a medium for writing
- ☐ **stylus**: _____; a pointed tool used for writing or marking on a surface
- ☐ **baked**: _____; cooked or hardened by heat
- ☐ **harden**: _____; become solid or firm
- ☐ **laws**: _____; rules or regulations established by a governing authority
- ☐ **recipes**: _____; instructions for preparing or cooking specific dishes
- ☐ **huge**: _____; extremely large or significant
- ☐ **development**: _____; the process of growth, progress, or advancement
- ☐ **humanity**: _____; the human race; all human beings collectively
- ☐ **allowed**: _____; permitted or made possible
- ☐ **keep records**: _____; maintain written accounts or documentation
- ☐ **pass down**: _____; transmit or hand down from one generation to another
- ☐ **generation**: _____; a group of individuals born and living at the same time
- ☐ **complex**: _____; intricate, involving many interconnected parts or elements
- ☐ **societies**: _____; organized groups of people living together under shared rules and norms
- ☐ **track**: _____; monitor or keep a record of
- ☐ **trade**: _____; the buying and selling of goods and services
- ☐ **taxes**: _____; mandatory contributions levied by governments to fund public expenditures
- ☐ **government**: _____; the governing body or system that exercises authority and control over a nation, state, or community
- ☐ **continued**: _____; ongoing; not stopping or ending
- ☐ **evolve**: _____; develop or change over time
- ☐ **conclusion**: _____; a final or closing part

DR. SIMON'S MAGIC ENGLISH

KEY VOCABULARY | LEVEL 700 - UNIT 5

- ☐ **astronomy**: _____ ; the scientific study of celestial objects, such as stars, planets, and galaxies
- ☐ **planets**: _____ ; celestial bodies that orbit around a star, such as the Earth, Mars, and Jupiter
- ☐ **celestial bodies**: _____ ; objects in space, such as stars, planets, and moons
- ☐ **ancient**: _____ ; belonging to a time long past, typically before the Middle Ages
- ☐ **modern-day**: _____ ; contemporary; existing or occurring at the present time
- ☐ **developed**: _____ ; created or advanced through a systematic process
- ☐ **sophisticated**: _____ ; complex or highly developed
- ☐ **system**: _____ ; a set of connected parts or elements working together to achieve a common purpose
- ☐ **predict**: _____ ; foretell or estimate a future event or occurrence
- ☐ **movements**: _____ ; actions or changes in position
- ☐ **recorded**: _____ ; documented or noted down
- ☐ **clay tablets**: _____ ; flat pieces of clay used as a medium for writing or recording information
- ☐ **preserved**: _____ ; kept safe or protected from harm or decay
- ☐ **calendar**: _____ ; a system for organizing and measuring time, typically based on the movements of celestial bodies
- ☐ **astronomical events**: _____ ; phenomena or occurrences related to celestial bodies, such as eclipses or comets
- ☐ **eclipse**: _____ ; the partial or total blocking of light from a celestial body by another celestial body
- ☐ **important**: _____ ; significant or of great value
- ☐ **divided**: _____ ; separated or split into parts or sections
- ☐ **equal**: _____ ; having the same quantity, size, or value
- ☐ **represented**: _____ ; symbolized or depicted
- ☐ **constellation**: _____ ; a group of stars forming a recognizable pattern or shape
- ☐ **zodiac**: _____ ; a band of the sky divided into twelve equal parts, each represented by a constellation and associated with specific astrological signs
- ☐ **astrology**: _____ ; the study of how the positions and movements of celestial bodies can influence human affairs and personality
- ☐ **influence**: _____ ; the power or effect of someone or something on another
- ☐ **human affairs**: _____ ; matters or events relating to human beings
- ☐ **positions**: _____ ; locations or placements
- ☐ **personality**: _____ ; the combination of characteristics or qualities that form an individual's distinctive character
- ☐ **destiny**: _____ ; the predetermined course of events in a person's life
- ☐ **contributions**: _____ ; valuable additions or contributions
- ☐ **astronomical**: _____ ; relating to astronomy or celestial objects
- ☐ **relationship**: _____ ; the connection, association, or link between two or more things or people

KEY VOCABULARY | LEVEL 700 - UNIT 6

- **famous**: _____; well-known or widely recognized
- **structures**: _____; buildings or constructions
- **huge**: _____; extremely large in size or amount
- **gods**: _____; deities or divine beings worshiped in religions
- **tombs**: _____; burial places or structures for the dead
- **consorts**: _____; spouses or partners
- **soul**: _____; the spiritual or immaterial essence of a person, believed to continue after death
- **ascend**: _____; rise or go up
- **afterlife**: _____; a realm or existence believed to occur after death
- **preserved**: _____; kept intact or protected from decay or damage
- **feat**: _____; an extraordinary or remarkable achievement
- **tools**: _____; implements or devices used to carry out a specific task or function
- **copper**: _____; a reddish-brown metallic element used for making tools and other objects
- **chisels**: _____; cutting tools with a shaped blade, used for carving or shaping materials
- **hammers**: _____; tools with a heavy head and a handle, used for striking or pounding
- **complete**: _____; finish or bring to an end
- **constructed**: _____; built or assembled
- **limestone**: _____; a sedimentary rock composed mainly of calcium carbonate
- **construction**: _____; the process or act of constructing or building something
- **required**: _____; necessary or needed
- **planning**: _____; the act or process of making plans or arrangements
- **organization**: _____; the action or process of organizing or arranging things in a structured manner
- **housed**: _____; provided with accommodation or shelter
- **fed**: _____; provided with food
- **transported**: _____; moved or conveyed from one place to another
- **quarries**: _____; places where stone or minerals are extracted or mined
- **developed**: _____; created or advanced through a systematic process
- **ramps**: _____; sloping or inclined surfaces used for ascending or descending
- **pulleys**: _____; simple machines consisting of a wheel and a rope or chain, used to lift or move heavy objects
- **process**: _____; a series of actions or steps taken to achieve a particular end
- **incredible**: _____; difficult to believe; extraordinary
- **achievement**: _____; a notable or remarkable accomplishment
- **reminder**: _____; something that causes one to remember or think about something else
- **civilization**: _____; an advanced stage of human development characterized by social, cultural, and technological progress
- **existed**: _____; was present or had being

DR. SIMON'S MAGIC ENGLISH

KEY VOCABULARY | LEVEL 700 - UNIT 7

- ☐ **code**: _____; a system of laws or regulations
- ☐ **ruled**: _____; governed or controlled
- ☐ **ancient**: _____; belonging to the distant past; very old
- ☐ **famous**: _____; well-known or widely recognized
- ☐ **creating**: _____; making or bringing into existence
- ☐ **laws**: _____; rules or regulations established by a governing authority
- ☐ **written**: _____; expressed or recorded in writing
- ☐ **huge**: _____; extremely large in size or amount
- ☐ **pillar**: _____; a tall, vertical structure or column
- ☐ **stela**: _____; an upright stone slab or pillar with inscriptions or carvings
- ☐ **placed**: _____; put or set in a particular position or location
- ☐ **center**: _____; the middle or central part of something
- ☐ **made up of**: _____; composed or constituted of
- ☐ **covered**: _____; included or dealt with
- ☐ **aspects**: _____; different facets or elements
- ☐ **property**: _____; belongings or possessions
- ☐ **rights**: _____; entitlements or privileges
- ☐ **relationships**: _____; connections or associations between people
- ☐ **included**: _____; contained or comprised
- ☐ **trade**: _____; the buying and selling of goods or services
- ☐ **agriculture**: _____; the practice of cultivating crops and rearing animals
- ☐ **crime**: _____; an illegal act or offense
- ☐ **harm**: _____; injury or damage caused to someone or something
- ☐ **punishment**: _____; a penalty imposed for wrongdoing
- ☐ **example**: _____; a specific instance or illustration
- ☐ **stole**: _____; took without permission or unlawfully
- ☐ **important**: _____; significant or of great importance
- ☐ **development**: _____; the process of growth or advancement
- ☐ **history**: _____; the study of past events or occurrences
- ☐ **applied**: _____; put into practice or implemented
- ☐ **social status**: _____; one's position or rank in society
- ☐ **enforced**: _____; ensured compliance or obedience
- ☐ **judges**: _____; officials who preside over courts of law
- ☐ **trained**: _____; educated or prepared through instruction or practice
- ☐ **interpret**: _____; explain or understand the meaning of something
- ☐ **conclusion**: _____; a final decision, opinion, or judgment

KEY VOCABULARY | LEVEL 700 - UNIT 8

- **caste**: _____; a social hierarchy or system of divisions based on birth, occupation, and social status
- **social**: _____; relating to society or its organization
- **hierarchy**: _____; a system of ranking or organizing in which people are divided into different levels or classes
- **organizing**: _____; arranging or structuring in a systematic manner
- **occupation**: _____; a person's regular or main job or profession
- **status**: _____; one's position or rank in a social hierarchy
- **specialize**: _____; concentrate on or become an expert in a particular subject or skill
- **trading**: _____; the act of buying and selling goods or services
- **priesthood**: _____; the role or occupation of being a priest or religious leader
- **customs**: _____; traditional practices or behaviors of a particular group or society
- **beliefs**: _____; ideas or principles accepted as true or held by a person or group
- **complex**: _____; intricate or consisting of many interconnected parts
- **rigid**: _____; inflexible or strict in structure or rules
- **highest**: _____; the greatest or most elevated in position, importance, or rank
- **priests**: _____; religious leaders or individuals authorized to perform religious rituals or ceremonies
- **scholars**: _____; learned or knowledgeable individuals
- **followed**: _____; came after or succeeded
- **warriors**: _____; fighters or soldiers
- **rulers**: _____; individuals who have authority or control over others
- **traders**: _____; individuals engaged in buying and selling goods or services
- **laborers**: _____; individuals who perform physical or manual work
- **servants**: _____; individuals employed to perform domestic or personal services for others
- **criticized**: _____; judged or evaluated negatively
- **discriminatory**: _____; showing prejudice or bias against a particular group
- **unfair**: _____; not just or equitable
- **blamed**: _____; held responsible or accountable for
- **perpetuating**: _____; causing to continue or endure
- **poverty**: _____; the state of being extremely poor or lacking resources
- **inequality**: _____; the condition of not being equal, especially in rights, opportunities, or distribution of wealth
- **recent**: _____; happening or having taken place not long ago
- **break down**: _____; dismantle or overcome barriers or divisions
- **barriers**: _____; obstacles or impediments
- **promote**: _____; support or advocate for
- **equality**: _____; the state of being equal in rights, status, or opportunities
- **social justice**: _____; the fair and equitable distribution of resources and opportunities in society

Dr. Simon's Magic English Level 700 | 189

DR. SIMON'S MAGIC ENGLISH

KEY VOCABULARY | **LEVEL 700 - UNIT 9**

- ☐ **militarism**: _____; a belief or policy that places a strong emphasis on military power, discipline, and readiness
- ☐ **city-state**: _____; an independent self-governing city and its surrounding territory
- ☐ **ancient**: _____; belonging to the distant past; very old
- ☐ **military**: _____; relating to armed forces or the profession of soldiers
- ☐ **prowess**: _____; great skill or expertise
- ☐ **soldiers**: _____; individuals who serve in an army or military
- ☐ **value**: _____; consider to be important or beneficial
- ☐ **discipline**: _____; strict training or control to develop obedience, self-control, and orderliness
- ☐ **bravery**: _____; courageous behavior or character
- ☐ **loyalty**: _____; faithfulness or allegiance to a person, group, or cause
- ☐ **state**: _____; a politically organized body of people in a defined territory
- ☐ **focus**: _____; directed attention or emphasis on a particular subject or activity
- ☐ **readiness**: _____; preparedness or willingness to act or respond quickly
- ☐ **barracks**: _____; buildings or facilities where soldiers live and train
- ☐ **march**: _____; walk or proceed with regular steps, especially as part of a military group
- ☐ **formation**: _____; an arrangement or organization of people or things
- ☐ **survive**: _____; continue to live or exist, especially in difficult conditions
- ☐ **toughness**: _____; the quality of being strong, durable, or resilient
- ☐ **willingness**: _____; readiness or eagerness to do something
- ☐ **endure**: _____; withstand or bear something difficult or challenging
- ☐ **hardship**: _____; severe suffering or deprivation
- ☐ **weakness**: _____; the state or condition of lacking strength or vigor
- ☐ **comrades**: _____; companions or colleagues, especially in a military context
- ☐ **army**: _____; a large organized group of soldiers trained for war
- ☐ **feared**: _____; regarded with great awe, reverence, or apprehension
- ☐ **phalanx**: _____; a military formation in which soldiers stood shoulder to shoulder in close ranks
- ☐ **enemy**: _____; a person or group that is hostile or opposed to another
- ☐ **penetrate**: _____; enter or pass through
- ☐ **critics**: _____; individuals who express their disapproval or objections
- ☐ **intense**: _____; very strong or extreme
- ☐ **harsh**: _____; severe or strict in manner, conditions, or treatment
- ☐ **unforgiving**: _____; not willing to forgive or show mercy
- ☐ **society**: _____; a community of individuals living together and sharing common customs, laws, and organizations
- ☐ **appreciate**: _____; recognize the value or significance of
- ☐ **culture**: _____; the customs, arts, social institutions, and achievements of a particular nation, people, or group

KEY VOCABULARY | LEVEL 700 - UNIT 10

- ☐ **electoral**: _____; relating to elections or the process of voting for representatives
- ☐ **democratic**: _____; relating to or advocating democracy, a form of government in which power is vested in the people
- ☐ **government**: _____; the governing body of a nation, state, or community
- ☐ **citizens**: _____; individuals who are recognized as members of a particular country or community and have certain rights and responsibilities
- ☐ **participate**: _____; take part in an activity or event
- ☐ **political**: _____; relating to the government, public affairs, and the exercise of power
- ☐ **voting**: _____; the process of expressing one's choice or opinion by marking a ballot or raising a hand
- ☐ **issues**: _____; subjects or topics that are matters of concern or dispute
- ☐ **electing**: _____; choosing or selecting by vote
- ☐ **officials**: _____; individuals who hold a position of authority or public trust
- ☐ **represent**: _____; act or speak on behalf of others
- ☐ **considered**: _____; regarded or thought of in a particular way
- ☐ **adult**: _____; a fully grown person who has reached the age of maturity
- ☐ **slaves**: _____; individuals who are owned and forced to work by others
- ☐ **foreigners**: _____; people from another country or nation
- ☐ **allowed**: _____; given permission or the right to do something
- ☐ **limited**: _____; restricted or constrained
- ☐ **random**: _____; chosen or occurring without a specific pattern, aim, or reason
- ☐ **selection**: _____; the action of choosing someone or something from a group
- ☐ **serve**: _____; perform duties or fulfill a function
- ☐ **juries**: _____; groups of citizens who are sworn to give a verdict in a legal case
- ☐ **council**: _____; a group of people who meet to discuss, advise, or make decisions
- ☐ **ensured**: _____; made certain or guaranteed
- ☐ **range**: _____; a variety or diversity
- ☐ **addition**: _____; the act or process of adding something
- ☐ **elections**: _____; the process of choosing individuals for public office through voting
- ☐ **qualifications**: _____; the requirements or criteria necessary for eligibility or suitability
- ☐ **perfect**: _____; flawless or without any faults
- ☐ **excluded**: _____; not included or allowed to be a part of something
- ☐ **limits**: _____; restrictions or boundaries
- ☐ **vote**: _____; express one's choice or opinion in an election or decision
- ☐ **inexperienced**: _____; lacking knowledge, skill, or experience
- ☐ **important**: _____; of great significance, value, or consequence
- ☐ **democracy**: _____; a system of government in which power is vested in the people and exercised through elected representatives

DR. SIMON'S MAGIC ENGLISH

KEY VOCABULARY | LEVEL 700 - UNIT 11

- ☐ **spiritual**: _____; relating to the soul, spirit, or religious matters
- ☐ **ancient**: _____; belonging to the distant past
- ☐ **modern-day**: _____; current or present-day
- ☐ **legend**: _____; a traditional story or narrative that is passed down through generations
- ☐ **tusks**: _____; long, curved teeth of certain animals, such as elephants
- ☐ **appeared**: _____; became visible or came into sight
- ☐ **sign**: _____; an indication or evidence of something
- ☐ **give birth**: _____; have a baby or deliver a child
- ☐ **pregnant**: _____; carrying an unborn child in the womb
- ☐ **rest**: _____; relax or take a break from activity
- ☐ **direction**: _____; the course or path along which something moves or points
- ☐ **declared**: _____; announced or stated firmly and confidently
- ☐ **chief**: _____; the leader or highest-ranking person in a group or organization
- ☐ **royal**: _____; relating to or belonging to a monarch or royal family
- ☐ **luxury**: _____; great comfort, elegance, or wealth
- ☐ **grew older**: _____; became older or more mature
- ☐ **teachings**: _____; ideas, principles, or instructions taught by a person
- ☐ **focused**: _____; directed attention or concentration towards something
- ☐ **achieving**: _____; successfully reaching or attaining a goal
- ☐ **enlightenment**: _____; the state of gaining deep knowledge, understanding, or insight
- ☐ **means**: _____; methods or ways of accomplishing something
- ☐ **becoming**: _____; developing or evolving into something
- ☐ **suffering**: _____; experiencing pain, distress, or hardship
- ☐ **finding**: _____; discovering or obtaining something
- ☐ **inner**: _____; relating to the mind, spirit, or personal thoughts and feelings
- ☐ **peace**: _____; a state of tranquility or harmony
- ☐ **followed**: _____; adhered to or observed
- ☐ **path**: _____; a course of action or way of life
- ☐ **major**: _____; significant or important
- ☐ **religions**: _____; systems of faith or worship
- ☐ **estimated**: _____; roughly calculated or approximated
- ☐ **followers**: _____; individuals who believe in and support a person, cause, or ideology
- ☐ **globally**: _____; worldwide or on a global scale
- ☐ **continue**: _____; persist or carry on without interruption
- ☐ **inspire**: _____; encourage, motivate, or stimulate
- ☐ **seek**: _____; search for or strive to obtain

KEY VOCABULARY | LEVEL 700 - UNIT 12

☐ **confucianism**: _____; a philosophy originated in ancient China
☐ **philosophy**: _____; a system of beliefs or principles
☐ **founded**: _____; established or created
☐ **Confucius**: _____; the name of the founder of Confucianism
☐ **importance**: _____; significance or value
☐ **education**: _____; the process of acquiring knowledge and skills
☐ **respect**: _____; admiration or esteem for someone or something
☐ **elders**: _____; older individuals or people of higher age
☐ **maintaining**: _____; preserving or upholding
☐ **social**: _____; relating to society or its organization
☐ **harmony**: _____; a state of peace, agreement, or cooperation
☐ **emphasizes**: _____; gives special importance or focus to
☐ **moral**: _____; relating to principles of right and wrong behavior
☐ **values**: _____; principles or standards considered worthwhile or desirable
☐ **ethics**: _____; principles of moral conduct or behavior
☐ **individuals**: _____; single persons or human beings
☐ **strive**: _____; make great efforts or struggle
☐ **treat**: _____; behave towards or deal with someone
☐ **kindness**: _____; being friendly, generous, or considerate
☐ **prosperous**: _____; successful, thriving, or wealthy
☐ **concept**: _____; an abstract or general idea
☐ **relationships**: _____; connections or associations between people
☐ **ruler**: _____; a person who governs or has authority
☐ **subject**: _____; a person under the rule or authority of another
☐ **profound**: _____; deep, intense, or significant
☐ **influence**: _____; the capacity to have an effect on someone or something
☐ **cultures**: _____; the customs, arts, and social institutions of a particular group
☐ **society**: _____; a community of individuals sharing common customs and values
☐ **shape**: _____; influence or mold
☐ **beliefs**: _____; ideas or convictions held by a person or group
☐ **generation**: _____; a group of individuals born and living at the same time
☐ **continues**: _____; persists or carries on without interruption
☐ **adapted**: _____; modified or adjusted to suit a new purpose or situation
☐ **incorporated**: _____; included or integrated into
☐ **aspects**: _____; different parts or features of something
☐ **politics**: _____; activities related to government and power

Dr. Simon's Magic English Level 700 | 193

DR. SIMON'S MAGIC ENGLISH

KEY VOCABULARY | **LEVEL 700 - UNIT 13**

- ☐ **wars**: _____; a series of battles
- ☐ **battles**: _____; conflicts or engagements between armed forces
- ☐ **significant**: _____; important or notable
- ☐ **impact**: _____; influence or effect
- ☐ **history**: _____; the study of past events
- ☐ **culture**: _____; customs, arts, and social institutions of a particular group
- ☐ **empire**: _____; a powerful state in ancient times
- ☐ **territory**: _____; land or region under control
- ☐ **conquering**: _____; subduing or taking control of
- ☐ **determined**: _____; having a strong resolve or purpose
- ☐ **defend**: _____; protect or guard against attack or threat
- ☐ **freedom**: _____; the state of being free or independent
- ☐ **way of life**: _____; a person's habits, customs, and values
- ☐ **divided**: _____; separated or split into parts
- ☐ **revolt**: _____; rebellion against the existing rule
- ☐ **rebellion**: _____; an act of resistance against authority
- ☐ **city-states**: _____; independent cities and their surrounding territories
- ☐ **rule**: _____; governance or control
- ☐ **invaded**: _____; entered forcefully or aggressively
- ☐ **victorious**: _____; having achieved victory or success
- ☐ **preserve**: _____; protect or maintain
- ☐ **independence**: _____; freedom or autonomy
- ☐ **strengthen**: _____; make stronger or more robust
- ☐ **sense of unity**: _____; feeling of togetherness or solidarity
- ☐ **development**: _____; growth or advancement
- ☐ **democratic**: _____; relating to a system of government where power is vested in the people
- ☐ **governments**: _____; systems or organizations for ruling a state or nation
- ☐ **rest of the world**: _____; other regions or countries
- ☐ **decline**: _____; gradual decrease or weakening
- ☐ **rise**: _____; ascension or emergence
- ☐ **spread**: _____; diffusion or dissemination
- ☐ **throughout**: _____; in every part or all over

KEY VOCABULARY | **LEVEL 700 - UNIT 14**

- ☐ **philosopher**: _____; a person who seeks wisdom and knowledge through rational inquiry
- ☐ **questions**: _____; inquiries or interrogations
- ☐ **truth**: _____; the state or quality of being in accordance with fact or reality
- ☐ **world**: _____; the planet Earth and everything that exists on it
- ☐ **asking**: _____; posing or inquiring about something
- ☐ **think**: _____; engage in mental activity or contemplation
- ☐ **deeply**: _____; profoundly or thoroughly
- ☐ **wrote**: _____; composed or recorded in written form
- ☐ **know**: _____; have knowledge or awareness of
- ☐ **famous**: _____; well-known or widely recognized
- ☐ **students**: _____; individuals who are taught by a teacher
- ☐ **ideas**: _____; concepts or thoughts
- ☐ **people**: _____; individuals or human beings
- ☐ **help**: _____; assist or aid
- ☐ **believe**: _____; have faith or confidence in something
- ☐ **ability**: _____; the power or skill to do something
- ☐ **care**: _____; be concerned or interested in
- ☐ **money**: _____; currency or wealth
- ☐ **material possessions**: _____; physical belongings or property
- ☐ **knowledge**: _____; information, understanding, or awareness
- ☐ **unfortunately**: _____; regrettably or sadly
- ☐ **some**: _____; a portion or number of people
- ☐ **trial**: _____; a formal examination of evidence in court
- ☐ **sentenced**: _____; declared punishment or penalty
- ☐ **death**: _____; the cessation of life
- ☐ **beliefs**: _____; convictions or opinions
- ☐ **powerful**: _____; having great influence or control
- ☐ **city**: _____; a large human settlement
- ☐ **drank**: _____; consumed liquid, specifically poison in this context
- ☐ **poison**: _____; a substance that can cause injury, illness, or death
- ☐ **died**: _____; ceased to live or exist
- ☐ **age**: _____; the length of time a person has lived
- ☐ **tragic**: _____; characterized by sorrow or suffering
- ☐ **remembered**: _____; kept in one's memory or honored
- ☐ **questioning**: _____; challenging or inquiring about something

DR. SIMON'S MAGIC ENGLISH

KEY VOCABULARY | LEVEL 700 - UNIT 15

- ☐ **emperor**: _____ ; a supreme ruler of an empire
- ☐ **unified**: _____ ; brought together or made into a single entity
- ☐ **ruler**: _____ ; a person who exercises power or authority over others
- ☐ **dynasty**: _____ ; a line of rulers from the same family
- ☐ **divided**: _____ ; separated or split into parts
- ☐ **states**: _____ ; distinct political entities or regions
- ☐ **war**: _____ ; armed conflict or hostilities
- ☐ **army**: _____ ; a large organized military force
- ☐ **conquer**: _____ ; defeat or subdue by force
- ☐ **unite**: _____ ; bring together or join as a whole
- ☐ **country**: _____ ; a nation or sovereign state
- ☐ **implemented**: _____ ; put into effect or action
- ☐ **changes**: _____ ; alterations or modifications
- ☐ **standardized**: _____ ; made uniform or consistent
- ☐ **language**: _____ ; a system of communication
- ☐ **currency**: _____ ; a form of money
- ☐ **measurements**: _____ ; units of size or quantity
- ☐ **public works**: _____ ; infrastructure projects for the benefit of the public
- ☐ **projects**: _____ ; planned and organized endeavors
- ☐ **roads**: _____ ; routes for transportation
- ☐ **canals**: _____ ; artificial waterways
- ☐ **tomb**: _____ ; a burial place or grave
- ☐ **terracotta**: _____ ; baked clay or ceramic
- ☐ **soldiers**: _____ ; individuals serving in the military
- ☐ **protect**: _____ ; safeguard or defend from harm
- ☐ **afterlife**: _____ ; the existence believed to follow death
- ☐ **attraction**: _____ ; something that draws interest or attention
- ☐ **controversial**: _____ ; causing disagreement or dispute
- ☐ **harsh**: _____ ; severe or cruel
- ☐ **treatment**: _____ ; the manner in which someone is dealt with
- ☐ **subjects**: _____ ; individuals under the rule or authority of a leader
- ☐ **executing**: _____ ; putting to death as a punishment
- ☐ **opposed**: _____ ; in conflict or disagreement with
- ☐ **ordered**: _____ ; commanded or directed
- ☐ **burning**: _____ ; setting on fire
- ☐ **critical**: _____ ; expressing disapproval or unfavorable opinions

KEY VOCABULARY | LEVEL 700 - UNIT 16

- ☐ **uprising**: _____ ; a rebellion or revolt against authority
- ☐ **gladiator**: _____ ; a person trained to fight in public games
- ☐ **slave**: _____ ; a person who is owned by another person and forced to work
- ☐ **revolt**: _____ ; a violent uprising against a ruler or authority
- ☐ **sold**: _____ ; transferred or traded in exchange for money or goods
- ☐ **slavery**: _____ ; the state of being owned and controlled by another person
- ☐ **trained**: _____ ; instructed or prepared for a specific purpose or skill
- ☐ **oppressors**: _____ ; those who subject others to cruel or unjust treatment
- ☐ **training school**: _____ ; an institution for instruction or preparation
- ☐ **gathered**: _____ ; assembled or brought together
- ☐ **followers**: _____ ; people who support and follow a leader or cause
- ☐ **army**: _____ ; a large organized military force
- ☐ **rebels**: _____ ; individuals who resist or oppose authority
- ☐ **defeated**: _____ ; overcome or beaten in a battle or contest
- ☐ **made up of**: _____ ; consisting of or composed of
- ☐ **freedom**: _____ ; the state of being free or liberated
- ☐ **support**: _____ ; assistance, backing, or endorsement
- ☐ **farmers**: _____ ; individuals who cultivate land and grow crops
- ☐ **urban workers**: _____ ; people employed in non-agricultural jobs in cities
- ☐ **unhappy**: _____ ; dissatisfied or not pleased
- ☐ **government**: _____ ; the system or group governing a state or nation
- ☐ **freedom fighter**: _____ ; a person who fights for liberty and against oppression
- ☐ **military strategist**: _____ ; an expert in planning and executing military operations
- ☐ **outnumbered**: _____ ; having fewer numbers or forces than the opponent
- ☐ **luck**: _____ ; fortunate circumstances or events
- ☐ **legacy**: _____ ; a lasting impact or influence left behind by someone
- ☐ **inspired**: _____ ; motivated or influenced by someone or something
- ☐ **resistance**: _____ ; the act of opposing or fighting against something
- ☐ **hope**: _____ ; a feeling of optimism or expectation

DR. SIMON'S MAGIC ENGLISH

KEY VOCABULARY | LEVEL 700 - UNIT 17

- ☐ **battle**: _____ ; a violent confrontation between opposing forces
- ☐ **naval**: _____ ; relating to the navy or warships
- ☐ **significant**: _____ ; important or noteworthy
- ☐ **Roman Emperor**: _____ ; the ruler of the Roman Empire
- ☐ **forces**: _____ ; military units or troops
- ☐ **allied**: _____ ; joined together in a cooperative relationship
- ☐ **powerful**: _____ ; having great strength or influence
- ☐ **empire**: _____ ; a group of territories ruled by a single authority
- ☐ **eastern**: _____ ; the region to the east
- ☐ **Mediterranean**: _____ ; the region surrounding the Mediterranean Sea
- ☐ **opposed**: _____ ; in conflict or disagreement with
- ☐ **Roman Senate**: _____ ; the governing body of ancient Rome
- ☐ **fleet**: _____ ; a group of ships
- ☐ **attacked**: _____ ; engaged in aggressive action against
- ☐ **ships**: _____ ; vessels used for transportation or warfare on water
- ☐ **superior**: _____ ; higher in quality, skill, or strength
- ☐ **tactics**: _____ ; strategies or methods used in a battle or conflict
- ☐ **better-trained**: _____ ; possessing superior training or instruction
- ☐ **sailors**: _____ ; individuals who navigate or operate ships at sea
- ☐ **retreated**: _____ ; withdrew or moved back
- ☐ **troops**: _____ ; soldiers or armed forces
- ☐ **decisive**: _____ ; settling an issue or dispute
- ☐ **victory**: _____ ; a triumph or success in a battle or contest
- ☐ **undisputed**: _____ ; accepted without question or dispute
- ☐ **ruler**: _____ ; a person who exercises authority or control
- ☐ **territories**: _____ ; regions or lands under the rule of a particular authority
- ☐ **defeat**: _____ ; the act of being overcome or vanquished
- ☐ **Roman Republic**: _____ ; the period of Roman history before the Roman Empire
- ☐ **beginning**: _____ ; the start or commencement
- ☐ **consequences**: _____ ; outcomes or results of an action or event
- ☐ **dominant**: _____ ; exercising control or influence over others
- ☐ **ambitions**: _____ ; aspirations or goals

KEY VOCABULARY | LEVEL 700 - UNIT 18

- ☐ **country**: _____; a defined geographic area with its own government
- ☐ **celebrated**: _____; observed or honored with festivities or ceremonies
- ☐ **holiday**: _____; a special day of celebration or observance
- ☐ **called**: _____; named or referred to as
- ☐ **visited**: _____; received a visit from someone
- ☐ **angel**: _____; a spiritual being often portrayed as a messenger of God
- ☐ **told**: _____; informed or conveyed information
- ☐ **special**: _____; unique, extraordinary, or exceptional
- ☐ **engaged**: _____; formally committed to marrying someone
- ☐ **traveled**: _____; journeyed or went on a trip
- ☐ **hometown**: _____; the town or city where a person was born or grew up
- ☐ **arrived**: _____; reached a destination or arrived at a place
- ☐ **found**: _____; discovered or came upon something
- ☐ **inns**: _____; establishments providing lodging or accommodations
- ☐ **full**: _____; occupied or at maximum capacity
- ☐ **stable**: _____; a building or structure for housing animals
- ☐ **swaddling clothes**: _____; strips of cloth used to wrap a baby
- ☐ **laid**: _____; placed or put down
- ☐ **manger**: _____; a trough or container for feeding animals
- ☐ **feeding trough**: _____; a container used for providing food to animals
- ☐ **appeared**: _____; became visible or made an appearance
- ☐ **shepherds**: _____; individuals who tend and care for sheep
- ☐ **flocks**: _____; groups of sheep or other animals
- ☐ **nearby**: _____; close or in close proximity
- ☐ **savior**: _____; a person who saves or delivers others from harm
- ☐ **hurried**: _____; moved quickly or rushed
- ☐ **filled**: _____; completely occupied or permeated
- ☐ **joy**: _____; a feeling of great happiness or delight
- ☐ **praised**: _____; expressed approval or admiration for someone or something
- ☐ **God**: _____; the supreme being or deity in monotheistic religions
- ☐ **wonderful**: _____; exceptionally good, marvelous, or remarkable
- ☐ **religion**: _____; a system of beliefs and practices concerning the divine or supernatural
- ☐ **reminds**: _____; brings something back to one's attention or memory
- ☐ **celebrate**: _____; observe or mark a special occasion with joy or festivity
- ☐ **kindness**: _____; the quality of being friendly, generous, or considerate

Dr. Simon's Magic English Level 700

DR. SIMON'S MAGIC ENGLISH

KEY VOCABULARY | **LEVEL 700 - UNIT 19**

- ☐ **essential**: _____; necessary or of great importance
- ☐ **material**: _____; a substance or matter used to create something
- ☐ **readily available**: _____; easily accessible or obtainable
- ☐ **different**: _____; not the same or distinct from others
- ☐ **record**: _____; document or preserve information
- ☐ **information**: _____; knowledge or data about something
- ☐ **papyrus**: _____; a material made from the stems of the papyrus plant, used for writing in ancient times
- ☐ **inventor**: _____; a person who creates or develops something new
- ☐ **imperial official**: _____; a person holding a position in the imperial government
- ☐ **expertise**: _____; specialized knowledge or skill in a particular field
- ☐ **textiles**: _____; materials or fabrics produced by weaving or knitting
- ☐ **tasked**: _____; assigned or given a specific duty or job
- ☐ **high demand**: _____; a situation where there is a great desire or need for something
- ☐ **experimented**: _____; conducted tests or trials to gather information
- ☐ **processes**: _____; a series of actions or steps to achieve a particular result
- ☐ **discovering**: _____; finding or uncovering something previously unknown
- ☐ **pulp**: _____; a soft, wet mixture of fibers
- ☐ **mulberry bark**: _____; the inner layer of the bark of the mulberry tree
- ☐ **rags**: _____; small pieces of cloth, typically old or torn
- ☐ **hemp fibers**: _____; strong fibers obtained from the hemp plant
- ☐ **pressed**: _____; squeezed or flattened with pressure
- ☐ **thin**: _____; having a small distance between opposite sides or surfaces
- ☐ **sheets**: _____; flat, thin pieces of material
- ☐ **refined**: _____; improved or made more precise
- ☐ **sizing agent**: _____; a substance added to control the absorption and strength of paper
- ☐ **durable**: _____; able to withstand wear, pressure, or damage
- ☐ **revolutionized**: _____; completely changed or transformed
- ☐ **communicated**: _____; conveyed or shared information or ideas
- ☐ **convenient**: _____; easy to use or access
- ☐ **affordable**: _____; reasonably priced or within financial reach
- ☐ **spread**: _____; extended or disseminated
- ☐ **countless**: _____; too numerous to be counted
- ☐ **purposes**: _____; reasons or intended uses
- ☐ **packaging**: _____; a material used to protect and contain products
- ☐ **innovative**: _____; characterized by introducing new ideas or methods

KEY VOCABULARY | LEVEL 700 - UNIT 20

- ☐ **edict**: _____; an official order or proclamation issued by a person in authority
- ☐ **important**: _____; significant or of great importance
- ☐ **event**: _____; a happening or occurrence
- ☐ **christianity**: _____; the religion based on the life and teachings of Jesus Christ
- ☐ **issued**: _____; formally released or published
- ☐ **granted**: _____; gave or allowed
- ☐ **religious tolerance**: _____; the acceptance and freedom of practicing different religions
- ☐ **empire**: _____; a group of territories under the rule of a single authority
- ☐ **persecuted**: _____; subjected to hostility or ill-treatment
- ☐ **authorities**: _____; those in power or in a position of control
- ☐ **threat**: _____; something that poses danger or harm
- ☐ **traditional**: _____; relating to or based on customs and practices that have been handed down through generations
- ☐ **religion**: _____; a system of beliefs and worship
- ☐ **emperor**: _____; the ruler of an empire
- ☐ **imprisoned**: _____; confined or held captive
- ☐ **places of worship**: _____; locations where religious ceremonies and practices take place
- ☐ **destroyed**: _____; ruined or completely demolished
- ☐ **vision**: _____; a supernatural or extraordinary perception
- ☐ **cross**: _____; a geometrical figure consisting of two intersecting lines
- ☐ **conquer**: _____; overcome or defeat
- ☐ **battle**: _____; a violent confrontation between opposing forces
- ☐ **support**: _____; endorse or assist
- ☐ **declared**: _____; officially announced or proclaimed
- ☐ **practice**: _____; engage in an activity or behavior
- ☐ **fear**: _____; a feeling of apprehension or unease
- ☐ **persecution**: _____; the act of subjecting someone to hostility or ill-treatment based on their beliefs
- ☐ **ordered**: _____; commanded or directed
- ☐ **return**: _____; give back or restore
- ☐ **confiscated**: _____; taken away or seized by authority
- ☐ **property**: _____; belongings or possessions
- ☐ **rebuilding**: _____; the act of constructing again or restoring
- ☐ **turning point**: _____; a moment of significant change or shift
- ☐ **recognized**: _____; acknowledged or identified
- ☐ **accepted**: _____; received with approval or agreement
- ☐ **paved the way**: _____; prepared the groundwork or created favorable conditions
- ☐ **dominant**: _____; having the greatest influence or control

Dr. Simon's Magic English Level 700 | 201

DR. SIMON'S MAGIC ENGLISH

KEY VOCABULARY | LEVEL 700 - UNIT 21

- ☐ **fall**: _____; the decline or downfall of something
- ☐ **empire**: _____; a group of territories under the rule of a single authority
- ☐ **powerful**: _____; having great strength or influence
- ☐ **history**: _____; the study of past events and their significance
- ☐ **collapsed**: _____; fell apart or disintegrated
- ☐ **factors**: _____; elements or circumstances that contribute to a result
- ☐ **economic**: _____; relating to the production, distribution, and consumption of goods and services
- ☐ **troubles**: _____; problems or difficulties
- ☐ **money**: _____; currency or wealth
- ☐ **spending**: _____; using money to buy goods or services
- ☐ **military**: _____; relating to armed forces or warfare
- ☐ **strong**: _____; powerful or capable
- ☐ **defend**: _____; protect from harm or danger
- ☐ **invaders**: _____; those who enter a territory by force
- ☐ **disease**: _____; an illness or medical condition
- ☐ **famine**: _____; a scarcity of food leading to widespread hunger and starvation
- ☐ **political**: _____; relating to government or the activities of those in power
- ☐ **corruption**: _____; dishonest or unethical behavior by those in positions of power
- ☐ **emperors**: _____; rulers of an empire
- ☐ **assassinated**: _____; killed or murdered
- ☐ **instability**: _____; lack of stability or constant change
- ☐ **final blow**: _____; the ultimate or decisive action that leads to a downfall
- ☐ **barbarian**: _____; a term used to describe a person from a non-Roman culture
- ☐ **overthrew**: _____; remove from power by force
- ☐ **exist**: _____; be present or continue to be in existence
- ☐ **collapse**: _____; fall apart or crumble
- ☐ **legacy**: _____; something handed down or inherited from the past
- ☐ **art**: _____; creative expression through visual or performing arts
- ☐ **literature**: _____; written works of artistic or intellectual value
- ☐ **philosophy**: _____; the study of fundamental questions about existence, knowledge, values, and reality
- ☐ **technology**: _____; the application of scientific knowledge for practical purposes
- ☐ **influence**: _____; the power to shape or affect something
- ☐ **Western civilization**: _____; the cultural, economic, and political heritage of Western Europe and countries influenced by it.

KEY VOCABULARY | LEVEL 700 - UNIT 22

- ☐ **migration period**: _____; a historical period characterized by the movement and migration of various Germanic tribes
- ☐ **barbarian invasions**: _____; another term used to refer to the Migration Period, highlighting the movements of Germanic tribes across Europe
- ☐ **tribe**: _____; a social group comprising families or communities linked by common culture, ancestry, and traditions
- ☐ **migrate**: _____; move from one region or place to another, often with the intention of settling in a new area
- ☐ **spread**: _____; extend or distribute over an area or among a group of people
- ☐ **continent**: _____; one of the main landmasses on Earth, usually identified as large and continuous
- ☐ **collapse**: _____; the sudden and complete breakdown or failure of a system, structure, or organization
- ☐ **reasons**: _____; causes or explanations for particular actions or events
- ☐ **entirely**: _____; completely or wholly
- ☐ **historians**: _____; scholars or experts who study and interpret the past
- ☐ **suggest**: _____; propose or put forward as a possibility or idea
- ☐ **searching**: _____; looking for or seeking something
- ☐ **settle**: _____; establish a permanent residence or community
- ☐ **fleeing**: _____; escaping or running away from a dangerous or threatening situation
- ☐ **invading**: _____; entering forcefully or aggressively with the intent to conquer or occupy
- ☐ **skilled**: _____; possessing a high level of ability or proficiency in a particular skill or field
- ☐ **warfare**: _____; the activity or process of engaging in armed conflict or war
- ☐ **excellent**: _____; exceptionally good or outstanding
- ☐ **horsemen**: _____; skilled riders or cavalry soldiers
- ☐ **clashed**: _____; engaged in conflict or fought against each other
- ☐ **conquered**: _____; defeated and gained control over a territory or people
- ☐ **sacked**: _____; attacked and plundered with great violence and destruction
- ☐ **emperor**: _____; the supreme ruler of an empire or state
- ☐ **overthrown**: _____; removed forcibly or ousted from power
- ☐ **thrive**: _____; grow, develop, or prosper vigorously
- ☐ **significant**: _____; important, notable, or having a considerable impact
- ☐ **impact**: _____; the effect or influence that something has on someone or something else
- ☐ **kingdoms**: _____; political entities ruled by a king or queen
- ☐ **emerged**: _____; came into existence or became known or visible
- ☐ **basis**: _____; the fundamental or underlying support or foundation
- ☐ **modern-day**: _____; pertaining to the present time or contemporary era

DR. SIMON'S MAGIC ENGLISH

KEY VOCABULARY | LEVEL 700 - UNIT 23

- ☐ **establishment**: _____ ; the act of establishing something or being established
- ☐ **feudal**: _____ ; relating to or characteristic of feudalism, a medieval European political and economic system
- ☐ **medieval**: _____ ; relating to the Middle Ages, the period in European history from the 5th to the 15th century
- ☐ **government**: _____ ; the governing body of a nation, state, or community
- ☐ **created**: _____ ; brought into existence
- ☐ **provide**: _____ ; make available for use; supply
- ☐ **protection**: _____ ; the action of protecting someone or something, or the state of being protected
- ☐ **organization**: _____ ; the action of organizing something
- ☐ **core**: _____ ; the central or most important part of something
- ☐ **hierarchy**: _____ ; a system or organization in which people or groups are ranked according to their status or authority
- ☐ **knight**: _____ ; a man who served his sovereign or lord as a mounted soldier in armor
- ☐ **peasant**: _____ ; a poor farmer of low social status who owns or rents a small piece of land for cultivation
- ☐ **grant**: _____ ; agree to give or allow something requested to
- ☐ **exchange**: _____ ; give something and receive something of the same kind in return
- ☐ **military**: _____ ; relating to or characteristic of soldiers or armed forces
- ☐ **shelter**: _____ ; a place giving temporary protection from bad weather or danger
- ☐ **return**: _____ ; come or go back to a place or person
- ☐ **bottom**: _____ ; the lowest point or part of something
- ☐ **laborer**: _____ ; a person doing unskilled manual work for wages
- ☐ **owned**: _____ ; had possession or ownership of
- ☐ **crop**: _____ ; a cultivated plant that is grown as food, especially a grain, fruit, or vegetable
- ☐ **rest**: _____ ; cease work or movement in order to relax, refresh oneself, or recover strength
- ☐ **society**: _____ ; the aggregate of people living together in a more or less ordered community
- ☐ **stability**: _____ ; the state of being stable; firmly established
- ☐ **freedom**: _____ ; the power or right to act, speak, or think as one wants without hindrance or restraint
- ☐ **station**: _____ ; a person's social position or rank in relation to others
- ☐ **evolved**: _____ ; developed gradually, especially from a simple to a more complex form
- ☐ **decline**: _____ ; become smaller, fewer, or less; decrease
- ☐ **replaced**: _____ ; took the place of
- ☐ **legacy**: _____ ; an amount of money or property left to someone in a will; a thing handed down by a predecessor
- ☐ **aspects**: _____ ; particular parts or features of something

KEY VOCABULARY | LEVEL 700 - UNIT 24

- ☐ **manorial**: _____; relating to or characteristic of a manor or the manorial system
- ☐ **organizing**: _____; arranging systematically; ordering
- ☐ **society**: _____; the aggregate of people living together in a more or less ordered community
- ☐ **middle ages**: _____; the period of European history from the 5th to the 15th century, often considered a time of cultural and societal transition
- ☐ **self-sufficient**: _____; able to supply one's own needs without external assistance
- ☐ **estate**: _____; a large area of land in the countryside, usually owned by a single person or family
- ☐ **lord**: _____; a man of noble rank or high social position
- ☐ **responsible**: _____; having an obligation to do something or take care of someone
- ☐ **providing**: _____; making available for use; supplying
- ☐ **peasant**: _____; a poor farmer of low social status who owns or rents a small piece of land for cultivation
- ☐ **protection**: _____; the action of protecting someone or something, or the state of being protected
- ☐ **justice**: _____; just behavior or treatment; fairness
- ☐ **exchange**: _____; give something and receive something of the same kind in return
- ☐ **labor**: _____; work, especially physical work
- ☐ **loyalty**: _____; a strong feeling of support or allegiance
- ☐ **divide**: _____; separate or be separated into parts
- ☐ **meadows**: _____; pieces of grassland, especially ones used for hay
- ☐ **village**: _____; a group of houses and associated buildings, larger than a hamlet and smaller than a town, situated in a rural area
- ☐ **task**: _____; a piece of work to be done or undertaken
- ☐ **assigned**: _____; allocated or designated
- ☐ **law**: _____; a system of rules recognized by a community or country as regulating the actions of its members
- ☐ **collect**: _____; bring or gather together
- ☐ **administer**: _____; manage and be responsible for the running of
- ☐ **right**: _____; a moral or legal entitlement to have or do something
- ☐ **required**: _____; needed to be done; compulsory
- ☐ **stability**: _____; the state of being stable; firmly established
- ☐ **security**: _____; the state of being free from danger or threat
- ☐ **perpetuated**: _____; made something, typically an undesirable situation or an unfounded belief continue indefinitely
- ☐ **inequality**: _____; lack of equality; disparity
- ☐ **limited**: _____; restricted in size, amount, or extent
- ☐ **individual**: _____; single; separate

DR. SIMON'S MAGIC ENGLISH

KEY VOCABULARY | **LEVEL 700 - UNIT 25**

- ☐ **founder**: _____; a person who establishes or originates something
- ☐ **islam**: _____; a monotheistic religion founded by Muhammad
- ☐ **practiced**: _____; engaged in a regular activity or custom
- ☐ **religion**: _____; a particular system of faith and worship
- ☐ **billion**: _____; a thousand million
- ☐ **founded**: _____; established or set up
- ☐ **shepherd**: _____; a person who tends and herds sheep
- ☐ **merchant**: _____; a person involved in trade or commerce
- ☐ **vision**: _____; an experience of seeing something in a dream or trance
- ☐ **angel**: _____; a spiritual being believed to act as a messenger of God
- ☐ **prophet**: _____; a person regarded as an inspired teacher or proclaimer of the will of God
- ☐ **preach**: _____; deliver a religious talk or discourse
- ☐ **received**: _____; be given, presented with, or paid
- ☐ **God**: _____; the supreme being, creator, and ruler of the universe
- ☐ **holy**: _____; dedicated or consecrated to God or a religious purpose
- ☐ **follow**: _____; go or come after a person or thing
- ☐ **righteous**: _____; morally right or justifiable
- ☐ **challenges**: _____; difficult tasks or situations that require effort to overcome
- ☐ **persecuted**: _____; subject to hostility and ill-treatment, especially because of religious or political beliefs
- ☐ **followers**: _____; people who believe in and support a particular person or cause
- ☐ **eventually**: _____; in the end, especially after a long delay, dispute, or series of problems
- ☐ **forced**: _____; compelled or coerced into doing something
- ☐ **leave**: _____; go away from a place
- ☐ **travel**: _____; go on a journey
- ☐ **journey**: _____; a traveling from one place to another, usually taking a long time
- ☐ **known**: _____; recognized, familiar, or within the scope of knowledge
- ☐ **beginning**: _____; the point in time or space at which something starts
- ☐ **calendar**: _____; a system of organizing and measuring time
- ☐ **continued**: _____; carried on or persisted in an activity or process
- ☐ **spread**: _____; extend over a large or increasing area or group of people
- ☐ **death**: _____; the permanent cessation of all vital functions
- ☐ **teachings**: _____; ideas or principles taught or advocated as a subject of instruction
- ☐ **major**: _____; important, serious, or significant

KEY VOCABULARY | LEVEL 700 - UNIT 26

- ☐ **islamic**: _____; relating to Islam, a monotheistic religion founded by Muhammad
- ☐ **empires**: _____; large political entities or states ruled by an emperor or empress
- ☐ **refer**: _____; mention or allude to
- ☐ **various**: _____; different kinds or types
- ☐ **prophet**: _____; a person regarded as an inspired teacher or proclaimer of the will of God
- ☐ **significant**: _____; important, meaningful, or notable
- ☐ **muslim**: _____; a follower of the religion of Islam
- ☐ **achievements**: _____; things accomplished or successfully completed
- ☐ **influence**: _____; the capacity to have an effect on the character, development, or behavior of someone or something
- ☐ **societies**: _____; organized groups of people with shared customs, values, and institutions
- ☐ **capital**: _____; the most important city or town of a country or region, usually the seat of government
- ☐ **scholarship**: _____; academic study or achievement; learning at a high level
- ☐ **translation**: _____; the act or process of rendering written or spoken text from one language into another
- ☐ **preserve**: _____; maintain or keep intact, protect from harm or loss
- ☐ **knowledge**: _____; information, skills, and understanding acquired through experience or education
- ☐ **military**: _____; relating to the armed forces or war
- ☐ **prowess**: _____; exceptional or superior skill or ability
- ☐ **expand**: _____; become larger in size, number, or amount; grow or extend
- ☐ **territory**: _____; an area of land under the jurisdiction of a ruler or state
- ☐ **conquests**: _____; acts of taking control or possession of a place through military force
- ☐ **renowned**: _____; famous or well-known for something
- ☐ **architecture**: _____; the art or practice of designing and constructing buildings
- ☐ **legacy**: _____; something handed down or inherited from a predecessor or the past
- ☐ **religious**: _____; relating to or concerned with religion
- ☐ **belief**: _____; acceptance that something is true or exists
- ☐ **promotion**: _____; the act of supporting, advocating, or advancing something
- ☐ **cultural**: _____; relating to the arts, customs, and social institutions of a particular group or society
- ☐ **contribution**: _____; a gift or payment made to a common fund or collection
- ☐ **development**: _____; the process of growing, evolving, or becoming more advanced
- ☐ **overall**: _____; considering or including everything or everyone
- ☐ **heritage**: _____; the traditions, achievements, beliefs, etc., that are part of the history of a group or nation

DR. SIMON'S MAGIC ENGLISH

KEY VOCABULARY | LEVEL 700 - UNIT 27

- ☐ **empress**: _____ ; a female ruler or monarch
- ☐ **concubine**: _____ ; a woman in a polygamous relationship with a man
- ☐ **nunnery**: _____ ; a place where nuns live and practice religious devotion
- ☐ **politics**: _____ ; the activities, actions, and policies used to gain and hold power in a government or to influence the government
- ☐ **intelligence**: _____ ; the ability to acquire, understand, and apply knowledge and skills
- ☐ **reforms**: _____ ; changes made to improve a system or institution
- ☐ **establishment**: _____ ; the creation or formation of something
- ☐ **secretariat**: _____ ; a department responsible for administrative or secretarial work
- ☐ **state affairs**: _____ ; matters relating to the administration and governance of a state or country
- ☐ **implementing**: _____ ; putting into effect or carrying out
- ☐ **policies**: _____ ; principles or rules used to guide decisions and actions
- ☐ **abolished**: _____ ; officially ended or put an end to
- ☐ **flogging**: _____ ; beating or whipping as a form of punishment
- ☐ **corporal punishment**: _____ ; physical punishment inflicted on a person's body as a penalty for an offense
- ☐ **merit-based**: _____ ; a system of evaluation or advancement based on individual abilities, achievements, or qualifications
- ☐ **conquests**: _____ ; acts of taking control or possession of a place through military force
- ☐ **trade route**: _____ ; a path or series of paths used for the transportation of goods between countries or regions
- ☐ **buddhist temples**: _____ ; places of worship for followers of Buddhism
- ☐ **monuments**: _____ ; structures or statues that commemorate or honor a person or event
- ☐ **patronage**: _____ ; support or financial assistance given to an individual or group, often for artistic or cultural purposes
- ☐ **opposition**: _____ ; resistance or disagreement
- ☐ **confucian scholars**: _____ ; scholars who adhere to the teachings and philosophy of Confucianism
- ☐ **political intrigue**: _____ ; secretive or complex political schemes or plots
- ☐ **accusations**: _____ ; claims or charges made against someone, often alleging wrongdoing
- ☐ **murder**: _____ ; the unlawful killing of a person
- ☐ **treachery**: _____ ; betrayal of trust or loyalty
- ☐ **legacy**: _____ ; something handed down or inherited from a predecessor or the past
- ☐ **ruthless**: _____ ; showing no mercy or compassion, harsh or cruel
- ☐ **dictator**: _____ ; a ruler who has complete control and power, often obtained and maintained by force
- ☐ **eliminated**: _____ ; removed or got rid of completely
- ☐ **opponents**: _____ ; individuals or groups who are against or compete with someone in a contest or conflict

KEY VOCABULARY | LEVEL 700 - UNIT 28

- ☐ **humiliation**: _____; the act of being made to feel ashamed, embarrassed, or degraded
- ☐ **medieval**: _____; relating to the Middle Ages, a period in European history between the 5th and 15th centuries
- ☐ **pope**: _____; the head of the Catholic Church
- ☐ **Holy Roman Emperor**: _____; the ruler of the Holy Roman Empire, a political entity in central Europe during the Middle Ages
- ☐ **conflict**: _____; a disagreement or struggle between two or more parties
- ☐ **power struggle**: _____; a competition or contest for authority or control
- ☐ **appoint**: _____; assign or designate someone to a position or role
- ☐ **bishops**: _____; high-ranking officials within the Catholic Church who oversee a specific region or diocese
- ☐ **excommunicated**: _____; formally expelled or banned from the Catholic Church
- ☐ **marched**: _____; moved forcefully or aggressively in a particular direction
- ☐ **depose**: _____; remove from power or position
- ☐ **trip**: _____; a journey or visit to a specific place
- ☐ **forgiveness**: _____; the act of pardoning or showing mercy to someone who has done wrong
- ☐ **snow**: _____; frozen precipitation in the form of white flakes
- ☐ **absolution**: _____; the formal forgiveness of sins by a priest or religious authority
- ☐ **turning point**: _____; a critical or decisive moment or event that marks a significant change
- ☐ **secular**: _____; relating to worldly or non-religious matters
- ☐ **rulers**: _____; individuals who exercise authority or control over others
- ☐ **Catholic Church**: _____; the Christian Church led by the pope and centered in Rome
- ☐ **papacy**: _____; the office or authority of the pope
- ☐ **monarchs**: _____; kings or queens who rule over a kingdom or empire
- ☐ **bend the knee**: _____; submit or yield to someone in a position of authority
- ☐ **authority**: _____; power or control over others, often based on position or expertise
- ☐ **kneel**: _____; bend one's knees and lower oneself as a sign of respect or submission
- ☐ **shift**: _____; a change or movement in direction or emphasis
- ☐ **marked**: _____; characterized or indicated by a distinguishing feature or event
- ☐ **dominate**: _____; exercise control, influence, or power over others
- ☐ **compete**: _____; strive or contend against others in a contest or rivalry
- ☐ **contest**: _____; a competition or struggle between individuals or groups
- ☐ **struggle**: _____; a vigorous effort or fight against difficulties or opposition
- ☐ **bitter**: _____; characterized by intense animosity or resentment
- ☐ **humiliating**: _____; causing someone to feel ashamed, embarrassed, or degraded
- ☐ **historical**: _____; relating to the past, especially in the context of events, people, or periods
- ☐ **event**: _____; a notable occurrence or happening

Dr. Simon's Magic English Level 700

DR. SIMON'S MAGIC ENGLISH

KEY VOCABULARY | **LEVEL 700 - UNIT 29**

- ☐ **crusades**: _____; a series of religious wars fought between Christians and Muslims
- ☐ **medieval**: _____; relating to the Middle Ages, a period in European history between the 5th and 15th centuries
- ☐ **pope**: _____; the head of the Roman Catholic Church
- ☐ **Holy Land**: _____; a region in the Middle East considered sacred by Judaism, Christianity, and Islam
- ☐ **kingdoms**: _____; monarchies and realms
- ☐ **trade routes**: _____; paths or networks used for commercial exchange
- ☐ **exchange**: _____; the act of giving or receiving something in return
- ☐ **crusaders**: _____; the Christian knights and nobles who participated in the Crusades
- ☐ **coats of arms**: _____; special symbols or designs worn on clothes to identify different groups
- ☐ **knights**: _____; warriors on horseback who served the feudal nobility
- ☐ **nobles**: _____; members of the privileged social class below the monarch
- ☐ **shields**: _____; protective devices held by soldiers to block attacks
- ☐ **weapons**: _____; instruments used for fighting or warfare
- ☐ **swords**: _____; long-bladed cutting weapons
- ☐ **spears**: _____; long weapons with pointed ends
- ☐ **bows**: _____; weapons used for shooting arrows
- ☐ **failed**: _____; not successful or achieving the desired result
- ☐ **permanently**: _____; in a lasting or enduring manner
- ☐ **retaking**: _____; reclaiming or recapturing something
- ☐ **violence**: _____; the use of physical force to cause harm or damage
- ☐ **brutality**: _____; extreme cruelty or harshness
- ☐ **atrocities**: _____; acts of extreme cruelty or violence
- ☐ **relationship**: _____; the way in which two or more people or groups are connected or interact
- ☐ **legacy**: _____; something handed down from the past that continues to have an impact or influence
- ☐ **occupation**: _____; the act of taking control or possession of a territory by a foreign power
- ☐ **holy**: _____; regarded as sacred or having a divine quality
- ☐ **noble cause**: _____; a morally justifiable or honorable purpose or goal
- ☐ **invasion**: _____; the act of forcefully entering and taking control of another's territory
- ☐ **religion**: _____; a system of beliefs and practices concerning the divine or supernatural
- ☐ **faith**: _____; a strong belief or trust in a particular religion or system of beliefs
- ☐ **expedition**: _____; a journey or voyage, often for a specific purpose
- ☐ **commercial**: _____; related to or engaged in business or trade
- ☐ **sacred**: _____; regarded with reverence and respect, often associated with the divine or religious significance

KEY VOCABULARY | LEVEL 700 - UNIT 30

- ☐ **develop**: _____; grow or cause to grow and become more advanced or mature
- ☐ **medieval**: _____; relating to the Middle Ages, a historical period between the 5th and 15th centuries
- ☐ **trade**: _____; the buying and selling of goods and services
- ☐ **guilds**: _____; associations of merchants and craftsmen who regulate their professions and protect the interests of their members
- ☐ **protection**: _____; the act of keeping someone or something safe from harm or danger
- ☐ **specialize**: _____; focus on a particular area or skill
- ☐ **blacksmithing**: _____; the craft or trade of shaping and forging iron and steel
- ☐ **carpentry**: _____; the trade or skill of working with wood and constructing buildings or wooden objects
- ☐ **weaving**: _____; the act or process of interlacing threads or yarns to create fabric
- ☐ **commerce**: _____; the activity of buying and selling goods and services
- ☐ **culture**: _____; the customs, arts, social institutions, and achievements of a particular group or society
- ☐ **education**: _____; the process of acquiring knowledge, skills, and values through teaching and learning
- ☐ **government**: _____; the system or group of people governing a community or nation
- ☐ **middle class**: _____; a social class between the upper class and the lower class, typically consisting of merchants and skilled workers
- ☐ **influence**: _____; the power to affect or shape someone or something
- ☐ **nobility**: _____; the class of people with high social or political status
- ☐ **opportunities**: _____; favorable circumstances or situations that can lead to success or advancement
- ☐ **women**: _____; adult human females
- ☐ **traders**: _____; people who engage in buying and selling goods or securities
- ☐ **artisans**: _____; skilled workers or craftsmen
- ☐ **city officials**: _____; individuals who hold positions of authority or responsibility in a city's government
- ☐ **urbanization**: _____; the process of population shift from rural areas to urban areas
- ☐ **transformed**: _____; did a significant change or alteration

DR. SIMON'S MAGIC ENGLISH

KEY VOCABULARY | **LEVEL 800 - UNIT 1**

- ☐ **invasion**: _____; an act of forcefully entering and taking control of a territory
- ☐ **warrior**: _____; a skilled fighter or soldier
- ☐ **leader**: _____; a person who guides or directs a group or organization
- ☐ **fierce**: _____; showing strong intensity or aggression
- ☐ **fighting skills**: _____; abilities and techniques used in combat
- ☐ **ride**: _____; sit and control the movement of a horse or other animal
- ☐ **horseback**: _____; the position of being on the back of a horse
- ☐ **defeat**: _____; overcome or prevail over an opponent
- ☐ **conquer**: _____; take control of or seize by force
- ☐ **attack**: _____; launch an offensive action against someone or something
- ☐ **destroy**: _____; cause severe damage or ruin
- ☐ **city**: _____; a large and important urban area
- ☐ **center**: _____; a place or location of significant activity or importance
- ☐ **learning**: _____; the acquisition of knowledge or skills
- ☐ **Siege of Baghdad**: _____; a historical event involving the Mongol attack and destruction of Baghdad
- ☐ **reputation**: _____; the beliefs or opinions that are generally held about someone or something
- ☐ **brutal**: _____; cruel, harsh, or violent
- ☐ **tolerant**: _____; accepting or respecting different beliefs, customs, or practices
- ☐ **cultures**: _____; the customs, arts, social institutions, and achievements of a particular group or society
- ☐ **religions**: _____; systems of faith and worship
- ☐ **tribute**: _____; payment or offering made to a ruler or conqueror
- ☐ **legacy**: _____; something left behind or inherited from the past
- ☐ **exists**: _____; has actual being or is present
- ☐ **ideas**: _____; concepts, thoughts, or notions
- ☐ **technology**: _____; the application of scientific knowledge for practical purposes
- ☐ **commerce**: _____; the activity of buying and selling goods and services
- ☐ **trade**: _____; the exchange of goods or services between individuals or entities

KEY VOCABULARY | LEVEL 800 - UNIT 2

- ☐ **document**: _____; a written or printed paper that provides information or evidence
- ☐ **history**: _____; the study of past events, particularly human affairs
- ☐ **signed**: _____; wrote one's name on a document to indicate agreement or endorsement
- ☐ **Magna Carta**: _____; "Great Charter" in Latin, a document signed by King John in 1215 in England
- ☐ **important**: _____; significant or of great significance
- ☐ **created**: _____; brought into existence or made
- ☐ **power**: _____; the ability or capacity to do something or act in a particular way
- ☐ **rights**: _____; entitlements or freedoms that are inherently possessed by individuals
- ☐ **protect**: _____; safeguard or defend from harm or danger
- ☐ **limit**: _____; set a boundary or restriction on something
- ☐ **ideas**: _____; concepts, thoughts, or notions
- ☐ **punished**: _____; imposed a penalty or consequence for wrongdoing
- ☐ **trial**: _____; a formal examination of evidence in a court of law to determine guilt or innocence
- ☐ **taxed**: _____; imposed a financial charge or levy on individuals or entities
- ☐ **consent**: _____; permission or agreement given voluntarily
- ☐ **money**: _____; a medium of exchange in the form of coins or banknotes
- ☐ **democratic**: _____; relating to or advocating democracy, a system of government by the people
- ☐ **government**: _____; the system or group of people governing a community, society, or nation
- ☐ **say**: _____; have a voice or influence in decision-making
- ☐ **run**: _____; control or manage the affairs of a country or organization
- ☐ **model**: _____; a representation or example to be followed or emulated
- ☐ **laws**: _____; rules and regulations established by a governing authority
- ☐ **countries**: _____; nations or sovereign states
- ☐ **used**: _____; employed or utilized something
- ☐ **own**: _____; belonging to or associated with oneself

DR. SIMON'S MAGIC ENGLISH

KEY VOCABULARY | LEVEL 800 - UNIT 3

- ☐ **papacy**: _____; the office or authority of the Pope as the head of the Roman Catholic Church
- ☐ **period**: _____; a specific length of time characterized by particular events or conditions
- ☐ **history**: _____; the study of past events, particularly human affairs
- ☐ **pope**: _____; the leader of the Roman Catholic Church
- ☐ **lived**: _____; resided or dwelled in a particular place
- ☐ **palace**: _____; a large and impressive residence, often occupied by a ruler or high-ranking individual
- ☐ **home**: _____; a place where one lives or feels a sense of belonging
- ☐ **country**: _____; a nation or sovereign state
- ☐ **power**: _____; the ability or capacity to influence or control
- ☐ **influence**: _____; the capacity to have an effect on the character, development, or behavior of someone or something
- ☐ **catholic church**: _____; the largest Christian church, led by the Pope, and comprising numerous religious denominations
- ☐ **people**: _____; individuals or human beings
- ☐ **based**: _____; having a foundation or originating from a particular place or source
- ☐ **kings**: _____; male rulers of a kingdom or monarchy
- ☐ **moved**: _____; relocated or transferred from one place to another
- ☐ **ended**: _____; brought to a conclusion or termination
- ☐ **talk**: _____; engage in conversation or discussion about a particular subject
- ☐ **powerful**: _____; having great power or influence
- ☐ **important**: _____; significant or of great significance

KEY VOCABULARY | LEVEL 800 - UNIT 4

- ☐ **travels**: _____; journeys or trips to different places
- ☐ **explorer**: _____; a person who travels to unknown or unfamiliar places to discover or investigate
- ☐ **lived**: _____; existed or resided in a particular place
- ☐ **century**: _____; a period of one hundred years
- ☐ **journey**: _____; a trip or travel from one place to another
- ☐ **teenager**: _____; a person aged between 13 and 19 years old
- ☐ **amazing**: _____; causing great surprise or wonder
- ☐ **powerful**: _____; having great power or influence
- ☐ **ruler**: _____; a person who has control or authority over others
- ☐ **named**: _____; having a particular name
- ☐ **leader**: _____; a person who leads or commands a group
- ☐ **empire**: _____; a group of states or countries under a single supreme authority
- ☐ **large**: _____; of considerable or relatively great size, extent, or capacity
- ☐ **included**: _____; comprising as part of a whole
- ☐ **countries**: _____; nations with its own government, occupying a particular territory
- ☐ **impressed**: _____; deeply or markedly affected or influenced
- ☐ **stay**: _____; remain in a particular place or state
- ☐ **agreed**: _____; gave consent or approval
- ☐ **working**: _____; engaging in paid employment or activities for a livelihood
- ☐ **culture**: _____; the customs, arts, social institutions, and achievements of a particular nation, people, or group
- ☐ **history**: _____; the study of past events, particularly in human affairs
- ☐ **returned**: _____; came or went back to a previous place or condition
- ☐ **important**: _____; of great significance or value
- ☐ **learn**: _____; gain or acquire knowledge of or skill in something by study, experience, or being taught
- ☐ **world**: _____; the earth, together with all of its countries, peoples, and natural features
- ☐ **outside**: _____; situated or moving beyond the boundaries or limits of something
- ☐ **own**: _____; belonging to oneself or itself
- ☐ **inspire**: _____; fill someone with the urge or ability to do or feel something, especially to do something creative
- ☐ **adventures**: _____; exciting or remarkable experiences
- ☐ **still**: _____; continuing to happen or be done; not finished or changed
- ☐ **famous**: _____; known about by many people

DR. SIMON'S MAGIC ENGLISH

KEY VOCABULARY | LEVEL 800 - UNIT 5

☐ **peasants**: _____; poor farmers or agricultural workers
☐ **rebellion**: _____; an act of open resistance or defiance against authority
☐ **pay**: _____; give money in exchange for goods or services
☐ **taxes**: _____; compulsory contributions to state revenue, levied by the government
☐ **lord**: _____; a man of noble rank or high social position
☐ **owned**: _____; possessed or had legal rights to something
☐ **difficult**: _____; needing much effort or skill to accomplish, deal with, or understand
☐ **struggled**: _____; made forceful or violent efforts to get free from restraint or constriction
☐ **ends**: _____; the final part of something
☐ **tired**: _____; in need of sleep or rest
☐ **treated**: _____; behaved toward or dealt with in a certain way
☐ **unfairly**: _____; in a manner lacking justice or impartiality
☐ **decided**: _____; made up one's mind
☐ **rebel**: _____; a person who rises in opposition or armed resistance against an established government or ruler
☐ **led**: _____; guided or directed
☐ **marched**: _____; walked steadily and with determination in a specified direction
☐ **demanded**: _____; asked authoritatively or forcefully
☐ **rights**: _____; moral or legal entitlements to have or do something
☐ **deal**: _____; take action to solve a problem or conflict
☐ **successful**: _____; accomplishing an aim or purpose
☐ **agreed**: _____; gave consent or approval
☐ **eventually**: _____; in the end, especially after a long delay, dispute, or series of problems
☐ **violent**: _____; using or involving physical force intended to hurt, damage, or kill someone or something
☐ **soldier**: _____; a person who serves in an army
☐ **despite**: _____; without being affected by; in spite of
☐ **impact**: _____; the action of one object coming forcibly into contact with another
☐ **society**: _____; the aggregate of people living together in a more or less ordered community
☐ **willing**: _____; ready, eager, or prepared to do something
☐ **accept**: _____; consent to receive something
☐ **situation**: _____; a set of circumstances in which one finds oneself
☐ **equality**: _____; the state of being equal, especially in status, rights, and opportunities
☐ **remembered**: _____; kept in one's mind as a memory or tribute
☐ **reminder**: _____; a thing that causes someone to remember something
☐ **difference**: _____; a point or way in which people or things are not the same
☐ **circumstances**: _____; the conditions or factors affecting a situation

KEY VOCABULARY | LEVEL 800 - UNIT 6

- ☐ **death**: _____; the permanent cessation of all vital functions
- ☐ **epidemic**: _____; a widespread occurrence of an infectious disease in a community at a particular time
- ☐ **century**: _____; a period of one hundred years
- ☐ **deadly**: _____; causing or able to cause death
- ☐ **disease**: _____; a disorder of structure or function in a human, animal, or plant
- ☐ **swept**: _____; moved or pushed something with force
- ☐ **bacteria**: _____; microscopic living organisms, typically one-celled, that can be found everywhere
- ☐ **spread**: _____; extend over a large area or between people
- ☐ **appeared**: _____; became visible or noticeable
- ☐ **contagious**: _____; capable of being transmitted from person to person
- ☐ **infected**: _____; affected with a disease-causing organism
- ☐ **symptoms**: _____; indications or signs of a disease or condition
- ☐ **fever**: _____; a temporary increase in body temperature
- ☐ **chills**: _____; feelings of coldness accompanied by shivering
- ☐ **swelling**: _____; an abnormal enlargement of a body part or area
- ☐ **lymph**: _____; a colorless fluid containing white blood cells
- ☐ **nodes**: _____; small rounded bodies or masses, such as those in the lymphatic system
- ☐ **terrifying**: _____; causing extreme fear or dread
- ☐ **impact**: _____; the action of one object coming forcibly into contact with another
- ☐ **caused**: _____; made something happen or exist
- ☐ **fear**: _____; an unpleasant emotion caused by the belief that someone or something is dangerous
- ☐ **panic**: _____; sudden uncontrollable fear or anxiety
- ☐ **punishment**: _____; the infliction or imposition of a penalty as retribution for an offense
- ☐ **society**: _____; the aggregate of people living together in a more or less ordered community
- ☐ **dying**: _____; ceasing to live
- ☐ **care**: _____; the provision of what is necessary for the health, welfare, maintenance, and protection of someone or something
- ☐ **crops**: _____; plants cultivated for food, typically referring to grain, vegetables, or fruit
- ☐ **medicine**: _____; the science or practice of the diagnosis, treatment, and prevention of disease
- ☐ **public**: _____; of or concerning the people as a whole
- ☐ **health**: _____; the state of being free from illness or injury
- ☐ **organized**: _____; arranged in a systematic way
- ☐ **demand**: _____; ask authoritatively or brusquely
- ☐ **conditions**: _____; the circumstances affecting the way people live or work
- ☐ **remember**: _____; have in or be able to bring to one's mind an awareness of someone or something from the past
- ☐ **deadliest**: _____; causing or capable of causing death in the highest degree
- ☐ **tragic**: _____; causing or characterized by extreme distress or sorrow
- ☐ **lasting**: _____; continuing or remaining in existence for a long time

DR. SIMON'S MAGIC ENGLISH

KEY VOCABULARY | **LEVEL 800 - UNIT 7**

- ☐ **witch**: _____; a person, typically a woman, who is believed to have magical powers and practices witchcraft
- ☐ **frenzy**: _____; a state or period of uncontrolled excitement or wild behavior
- ☐ **fear**: _____; an unpleasant emotion caused by the belief that someone or something is dangerous
- ☐ **suspicion**: _____; a feeling or thought that someone is possibly guilty of wrongdoing or that something is wrong or dangerous
- ☐ **period**: _____; a length or portion of time
- ☐ **accused**: _____; charged with or declared to have committed a crime or offense
- ☐ **trial**: _____; a formal examination of evidence before a judge, typically in order to decide guilt in a criminal or civil case
- ☐ **punished**: _____; subjected to a penalty or other form of retribution
- ☐ **fueled**: _____; provided with energy or support
- ☐ **superstition**: _____; excessively credulous belief in and reverence for supernatural beings
- ☐ **cause**: _____; make something happen
- ☐ **harm**: _____; physical or mental damage or injury
- ☐ **cast**: _____; cause to be, distribute, or perform in a specified way
- ☐ **spell**: _____; a form of words used as a magical charm or incantation
- ☐ **illness**: _____; a disease or period of sickness affecting the body or mind
- ☐ **crop**: _____; a cultivated plant that is grown as food, especially a grain, fruit, or vegetable
- ☐ **result**: _____; a consequence or outcome of something
- ☐ **belief**: _____; acceptance that something exists or is true, especially without proof
- ☐ **appearance**: _____; the way that someone or something looks
- ☐ **vulnerable**: _____; susceptible to physical or emotional attack or harm
- ☐ **influence**: _____; the capacity to have an effect on the character, development, or behavior of someone or something
- ☐ **devil**: _____; the supreme spirit of evil
- ☐ **witchcraft**: _____; the practice of magic, especially black magic
- ☐ **subjected**: _____; cause or force to undergo a particular experience, especially one that is unpleasant or unwelcome
- ☐ **treatment**: _____; medical care given to a patient for an illness or injury
- ☐ **interrogated**: _____; asked questions of (someone) closely, aggressively, or formally
- ☐ **tortured**: _____; subjected to severe physical or mental suffering
- ☐ **confess**: _____; admit or state that one has committed a crime or is at fault in some way
- ☐ **stake**: _____; a wooden or metal post with a pointed end that is driven into the ground to support something or mark a position
- ☐ **cruelty**: _____; behavior that causes physical or mental harm to others
- ☐ **profound**: _____; very great or intense
- ☐ **impact**: _____; a marked effect or influence
- ☐ **respect**: _____; a feeling of deep admiration for someone or something elicited by their abilities, qualities, or achievements
- ☐ **dignity**: _____; the state or quality of being worthy of honor or respect

KEY VOCABULARY | LEVEL 800 - UNIT 8

- ☐ **period**: _____ ; a length or portion of time
- ☐ **innovation**: _____ ; the introduction of something new
- ☐ **creativity**: _____ ; the use of imagination or original ideas to create something
- ☐ **literature**: _____ ; written works, especially those considered of superior or lasting artistic merit
- ☐ **philosophy**: _____ ; the study of fundamental questions about existence, knowledge, values, reason, and more
- ☐ **renewed**: _____ ; resumed or restored to a previous state or condition
- ☐ **classical**: _____ ; relating to ancient Greek or Roman literature, art, or culture
- ☐ **ancient**: _____ ; belonging to the very distant past
- ☐ **experiment**: _____ ; a scientific procedure undertaken to make a discovery, test a hypothesis, or demonstrate a known fact
- ☐ **innovative**: _____ ; introducing or using new ideas or methods
- ☐ **advancements**: _____ ; progress or improvements in a particular field
- ☐ **inventors**: _____ ; individuals who create or design new inventions or devices
- ☐ **discoveries**: _____ ; finding or learning something for the first time
- ☐ **inventions**: _____ ; unique or novel devices, methods, or processes developed through study and experimentation
- ☐ **printing press**: _____ ; a machine for printing text or pictures from type or plates
- ☐ **produce**: _____ ; create, make, or manufacture
- ☐ **cheaply**: _____ ; at a low cost or price
- ☐ **thinkers**: _____ ; individuals who engage in thinking, reasoning, or contemplation
- ☐ **innovators**: _____ ; individuals who introduce or adopt new ideas, methods, or techniques
- ☐ **significant**: _____ ; important or noteworthy
- ☐ **contribution**: _____ ; the act of giving or supplying something, such as money, resources, or ideas, to a common purpose or cause
- ☐ **impact**: _____ ; a marked effect or influence
- ☐ **cultural**: _____ ; relating to the ideas, customs, and social behavior of a particular people or society
- ☐ **intellectual**: _____ ; relating to the intellect or understanding
- ☐ **enlightenment**: _____ ; a philosophical and intellectual movement in Europe during the 17th and 18th centuries that emphasized reason, science, and individual rights
- ☐ **scientific revolution**: _____ ; a period of rapid advancements in scientific knowledge and understanding that took place from the 16th to the 18th centuries
- ☐ **achievement**: _____ ; a thing done successfully with effort, skill, or courage
- ☐ **progress**: _____ ; forward or onward movement toward a destination or goal
- ☐ **poverty**: _____ ; the state of being extremely poor
- ☐ **inequality**: _____ ; the state of not being equal, especially in status, rights, or opportunities
- ☐ **overall**: _____ ; taking everything into account
- ☐ **celebrated**: _____ ; widely recognized, honored, or praised

DR. SIMON'S MAGIC ENGLISH

KEY VOCABULARY | LEVEL 800 - UNIT 9

- ☐ **printing press**: _____; a machine used for printing, typically involving the transfer of ink from a plate or type onto paper or other material
- ☐ **inventions**: _____; unique or novel devices, methods, processes, or discoveries
- ☐ **invented**: _____; created or developed something for the first time
- ☐ **expensive**: _____; costing a lot of money
- ☐ **process**: _____; a series of actions or steps taken to achieve a particular end
- ☐ **afford**: _____; have enough money or resources to be able to pay for or obtain
- ☐ **access**: _____; the ability or right to approach, enter, or make use of something
- ☐ **available**: _____; able to be used, obtained, or accessed
- ☐ **explosion**: _____; a sudden and rapid increase or growth
- ☐ **knowledge**: _____; facts, information, and skills acquired through experience, education, or training
- ☐ **literacy**: _____; the ability to read and write
- ☐ **revolutionized**: _____; radically changed or transformed
- ☐ **spread**: _____; extend over a large or increasing area
- ☐ **previously**: _____; before a particular time or event
- ☐ **travel**: _____; move or go from one place to another
- ☐ **carry**: _____; transport or support from one place to another
- ☐ **printed**: _____; reproduced or produced in printed form
- ☐ **distributed**: _____; spread or delivered over a wide area
- ☐ **vast**: _____; very great in extent, size, or quantity
- ☐ **distance**: _____; the amount of space between two points or things
- ☐ **sparking**: _____; igniting or causing the start or development of something
- ☐ **paved the way**: _____; prepared the ground or made progress easier for subsequent developments or achievements
- ☐ **advancements**: _____; progresses or improvements in a particular area or field
- ☐ **including**: _____; comprising as part of a whole
- ☐ **book industry**: _____; the business or trade of publishing, printing, and distributing books
- ☐ **played a key role**: _____; had a significant influence or importance
- ☐ **development**: _____; the process of growing, progressing, or improving
- ☐ **technology**: _____; the application of scientific knowledge for practical purposes
- ☐ **outdated**: _____; no longer in use or no longer useful or relevant
- ☐ **impact**: _____; a marked effect or influence
- ☐ **undeniable**: _____; impossible to deny or dispute
- ☐ **reminder**: _____; something that serves to keep someone aware of, or bring something to their attention again
- ☐ **innovation**: _____; the introduction of something new or a new idea, method, or device
- ☐ **information**: _____; facts, data, or details about something

KEY VOCABULARY | LEVEL 800 - UNIT 10

☐ **explorer**: _____ ; a person who travels to unknown places to discover new things
☐ **famous**: _____ ; well-known or widely recognized
☐ **discovery**: _____ ; the act or process of finding or uncovering something previously unknown
☐ **sailed**: _____ ; traveled by boat or ship
☐ **trade route**: _____ ; a path or course followed by traders to conduct commerce
☐ **instead**: _____ ; in place of, as an alternative or substitute
☐ **finding**: _____ ; discovering or coming across something
☐ **island**: _____ ; a piece of land surrounded by water
☐ **named**: _____ ; gave a name to
☐ **continued**: _____ ; kept going or proceeding
☐ **explore**: _____ ; travel through an unfamiliar area in order to learn about it
☐ **coast**: _____ ; the land along the edge of a sea or ocean
☐ **profound**: _____ ; having a deep or far-reaching effect
☐ **impact**: _____ ; a significant or major effect or influence
☐ **world history**: _____ ; the history of human civilizations and societies on a global scale
☐ **exchange**: _____ ; the act of giving or receiving something in return for something else
☐ **foods**: _____ ; substances that people eat for nourishment
☐ **animals**: _____ ; living organisms that can move, consume food, and reproduce
☐ **plants**: _____ ; living organisms that typically have roots, stems, leaves, and reproduce by seeds or spores
☐ **colonization**: _____ ; the act of establishing colonies or settling in a new territory
☐ **indigenous peoples**: _____ ; the original inhabitants of a particular region or land
☐ **enslaved**: _____ ; held in slavery or bondage
☐ **displaced**: _____ ; forced to leave their homes or original location
☐ **killed**: _____ ; caused the death of
☐ **parts**: _____ ; regions or areas
☐ **negative**: _____ ; unfavorable or harmful
☐ **choose**: _____ ; decide or select
☐ **celebrate**: _____ ; observe or commemorate a significant event or occasion

Dr. Simon's Magic English Level 800 | 221

DR. SIMON'S MAGIC ENGLISH

KEY VOCABULARY | LEVEL 800 - UNIT 11

- ☐ **explorer**: _____; a person who travels to unknown places to discover new things
- ☐ **new route**: _____; a different path or course
- ☐ **spice islands**: _____; islands in Southeast Asia known for their valuable spices
- ☐ **voyage**: _____; a long journey, especially by sea or air
- ☐ **journey**: _____; a long trip or expedition
- ☐ **difficult**: _____; not easy; challenging
- ☐ **faced**: _____; confronted or encountered
- ☐ **storms**: _____; violent weather conditions with strong winds and precipitation
- ☐ **strong winds**: _____; powerful air currents
- ☐ **rough seas**: _____; turbulent or agitated waters
- ☐ **crew**: _____; a group of people working together on a ship or aircraft
- ☐ **sick**: _____; unwell or ill
- ☐ **lack**: _____; absence or shortage of something
- ☐ **shipwrecked**: _____; a ship that has been destroyed or damaged by a storm or accident
- ☐ **left behind**: _____; abandoned or not taken along
- ☐ **eventually**: _____; after a period of time; in the end
- ☐ **reached**: _____; arrived at a destination
- ☐ **battle**: _____; a violent encounter or conflict between opposing forces
- ☐ **natives**: _____; indigenous or original inhabitants of a place
- ☐ **remaining**: _____; still existing or left after others have gone
- ☐ **sailed**: _____; traveled by boat or ship
- ☐ **traded**: _____; exchanged goods or services
- ☐ **valuable**: _____; having great worth or importance
- ☐ **spices**: _____; aromatic substances used to flavor food or for medicinal purposes
- ☐ **headed back**: _____; started the journey back
- ☐ **rounding**: _____; going around or circling
- ☐ **Cape of Good Hope**: _____; a rocky headland on the Atlantic coast of South Africa
- ☐ **arrived**: _____; reached a destination
- ☐ **completing**: _____; finishing or concluding
- ☐ **first-ever**: _____; the very first of its kind
- ☐ **proved**: _____; demonstrated or showed to be true
- ☐ **flat**: _____; having a level surface; not curved or sloping
- ☐ **believed**: _____; accepted or regarded as true
- ☐ **opened up**: _____; created or made accessible
- ☐ **trade routes**: _____; established paths for the exchange of goods and services
- ☐ **expanded**: _____; increased in size, scope, or significance
- ☐ **exploration**: _____; the act of traveling to new places for discovery or research

KEY VOCABULARY | LEVEL 800 - UNIT 12

- ☐ **movement**: _____ ; a group of people working together to achieve a common goal
- ☐ **protestant**: _____ ; a member of a Christian group that separated from the Roman Catholic Church during the Reformation
- ☐ **reformation**: _____ ; a 16th-century religious movement aimed at reforming the Catholic Church and establishing new Christian churches
- ☐ **worshipped**: _____ ; showed reverence or devotion to a deity or religious entity
- ☐ **god**: _____ ; a supreme being or deity
- ☐ **catholic**: _____ ; relating to the Roman Catholic Church or its members
- ☐ **church**: _____ ; a religious institution or building used for Christian worship
- ☐ **doing things wrong**: _____ ; acting in a manner that is considered incorrect or improper
- ☐ **monk**: _____ ; a member of a religious community of men who typically live in a monastery and dedicate themselves to a life of prayer and devotion
- ☐ **ideas**: _____ ; thoughts or concepts
- ☐ **nailed**: _____ ; affixed or attached firmly
- ☐ **language**: _____ ; a system of communication consisting of words, gestures, or symbols
- ☐ **personal relationship**: _____ ; an individual connection or bond between two people
- ☐ **spread**: _____ ; extend over a larger area or affect a greater number of people
- ☐ **joined**: _____ ; became a member of or participated in
- ☐ **religion**: _____ ; a system of faith and worship
- ☐ **similar**: _____ ; having qualities in common; alike
- ☐ **differences**: _____ ; distinctions or variations
- ☐ **decided**: _____ ; determined or settled
- ☐ **heaven**: _____ ; a spiritual realm or afterlife believed to be the dwelling place of God and the blessed
- ☐ **creation**: _____ ; the act of bringing something into existence
- ☐ **different**: _____ ; not the same; distinct or separate
- ☐ **christian**: _____ ; relating to or professing Christianity
- ☐ **like**: _____ ; similar to or resembling
- ☐ **lutheran**: _____ ; relating to or characteristic of Lutheranism, a branch of Protestant Christianity
- ☐ **presbyterian**: _____ ; relating to or characteristic of Presbyterianism, a branch of Protestant Christianity
- ☐ **baptist**: _____ ; relating to or characteristic of Baptists, a branch of Protestant Christianity
- ☐ **thought**: _____ ; a mental process of considering or contemplating something
- ☐ **most important**: _____ ; of greatest significance or value

DR. SIMON'S MAGIC ENGLISH

KEY VOCABULARY | LEVEL 800 - UNIT 13

- ☐ **religion**: _____; a system of faith and worship
- ☐ **protestant**: _____; a member of a Christian group that separated from the Roman Catholic Church during the Reformation
- ☐ **reformation**: _____; a 16th-century religious movement aimed at reforming the Catholic Church and establishing new Christian churches
- ☐ **founded**: _____; established or created
- ☐ **based**: _____; founded or established on a particular principle, idea, or belief
- ☐ **idea**: _____; a thought, belief, or concept
- ☐ **god**: _____; a supreme being or deity
- ☐ **all-powerful**: _____; having unlimited or supreme power
- ☐ **future**: _____; the time or period of time following the present
- ☐ **already**: _____; before a specified time or event
- ☐ **heaven**: _____; a spiritual realm or afterlife believed to be the dwelling place of God and the blessed
- ☐ **chosen**: _____; selected or elected
- ☐ **change**: _____; alter or modify
- ☐ **importance**: _____; significance or value
- ☐ **hard work**: _____; diligent and strenuous effort
- ☐ **good behavior**: _____; moral conduct or actions
- ☐ **popular**: _____; widely liked, admired, or followed
- ☐ **parts**: _____; regions or areas
- ☐ **world**: _____; the planet Earth and all its inhabitants
- ☐ **practice**: _____; engage in or perform regularly
- ☐ **predestination**: _____; the belief that God has already determined the fate or eternal destiny of individuals
- ☐ **decided**: _____; determined or settled
- ☐ **emphasizes**: _____; places special importance or focus on
- ☐ **type**: _____; category or kind
- ☐ **christianity**: _____; the religion based on the life, teachings, and beliefs of Jesus Christ
- ☐ **beliefs**: _____; convictions or principles accepted and held by an individual or group
- ☐ **learn**: _____; acquire knowledge or information

KEY VOCABULARY | LEVEL 800 - UNIT 14

- ☐ **millions**: _____; a very large number
- ☐ **fell**: _____; declined or collapsed
- ☐ **explorers**: _____; individuals who travel to discover new places or learn about the unknown
- ☐ **take over**: _____; assume control or possession of
- ☐ **wealth**: _____; abundance of valuable resources or possessions
- ☐ **thought**: _____; believed or considered
- ☐ **weak**: _____; lacking strength or power
- ☐ **conquer**: _____; defeat or overcome by force
- ☐ **brave**: _____; courageous or fearless
- ☐ **warriors**: _____; skilled fighters or soldiers
- ☐ **fought back**: _____; resisted or defended against an attack
- ☐ **outnumbered**: _____; having a smaller number compared to the opposing side
- ☐ **outgunned**: _____; having fewer or less powerful weapons compared to the opposing side
- ☐ **disease**: _____; an illness or medical condition
- ☐ **captured**: _____; seized or taken as a prisoner
- ☐ **emperor**: _____; the ruler of an empire
- ☐ **held**: _____; kept in custody or possession
- ☐ **ransom**: _____; a sum of money or payment demanded in exchange for the release of a captive
- ☐ **demanding**: _____; requiring or insisting upon something
- ☐ **gathered**: _____; collected or assembled
- ☐ **death**: _____; the end of life
- ☐ **apart**: _____; separated or divided
- ☐ **destroyed**: _____; ruined or demolished
- ☐ **cities**: _____; large and important urban areas
- ☐ **temples**: _____; buildings used for religious worship
- ☐ **leaders**: _____; individuals who guide or direct a group or nation
- ☐ **forced**: _____; compelled or coerced
- ☐ **convert**: _____; change one's beliefs or religion
- ☐ **christianity**: _____; the religion based on the life, teachings, and beliefs of Jesus Christ
- ☐ **language**: _____; a system of communication used by a particular country or community
- ☐ **culture**: _____; the customs, arts, and achievements of a particular group or society
- ☐ **way of life**: _____; the manner in which a person or group lives
- ☐ **alive**: _____; living or in existence
- ☐ **minority**: _____; a small number or group within a larger community
- ☐ **land**: _____; the earth's surface or a specified territory
- ☐ **fighting**: _____; struggling or striving
- ☐ **preserve**: _____; protect or maintain in its original state
- ☐ **traditions**: _____; customs or beliefs passed down through generations

Dr. Simon's Magic English Level 800 | 225

DR. SIMON'S MAGIC ENGLISH

KEY VOCABULARY | **LEVEL 800 - UNIT 15**

- ☐ **centuries**: _____ ; periods of one hundred years
- ☐ **believed**: _____ ; held as true or real
- ☐ **earth**: _____ ; the planet we live on
- ☐ **center**: _____ ; the middle point or core
- ☐ **universe**: _____ ; all existing matter and space
- ☐ **sun**: _____ ; the star at the center of our solar system
- ☐ **planets**: _____ ; celestial bodies that orbit around a star
- ☐ **revolved**: _____ ; moved in a circular path
- ☐ **theory**: _____ ; a well-substantiated explanation or principle
- ☐ **geocentric**: _____ ; having the belief that the Earth is the center of the universe
- ☐ **proposed**: _____ ; suggested or put forward for consideration
- ☐ **heliocentric**: _____ ; having the belief that the sun is the center of the universe
- ☐ **astronomer**: _____ ; a scientist who studies celestial bodies
- ☐ **viewed**: _____ ; perceived or regarded in a certain way
- ☐ **forever**: _____ ; for all future time; always
- ☐ **stated**: _____ ; expressed or declared
- ☐ **according to**: _____ ; as stated or indicated by
- ☐ **circular**: _____ ; having the shape of a circle
- ☐ **orbits**: _____ ; the curved paths of a celestial object around another object
- ☐ **revolutionary**: _____ ; causing a complete or dramatic change
- ☐ **widely accepted**: _____ ; acknowledged or believed by many people
- ☐ **rejected**: _____ ; refused to accept or consider
- ☐ **powerful**: _____ ; having great influence or control
- ☐ **bible**: _____ ; the sacred text of Christianity
- ☐ **telescope**: _____ ; an instrument used for observing distant objects
- ☐ **observe**: _____ ; watch or study carefully
- ☐ **gather**: _____ ; collect or assemble
- ☐ **evidence**: _____ ; facts or information supporting a claim or belief
- ☐ **supported**: _____ ; provided evidence or justification for
- ☐ **discovered**: _____ ; found or learned something new
- ☐ **Jupiter**: _____ ; the largest planet in our solar system
- ☐ **moons**: _____ ; natural satellites that orbit around a planet
- ☐ **today**: _____ ; the present time
- ☐ **true**: _____ ; in accordance with fact or reality
- ☐ **solar system**: _____ ; the collection of planets and other celestial bodies that orbit around the sun
- ☐ **knowledge**: _____ ; information, skills, or awareness acquired through experience or education
- ☐ **helped**: _____ ; assisted or contributed to

KEY VOCABULARY | LEVEL 800 - UNIT 16

- ☐ **era**: _____; a period of time marked by particular characteristics or events
- ☐ **absolute monarchy**: _____; a system of government where a monarch has complete control and power
- ☐ **complete control**: _____; having total authority or power
- ☐ **countries**: _____; political entities with defined territories and governments
- ☐ **period**: _____; a specific length of time
- ☐ **marked by**: _____; characterized by
- ☐ **rise**: _____; an increase or growth
- ☐ **powerful**: _____; having great influence or control
- ☐ **iron fist**: _____; ; strict and oppressive rule
- ☐ **monarchs**: _____; rulers, typically kings or queens
- ☐ **subjects**: _____; individuals under the rule of a monarch
- ☐ **decisions**: _____; choices or judgments
- ☐ **consequences**: _____; outcomes or results
- ☐ **tax**: _____; impose a financial charge on citizens
- ☐ **laws**: _____; rules or regulations
- ☐ **declare war**: _____; officially announce a state of war
- ☐ **approval**: _____; agreement or consent
- ☐ **famous**: _____; well-known or widely recognized
- ☐ **divine right of kings**: _____; the belief that a monarch's authority comes from God
- ☐ **chosen**: _____; selected or appointed
- ☐ **rule**: _____; govern or control
- ☐ **symbol**: _____; a representation or emblem
- ☐ **power**: _____; authority or control
- ☐ **wealth**: _____; abundance of valuable possessions or resources
- ☐ **came to an end**: _____; concluded or finished
- ☐ **Age of Enlightenment**: _____; a period of intellectual and philosophical movement
- ☐ **question**: _____; challenge or doubt
- ☐ **authority**: _____; power or control
- ☐ **demand**: _____; request or insist on
- ☐ **rights**: _____; entitlements or privileges
- ☐ **freedoms**: _____; liberties or independence
- ☐ **governed**: _____; ruled or managed
- ☐ **democratically elected officials**: _____; leaders chosen by the people through voting
- ☐ **vote**: _____; express a choice or opinion through a formal process
- ☐ **affect**: _____; influence or impact
- ☐ **lives**: _____; individual existences or personal experiences
- ☐ **big change**: _____; significant transformation or shift

Dr. Simon's Magic English Level 800 | 227

DR. SIMON'S MAGIC ENGLISH

KEY VOCABULARY | LEVEL 800 - UNIT 17

- ☐ **puritan revolution**: _____ ; a period in English history when Puritans rebelled against the king and sought to reform the Church of England
- ☐ **group**: _____ ; a collection of individuals
- ☐ **rebelled**: _____ ; resisted or opposed authority
- ☐ **Church of England**: _____ ; the established Christian church in England
- ☐ **purified**: _____ ; cleansed or removed impurities
- ☐ **Roman Catholic Church**: _____ ; the Christian church headed by the pope in Rome
- ☐ **disagreed**: _____ ; had a difference of opinion or belief
- ☐ **bible**: _____ ; the sacred scripture of Christianity
- ☐ **religious practices**: _____ ; rituals or customs related to worship
- ☐ **forced**: _____ ; compelled or coerced
- ☐ **simple living**: _____ ; a lifestyle characterized by frugality and minimalism
- ☐ **hard work**: _____ ; labor or effort expended
- ☐ **rebels**: _____ ; individuals who oppose or resist authority
- ☐ **roundheads**: _____ ; the parliamentary forces during the English Civil War
- ☐ **king's army**: _____ ; the military forces loyal to the king
- ☐ **cavaliers**: _____ ; the royalist forces during the English Civil War
- ☐ **war**: _____ ; a conflict between organized groups or nations
- ☐ **bloody**: _____ ; characterized by violence and bloodshed
- ☐ **won**: _____ ; emerged victorious or succeeded
- ☐ **executed**: _____ ; put to death, usually by legal authority
- ☐ **established**: _____ ; founded or created
- ☐ **government**: _____ ; the system or body governing a state or community
- ☐ **commonwealth**: _____ ; a political entity founded for the common welfare
- ☐ **republic**: _____ ; a form of government where power rests with the people and their elected representatives
- ☐ **elected representatives**: _____ ; individuals chosen by the people to represent their interests
- ☐ **religious beliefs**: _____ ; personal convictions or faith
- ☐ **law of the land**: _____ ; legal principles or regulations enforced in a country
- ☐ **impact**: _____ ; influence or effect
- ☐ **idea**: _____ ; a thought, belief, or concept
- ☐ **governed**: _____ ; ruled or controlled
- ☐ **religious freedom**: _____ ; the right to practice one's religion without interference

KEY VOCABULARY | LEVEL 800 - UNIT 18

☐ **emperor**: _____ ; a male ruler of an empire
☐ **reforms**: _____ ; changes made to improve or modernize something
☐ **modernize**: _____ ; bring up to date or make more modern
☐ **stronger**: _____ ; more powerful or robust
☐ **nation**: _____ ; a sovereign state or country
☐ **determined**: _____ ; having a firm or fixed purpose
☐ **traveled**: _____ ; journeyed or went on a trip
☐ **customs**: _____ ; traditions or practices of a particular group
☐ **technology**: _____ ; the application of scientific knowledge for practical purposes
☐ **government**: _____ ; the system or body governing a state or community
☐ **accomplishments**: _____ ; achievements or successes
☐ **capital city**: _____ ; the main city or seat of government of a country
☐ **trade**: _____ ; the exchange of goods or services
☐ **modernized**: _____ ; made more modern or up to date
☐ **army**: _____ ; a military organization trained for warfare
☐ **navy**: _____ ; the branch of a nation's armed forces that conducts naval operations
☐ **reorganized**: _____ ; rearranged or restructured
☐ **weapons**: _____ ; instruments or devices used for defense or attack
☐ **tactics**: _____ ; strategies or maneuvers used in a battle or conflict
☐ **victories**: _____ ; successful outcomes or wins
☐ **social reforms**: _____ ; changes made to improve society or social conditions
☐ **education**: _____ ; the process of acquiring knowledge and skills
☐ **established**: _____ ; founded or set up
☐ **university**: _____ ; an institution of higher education and research
☐ **orthodox church**: _____ ; the predominant religious denomination in Russia
☐ **alphabet**: _____ ; a set of letters or characters used in writing
☐ **style**: _____ ; particular manner or mode of expression
☐ **clothing**: _____ ; garments or attire
☐ **etiquette**: _____ ; rules or customs governing polite behavior
☐ **legacy**: _____ ; something handed down from the past or inherited
☐ **remembered**: _____ ; recalled or kept in memory

Dr. Simon's Magic English Level 800 | 229

DR. SIMON'S MAGIC ENGLISH

KEY VOCABULARY | **LEVEL 800 - UNIT 19**

- ☐ **glorious revolution**: _____; an event that happened in England in 1688, known for being peaceful and not involving fighting or bloodshed
- ☐ **event**: _____; a notable occurrence or happening
- ☐ **unpopular**: _____; not liked or favored by many people
- ☐ **religious beliefs**: _____; personal convictions or faith system
- ☐ **subjects**: _____; the people who are under the rule of a monarch
- ☐ **limit**: _____; restrict or set boundaries on something
- ☐ **power of parliament**: _____; the authority and influence of the legislative body in England
- ☐ **nobles**: _____; powerful members of the aristocracy
- ☐ **daughter**: _____; a female child of a parent
- ☐ **husband**: _____; a married man in relation to his spouse
- ☐ **protestants**: _____; Christians who belong to the Western Christian tradition and are not members of the Roman Catholic Church
- ☐ **respect**: _____; hold in high regard or esteem
- ☐ **arrived**: _____; came or reached a destination
- ☐ **welcomed**: _____; received with pleasure or hospitality
- ☐ **rule**: _____; govern or control
- ☐ **flee**: _____; run away or escape
- ☐ **crowned**: _____; ceremonially made king or queen
- ☐ **consent**: _____; agreement or permission
- ☐ **parliament**: _____; the legislative body of a country
- ☐ **important decisions**: _____; significant choices or actions
- ☐ **approval**: _____; consent or agreement
- ☐ **principle**: _____; a fundamental truth or guideline
- ☐ **constitutional monarchy**: _____; a form of government in which the monarch's power is limited by a constitution or laws
- ☐ **limited**: _____; restricted or restrained
- ☐ **law**: _____; a set of rules established by a governing authority
- ☐ **representatives**: _____; individuals chosen to act or speak on behalf of others
- ☐ **governed**: _____; controlled or directed

KEY VOCABULARY | LEVEL 800 - UNIT 20

- ☐ **Boston tea party**: _____; a protest that took place in Boston, Massachusetts in 1773 against British taxation
- ☐ **protest**: _____; an expression of objection or disapproval
- ☐ **American colonies**: _____; the colonies established by the British in North America before the American Revolution
- ☐ **colonists**: _____; people who settled in and were living in the American colonies
- ☐ **taxed unfairly**: _____; subjected to unjust or inequitable taxation
- ☐ **upset**: _____; feeling of dissatisfaction or annoyance
- ☐ **tax**: _____; a financial charge imposed by the government on individuals or entities
- ☐ **tea**: _____; a hot or cold beverage made from the leaves of the Camellia sinensis plant
- ☐ **government**: _____; the governing body of a nation or state
- ☐ **monopoly**: _____; exclusive control or possession of a product or service in a particular market
- ☐ **expensive**: _____; costing a lot of money
- ☐ **dressed up**: _____; wearing special clothing or costumes
- ☐ **native Americans**: _____; the indigenous people of the Americas
- ☐ **snuck**: _____; moved quietly or surreptitiously
- ☐ **aboard**: _____; on or onto a ship, aircraft, or other vehicle
- ☐ **ships**: _____; large vessels used for transportation on water
- ☐ **dumped**: _____; emptied or got rid of something in a careless or hurried manner
- ☐ **Boston harbor**: _____; a harbor in Boston, Massachusetts
- ☐ **destroying**: _____; causing severe damage or ruin
- ☐ **unusable**: _____; not able to be used or utilized
- ☐ **outraged**: _____; extremely angry or resentful
- ☐ **act of rebellion**: _____; an action against established authority or control
- ☐ **coercive acts**: _____; a series of laws passed by the British government in response to the Boston Tea Party, aimed at punishing the colonists
- ☐ **response**: _____; a reaction or answer to something
- ☐ **important event**: _____; a significant happening or occurrence
- ☐ **American Revolution**: _____; the war fought by the American colonies to gain independence from Great Britain
- ☐ **spark**: _____; ignite or stimulate
- ☐ **stand up for**: _____; defend or support
- ☐ **rights**: _____; entitlements or privileges that individuals possess
- ☐ **extreme measures**: _____; drastic or radical actions

DR. SIMON'S MAGIC ENGLISH

KEY VOCABULARY | **LEVEL 800 - UNIT 21**

- ☐ **founding**: _____ ; the act of establishing or creating something
- ☐ **country**: _____ ; a political and geographic entity with its own government and borders
- ☐ **inhabited**: _____ ; lived in or occupied by people or animals
- ☐ **native Americans**: _____ ; the indigenous people of the Americas
- ☐ **thousands of years**: _____ ; a long period of time consisting of thousands of years
- ☐ **European explorers**: _____ ; individuals from Europe who traveled to new lands for discovery or colonization
- ☐ **build settlements**: _____ ; establish communities or towns
- ☐ **13 colonies**: _____ ; the original British colonies in North America that later formed the United States
- ☐ **ruled**: _____ ; governed or controlled
- ☐ **Great Britain**: _____ ; a country in Europe that colonized and ruled over the American colonies
- ☐ **freedom**: _____ ; the state of being free, having liberty or independence
- ☐ **say**: _____ ; an opportunity to express one's opinion or make decisions
- ☐ **government**: _____ ; the governing body of a nation or state
- ☐ **declare**: _____ ; publicly announce or proclaim
- ☐ **independence**: _____ ; freedom from control or influence of others
- ☐ **declaration of independence**: _____ ; a document written by Thomas Jefferson in 1776 to proclaim the independence of the American colonies from Great Britain
- ☐ **signed**: _____ ; written one's signature on a document to indicate approval or agreement
- ☐ **war**: _____ ; a conflict or struggle between two or more groups or nations
- ☐ **American Revolution**: _____ ; the war fought by the American colonies to gain independence from Great Britain
- ☐ **president**: _____ ; the elected head of state of a country
- ☐ **constitution**: _____ ; a set of fundamental principles or rules that define the structure and governance of a country
- ☐ **protects**: _____ ; safeguards or defends
- ☐ **rights**: _____ ; entitlements or privileges that individuals possess
- ☐ **diverse**: _____ ; consisting of different or varied elements or qualities
- ☐ **50 states**: _____ ; the individual political divisions of the United States
- ☐ **known for**: _____ ; recognized or famous for
- ☐ **democracy**: _____ ; a system of government where power is vested in the people, who exercise it through voting or elected representatives
- ☐ **opportunity**: _____ ; a chance or favorable circumstance
- ☐ **achieve**: _____ ; successfully accomplish or reach a goal
- ☐ **dreams**: _____ ; aspirations or goals

KEY VOCABULARY | LEVEL 800 - UNIT 22

- ☐ **French Revolution**: _____; a period of radical social and political change in France from 1789 to 1799
- ☐ **time**: _____; a period or era
- ☐ **French history**: _____; the history of France
- ☐ **people**: _____; the general population or citizens
- ☐ **say**: _____; an opportunity to express one's opinion or make decisions
- ☐ **country**: _____; a political and geographic entity with its own government and borders
- ☐ **ruled**: _____; governed or controlled
- ☐ **king**: _____; a male monarch who inherits the position
- ☐ **rights**: _____; entitlements or privileges that individuals possess
- ☐ **nobles**: _____; members of the noble class or aristocracy
- ☐ **freedom**: _____; the state of being free, having liberty or independence
- ☐ **listen**: _____; pay attention or give heed to someone's concerns or opinions
- ☐ **take action**: _____; do something in response to a situation or problem
- ☐ **stormed**: _____; forcefully or aggressively entered
- ☐ **start**: _____; the beginning or commencement
- ☐ **change**: _____; the act or process of becoming different
- ☐ **government**: _____; the governing body of a nation or state
- ☐ **fair**: _____; just or equitable
- ☐ **equal**: _____; having the same rights or status
- ☐ **flag**: _____; a piece of cloth with distinctive colors and designs representing a country or organization
- ☐ **red**: _____; a color symbolizing revolution or bravery
- ☐ **white**: _____; a color symbolizing purity or innocence
- ☐ **blue**: _____; a color symbolizing liberty or loyalty
- ☐ **violence**: _____; behavior involving physical force intended to hurt, damage, or kill
- ☐ **killed**: _____; caused the death of
- ☐ **queen**: _____; a female monarch who inherits the position
- ☐ **end**: _____; the conclusion or termination
- ☐ **leader**: _____; a person who leads or guides others
- ☐ **today**: _____; the present time or current era
- ☐ **democracy**: _____; a system of government where power is vested in the people, who exercise it through voting or elected representatives
- ☐ **pave the way**: _____; make progress or create favorable conditions for something

DR. SIMON'S MAGIC ENGLISH

KEY VOCABULARY | LEVEL 800 - UNIT 23

- ☐ **French Revolution**: _____; a period of radical social and political change in France from 1789 to 1799
- ☐ **famous**: _____; well-known or widely recognized
- ☐ **victories**: _____; successes in battles or conflicts
- ☐ **battles**: _____; military engagements or fights
- ☐ **born**: _____; brought into existence through birth
- ☐ **island**: _____; a landmass surrounded by water
- ☐ **ambitious**: _____; having a strong desire for success or achievement
- ☐ **great power**: _____; a nation with significant influence and capabilities on the global stage
- ☐ **successful**: _____; achieving the desired results or outcomes
- ☐ **military campaigns**: _____; organized operations or strategies conducted by the military
- ☐ **conquered**: _____; gained control over or subjugated
- ☐ **reforms**: _____; changes or improvements made to a system or institution
- ☐ **legal system**: _____; the framework of laws and regulations governing a society
- ☐ **Napoleonic code**: _____; a legal system established by Napoleon, based on equality before the law
- ☐ **laws**: _____; rules or regulations enforced by a governing authority
- ☐ **improved**: _____; made better or enhanced
- ☐ **education**: _____; the process of acquiring knowledge and skills
- ☐ **economy**: _____; the system of production, distribution, and consumption of goods and services
- ☐ **peaceful**: _____; characterized by a lack of violence or conflict
- ☐ **wars**: _____; conflicts or hostilities between nations or groups
- ☐ **enemies**: _____; individuals or nations who are hostile or opposed
- ☐ **downfall**: _____; the sudden loss of power or position
- ☐ **invaded**: _____; forcefully entered or occupied
- ☐ **unsuccessful**: _____; not achieving the desired goals or outcomes
- ☐ **defeated**: _____; overcome or beaten in battle or conflict
- ☐ **abdicate**: _____; relinquish or give up power or authority
- ☐ **exiled**: _____; forced to live away from one's own country or homeland
- ☐ **escaped**: _____; managed to get away or break free
- ☐ **died**: _____; ceased to live or exist
- ☐ **accomplishments**: _____; achievements or successes
- ☐ **remembered**: _____; recalled or kept in memory
- ☐ **lives lost**: _____; casualties or fatalities in wars or conflicts

KEY VOCABULARY | LEVEL 800 - UNIT 24

- ☐ **industrial revolution**: _____; a period of rapid industrialization and technological advancement
- ☐ **change**: _____; the act or process of becoming different
- ☐ **world**: _____; the planet Earth and all its inhabitants
- ☐ **century**: _____; a period of 100 years
- ☐ **inventions**: _____; new creations or discoveries
- ☐ **lived**: _____; existed or resided
- ☐ **worked**: _____; engaged in labor or employment
- ☐ **forever**: _____; for all time; permanently
- ☐ **made**: _____; produced or created
- ☐ **expensive**: _____; costing a lot of money
- ☐ **machines**: _____; mechanical devices or contraptions
- ☐ **faster**: _____; at a greater speed or rate
- ☐ **cheaper**: _____; costing less money
- ☐ **factories**: _____; buildings where goods are produced on a large scale
- ☐ **goods**: _____; products or items
- ☐ **textiles**: _____; fabrics or cloth materials
- ☐ **iron**: _____; a strong and malleable metal
- ☐ **buy**: _____; acquire in exchange for money
- ☐ **clothes**: _____; garments or attire
- ☐ **toys**: _____; objects for play or amusement
- ☐ **cities**: _____; large urban areas
- ☐ **grew**: _____; increased in size or population
- ☐ **bigger**: _____; larger in size or magnitude
- ☐ **countryside**: _____; rural areas or regions
- ☐ **working conditions**: _____; the environment and circumstances of work
- ☐ **crowded**: _____; filled with a large number of people or things
- ☐ **unhealthy**: _____; detrimental to health or well-being
- ☐ **impact**: _____; the effect or influence of something
- ☐ **environment**: _____; the natural world and surroundings
- ☐ **pollution**: _____; the presence of harmful substances in the environment
- ☐ **forests**: _____; large areas covered with trees
- ☐ **cut down**: _____; fell or remove trees
- ☐ **room**: _____; space or area
- ☐ **lasting**: _____; enduring or continuing for a long time
- ☐ **modern conveniences**: _____; contemporary amenities or comforts
- ☐ **enjoy**: _____; derive pleasure or satisfaction from

Dr. Simon's Magic English Level 800

DR. SIMON'S MAGIC ENGLISH

KEY VOCABULARY | **LEVEL 800 - UNIT 25**

- ☐ **capitalist society**: _____; an economic system where private individuals own and control the means of production for profit
- ☐ **economic system**: _____; a way of organizing and distributing resources and goods within a society
- ☐ **private individuals**: _____; individuals who are not part of the government or public sector
- ☐ **government**: _____; the governing body of a nation or state
- ☐ **means of production**: _____; the resources and facilities used to produce goods and services
- ☐ **factories**: _____; buildings where goods are manufactured or produced
- ☐ **land**: _____; the surface of the earth, including its natural resources
- ☐ **businesses**: _____; organizations engaged in commercial, industrial, or professional activities
- ☐ **sell**: _____; exchange goods or services for money
- ☐ **goods**: _____; products or items that are tangible and can be traded
- ☐ **services**: _____; intangible actions or efforts provided to fulfill a need or desire
- ☐ **profit**: _____; the financial gain or benefit obtained from a business activity
- ☐ **emerge**: _____; come into existence or become known
- ☐ **merchants**: _____; individuals engaged in trade or commerce
- ☐ **traders**: _____; individuals involved in buying and selling goods
- ☐ **accumulate**: _____; gather or collect over time
- ☐ **wealth**: _____; abundance of valuable possessions or resources
- ☐ **formation**: _____; the act or process of being formed or created
- ☐ **feature**: _____; a distinctive attribute or characteristic
- ☐ **competition**: _____; the act of striving against others for the same goal or prize
- ☐ **attract**: _____; draw the attention or interest of
- ☐ **innovation**: _____; the introduction of something new or improved
- ☐ **efficiency**: _____; the ability to accomplish a task or produce a desired result with minimal waste
- ☐ **improve**: _____; make or become better
- ☐ **products**: _____; items created or manufactured for sale
- ☐ **price**: _____; the amount of money required to purchase something
- ☐ **supply and demand**: _____; the relationship between the availability of goods and the desire or demand for those goods
- ☐ **determined**: _____; decided or fixed
- ☐ **scarcity**: _____; a limited supply of resources or goods
- ☐ **popularity**: _____; the state of being widely liked, admired, or sought after
- ☐ **prosperity**: _____; the state of being successful, flourishing, or wealthy
- ☐ **lift**: _____; raise or elevate
- ☐ **poverty**: _____; the state of being extremely poor or lacking basic necessities

KEY VOCABULARY | LEVEL 800 - UNIT 26

- ☐ **conflict**: _____; a serious disagreement or struggle between two or more parties
- ☐ **importing**: _____; bringing goods or products from another country
- ☐ **tea**: _____; a popular beverage made from the leaves of the Camellia sinensis plant
- ☐ **buy**: _____; acquire in exchange for money or goods
- ☐ **selling**: _____; exchanging goods or services for money
- ☐ **opium**: _____; a highly addictive narcotic drug derived from the opium poppy plant
- ☐ **threat**: _____; something that is likely to cause harm or danger
- ☐ **society**: _____; a group of individuals living together in a community
- ☐ **trade**: _____; the buying and selling of goods and services
- ☐ **military power**: _____; the strength and capability of a country's armed forces
- ☐ **protect**: _____; guard or defend against harm or danger
- ☐ **equipped**: _____; supplied or provided with necessary tools or resources
- ☐ **trained**: _____; educated or prepared for a specific purpose or task
- ☐ **defeated**: _____; overcome or beaten in a battle or competition
- ☐ **army**: _____; a large organized group of armed individuals trained for warfare
- ☐ **result**: _____; the outcome or consequence of an action or event
- ☐ **forced**: _____; compelled or coerced to do something against one's will
- ☐ **sign**: _____; formally agree to or authorize a document or agreement
- ☐ **treaty**: _____; a formal agreement between nations or states
- ☐ **control**: _____; having power or authority over something
- ☐ **ports**: _____; designated locations where ships can load and unload cargo
- ☐ **profound**: _____; having deep meaning or significance
- ☐ **impact**: _____; a strong effect or influence on someone or something
- ☐ **decline**: _____; a gradual or continuous decrease or deterioration
- ☐ **humiliation**: _____; the act of causing someone to feel ashamed or embarrassed
- ☐ **contributed**: _____; played a part in or had an influence on
- ☐ **widespread**: _____; existing or happening over a large area or among many people
- ☐ **addiction**: _____; a physical or psychological dependence on a substance or activity
- ☐ **devastating**: _____; causing severe damage or destruction
- ☐ **effects**: _____; the results or consequences of an action or event
- ☐ **generations**: _____; groups of individuals born and living at the same time
- ☐ **contemporary**: _____; existing or occurring at the present time
- ☐ **demonstration**: _____; a public display or show of a particular quality or behavior
- ☐ **perils**: _____; dangers or risks associated with something
- ☐ **dependency**: _____; reliance on a particular substance or activity
- ☐ **outcomes**: _____; the results or consequences of a situation or event
- ☐ **worldwide**: _____; occurring or extending throughout the world
- ☐ **commerce**: _____; the activity of buying and selling goods and services
- ☐ **political relations**: _____; interactions and connections between different political entities

Dr. Simon's Magic English Level 800

DR. SIMON'S MAGIC ENGLISH

KEY VOCABULARY | **LEVEL 800 - UNIT 27**

- ☐ **communist manifesto**: _____ ; a political document written by Karl Marx and Friedrich Engels in 1848, advocating for communism
- ☐ **political**: _____ ; relating to the government, public affairs, or the actions and policies of a governing body
- ☐ **document**: _____ ; a written or printed record that provides information or evidence
- ☐ **written**: _____ ; expressed or communicated in written form
- ☐ **outlined**: _____ ; presented or described the main points or features of something
- ☐ **vision**: _____ ; an imagined plan or idea for the future
- ☐ **society**: _____ ; a group of individuals living together in a community
- ☐ **communism**: _____ ; a socioeconomic system in which there is common ownership of the means of production and resources are shared equally
- ☐ **system**: _____ ; a set of principles or procedures for governing or organizing something
- ☐ **works**: _____ ; engages in productive activity for a specific purpose or goal
- ☐ **shares**: _____ ; divides or distributes something among multiple individuals
- ☐ **resources**: _____ ; materials, assets, or other sources of support or aid
- ☐ **equally**: _____ ; in a manner that is fair and without discrimination or favoritism
- ☐ **capitalism**: _____ ; an economic system characterized by private ownership of the means of production and profit-driven competition
- ☐ **unfair**: _____ ; not just or equitable; not based on principles of equality or impartiality
- ☐ **inequality**: _____ ; a state of unequal distribution or treatment, often related to social or economic factors
- ☐ **exploitation**: _____ ; the action or process of treating someone unfairly to benefit from their labor or resources
- ☐ **provides**: _____ ; gives or supplies something
- ☐ **opportunities**: _____ ; chances or possibilities for advancement, growth, or success
- ☐ **fulfilling**: _____ ; satisfying or meeting one's needs or desires
- ☐ **significant**: _____ ; important or notable; having meaning or consequence
- ☐ **impact**: _____ ; a strong effect or influence on someone or something
- ☐ **politics**: _____ ; the activities, actions, and policies used to gain and hold power in a government or to influence the government
- ☐ **countries**: _____ ; sovereign states or nations
- ☐ **implemented**: _____ ; put into effect or action
- ☐ **resistance**: _____ ; opposition or refusal to accept something
- ☐ **criticism**: _____ ; the act of expressing disapproval or pointing out faults or shortcomings
- ☐ **controversial**: _____ ; causing disagreement or dispute
- ☐ **remains**: _____ ; continues to exist or be relevant
- ☐ **important**: _____ ; significant or of great importance
- ☐ **thought**: _____ ; the process of thinking or reasoning
- ☐ **continues**: _____ ; persists or goes on without interruption or cessation
- ☐ **debated**: _____ ; discussed or argued about, often with differing opinions

KEY VOCABULARY | LEVEL 800 - UNIT 28

☐ **Taiping heavenly rebellion**: _____; a massive conflict that took place in China during the mid-19th century

☐ **massive**: _____; very large in size, extent, or amount

☐ **conflict**: _____; a serious disagreement or struggle between opposing forces

☐ **declared**: _____; publicly announced or proclaimed

☐ **followers**: _____; people who believe in and support a leader or cause

☐ **ruling**: _____; governing or controlling

☐ **establish**: _____; set up or create

☐ **prosperity**: _____; the state of being successful or thriving, especially economically

☐ **controlled**: _____; governed or had authority over

☐ **major cities**: _____; large and important urban areas

☐ **rebels**: _____; individuals who rise in opposition or armed resistance against an established authority or government

☐ **series**: _____; a number of events or actions that are connected or follow one after another

☐ **battles**: _____; military encounters or conflicts

☐ **initial**: _____; occurring at the beginning or first stage

☐ **successes**: _____; achievements or favorable outcomes

☐ **ultimately**: _____; in the end; finally

☐ **defeated**: _____; overcome or beaten in a battle or contest

☐ **incredibly**: _____; to an extraordinary or remarkable degree

☐ **violent**: _____; involving physical force, especially to cause injury or death

☐ **estimates**: _____; approximations or educated guesses

☐ **suggesting**: _____; proposing or indicating

☐ **result**: _____; consequence or outcome

☐ **famine**: _____; extreme scarcity of food, often resulting in starvation and malnutrition

☐ **disease**: _____; a disorder of structure or function in a living organism, often causing illness or abnormality

☐ **significant**: _____; important or notable; having meaning or consequence

☐ **impact**: _____; a strong effect or influence on someone or something

☐ **society**: _____; a group of individuals living together in a community

☐ **leading**: _____; having a prominent role or position

☐ **religion**: _____; a system of beliefs and practices related to the divine or supernatural

☐ **achieve**: _____; accomplish or attain

☐ **remains**: _____; continues to exist or be relevant

☐ **scale**: _____; the size or extent of something

☐ **devastation**: _____; severe destruction or damage

☐ **innovative**: _____; introducing or using new methods, ideas, or products

☐ **proposed**: _____; put forward for consideration or discussion

☐ **gender equality**: _____; the belief in equal rights, opportunities, and treatment regardless of gender

☐ **land redistribution**: _____; the act of reallocating land ownership or access

Dr. Simon's Magic English Level 800 | 239

DR. SIMON'S MAGIC ENGLISH

KEY VOCABULARY | **LEVEL 800 - UNIT 29**

- ☐ **Sepoys**: _____; Indian soldiers
- ☐ **mutiny**: _____; a revolt or rebellion against authority, typically by soldiers or sailors
- ☐ **indian rebellion**: _____; a significant event in Indian history, also known as the Sepoy Mutiny or the Indian Rebellion of 1857
- ☐ **significant**: _____; important or noteworthy
- ☐ **event**: _____; a notable occurrence or happening
- ☐ **rebelled**: _____; rose in opposition or resistance against authority
- ☐ **British officers**: _____; individuals in positions of command or leadership within the British military
- ☐ **angry**: _____; feeling or showing strong displeasure or resentment
- ☐ **animal fat**: _____; fat derived from animals
- ☐ **cartridges**: _____; containers or casings holding bullets or ammunition
- ☐ **rifles**: _____; long-barreled firearms designed for accuracy and range
- ☐ **religious beliefs**: _____; personal or cultural convictions or principles regarding spirituality or faith
- ☐ **spread**: _____; extended or expanded over an area or population
- ☐ **joining**: _____; becoming a part of or uniting with
- ☐ **attack**: _____; launch an assault or offensive action against
- ☐ **forts**: _____; fortified structures or buildings used for defense
- ☐ **cities**: _____; large urban areas
- ☐ **violent**: _____; involving physical force or aggression
- ☐ **clashes**: _____; violent conflicts or confrontations
- ☐ **regain**: _____; recover or recapture control or possession of something
- ☐ **control**: _____; authority or power over something or someone
- ☐ **sent**: _____; dispatched or conveyed to a destination
- ☐ **troops**: _____; military personnel or armed forces
- ☐ **crush**: _____; suppress or defeat by force or overwhelming pressure
- ☐ **end**: _____; conclusion or termination
- ☐ **rule**: _____; exercise authority or control over a country or region
- ☐ **beginning**: _____; the starting point or initial stage
- ☐ **direct**: _____; immediate or without intermediaries
- ☐ **turning point**: _____; a moment of significant change or shift
- ☐ **political**: _____; relating to government, politics, or public affairs
- ☐ **social structures**: _____; the patterns or organization of relationships within a society
- ☐ **highlighted**: _____; emphasized or brought attention to
- ☐ **tensions**: _____; conflicts, disagreements, or strains
- ☐ **rulers**: _____; those who have authority or control over a country or people
- ☐ **continue**: _____; persist or endure

KEY VOCABULARY | LEVEL 800 - UNIT 30

- ☐ **theory**: _____; a well-substantiated explanation or framework that explains a phenomenon
- ☐ **evolution**: _____; the process of gradual and cumulative change in living organisms over successive generations
- ☐ **living things**: _____; organisms that have the characteristics of life, such as plants and animals
- ☐ **evolved**: _____; developed or changed gradually over time
- ☐ **common ancestor**: _____; an organism from which two or more different species have descended
- ☐ **natural selection**: _____; the process by which certain traits or characteristics become more or less common in a population due to their impact on survival and reproduction
- ☐ **adapted**: _____; adjusted or modified to fit a particular environment or circumstances
- ☐ **environment**: _____; the surroundings or conditions in which an organism exists
- ☐ **survive**: _____; continue to live or exist
- ☐ **reproduce**: _____; produce offspring or create new individuals of the same species
- ☐ **traits**: _____; distinguishing characteristics or features
- ☐ **offspring**: _____; the descendants or children of an organism
- ☐ **species**: _____; a group of organisms capable of interbreeding and producing fertile offspring
- ☐ **controversial**: _____; causing disagreement or debate
- ☐ **challenged**: _____; questioned or called into doubt
- ☐ **created**: _____; brought into existence or made
- ☐ **god**: _____; a deity or higher power often associated with religious beliefs
- ☐ **form**: _____; the structure or shape of something
- ☐ **accepted**: _____; acknowledged or recognized as true or valid
- ☐ **foundation**: _____; the basis or groundwork on which something is built or developed
- ☐ **modern biology**: _____; the study of living organisms and their interactions based on current scientific knowledge
- ☐ **examples**: _____; instances or illustrations used to explain or support a statement
- ☐ **peppered moth**: _____; a species of moth that exhibits color variation in response to environmental changes
- ☐ **industrial revolution**: _____; a period of rapid industrialization and societal transformation in the 18th and 19th centuries
- ☐ **pollution**: _____; the presence of harmful or undesirable substances in the environment
- ☐ **factories**: _____; industrial buildings where goods are manufactured or processed
- ☐ **darkened**: _____; made or became darker in color or appearance
- ☐ **common**: _____; occurring or existing frequently or widely
- ☐ **camouflaged**: _____; disguised or concealed to blend in with the surroundings
- ☐ **impact**: _____; the effect or influence of one thing on another
- ☐ **understanding**: _____; comprehension or knowledge about a particular subject or concept
- ☐ **natural world**: _____; the physical universe, including all living organisms and the environments they inhabit
- ☐ **connected**: _____; linked or joined together

Dr. Simon's Magic English Level 800 | 241

DR. SIMON'S MAGIC ENGLISH

KEY VOCABULARY | **LEVEL 900 - UNIT 1**

- ☐ **American Civil War**: _____; a conflict that occurred from 1861 to 1865 between the United States and the Confederate States of America
- ☐ **conflict**: _____; a struggle or disagreement between two or more parties
- ☐ **took place**: _____; occurred or happened
- ☐ **union**: _____; the United States of America, the northern states during the Civil War
- ☐ **confederate**: _____; a person who helps someone do something
- ☐ **slavery**: _____; the practice of owning and treating people as property, typically for forced labor
- ☐ **abolished**: _____; officially ended or eliminated
- ☐ **right**: _____; a moral or legal entitlement or claim
- ☐ **states' rights**: _____; the belief that states have certain powers and rights separate from the federal government
- ☐ **economic differences**: _____; variations or disparities in economic conditions or systems
- ☐ **bloody**: _____; involving a large amount of violence or bloodshed
- ☐ **devastating**: _____; causing great damage or destruction
- ☐ **soldiers**: _____; individuals who serve in the military
- ☐ **losing their lives**: _____; dying or being killed
- ☐ **victorious**: _____; having won a victory or achieved success
- ☐ **significant**: _____; important or notable
- ☐ **impact**: _____; the effect or influence of something
- ☐ **country**: _____; a nation or sovereign state
- ☐ **federal government**: _____; the central authority or governing body of a federation or nation
- ☐ **reconstruction**: _____; the period after the Civil War in which the United States worked to rebuild and reintegrate the Southern states
- ☐ **remembered**: _____; recalled or commemorated
- ☐ **pivotal**: _____; crucial or essential
- ☐ **moment**: _____; a brief or specific period of time
- ☐ **reminder**: _____; something that serves to keep a fact or idea in one's memory
- ☐ **importance**: _____; the quality or state of being significant or valuable
- ☐ **standing up for**: _____; supporting or defending a cause or principle
- ☐ **cost**: _____; the price or sacrifice required to achieve something
- ☐ **freedom**: _____; the state of being free, without restrictions or oppression

KEY VOCABULARY | LEVEL 900 - UNIT 2

- ☐ **blood and iron policy**: _____; a political strategy adopted by Otto von Bismarck in Germany
- ☐ **political**: _____; relating to government, politics, or public affairs
- ☐ **strategy**: _____; a plan or course of action designed to achieve a particular goal
- ☐ **adopted**: _____; accepted or implemented
- ☐ **prominent**: _____; well-known or widely recognized
- ☐ **statesman**: _____; a skilled and experienced political leader
- ☐ **military force**: _____; the use of armed forces to achieve a military objective or goal
- ☐ **industrial strength**: _____; the level of power or capability in industrial production and technology
- ☐ **achieve**: _____; successfully reach or accomplish a goal
- ☐ **speech**: _____; a formal address or presentation
- ☐ **great questions**: _____; important or significant issues or challenges
- ☐ **decided**: _____; settled or resolved
- ☐ **declaration**: _____; a formal statement or announcement
- ☐ **intentions**: _____; aims, goals, or purposes
- ☐ **unite**: _____; bring together or join into a single entity or whole
- ☐ **establishment**: _____; the act of creating or setting up something
- ☐ **empire**: _____; a group of territories or nations under a single authority or ruler
- ☐ **downsides**: _____; disadvantages or negative aspects
- ☐ **focus**: _____; concentration or emphasis
- ☐ **militarism**: _____; the belief or policy of maintaining a strong military capability and being prepared to use it aggressively to defend or promote national interests
- ☐ **neglect**: _____; fail to give proper attention or care to something
- ☐ **social and economic issues**: _____; concerns or problems related to society and the economy
- ☐ **contributed**: _____; added to or had an effect on
- ☐ **tensions**: _____; conflicts or strained relations
- ☐ **important**: _____; significant or of great importance
- ☐ **balancing**: _____; finding a proper or desirable proportion or combination
- ☐ **development**: _____; growth or progress
- ☐ **dangers**: _____; risks or potential harm
- ☐ **relying**: _____; depending or placing trust or confidence in something or someone
- ☐ **heavily**: _____; to a great extent or degree
- ☐ **international relations**: _____; interactions and dealings between nations

DR. SIMON'S MAGIC ENGLISH

KEY VOCABULARY | LEVEL 900 - UNIT 3

- ☐ **Paris Commune**: _____; a revolutionary government that ruled the city of Paris from March to May 1871
- ☐ **government**: _____; a system or body of people governing a state or community
- ☐ **ruled**: _____; governed or controlled
- ☐ **revolutionary**: _____; relating to or characteristic of a political revolution
- ☐ **formed**: _____; established or created
- ☐ **defeat**: _____; loss or failure in a battle or conflict
- ☐ **ordinary**: _____; common or average
- ☐ **Parisians**: _____; residents or inhabitants of Paris
- ☐ **run**: _____; managed or operated
- ☐ **rights**: _____; entitlements or freedoms that are protected by law
- ☐ **freedoms**: _____; liberties or privileges
- ☐ **working class**: _____; the social group consisting of people who work for wages, usually in manual labor or low-skilled jobs
- ☐ **create**: _____; bring into existence or make
- ☐ **society**: _____; a group of individuals living together in a community and sharing common customs, values, and institutions
- ☐ **equality**: _____; the state of being equal in rights, opportunities, or status
- ☐ **fairness**: _____; the quality of being just, impartial, or reasonable
- ☐ **abolished**: _____; officially ended or eliminated
- ☐ **death penalty**: _____; a legal punishment by death for a crime
- ☐ **separated**: _____; divided or detached
- ☐ **church and state**: _____; the separation or independence of religious institutions and government authorities
- ☐ **established**: _____; set up or founded
- ☐ **implemented**: _____; put into effect or action
- ☐ **policies**: _____; plans or courses of action adopted by a government or organization
- ☐ **medical care**: _____; healthcare or medical treatment
- ☐ **housing**: _____; shelter or accommodation
- ☐ **troops**: _____; a group of soldiers or armed forces
- ☐ **retake**: _____; regain or recapture
- ☐ **attacked**: _____; launched a hostile action against
- ☐ **defeated**: _____; beaten or overcome
- ☐ **executed**: _____; put to death as a legal punishment
- ☐ **remembered**: _____; recalled or commemorated
- ☐ **struggle**: _____; a hard-fought or difficult effort
- ☐ **social justice**: _____; the fair distribution of wealth, opportunities, and privileges in society
- ☐ **inspire**: _____; fill with the urge or ability to do or feel something
- ☐ **principles**: _____; fundamental truths or guidelines

KEY VOCABULARY | LEVEL 900 - UNIT 4

- ☐ **light bulb**: _____; an electric lamp consisting of a bulb containing a wire filament
- ☐ **inventions**: _____; newly created devices, methods, or processes
- ☐ **lives**: _____; plural form of "life," referring to one's existence or way of living
- ☐ **goes down**: _____; sets below the horizon
- ☐ **process**: _____; a series of actions or steps taken to achieve a particular end
- ☐ **involved**: _____; included or participated in
- ☐ **achieved**: _____; accomplished or attained
- ☐ **candles**: _____; cylindrical pieces of wax with a wick in the middle that can be lit to provide light
- ☐ **workplaces**: _____; locations where people work
- ☐ **gave off**: _____; emitted or released
- ☐ **required**: _____; needed or demanded
- ☐ **maintenance**: _____; the process of maintaining or preserving something
- ☐ **wicks**: _____; pieces of cord or fiberglass that draw up fuel in a lamp or candle
- ☐ **trimmed**: _____; cut or removed the excess part of something
- ☐ **refilled**: _____; filled again or replenished
- ☐ **frequently**: _____; often or regularly
- ☐ **determined**: _____; strongly motivated or resolved
- ☐ **spent**: _____; used or consumed
- ☐ **experimenting**: _____; conducting tests or trials to discover or prove something
- ☐ **materials**: _____; substances or matter used in the production or construction of something
- ☐ **designs**: _____; plans or drawings produced to show the look and function of something before it is built or made
- ☐ **create**: _____; bring into existence or make
- ☐ **burn**: _____; undergo combustion or be consumed as fuel
- ☐ **brightly**: _____; with a high degree of light or luminosity
- ☐ **last**: _____; continue or endure
- ☐ **huge**: _____; very large or extensive
- ☐ **improvement**: _____; an action or process of enhancing or bettering something
- ☐ **game-changer**: _____; something or someone that dramatically changes the nature of a particular activity or situation
- ☐ **paved**: _____; prepared or made a way for
- ☐ **electric power grids**: _____; interconnected networks for generating, transmitting, and distributing electricity
- ☐ **appliances**: _____; devices or machines designed to perform specific tasks, typically in households
- ☐ **item**: _____; an individual article or unit
- ☐ **take for granted**: _____; fail to appreciate the value or importance of something
- ☐ **remember**: _____; recall or bring back to mind
- ☐ **dedication**: _____; commitment or devotion to a particular purpose or cause
- ☐ **safe**: _____; protected from danger or harm

DR. SIMON'S MAGIC ENGLISH

KEY VOCABULARY | LEVEL 900 - UNIT 5

- ☐ **massive**: _____; extremely large or significant in scale
- ☐ **global**: _____; relating to or encompassing the whole world
- ☐ **conflict**: _____; a prolonged struggle or battle
- ☐ **lasted**: _____; continued or endured for a specific period of time
- ☐ **major**: _____; significant or important
- ☐ **alliances**: _____; formal agreements or partnerships between nations
- ☐ **included**: _____; comprised or contained
- ☐ **assassinated**: _____; killed or murdered
- ☐ **nationalist**: _____; a person who advocates for the interests or independence of one's nation
- ☐ **triggered**: _____; caused or initiated
- ☐ **series**: _____; a sequence or chain of events
- ☐ **declarations**: _____; formal announcements or statements
- ☐ **embroiled**: _____; involved or entangled in a difficult situation
- ☐ **spread**: _____; extended or expanded
- ☐ **globe**: _____; the earth or the world
- ☐ **marked**: _____; characterized or distinguished
- ☐ **weapons**: _____; instruments or devices used for defense or attack
- ☐ **tactics**: _____; strategies or methods employed in a battle or conflict
- ☐ **poisonous gas**: _____; chemical substances released in gaseous form that are toxic to humans and animals
- ☐ **soldiers**: _____; military personnel who fight on land
- ☐ **civilians**: _____; non-military individuals or population
- ☐ **wounded**: _____; injured or harmed, especially by a weapon
- ☐ **suffered**: _____; experienced pain, distress, or adversity
- ☐ **long-term**: _____; over a significant period of time
- ☐ **effects**: _____; consequences or outcomes
- ☐ **significant**: _____; important or notable
- ☐ **impact**: _____; a strong effect or influence
- ☐ **leading to**: _____; causing or resulting in
- ☐ **downfall**: _____; the collapse or end of something
- ☐ **several**: _____; more than two but not many
- ☐ **empires**: _____; large and powerful territories or nations
- ☐ **armistice agreement**: _____; a formal agreement to cease fighting or hostilities
- ☐ **formally**: _____; officially or in a formal manner
- ☐ **turning point**: _____; a critical or decisive moment that leads to a notable change
- ☐ **political**: _____; relating to government, politics, or public affairs
- ☐ **landscape**: _____; the visible features of an area or territory

KEY VOCABULARY | LEVEL 900 - UNIT 6

- ☐ **armored**: _____ ; protected with metal plates or armor
- ☐ **vehicle**: _____ ; a means of transportation
- ☐ **military**: _____ ; relating to armed forces or warfare
- ☐ **purposes**: _____ ; intentions or objectives
- ☐ **appearance**: _____ ; the act of coming into view or being seen
- ☐ **warfare**: _____ ; the act of engaging in war or conflict
- ☐ **invented**: _____ ; created or brought into existence
- ☐ **soldiers**: _____ ; military personnel
- ☐ **horseback**: _____ ; on the back of a horse
- ☐ **vulnerable**: _____ ; susceptible to harm or attack
- ☐ **enemy**: _____ ; a person or group that opposes or threatens
- ☐ **difficult**: _____ ; not easy; challenging
- ☐ **battlefield**: _____ ; an area where a battle is fought
- ☐ **designed**: _____ ; planned or created with a specific purpose
- ☐ **solve**: _____ ; find a solution to a problem
- ☐ **problems**: _____ ; difficulties or challenges
- ☐ **protects**: _____ ; shields or defends from harm
- ☐ **equipped**: _____ ; provided with necessary tools or resources
- ☐ **allows**: _____ ; permits or enables
- ☐ **unreliable**: _____ ; not dependable or trustworthy
- ☐ **break through**: _____ ; penetrate or overcome
- ☐ **lines**: _____ ; military positions or defensive boundaries
- ☐ **provide**: _____ ; supply or furnish
- ☐ **infantry**: _____ ; foot soldiers or ground forces
- ☐ **continued**: _____ ; persisted or carried on
- ☐ **developed**: _____ ; advanced or progressed
- ☐ **improved**: _____ ; enhanced or made better
- ☐ **extensively**: _____ ; to a great extent or degree
- ☐ **Allied**: _____ ; the group of nations that fought against the Axis powers in World War II
- ☐ **Axis**: _____ ; the group of nations that fought against the Allies in World War II
- ☐ **support**: _____ ; provide assistance or help
- ☐ **ground troops**: _____ ; soldiers who fight on land
- ☐ **destroy**: _____ ; cause severe damage or ruin
- ☐ **fortifications**: _____ ; structures or defenses built for protection
- ☐ **significant**: _____ ; important or notable
- ☐ **development**: _____ ; the process of growing, progressing, or evolving
- ☐ **safer**: _____ ; free from danger or risk

Dr. Simon's Magic English Level 900 | 247

DR. SIMON'S MAGIC ENGLISH

KEY VOCABULARY | LEVEL 900 - UNIT 7

- ☐ **revolution**: _____; a forcible overthrow of a government or social order
- ☐ **political**: _____; relating to the government or public affairs
- ☐ **took place**: _____; occurred or happened
- ☐ **led**: _____; guided or directed
- ☐ **socialist**: _____; a person who advocates for a social and economic system based on collective ownership and control of resources
- ☐ **revolutionaries**: _____; individuals who actively participate in or support a revolution
- ☐ **tsar**: _____; the emperor of Russia before the Russian Revolution
- ☐ **absolute**: _____; complete or total
- ☐ **rule**: _____; govern or control
- ☐ **living**: _____; existing or experiencing life
- ☐ **poverty**: _____; the state of being extremely poor
- ☐ **suffering**: _____; experiencing pain or distress
- ☐ **promised**: _____; made a declaration to do or provide something
- ☐ **create**: _____; bring into existence or bring about
- ☐ **government**: _____; the governing body of a nation, state, or community
- ☐ **fair**: _____; just or equitable
- ☐ **equal**: _____; having the same rights, status, or opportunities
- ☐ **launched**: _____; started or initiated
- ☐ **stormed**: _____; attacked or rushed suddenly and forcefully
- ☐ **overthrew**: _____; removed from power or authority by force
- ☐ **established**: _____; set up or created
- ☐ **communist**: _____; a person relating to or advocating for a society in which all property is publicly owned
- ☐ **country**: _____; a nation or state
- ☐ **significant**: _____; important or noteworthy
- ☐ **impact**: _____; the effect or influence of one thing on another
- ☐ **rest of the world**: _____; other parts of the world outside of Russia
- ☐ **marked**: _____; indicated or represented
- ☐ **beginning**: _____; the start or commencement of something
- ☐ **era**: _____; a particular period in history
- ☐ **profound**: _____; having deep meaning or significance
- ☐ **influence**: _____; the capacity to have an effect on the character, development, or behavior of someone or something
- ☐ **development**: _____; the process of growth or advancement

KEY VOCABULARY | LEVEL 900 - UNIT 8

- ☐ **treaty**: _____ ; a formal agreement between countries
- ☐ **signed**: _____ ; put one's signature on a document to indicate approval or agreement
- ☐ **countries**: _____ ; nations or states
- ☐ **goal**: _____ ; an aim or objective
- ☐ **establish**: _____ ; set up or create
- ☐ **peace**: _____ ; a state of tranquility or harmony
- ☐ **prevent**: _____ ; stop or hinder something from happening
- ☐ **punished**: _____ ; subjected to a penalty or consequence for wrongdoing
- ☐ **forced**: _____ ; compelled or made to do something against one's will
- ☐ **give up**: _____ ; surrender or relinquish
- ☐ **pay**: _____ ; give money in exchange for goods or services
- ☐ **organization**: _____ ; a group of people with a particular purpose or structure
- ☐ **League of Nations**: _____ ; an international organization established after World War I to promote peace and cooperation among nations
- ☐ **solve**: _____ ; find a solution or answer to a problem
- ☐ **problems**: _____ ; difficulties or challenges
- ☐ **peacefully**: _____ ; in a nonviolent or harmonious manner
- ☐ **controversial**: _____ ; causing disagreement or dispute
- ☐ **harsh**: _____ ; severe or strict
- ☐ **lead to**: _____ ; result in or cause something to happen
- ☐ **severely**: _____ ; to a great degree or extent
- ☐ **unfortunately**: _____ ; regrettably or unluckily
- ☐ **achieve**: _____ ; accomplish or attain
- ☐ **preventing**: _____ ; stopping or hindering something from happening
- ☐ **historians**: _____ ; scholars or experts in history
- ☐ **terms**: _____ ; conditions or stipulations
- ☐ **contributed**: _____ ; played a part in or had an effect on
- ☐ **lesson**: _____ ; an experience or observation that imparts knowledge or skill
- ☐ **importance**: _____ ; significance or value
- ☐ **treating**: _____ ; dealing with or handling
- ☐ **defeated**: _____ ; having been overcome in a battle or contest
- ☐ **fairly**: _____ ; in an equitable or just manner
- ☐ **remember**: _____ ; recall from memory or bring to mind
- ☐ **consequences**: _____ ; results or effects of an action or event
- ☐ **easy**: _____ ; not difficult or challenging to do or achieve

DR. SIMON'S MAGIC ENGLISH

KEY VOCABULARY | LEVEL 900 - UNIT 9

- ☐ **political**: _____ ; relating to government or the activities of the government
- ☐ **cultural**: _____ ; relating to the customs, beliefs, and practices of a particular group
- ☐ **emerged**: _____ ; came into existence or became known
- ☐ **concluded**: _____ ; brought to a close or finalized
- ☐ **nationwide**: _____ ; occurring or affecting an entire nation
- ☐ **protests**: _____ ; expressions of objection or disapproval
- ☐ **erupted**: _____ ; broke out suddenly or violently
- ☐ **response**: _____ ; a reaction or reply to something
- ☐ **perceived**: _____ ; recognized or understood
- ☐ **betrayal**: _____ ; an act of being disloyal or unfaithful
- ☐ **awarded**: _____ ; given or granted
- ☐ **territories**: _____ ; areas of land or regions
- ☐ **previously**: _____ ; before a particular time or event
- ☐ **turning point**: _____ ; a critical or decisive moment
- ☐ **intellectual**: _____ ; a person who engages in or is highly interested in intellectual activities
- ☐ **reject**: _____ ; refuse to accept or consider
- ☐ **traditional**: _____ ; relating to customs, beliefs, or practices that have been established over time
- ☐ **confucianism**: _____ ; the teachings of Confucius, emphasizing moral values and social harmony
- ☐ **embrace**: _____ ; accept or support enthusiastically
- ☐ **democracy**: _____ ; a system of government in which power is vested in the people
- ☐ **individual rights**: _____ ; the rights and freedoms that individuals are entitled to
- ☐ **student-led**: _____ ; led or organized by students
- ☐ **strikes**: _____ ; organized work stoppages as a form of protest
- ☐ **demanding**: _____ ; insisting or asking for something forcefully
- ☐ **reforms**: _____ ; changes or improvements in practices or traditions
- ☐ **fueled**: _____ ; provided motivation or energy for something
- ☐ **publication**: _____ ; the act of making something publicly available, such as a book or article
- ☐ **literary works**: _____ ; written pieces of literature
- ☐ **challenged**: _____ ; questioned or confronted
- ☐ **values**: _____ ; principles or standards of behavior
- ☐ **promoted**: _____ ; supported or advanced
- ☐ **galvanize**: _____ ; shock or excite someone into taking action
- ☐ **major role**: _____ ; significant or influential position or function
- ☐ **shaping**: _____ ; influencing the form or development of
- ☐ **influencing**: _____ ; affecting or shaping something in an indirect or gradual way
- ☐ **education**: _____ ; the process of receiving or giving systematic instruction

KEY VOCABULARY | LEVEL 900 - UNIT 10

- ☐ **Great Depression**: _____; a period of severe economic hardship that began in the United States in 1929
- ☐ **period**: _____; a specific length of time
- ☐ **severe**: _____; extremely bad or serious
- ☐ **economic hardship**: _____; financial difficulties or struggles
- ☐ **decade**: _____; a period of ten years
- ☐ **combination**: _____; a mixture or blend of different elements
- ☐ **factors**: _____; elements or circumstances that contribute to a result
- ☐ **stock market crash**: _____; a sudden and significant decline in stock prices
- ☐ **bank failures**: _____; the collapse or closure of banks
- ☐ **reduction**: _____; a decrease or lowering of something
- ☐ **consumer spending**: _____; the amount of money people spend on goods and services
- ☐ **savings**: _____; money set aside for the future
- ☐ **unemployment rate**: _____; the percentage of the workforce that is unemployed
- ☐ **reached**: _____; attained or arrived at a particular point or level
- ☐ **charity**: _____; assistance or help provided to those in need
- ☐ **basic necessities**: _____; essential items or things needed for survival
- ☐ **profound impact**: _____; a significant and deep influence or effect
- ☐ **extremist political movements**: _____; radical or extreme ideologies in politics
- ☐ **fascism**: _____; a political ideology characterized by dictatorial power and suppression of opposition
- ☐ **communism**: _____; a political ideology advocating for common ownership of resources and the absence of social classes
- ☐ **outbreak**: _____; the sudden occurrence or emergence of something
- ☐ **policies**: _____; principles or rules guiding decision-making and actions
- ☐ **ease**: _____; alleviate or lessen
- ☐ **suffering**: _____; the state of undergoing pain, distress, or hardship
- ☐ **foundation**: _____; the basis or groundwork for something
- ☐ **hardships**: _____; difficulties or challenges
- ☐ **shared purpose**: _____; a common objective or goal
- ☐ **institutions**: _____; organizations or establishments
- ☐ **value**: _____; consider something important or beneficial
- ☐ **importance**: _____; significance or relevance
- ☐ **cooperation**: _____; working together for a common goal
- ☐ **solidarity**: _____; unity or mutual support
- ☐ **adversity**: _____; difficulties or hardships

Dr. Simon's Magic English Level 900

DR. SIMON'S MAGIC ENGLISH

KEY VOCABULARY | **LEVEL 900 - UNIT 11**

☐ **struggle**: _____; a difficult or challenging endeavor
☐ **gain**: _____; obtain or acquire
☐ **independence**: _____; freedom from control or influence
☐ **sparked**: _____; ignited or initiated
☐ **colonization**: _____; the act of establishing control over a territory and its people
☐ **century**: _____; a period of one hundred years
☐ **momentum**: _____; the force or speed of movement
☐ **efforts**: _____; actions or endeavors made to achieve a goal
☐ **prominent**: _____; well-known or distinguished
☐ **leaders**: _____; individuals who guide or direct others
☐ **non-violent**: _____; peaceful or without the use of physical force
☐ **character**: _____; the distinguishing qualities or features of something
☐ **advocating**: _____; supporting or promoting
☐ **peaceful protests**: _____; demonstrations or actions that are peaceful and non-aggressive
☐ **boycotts**: _____; refusals to participate in or buy certain goods or services
☐ **civil disobedience**: _____; the deliberate refusal to obey laws as a form of protest
☐ **challenging**: _____; difficult or demanding
☐ **authority**: _____; power or control
☐ **assert**: _____; state or declare with confidence
☐ **rights**: _____; entitlements or privileges
☐ **significant events**: _____; important occurrences or incidents
☐ **Salt March**: _____; a protest led by Mahatma Gandhi against the British salt monopoly
☐ **partition of India**: _____; the division of British India into India and Pakistan
☐ **creation**: _____; the act of bringing something into existence
☐ **successful**: _____; achieving or accomplishing a desired outcome
☐ **achieve**: _____; attain or accomplish
☐ **perseverance**: _____; persistence or determination
☐ **sacrifice**: _____; giving up something for a greater cause
☐ **citizens**: _____; individuals who belong to a particular country

KEY VOCABULARY | LEVEL 900 - UNIT 12

- ☐ **New Deal**: _____ ; a series of programs and policies implemented by the United States government during the 1930s in response to the Great Depression
- ☐ **series**: _____ ; a number of events or actions that are connected or related
- ☐ **programs**: _____ ; sets of planned actions or initiatives
- ☐ **policies**: _____ ; guidelines or principles adopted by a government or organization
- ☐ **implemented**: _____ ; put into effect or action
- ☐ **goal**: _____ ; an aim or objective
- ☐ **provide**: _____ ; supply or make available
- ☐ **relief**: _____ ; assistance or support to alleviate hardship
- ☐ **recovery**: _____ ; the process of returning to a normal or improved state
- ☐ **reform**: _____ ; changes made to improve a system or situation
- ☐ **economic crisis**: _____ ; a period of severe economic difficulties
- ☐ **driving force**: _____ ; the main factor or person that causes something to happen
- ☐ **responsibility**: _____ ; the duty or obligation to take care of something or someone
- ☐ **citizens**: _____ ; individuals who belong to a particular country
- ☐ **tough times**: _____ ; challenging or difficult periods
- ☐ **different**: _____ ; not the same; distinct or separate
- ☐ **social security act**: _____ ; a law that provided retirement benefits for workers and their families
- ☐ **still in place**: _____ ; currently existing or operational
- ☐ **retirement benefits**: _____ ; financial support or payments for retired individuals
- ☐ **increased**: _____ ; made greater or larger
- ☐ **regulation**: _____ ; the act of controlling or directing something
- ☐ **economy**: _____ ; the system of production, distribution, and consumption of goods and services
- ☐ **expanded**: _____ ; made larger or more extensive
- ☐ **social welfare programs**: _____ ; government programs that provide assistance and support to individuals in need
- ☐ **legacy**: _____ ; something that is left behind or inherited from the past
- ☐ **government programs**: _____ ; initiatives or actions implemented by the government to address specific needs or issues
- ☐ **reminder**: _____ ; something that serves to jog one's memory or bring something to mind
- ☐ **importance**: _____ ; the quality or state of being significant or valuable
- ☐ **action**: _____ ; the process of doing something or taking steps to achieve a goal
- ☐ **economic stability**: _____ ; a state of consistent and balanced economic conditions
- ☐ **growth**: _____ ; an increase in size, quantity, or importance

Dr. Simon's Magic English Level 900

DR. SIMON'S MAGIC ENGLISH

KEY VOCABULARY | LEVEL 900 - UNIT 13

- ☐ **global**: _____ ; relating to the whole world; worldwide
- ☐ **war**: _____ ; a state of armed conflict between nations or groups
- ☐ **deadliest**: _____ ; causing the most deaths
- ☐ **conflict**: _____ ; a serious disagreement or struggle
- ☐ **human history**: _____ ; the recorded events and experiences of humanity
- ☐ **fatalities**: _____ ; deaths resulting from a disaster, accident, or war
- ☐ **fought**: _____ ; engaged in battle or warfare
- ☐ **axis powers**: _____ ; the alliance of Germany, Japan, and Italy during World War II
- ☐ **allies**: _____ ; the alliance of the United States, the United Kingdom, and the Soviet Union during World War II
- ☐ **origin**: _____ ; the beginning or source of something
- ☐ **aftermath**: _____ ; the period following an event or war
- ☐ **humiliated**: _____ ; made to feel ashamed or embarrassed
- ☐ **reparations**: _____ ; payments or compensation made by a defeated country after a war
- ☐ **territorial losses**: _____ ; the land or territory lost by a country in a war
- ☐ **rose to power**: _____ ; gained authority or control
- ☐ **reverse**: _____ ; change or undo something
- ☐ **empire**: _____ ; a group of territories or countries under a single authority
- ☐ **conquest**: _____ ; the act of taking control of a territory or country by force
- ☐ **invaded**: _____ ; entered forcefully with an army or military
- ☐ **response**: _____ ; a reaction or reply to something
- ☐ **spread**: _____ ; extended or expanded in all directions
- ☐ **notable**: _____ ; worthy of attention or remarkable
- ☐ **D-day invasion**: _____ ; the Allied invasion of Normandy, France, on June 6, 1944
- ☐ **effort**: _____ ; a vigorous or determined attempt
- ☐ **liberate**: _____ ; set free or release from enemy occupation
- ☐ **occupation**: _____ ; the control and possession of a territory by foreign forces
- ☐ **dropping**: _____ ; releasing or delivering something from the air
- ☐ **atomic bombs**: _____ ; powerful explosive devices that use nuclear reactions
- ☐ **cities**: _____ ; large urban areas with a high population density
- ☐ **surrender**: _____ ; yield or give up in a battle or conflict
- ☐ **profound**: _____ ; having deep meaning or significance
- ☐ **formation**: _____ ; the act of coming together or establishing
- ☐ **establishment**: _____ ; the creation or founding of something
- ☐ **global superpower**: _____ ; a dominant and influential country on a global scale
- ☐ **Cold War**: _____ ; a state of political and military tension between the Western powers and the Soviet Union

KEY VOCABULARY | LEVEL 900 - UNIT 14

- ☐ **regime**: _____; a form of government; a particular government
- ☐ **death**: _____; the end of life or the state of being dead
- ☐ **racist**: _____; showing or expressing discrimination or prejudice based on race
- ☐ **anti-semitic**: _____; having or showing hostility or prejudice against Jewish people
- ☐ **charisma**: _____; a compelling charm or attractiveness that inspires devotion or loyalty
- ☐ **speeches**: _____; formal spoken presentations
- ☐ **promise**: _____; a declaration or assurance that one will do a particular thing or that a particular thing will happen
- ☐ **restore**: _____; bring back or return to a previous or better condition
- ☐ **implement**: _____; put into effect or action
- ☐ **policies**: _____; principles or rules adopted or followed by a government, organization, or individual
- ☐ **pure**: _____; free from contamination or impurities
- ☐ **jews**: _____; a term referring to individuals of Jewish descent or faith
- ☐ **homosexuals**: _____; individuals who are sexually attracted to people of the same sex
- ☐ **undesirables**: _____; people considered to be unacceptable or unwelcome
- ☐ **eliminated**: _____; removed or got rid of completely
- ☐ **holocaust**: _____; the systematic murder of six million Jews and millions of others during World War II
- ☐ **systematic**: _____; carried out according to a fixed plan or system
- ☐ **oppression**: _____; prolonged cruel or unjust treatment or control
- ☐ **initiated**: _____; caused or started something
- ☐ **conflicts**: _____; prolonged armed struggles or disputes
- ☐ **propaganda**: _____; information, especially biased or misleading, used to promote a political cause or point of view
- ☐ **violence**: _____; behavior involving physical force intended to hurt, damage, or kill
- ☐ **suppress**: _____; forcibly put an end to something
- ☐ **opposition**: _____; resistance or dissent, especially against a ruling authority
- ☐ **gestapo**: _____; the secret police force of the Nazi regime
- ☐ **arresting**: _____; taking someone into custody, usually by legal authority
- ☐ **executing**: _____; carrying out a sentence of death on a person
- ☐ **collapsed**: _____; fell down or gave way suddenly
- ☐ **suicide**: _____; the act of intentionally taking one's own life
- ☐ **devastation**: _____; severe destruction or damage
- ☐ **wrought**: _____; caused or brought about
- ☐ **atrocities**: _____; extremely cruel, brutal, or wicked actions

DR. SIMON'S MAGIC ENGLISH

KEY VOCABULARY | **LEVEL 900 - UNIT 15**

- ☐ **Pacific War**: _____; a major conflict that took place during World War II in the Pacific Ocean and East Asia
- ☐ **Asia-Pacific war**: _____; an alternative name for the Pacific War, emphasizing its scope in the Asia-Pacific region
- ☐ **conflict**: _____; a serious disagreement or struggle between opposing forces
- ☐ **allies**: _____; countries or groups that join together for a common purpose or goal
- ☐ **Empire of Japan**: _____; the historical Japanese state from the Meiji Restoration in 1868 to the end of World War II in 1945
- ☐ **surprise attack**: _____; an unexpected and sudden assault
- ☐ **naval base**: _____; a military installation for the Navy
- ☐ **Pearl Harbor**: _____; a harbor in Hawaii where the Japanese attacked the US naval base on December 7, 1941
- ☐ **land**: _____; the solid part of the Earth's surface
- ☐ **sea**: _____; a large body of saltwater partially enclosed by land
- ☐ **air**: _____; the invisible gaseous substance surrounding the Earth, consisting mainly of oxygen and nitrogen
- ☐ **jungles**: _____; dense, tropical forests
- ☐ **island-hopping campaigns**: _____; a military strategy used by the Allies in the Pacific War to capture strategic islands and bypass heavily defended ones
- ☐ **surrendered**: _____; gave up resistance and submitted to an enemy or opponent
- ☐ **atomic bombs**: _____; powerful explosive devices that use nuclear reactions as their source of energy
- ☐ **impact**: _____; a powerful effect or influence
- ☐ **imperial expansion**: _____; the growth and territorial acquisition of an empire
- ☐ **superpower**: _____; a nation with dominant power and influence on a global scale
- ☐ **Cold War**: _____; a state of political and military tension between the United States and the Soviet Union
- ☐ **tensions**: _____; strained relations or feelings of hostility between individuals, groups, or nations

KEY VOCABULARY | LEVEL 900 - UNIT 16

☐ **atomic bombs**: _____; highly destructive weapons that release a large amount of energy through nuclear reactions
☐ **dropped**: _____; released or delivered in a controlled manner from an aircraft or other platform
☐ **cities**: _____; large human settlements characterized by significant infrastructure and population density
☐ **warfare**: _____; the engagement in or conduct of war or conflict
☐ **devastating**: _____; causing severe damage or destruction
☐ **bombing**: _____; the act of attacking with bombs or explosives
☐ **bomber**: _____; an aircraft designed to carry and drop bombs
☐ **exploded**: _____; rapidly released energy, causing a violent expansion or disruption
☐ **fireball**: _____; a ball of fire created by an explosion
☐ **blast wave**: _____; a shock wave generated by an explosion, causing intense air pressure and damage
☐ **destroyed**: _____; severely damaged or completely ruined
☐ **radius**: _____; the distance from the center of a circle to its outer edge
☐ **killed**: _____; caused the death of
☐ **injured**: _____; harmed or wounded
☐ **second**: _____; occurring after the first in a series or sequence
☐ **powerful**: _____; having great strength or force
☐ **morality**: _____; a principle concerning the distinction between right and wrong conduct
☐ **devastating weapons**: _____; highly destructive tools or instruments of warfare
☐ **frankly**: _____; honestly or bluntly speaking
☐ **helped**: _____; contributed to or assisted in
☐ **bring an end**: _____; cause the conclusion or termination of
☐ **war**: _____; a state of armed conflict between nations or groups
☐ **surrendered**: _____; yielded or gave up control or authority
☐ **new era**: _____; a new period or phase
☐ **nuclear warfare**: _____; the use of nuclear weapons in armed conflict

Dr. Simon's Magic English Level 900 | 257

DR. SIMON'S MAGIC ENGLISH

KEY VOCABULARY | **LEVEL 900 - UNIT 17**

- ☐ **United Nations**: _____ ; an international organization formed to promote cooperation and maintain peace, security, and prosperity
- ☐ **international organization**: _____ ; a group or entity consisting of multiple nations or countries working together towards common goals
- ☐ **founded**: _____ ; established or created
- ☐ **promote**: _____ ; support or encourage the advancement of
- ☐ **cooperation**: _____ ; the act of working together towards a common goal or objective
- ☐ **maintain**: _____ ; preserve or keep in a certain state or condition
- ☐ **security**: _____ ; protection from danger or harm
- ☐ **prosperity**: _____ ; the state of being successful, wealthy, or flourishing
- ☐ **headquarters**: _____ ; the main administrative center or office
- ☐ **prevent**: _____ ; stop or hinder from happening
- ☐ **resolve**: _____ ; settle or find a solution to
- ☐ **diplomacy**: _____ ; the practice of conducting negotiations and maintaining relationships between nations
- ☐ **negotiation**: _____ ; the process of discussing and reaching an agreement through compromise
- ☐ **peacekeeping forces**: _____ ; military or civilian personnel deployed to maintain peace and security in conflict areas
- ☐ **human rights**: _____ ; fundamental rights and freedoms to which all individuals are entitled
- ☐ **protect**: _____ ; safeguard or defend from harm or danger
- ☐ **environment**: _____ ; the natural surroundings or ecosystem
- ☐ **humanitarian aid**: _____ ; assistance provided to people in need, particularly during emergencies or crises
- ☐ **sustainable development goals**: _____ ; a set of global objectives adopted by the UN to address social, economic, and environmental challenges
- ☐ **eliminate**: _____ ; eradicate or remove completely
- ☐ **poverty**: _____ ; the state of lacking basic necessities and resources
- ☐ **ensure**: _____ ; guarantee or make certain of
- ☐ **access**: _____ ; the ability to obtain or use something
- ☐ **basic needs**: _____ ; fundamental requirements for survival and well-being
- ☐ **education**: _____ ; the process of acquiring knowledge, skills, and values through learning
- ☐ **healthcare**: _____ ; the maintenance and improvement of physical and mental health through medical services
- ☐ **general assembly**: _____ ; the main deliberative body composed of all member states
- ☐ **security council**: _____ ; a principal organ responsible for maintaining international peace and security
- ☐ **international court of justice**: _____ ; the principal judicial organ that settles legal disputes between states
- ☐ **secretariat**: _____ ; the administrative arm of the UN responsible for coordinating activities and providing support
- ☐ **achieve**: _____ ; accomplish or attain
- ☐ **create**: _____ ; bring into existence or make something new
- ☐ **prosperous**: _____ ; thriving or successful

KEY VOCABULARY | **LEVEL 900 - UNIT 18**

- ☐ **founding**: _____; the act or process of establishing or creating
- ☐ **founded**: _____; established or created
- ☐ **civil war**: _____; a war between different groups or factions within the same country
- ☐ **emerged**: _____; appeared or came forth
- ☐ **victorious**: _____; having won or achieved victory
- ☐ **declared**: _____; announced or proclaimed
- ☐ **establishment**: _____; the act of creating or setting up something
- ☐ **nation**: _____; a sovereign state or country
- ☐ **marked**: _____; indicated or signified
- ☐ **end**: _____; the conclusion or termination of something
- ☐ **feudalism**: _____; a social system based on land ownership and hierarchical relationships
- ☐ **warlordism**: _____; a period of regional military rule by warlords
- ☐ **imperialism**: _____; the policy of extending a nation's power and influence through colonization or military force
- ☐ **implementing**: _____; putting into effect or carrying out
- ☐ **policies**: _____; sets of principles or rules adopted by an organization or government
- ☐ **improve**: _____; enhance or make better
- ☐ **land reforms**: _____; changes or redistributions of land ownership or use
- ☐ **promotion**: _____; the act of advancing or advocating for something
- ☐ **gender equality**: _____; the principle of equal treatment and opportunities for all genders
- ☐ **comprehensive**: _____; complete or including all aspects or elements
- ☐ **education system**: _____; the framework and institutions for providing education
- ☐ **experienced**: _____; undergone or lived through
- ☐ **growth**: _____; the process of increasing in size, quantity, or quality
- ☐ **development**: _____; the act of progressing or advancing
- ☐ **leadership**: _____; the position or function of a leader
- ☐ **major**: _____; significant or important
- ☐ **global politics**: _____; the interactions and relations between nations on a worldwide scale
- ☐ **challenges**: _____; difficulties or obstacles
- ☐ **criticisms**: _____; negative comments or evaluations
- ☐ **human rights**: _____; fundamental rights and freedoms to which all individuals are entitled
- ☐ **government**: _____; the system or group of individuals governing a state or nation
- ☐ **maintained**: _____; asserted or upheld
- ☐ **significant**: _____; important or noteworthy
- ☐ **course**: _____; the direction or path of something
- ☐ **continues**: _____; persists or carries on

DR. SIMON'S MAGIC ENGLISH

KEY VOCABULARY | **LEVEL 900 - UNIT 19**

- ☐ **fought**: _____; engaged in battle or warfare
- ☐ **divided**: _____; separated or split into parts
- ☐ **communist**: _____; a person relating to a political ideology advocating for the common ownership of resources and the absence of social classes
- ☐ **democratic**: _____; relating to a political system where power is held by the people and exercised through elected representatives
- ☐ **invaded**: _____; entered forcefully or aggressively
- ☐ **uniting**: _____; bringing together or joining as one
- ☐ **country**: _____; a nation or sovereign state
- ☐ **rule**: _____; the exercise of authority or control
- ☐ **aid**: _____; assistance or support
- ☐ **mainly**: _____; predominantly or primarily
- ☐ **peninsula**: _____; a piece of land surrounded by water on three sides
- ☐ **lasted**: _____; continued or endured for a certain period of time
- ☐ **fighting**: _____; engaging in battle or warfare
- ☐ **intense**: _____; extremely strong or severe
- ☐ **brutal**: _____; cruel or savage
- ☐ **casualties**: _____; people killed or injured in a war or accident
- ☐ **decisive**: _____; settling an issue or producing a definite result
- ☐ **victory**: _____; a triumph or success in a battle or competition
- ☐ **ceasefire**: _____; a temporary suspension of fighting
- ☐ **signed**: _____; put one's signature on a document
- ☐ **established**: _____; created or set up
- ☐ **heavily guarded**: _____; strongly protected or secured
- ☐ **borders**: _____; the boundaries between countries or regions
- ☐ **significant**: _____; important or notable
- ☐ **impact**: _____; the effect or influence of something
- ☐ **conflicts**: _____; disputes or clashes
- ☐ **Cold War**: _____; the period of geopolitical tension between the Soviet Union and the United States and their respective allies
- ☐ **military engagement**: _____; a military operation or battle
- ☐ **global superpower**: _____; a country with significant influence and power on a worldwide scale
- ☐ **profound**: _____; deep or far-reaching
- ☐ **effect**: _____; a result or consequence
- ☐ **continue**: _____; persist or endure
- ☐ **division**: _____; the act or process of separating or dividing

KEY VOCABULARY | LEVEL 900 - UNIT 20

- ☐ **period**: _____ ; a specific length of time
- ☐ **political**: _____ ; relating to the government or public affairs of a country
- ☐ **tension**: _____ ; a state of strained relations or unease
- ☐ **rivalry**: _____ ; competition or conflict between individuals or groups
- ☐ **conflict**: _____ ; a disagreement or struggle between opposing forces
- ☐ **collapsed**: _____ ; ceased to function or exist
- ☐ **established**: _____ ; created or set up
- ☐ **communist**: _____ ; a person relating to a political ideology advocating for the common ownership of resources and the absence of social classes
- ☐ **responded**: _____ ; reacted or answered
- ☐ **containment**: _____ ; the policy of preventing the spread of communism or aggression
- ☐ **aimed**: _____ ; directed or intended
- ☐ **spread**: _____ ; the expansion or dissemination of something
- ☐ **military forces**: _____ ; armed forces or defense personnel
- ☐ **engaged**: _____ ; involved or participated
- ☐ **develop**: _____ ; create or produce
- ☐ **advanced**: _____ ; highly developed or sophisticated
- ☐ **proxy wars**: _____ ; conflicts in which opposing sides are supported by external powers
- ☐ **supported**: _____ ; provided assistance or backing
- ☐ **cultural**: _____ ; relating to the arts, customs, and social behaviors of a particular group
- ☐ **ideological**: _____ ; relating to a system of ideas or beliefs
- ☐ **dimensions**: _____ ; aspects or elements
- ☐ **allies**: _____ ; countries or groups joined in a common purpose or goal
- ☐ **emphasized**: _____ ; highlighted or stressed
- ☐ **democracy**: _____ ; a system of government by the people, often through elected representatives
- ☐ **promoted**: _____ ; advocated or supported
- ☐ **socialism**: _____ ; a political and economic system based on collective ownership and control of resources
- ☐ **collective**: _____ ; shared or done by a group of people
- ☐ **ownership**: _____ ; the state of having legal possession or control
- ☐ **resources**: _____ ; assets or materials that can be used
- ☐ **crisis**: _____ ; a time of intense difficulty or danger
- ☐ **nuclear war**: _____ ; a conflict involving the use of nuclear weapons
- ☐ **ultimately**: _____ ; finally or in the end
- ☐ **avoided**: _____ ; prevented or averted

DR. SIMON'S MAGIC ENGLISH

KEY VOCABULARY | LEVEL 900 - UNIT 21

- ☐ **Asia-Africa conference**: _____ ; a meeting of Asian and African nations
- ☐ **took place**: _____ ; occurred or happened
- ☐ **significant**: _____ ; important or noteworthy
- ☐ **marked**: _____ ; indicated or symbolized
- ☐ **leaders**: _____ ; individuals in positions of authority or influence
- ☐ **newly independent**: _____ ; recently liberated or self-governing
- ☐ **discuss**: _____ ; talk about or exchange views on
- ☐ **issues**: _____ ; topics or subjects of concern
- ☐ **shared**: _____ ; common or mutual
- ☐ **colonization**: _____ ; the act of establishing control over a territory and its people
- ☐ **explore**: _____ ; investigate or examine
- ☐ **possibilities**: _____ ; potential or options
- ☐ **cooperation**: _____ ; working together or collaboration
- ☐ **collaboration**: _____ ; joint effort or cooperation
- ☐ **representatives**: _____ ; individuals chosen to act or speak on behalf of others
- ☐ **discussions**: _____ ; conversations or deliberations
- ☐ **focused**: _____ ; centered or concentrated
- ☐ **political**: _____ ; relating to government or public affairs
- ☐ **economic**: _____ ; pertaining to the production, distribution, and consumption of goods and services
- ☐ **security**: _____ ; protection or safety
- ☐ **cultural exchange**: _____ ; the sharing of customs, ideas, and practices between different cultures
- ☐ **outcomes**: _____ ; results or consequences
- ☐ **adoption**: _____ ; the act of accepting or approving something
- ☐ **declaration**: _____ ; a statement adopted at the conference
- ☐ **commitment**: _____ ; dedication or pledge
- ☐ **promoting**: _____ ; advocating or supporting
- ☐ **respecting**: _____ ; showing regard or consideration for
- ☐ **principles**: _____ ; fundamental truths or beliefs
- ☐ **sovereignty**: _____ ; supreme authority or power
- ☐ **non-interference**: _____ ; refraining from interfering in the affairs of others
- ☐ **internal affairs**: _____ ; matters concerning the domestic affairs of a country
- ☐ **milestone**: _____ ; a significant event or achievement
- ☐ **post-colonial**: _____ ; occurring after the end of colonial rule
- ☐ **oppressed**: _____ ; subjected to unjust or cruel treatment
- ☐ **pave the way**: _____ ; prepare the groundwork or facilitate
- ☐ **non-aligned movement**: _____ ; a political organization of neutral countries during the Cold War

KEY VOCABULARY | LEVEL 900 - UNIT 22

- ☐ **conflict**: _____; a struggle or fight between opposing forces
- ☐ **took place**: _____; occurred or happened
- ☐ **fought**: _____; engaged in battle or warfare
- ☐ **unify**: _____; bring together or make into one
- ☐ **communist**: _____; a person relating to a political ideology advocating for a classless society and collective ownership of resources
- ☐ **rule**: 지배하다, _____; govern or control
- ☐ **independent**: _____; free or self-governing
- ☐ **democratic**: _____; relating to a system of government where power is vested in the people and exercised through voting
- ☐ **involved**: _____; participating or taking part
- ☐ **supporting**: _____; providing assistance or aid
- ☐ **troops**: _____; soldiers or armed forces
- ☐ **weapons**: _____; tools or devices used for fighting or defense
- ☐ **resources**: _____; assets or materials that can be used to achieve a purpose
- ☐ **controversial**: _____; causing disagreement or debate
- ☐ **support**: _____; never oppose or disapprove of
- ☐ **costly**: _____; expensive or requiring great sacrifice
- ☐ **lives**: _____; human beings or individuals
- ☐ **intervene**: _____; interfere or get involved
- ☐ **affairs**: _____; matters or events
- ☐ **difficult**: _____; challenging or not easy
- ☐ **conditions**: _____; circumstances or situations
- ☐ **dense**: _____; thick or closely packed
- ☐ **jungles**: _____; dense forests with thick vegetation
- ☐ **soldiers**: _____; military personnel or combatants
- ☐ **casualties**: _____; people who are killed, wounded, or missing in action during a war
- ☐ **toll**: _____; the negative impact or cost
- ☐ **civilians**: _____; non-military individuals or ordinary people
- ☐ **displaced**: _____; forced to leave or move from their original location
- ☐ **peace agreement**: _____; a formal agreement to end hostilities and establish peace
- ☐ **withdraw**: _____; remove or pull back
- ☐ **fighting**: _____; engaging in battle or conflict
- ☐ **captured**: _____; seized or taken by force
- ☐ **capital**: _____; the main city or seat of government
- ☐ **marked**: _____; indicated or signaled
- ☐ **era**: _____; a distinct period of time

Dr. Simon's Magic English Level 900

DR. SIMON'S MAGIC ENGLISH

KEY VOCABULARY | **LEVEL 900 - UNIT 23**

- ☐ **cultural revolution**: _____; a period of political and social upheaval in China
- ☐ **period**: _____; a specific span of time
- ☐ **upheaval**: _____; a state of disruption or chaos
- ☐ **initiated**: _____; started or began
- ☐ **aimed**: _____; intended or directed towards a goal
- ☐ **revive**: _____; bring back to life or restore
- ☐ **revolutionary**: _____; relating to a major change or overthrow of established norms or systems
- ☐ **fervor**: _____; intense passion or enthusiasm
- ☐ **purge**: _____; eliminate or remove
- ☐ **capitalist**: _____; relating to an economic system based on private ownership and profit
- ☐ **traditional**: _____; customary or long-established
- ☐ **elements**: _____; components or aspects
- ☐ **citizens**: _____; members of a country or state
- ☐ **mobilized**: _____; organized or activated
- ☐ **uphold**: _____; support or maintain
- ☐ **ideology**: _____; a system of ideas or beliefs
- ☐ **counterrevolutionary**: _____; opposing a revolution or revolutionary principles
- ☐ **intellectuals**: _____; highly educated or knowledgeable individuals
- ☐ **targeted**: _____; singled out or focused on
- ☐ **criticism**: _____; the act of analyzing or evaluating something negatively
- ☐ **persecution**: _____; mistreatment or harassment
- ☐ **traditional cultural artifacts**: _____; objects representing cultural heritage
- ☐ **destroyed**: _____; damaged beyond repair or ruined
- ☐ **profound**: _____; deep or significant
- ☐ **widespread**: _____; extensive or prevalent
- ☐ **dislocation**: _____; disturbance or disruption
- ☐ **torn apart**: _____; separated or divided
- ☐ **publicly confess**: _____; admit or acknowledge something in a public setting
- ☐ **crimes**: _____; illegal or immoral acts
- ☐ **suffered**: _____; experienced hardship or loss
- ☐ **economic growth**: _____; increase in the production and consumption of goods and services
- ☐ **stalling**: _____; slowing down or halting progress
- ☐ **grinding to a halt**: _____; coming to a complete stop
- ☐ **negative impact**: _____; adverse effect or consequence
- ☐ **significant**: _____; important or meaningful
- ☐ **legacy**: _____; a lasting impact or inheritance

KEY VOCABULARY | LEVEL 900 - UNIT 24

☐ **significant**: _____; important or noteworthy
☐ **achievement**: _____; a notable accomplishment or success
☐ **history**: _____; the study of past events
☐ **space exploration**: _____; the investigation and discovery of celestial bodies
☐ **NASA**: _____; National Aeronautics and Space Administration
☐ **launched**: _____; sent or set in motion
☐ **spacecraft**: _____; a vehicle designed for travel in outer space
☐ **astronauts**: _____; individuals who travel and work in space
☐ **moon**: _____; Earth's natural satellite
☐ **land**: _____; touch down or set foot on a surface
☐ **surface**: _____; the outer layer or exterior of something
☐ **collect**: _____; gather or acquire
☐ **samples**: _____; small portions or specimens for analysis
☐ **research**: _____; systematic investigation or study
☐ **set foot**: _____; step or walk
☐ **mankind**: _____; humanity or the human race
☐ **join**: _____; come together or meet up
☐ **spend**: _____; pass or use time
☐ **hours**: _____; units of time
☐ **monitor**: _____; observe or keep track of
☐ **above**: _____; at a higher position or level
☐ **return**: _____; come back or go back
☐ **journey**: _____; a trip or travel
☐ **splash down**: _____; land in water
☐ **tremendous**: _____; enormous or extraordinary
☐ **human ingenuity**: _____; creative and resourceful thinking by humans
☐ **courage**: _____; bravery or boldness
☐ **determination**: _____; firmness of purpose or resoluteness
☐ **risked**: _____; exposed to danger or uncertainty
☐ **explore**: _____; investigate or discover
☐ **unknown**: _____; unfamiliar or unexplored territory

DR. SIMON'S MAGIC ENGLISH

KEY VOCABULARY | **LEVEL 900 - UNIT 25**

- ☐ **oil shock**: _____ ; a sudden and significant increase in the price of oil
- ☐ **crisis**: _____ ; a time of intense difficulty or danger
- ☐ **price**: _____ ; the amount of money required or given in exchange for something
- ☐ **suddenly**: _____ ; happening quickly or unexpectedly
- ☐ **skyrocketed**: _____ ; rose rapidly or sharply
- ☐ **largest producers**: _____ ; countries that generate the most quantity of a specific product
- ☐ **stop selling**: _____ ; cease the act of selling or providing
- ☐ **support**: _____ ; back or assist
- ☐ **immediate**: _____ ; happening without delay or hesitation
- ☐ **shortage**: _____ ; a lack or deficiency of something
- ☐ **increase**: _____ ; a rise or growth in quantity, size, or importance
- ☐ **economic problems**: _____ ; difficulties or challenges related to the economy
- ☐ **long lines**: _____ ; queues or waiting lines that are lengthy
- ☐ **buy**: _____ ; purchase or acquire in exchange for money
- ☐ **gasoline**: _____ ; a fuel commonly used in automobiles
- ☐ **wait**: _____ ; delay or remain in a state of readiness
- ☐ **small amount**: _____ ; a limited quantity or portion
- ☐ **fuel**: _____ ; a substance used to produce energy, such as gasoline
- ☐ **major impact**: _____ ; a significant effect or influence
- ☐ **world economy**: _____ ; the global system of production, trade, and consumption of goods and services
- ☐ **change**: _____ ; alteration or modification
- ☐ **think**: _____ ; have a particular belief or opinion
- ☐ **energy**: _____ ; the capacity to do work or produce power
- ☐ **alternative sources**: _____ ; different options or choices
- ☐ **invest**: _____ ; allocate resources or money for future benefits
- ☐ **renewable energy**: _____ ; energy obtained from sources that can be replenished naturally
- ☐ **conserve**: _____ ; save or use sparingly
- ☐ **efficiently**: _____ ; in a way that maximizes productivity or minimizes waste
- ☐ **significant**: _____ ; important or notable
- ☐ **event**: _____ ; a happening or occurrence
- ☐ **affect**: _____ ; have an influence on or cause a change in
- ☐ **positive**: _____ ; beneficial or advantageous
- ☐ **environment**: _____ ; the natural surroundings or conditions

KEY VOCABULARY | LEVEL 900 - UNIT 26

- ☐ **political**: _____; related to government or public affairs
- ☐ **economic systems**: _____; the structures and mechanisms governing the production, distribution, and consumption of goods and services
- ☐ **falling behind**: _____; lagging or not keeping pace with others
- ☐ **technology**: _____; the application of scientific knowledge for practical purposes
- ☐ **economics**: _____; the study of the production, distribution, and consumption of goods and services
- ☐ **address**: _____; deal with or confront
- ☐ **significant**: _____; important or notable
- ☐ **introduction**: _____; the act of bringing something new into existence or use
- ☐ **capitalist principles**: _____; the beliefs and practices associated with capitalism, such as private ownership and competition
- ☐ **private ownership**: _____; the state of having personal or individual ownership of property or assets
- ☐ **competition**: _____; the rivalry between individuals or entities in a market or industry
- ☐ **prosperous**: _____; successful or thriving
- ☐ **challenges**: _____; difficulties or obstacles
- ☐ **accustomed**: _____; familiar with or used to
- ☐ **embrace**: _____; accept or adopt willingly
- ☐ **political system**: _____; the structure and organization of government and political processes
- ☐ **open debate**: _____; discussion characterized by free expression of ideas and opinions
- ☐ **discussion**: _____; conversation or dialogue
- ☐ **democratic practices**: _____; actions or processes aligned with democratic principles and ideals
- ☐ **government**: _____; the governing body of a nation, state, or community
- ☐ **emergence**: _____; the process of coming into existence or becoming known
- ☐ **political parties**: _____; organized groups that represent specific political ideologies or interests
- ☐ **movements**: _____; organized efforts or campaigns to achieve social or political change
- ☐ **overall**: _____; considering everything or taken as a whole
- ☐ **period**: _____; a specific length of time
- ☐ **experimentation**: _____; the act of trying out new ideas or methods
- ☐ **positive changes**: _____; beneficial or advantageous alterations
- ☐ **freedom of speech**: _____; the right to express opinions and ideas without censorship or restraint
- ☐ **economic opportunity**: _____; chances or possibilities for economic advancement or success
- ☐ **political instability**: _____; a state of uncertainty or vulnerability in the political system
- ☐ **economic turmoil**: _____; a state of confusion or disorder in the economy
- ☐ **short term**: _____; a brief or temporary period

Dr. Simon's Magic English Level 900 | 267

DR. SIMON'S MAGIC ENGLISH

KEY VOCABULARY | **LEVEL 900 - UNIT 27**

- ☐ **reunification**: _____ ; the act or process of reuniting or bringing together again
- ☐ **divided**: _____ ; separated into parts or sections
- ☐ **separate**: _____ ; set apart or divide into distinct parts
- ☐ **countries**: _____ ; sovereign states or nations
- ☐ **taken down**: _____ ; removed or dismantled
- ☐ **fall**: _____ ; the collapse or downfall
- ☐ **pivotal moment**: _____ ; a crucial or significant turning point
- ☐ **communist country**: _____ ; a country that follows a political ideology based on communal ownership and control of resources
- ☐ **limited freedoms**: _____ ; restrictions on personal liberties or rights
- ☐ **poor living conditions**: _____ ; unfavorable or substandard quality of life
- ☐ **symbol of hope**: _____ ; an object or event that represents optimism or a positive outlook
- ☐ **reunited**: _____ ; brought back together or reconnected
- ☐ **families**: _____ ; groups of related individuals
- ☐ **friends**: _____ ; individuals with a close personal bond
- ☐ **tension**: _____ ; strained or uneasy relations
- ☐ **negotiations**: _____ ; discussions or talks aimed at reaching an agreement
- ☐ **allies**: _____ ; countries or entities joined in a common cause or purpose
- ☐ **officially declared**: _____ ; publicly announced or proclaimed
- ☐ **historic moment**: _____ ; a significant or memorable event in history
- ☐ **celebration**: _____ ; a joyful or festive gathering
- ☐ **today**: _____ ; the present time or era
- ☐ **thriving**: _____ ; flourishing or prospering
- ☐ **strong economy**: _____ ; a robust or prosperous financial system
- ☐ **rich culture**: _____ ; a diverse and vibrant cultural heritage
- ☐ **significant event**: _____ ; an important or noteworthy occurrence
- ☐ **division**: _____ ; the act of separating or creating a distinction
- ☐ **come together**: _____ ; unite or join as a group or community

KEY VOCABULARY | LEVEL 900 - UNIT 28

- ☐ **conflict**: _____; a state of disagreement or hostility between parties
- ☐ **coalition**: _____; an alliance or union of different groups or countries
- ☐ **countries**: _____; sovereign states or nations
- ☐ **invasion**: _____; the act of forcefully entering or taking over a territory
- ☐ **international condemnation**: _____; widespread disapproval or criticism from the international community
- ☐ **United Nations Security Council**: _____; the principal organ of the United Nations responsible for maintaining international peace and security
- ☐ **resolution**: _____; a formal decision or course of action adopted by an organization or an institution
- ☐ **force**: _____; physical strength or power
- ☐ **remove**: _____; eliminate or take away
- ☐ **military operation**: _____; a coordinated military action or campaign
- ☐ **air campaign**: _____; a series of military operations conducted by air forces
- ☐ **aircraft**: _____; vehicles that can fly, such as planes or helicopters
- ☐ **military infrastructure**: _____; facilities and structures used by the military
- ☐ **communication systems**: _____; networks and equipment used for transmitting information
- ☐ **military units**: _____; organized groups of soldiers or military personnel
- ☐ **ground offensive**: _____; a military operation conducted by land forces
- ☐ **military victory**: _____; a successful outcome or achievement in warfare
- ☐ **turning point**: _____; a decisive moment or event that causes a significant change
- ☐ **military capabilities**: _____; the military strength, resources, and abilities of a country or armed forces
- ☐ **intervene**: _____; get involved or take action in a situation
- ☐ **protect**: _____; guard or defend against harm or danger
- ☐ **interests**: _____; concerns, benefits, or objectives
- ☐ **allies**: _____; countries or entities joined in a common cause or purpose
- ☐ **far-reaching effects**: _____; extensive or widespread consequences
- ☐ **establishment**: _____; the creation or formation of something
- ☐ **no-fly zone**: _____; an area where aircraft are prohibited from flying
- ☐ **economic sanctions**: _____; measures imposed by one country or a group of countries to restrict trade or economic activity

DR. SIMON'S MAGIC ENGLISH

KEY VOCABULARY | LEVEL 900 - UNIT 29

- ☐ **dissolution**: _____; the act of formally ending or disbanding an organization or entity
- ☐ **communist state**: _____; a state that is governed by a single communist party and operates under a socialist economic system
- ☐ **republics**: _____; autonomous regions or states within a larger country or federation
- ☐ **powerful**: _____; having great strength, influence, or control
- ☐ **repressive government**: _____; a government that exercises strict control over its citizens and suppresses dissent or opposition
- ☐ **individual freedoms**: _____; personal rights and liberties enjoyed by individuals in a society
- ☐ **economic struggles**: _____; difficulties or challenges related to the economy, such as unemployment, inflation, or economic decline
- ☐ **problems**: _____; issues or challenges that need to be addressed or resolved
- ☐ **leader**: _____; a person who has authority or influence over others
- ☐ **reform**: _____; the process of making changes or improvements
- ☐ **transparent**: _____; open and clear, without hidden agendas or secrets
- ☐ **economy**: _____; the system of production, distribution, and consumption of goods and services in a country or region
- ☐ **freedom**: _____; the state of being able to act, speak, or think without constraint or control
- ☐ **save**: _____; prevent from being destroyed or lost
- ☐ **leaders**: _____; individuals who hold positions of authority or influence
- ☐ **agreement**: _____; a formal understanding or arrangement reached between parties
- ☐ **dissolved**: _____; brought to an end or disintegrated
- ☐ **commonwealth of independent states**: _____; an organization formed by the former Soviet republics after the dissolution of the USSR
- ☐ **central control**: _____; the level of authority and decision-making power held by a central government or organization
- ☐ **significant**: _____; important or noteworthy
- ☐ **Cold War**: _____; a period of political tension and rivalry between the United States and the Soviet Union after World War II
- ☐ **era**: _____; a period of time characterized by particular events, developments, or conditions
- ☐ **international relations**: _____; interactions and relationships between countries and nations
- ☐ **decisions**: _____; choices or determinations made after careful consideration
- ☐ **chart**: _____; plan or map out a course of action or direction

KEY VOCABULARY | LEVEL 900 - UNIT 30

- ☐ **coordinated**: _____; organized or planned in a unified manner
- ☐ **terrorist attack**: _____; a violent act that is intended to create fear and terror among the population, often for political or religious purposes
- ☐ **extremist group**: _____; a group that holds extreme views and is willing to use violent means to achieve its goals
- ☐ **hijacked**: _____; forcefully taking control of a vehicle, such as an airplane, and using it for illegal purposes
- ☐ **intentionally**: _____; deliberately, on purpose
- ☐ **deaths**: _____; the number of people who lost their lives as a result of the 9/11 terrorist attacks
- ☐ **military campaign**: _____; a series of military operations carried out by a nation or alliance to achieve a specific military or political objective
- ☐ **combat**: _____; fight against or oppose, often in a military context
- ☐ **invasion**: _____; a military operation in which a country or group enters another country or territory by force, with the aim of occupying and controlling it
- ☐ **security measures**: _____; actions taken to protect against potential threats, such as terrorism or crime
- ☐ **implemented**: _____; put into effect, applied
- ☐ **immigration policies**: _____; laws and regulations related to the movement of people across international borders
- ☐ **civil liberties**: _____; individual rights and freedoms that are protected by law, such as freedom of speech and the right to privacy
- ☐ **international relations**: _____; the study of relationships between countries, including political, economic, and cultural interactions
- ☐ **remembered**: _____; to keep the memory of something or someone alive
- ☐ **annually**: _____; once a year, every year
- ☐ **honor**: _____; show respect and admiration for someone or something
- ☐ **victims**: _____; people who suffered harm or injury as a result of the 9/11 terrorist attacks
- ☐ **heroes**: _____; individuals who demonstrated bravery and selflessness during the 9/11 terrorist attacks
- ☐ **unity**: _____; the state of being united or joined together as a group, often in the face of adversity
- ☐ **resilience**: _____; the ability to recover quickly from difficulties or setbacks
- ☐ **tragedy**: _____; a terrible event or disaster that causes great suffering, loss, or sadness
- ☐ **adversity**: _____; a difficult or unpleasant situation, often involving hardship or struggle

사이먼 미국교과서 100에서 900까지 어휘 총정리

발행일	2024년 6월 10일 1쇄 발행
지은이	Dr. Simon
발행인	손건
편집기획	김상배, 장수경
마케팅	최관호, 김재명
디자인	보스코
제작	최승용
인쇄	선경프린테크
발행처	랭컴
주소	서울시 영등포구 영등포동 4가 146-5
등록번호	312-2006-00060
도서구입문의	전화 02-2636-0895 팩스 02-2636-0896

ⓒ랭컴 2023
ISBN   979-11-7142-050-6 73740

✖ 이 책은 국제 저작권법에 따라 보호받는 저작물이므로 복사 및 무단복제와 무단전재를 금하며, 전자적 사용과 유료 및 무료 동영상과 같은 2차 저작물로의 사용도 금합니다.
✚ 학교 및 학원에서의 수업용 교재 채택은 서면동의 없이 허용하며, 적극 장려합니다.
✚ 학교 및 학원에서의 사용시 도서구입문의처로 문의하시면 다양한 부가혜택이 제공됩니다.
✚ 파본은 구입처에서 교환해 드립니다. 책값은 뒤 표지에 있습니다.